Hegel's Ethical Thought

Hegel's
Ethical Thought

ALLEN W. WOOD

CAMBRIDGE
UNIVERSITY PRESS

Published by the Press Syndicate of the University of Cambridge
The Pitt Building, Trumpington Street, Cambridge CB2 1RP
40 West 20th Street, New York, NY 10011-4211, USA
10 Stamford Road, Oakleigh, Melbourne 3166, Australia

First published 1990
Reprinted 1991, 1993, 1995

Library of Congress Cataloging-in-Publication Data
Wood, Allen W.
Hegel's ethical thought / Allen W. Wood.
p. cm.
Includes bibliographical references.
ISBN 0-521-37432-4. – ISBN 0-521-37782-X (pbk.)
1. Hegel, Georg Wilhelm Friedrich, 1770–1831 – Ethics. 2. Ethics,
Modern – 18th century. 3. Ethics, Modern – 19th century. 4. Ethics,
German. I. Title.
B2949.E8W66 1990
170'.92 – dc20   89-77466

British Library Cataloguing in Publication Data
Wood, Allen W.
Hegel's ethical thought.
1. Ethics. Theories of Hegel, Georg Wilhelm Friedrich,
1770–1831
I. Title
170.92

ISBN 0-521-37432-4 hardback
ISBN 0-521-37782-X paperback

Transferred to digital printing 2002

To Forrest,
Henry, and Stephen

Contents

CONTENTS

Part IV: Ethical life

Preface

Hegel's social and political thought has been studied by philosophers, even more by political theorists and historians of ideas. Treatments of it have usually neglected the philosophical foundations of Hegel's theory of society and politics. By "philosophical foundations" I do not mean Hegel's speculative metaphysics. I suspect that one of the reasons why Hegel's ethical theory has been neglected is that it has been supposed that this is what "philosophical foundations" has to mean in his case. If you decide to examine *those* foundations more closely, you know before long that you are in for a difficult and generally unrewarding time of it, at least from the standpoint of social and political theory. If you are sensible, you will try to avoid that. If you are not so sensible, you will humbug yourself into thinking that there is some esoteric truth in Hegelian dialectical logic which provides a hidden key to his social thought.

What I mean by "philosophical foundations" is the *ethical theory* on which Hegel rests his critical reflections on modern social and political life. This subject has been neglected partly because some believe it to be nonexistent. I hope to show that such beliefs are seriously in error. Hegel's philosophical orientation does tend to obscure his ethical theory, and that ethical theory does not fall into the familiar patterns of consequentialism and deontologism, but involves a critique of them. Nevertheless, there is such a thing as Hegelian ethical theory, and it is a powerful and important theory, which should be taken seriously by moral philosophers as well as by those who are interested in Hegel's social and political thought.

In the late twentieth century, everybody knows that Hegel is an important thinker who cannot be ignored or easily dismissed. But the broad outlines of Hegel's thought are much oftener discussed with sophistication than his writings are read with comprehension. English-speaking philosophers still often have very simplistic and distorted images of Hegel, suggested by the thoughts that Hegel was a figure of the Romantic period, a German idealist with a gnostical metaphysics of obscurely religious intent, a proponent of communitarian ethical thought, and a critic of Kant and Enlightenment liberalism. Hegel is all these things, of course. But the associations they set off in the minds of English-speaking philosophers, separated from Hegel's milieu by nearly two centuries and (more importantly) by the propaganda of two world wars and a cold war, are often nothing but misleading stereotypes. They reinforce the very ideologies that the study of Hegel might help us to unlearn.

xiii

Hegel's era was the era of German Romanticism, but Hegel himself was an opponent of the Romantic movement. He was always much more favorably disposed to Kant and the Enlightenment than to the likes of Schlegel and Novalis. Hegel's critique of liberal individualism is not a reactionary or irrationalist repudiation of its concern for individual rights and civil liberty – which mattered as much to the bourgeois Hegel as they do to liberals. Instead, it was a rejection of the formalistic and ahistorical conceptions of human nature, society, and reason in terms of which the Enlightenment conceived and attempted to defend these values. Much of Hegel's critique of the liberal tradition is still valid today, but Hegel's thought equally serves as basis for criticizing various forms of irrationalist and relativist thought in behalf of which Hegel's own name is often ignorantly invoked.

The infamous obscurity of Hegel's writings makes common misunderstandings all the more difficult to correct. Even the most acute and well-intentioned may lack the leisure and the patience to penetrate Hegel's pretentious style and abstract jargon. Partly for this reason, Hegel's influence tends to perpetuate itself through familiar (and often malicious) caricatures and bowdlerizations. Even the most grossly inaccurate of them are often difficult to expose unless one puts forth more effort than can be lightly afforded by those with only a casual or moderate interest in Hegel's thought.

Unfortunately, there is no radical remedy for the problem, no royal road through the Hegelian brambles. The currency of Hegel's thought has produced some helpful scholarship on his philosophy. More broadly, scholarship even in English is beginning to shed much needed light on the most important period of philosophical activity in modern times, the movement of German philosophy between 1781 and 1820. To understand this period better is to get a better grasp on the issues that still most trouble and rend Western culture; twentieth-century philosophy, at least English-speaking philosophy, has suffered greatly from its failure to realize this. The present book is my attempt to contribute to that understanding.

Much light has been shed on Hegel's ethical and political thought by the recent publication of his lecture transcriptions over a period of years (1817–1831). I have kept in mind the distinction between these texts and Hegel's published writings, but I have not hesitated in the least to use the lecture materials. As Hegel himself saw it, lecturing was probably the most important part of his philosophical activity. All his major writings after 1817 were merely outlines to be lectured upon. Eduard Gans appreciated this point when he devoted a sizable proportion of the first edition of Hegel's collected writings to Hegel's lecture transcriptions on history, art, religion, and philosophy. Editors of subsequent editions have correctly followed him in this. There are a number of topics, including those dealt with in Chapter 13 and Chapter 14, §§ 7–11, which are dealt with in much greater detail in lecture transcriptions than in the writings Hegel published. These discussions represent some of Hegel's boldest and most interesting forays as a thinker, and it is perhaps understandable that he might have undertaken them in lectures rather than in published writings. To deprive ourselves of them on narrow philological grounds would be to impoverish our appreciation of Hegel's ethical thought.

This book has taken me a long time to write. I first taught Hegel's *Philosophy of Right* at the University of Michigan in 1973, and recall with pride that Bernard Cullen and Charles Beitz were among my students then. Different embryonic versions of some of my thoughts about Hegel's ethical theory were presented at the Inter-University Centre in Dubrovnik in 1975 and at the University of Helsinki, Finland in 1981. I began to work seriously on the book only in 1983–1984 in Berlin, supported by a fellowship from the John Simon Guggenheim Foundation. Facilities for my research at the Institut für Philosophie, Freie Universität, Berlin in 1983–1984 were provided through the generous assistance of Professor Ernst Tugendhat. Considerable momentum was given to my work on it by my association with stimulating colleagues and students at the University of California at San Diego in 1986. My students, both there and at Cornell University, enriched my study of Hegel. Portions of the book have been presented to and discussed with groups of philosophers from many different institutions, including the four to which I feel closest: Cornell University, the Freie Universität in Berlin, the University of California at San Diego, and Reed College. The relevant chapters were invariably improved as a result of these discussions.

Many individuals have helped me to write this book through discussions or correspondence, or by giving me comments, oral or written, on drafts of various parts of it. I list (in alphabetical order) those to whom I feel especially obliged for information, suggestions, or criticisms: Henry Allison, Emil Angehrn, Anthony Appiah, Lewis White Beck, John G. Bennett, Felmon Davis, Alan Donagan, Andreas Eshete, Richard Farr, Richard Feldman, Carl Ginet, Paul Guyer, Jean Hampton, Michael Hardimon, Harold Hodes, Terence Irwin, Chris Kern, Harald Köhl, Christine Korsgaard, Anton Leist, David Lyons, Julie Maybee, John McCumber, George Myro, Kai Nielsen, William Peck, Robert Pippin, Thomas Pogge, Allen Rosen, John Russell, Gottfried Seebass, John Simmons, Sydney Shoemaker, Robert Stalnaker, Peter Steinberger, Nicholas Sturgeon, Michael Theunissen, Neil Thomason, Ernst Tugendhat, Milton Wachsberg, Christopher Wagner, Robert Wallace, Andreas Wildt, Ursula Wolf, and Rega Wood.

Abbreviations

All translations from the works listed below are my own. Standard English translations will normally be cited along with the original, with English pagination following German pagination, separated by a slash (/).

Writings of G. W. F. Hegel (1770–1831)

Werke   *Hegel: Werke: Theorie Werkausgabe.* Frankfurt: Suhrkamp Verlag, 1970. Cited by volume.

B   *Hegels Briefe,* edited by Johannes Hoffmeister and Friedhelm Nicolin. Hamburg: Felix Meiner Verlag, 1981. Cited by volume and page number.

    Hegel: The Letters, translated by Clark Butler and Christiane Seiler. Bloomington: Indiana University Press, 1984. Cited by page number.

D   *Differenz des Fichte'schen und Schelling'schen Systems der Philosophie* (1801), *Werke 2.*

    The Difference Between Fichte's and Schelling's System of Philosophy, translated by H. S. Harris and Walter Cerf. Albany: SUNY Press, 1977.

DV   *Die Verfassung Deutschlands, Werke 1.*

    "The German Constitution," in *Hegel's Political Writings,* translated by T. M. Knox. Oxford: the Clarendon Press, 1964.

EL   *Enzyklopädie der philosophischen Wissenschaften I* (1817, rev. 1827, 1830), *Werke 8.*

    Hegel's Logic, translated by William Wallace. Oxford: Oxford University Press, 1975. Cited by paragraph (§) number. Additions are indicated by an "A".

EN   *Enzyklopädie der philosophischen Wissenschaften II* (1817, rev. 1827, 1830), *Werke 9.*

    Hegel's Philosophy of Nature, translated by Michael J. Petry. New York: Humanities Press, 1970. Cited by paragraph (§) number.

EG   *Enzyklopädie der philosophischen Wissenschaften III* (1817, rev. 1827, 1830), *Werke 10.*

    Hegel's Philosophy of Mind, translated by William Wallace and A. V. Miller. Oxford: Oxford University Press, 1971. Cited by paragraph (§) number. Additions are indicated by an "A".

EH   *Enzyklopädie der Philosophischen Wissenschaften* (1817 Heidelberg version). *Hegels Sämtliche Werke, 4*. Auflage der Jubiläumsausgabe, edited by Hermann Glockner. Stuttgart: Friedrich Frommann Verlag, 1968, Volume 6. Cited by paragraph (§) number.

GW   *Glauben und Wissen* (1802), *Werke 2*.

        Faith and Knowledge, translated by Walter Cerf and H. S. Harris. Albany: SUNY Press, 1977.

JR   *Jenaer Realphilosophie* (1805–1806) (previous title: *Jenenser Realphilosophie II*), edited by J. Hoffmeister. Hamburg: Felix Meiner Verlag, 1969.

        Hegel and the Human Spirit, translated by Leo Rauch. Detroit: Wayne State University Press, 1983. Cited by page number.

JR 1   *Jenenser Realphilosophie I* (1803–1804), edited by J. Hoffmeister. Hamburg: Felix Meiner Verlag, 1930. Cited by page number.

        System of Ethical Life and First Philosophy of Spirit, translated by H. S. Harris. Albany: SUNY Press, 1979. Cited by page number.

NP   *Nürnberger Propädeutik* (1808–1811), *Werke 4*.

NR   *Über die wissenschaftliche Behandlungsarten des Naturrechts* (1802), *Werke 2*.

        Natural Law, translated by T. M. Knox. Philadelphia: University of Pennsylvania Press, 1975. Cited by page number.

PhG   *Phänomenologie des Geistes* (1807), *Werke 3*.

        Phenomenology of Spirit, translated by A. V. Miller. Oxford: Oxford University Press, 1977. Cited by paragraph (¶) number.

PR   *Philosophie des Rechts* (1821), *Werke 7*.

        Hegel's Philosophy of Right, translated by H. B. Nisbet, edited by Allen W. Wood. Cambridge: Cambridge University Press, forthcoming in 1992. Cited by paragraph (§) number. Remarks are indicated by an "R," additions by an "A." Preface and sometimes longer paragraphs cited by page number in German edition only.

SS   *System der Sittlichkeit* (1802), edited by G. Lasson. Hamburg: Felix Meiner Verlag, 1967.

        System of Ethical Life and First Philosophy of Spirit, translated by H. S. Harris. Albany: SUNY Press, 1979. Cited by page number.

TJ   *Theologische Jugendschriften* (1793–1800), *Werke 1*.

TE   *Hegel: Three Essays, 1793–1795*, translated by Peter Fuss and John Dobbins. Notre Dame: University of Notre Dame Press, 1984.

ETW   *Early Theological Writings*, translated by T. M. Knox. Philadelphia: University of Pennsylvania Press, 1971. Cited by page number.

VA   *Vorlesungen über Ästhetik*, *Werke 13–16*.

        The Philosophy of Fine Art, translated by F. P. B. Osmaston. New York: Hacker, 1975. Cited by volume and page number.

VG   *Die Vernunft in der Geschichte*, edited by J. Hoffmeister. Hamburg: Felix Meiner Verlag 1955.

Lectures on the Philosophy of World History: Introduction, translated by H. B. Nisbet. Cambridge: Cambridge University Press, 1975. Cited by page number.

VGP   *Vorlesungen über die Geschichte der Philosophie,* Bd. 1–3. *Werke 18–20.*

Lectures on the History of Philosophy, translated by Elizabeth Haldane. New York: Humanities Press, 1968. Cited by volume and page.

VPG   *Vorlesungen über die Geschichte der Philosophie, Werke 12.*

The Philosophy of History, translated by J. Sibree. New York: Dover, 1956. Cited by page number.

VPR   *Vorlesungen über Rechtsphilosophie,* edited by K.-H. Ilting. Stuttgart: Frommann Verlag, 1974. Including notes and transcriptions from Hegel's lectures of 1818–1819 (transcription by C. G. Homeyer), 1821–1822, 1822–1823 (transcription by H. G. Hotho), 1824–1825 (transcription by K. G. von Griesheim), 1831 (transcription by D. F. Strauss). Cited by volume and page number.

VPR17   *Die Philosophie des Rechts: Die Mitschriften Wannenmann (Heidelberg 1817–1818) und Homeyer (Berlin 1818/19),* edited by von K.-H. Ilting. Stuttgart: Klett-Cotta Verlag, 1983. Cited by page number.

VPR19   *Philosophie des Rechts: Die Vorlesung von 1819/1820,* anonymous transcription or transcriptions edited by Dieter Henrich. Frankfurt: Suhrkamp Verlag, 1983. Cited by page number.

VR   *Vorlesungen über die Philosophie der Religion, Werke 16–17.*

Lectures on the Philosophy of Religion, translated by E. B. Speirs and J. B. Sanderson. London: Routledge & Kegan Paul, 1895. 3 vols. Cited by volume and page number.

WL   *Wissenschaft der Logik* (1812–1816), *Werke* 5–6. Cited by volume and page number.

Hegel's Science of Logic, translated by A. V. Miller. London: George Allen & Unwin, 1969. Cited by page number.

In writings cited by paragraph (§), a comma used before "R" or "A" means "and." Thus: "PR § 33,A" means: "PR § 33 and the addition to § 33"; "PR § 270,R,A" means: "PR § 270 and the remark to § 270 and the addition to § 270."

Writings of Immanuel Kant (1724–1804)

GS   *Kants Gesammelte Schriften.* Berlin: Ausgabe der königlich preussischen Akademie der Wissenschaften, 1910–. Cited by volume and page number.

A/B   *Kritik der reinen Vernunft* (1781/1787), edited by Raymund Schmidt. Hamburg: Meiner, 1956.

Immanuel Kant's Critique of Pure Reason, translated by Norman Kemp Smith. New York: St. Martin's, 1963. Cited by first edition (A) and second edition (B) page numbers.

BSE   *Beobachtungen über das Gefühl des Schönen und Erhabenen* (1764), *GS 2.*

Observations on the Beautiful and Sublime, translated by J. Goldthwait. Berkeley: University of California Press, 1981.

G   *Grundlegung der Metaphysik der Sitten* (1785), *GS 4.*

Foundations of the Metaphysics of Morals, translated by Lewis White Beck. Indianapolis: Bobbs-Merrill, 1959. Cited by page number.

IG   *Idee zu einer allgemeinen Geschichte in weltbürgerlicher Absicht* (1784), *GS 8.*

"Idea for a Universal History with a Cosmopolitan Purpose," translated by H. B. Nisbet, in *Kant's Political Writings*, edited by H. Reiss. Cambridge: Cambridge University Press, 1970.

KpV   *Kritik der praktischen Vernunft* (1788), *GS 5.*

Critique of Practical Reason, translated by Lewis White Beck. Indianapolis: Bobbs-Merrill, 1956. Cited by page number.

R   *Religion innerhalb der Grenzen der blossen Vernunft* (1793–1794), *GS 6.*

Religion Within the Limits of Reason Alone, translated by Theodore M. Greene and Hoyt H. Hudson. New York: Harper & Row, 1960. Cited by page number.

RL   *Metaphysik der Sitten* (1797): Rechtslehre, *GS 6.*

Metaphysical Elements of Justice, translated by John Ladd. Indianapolis: Bobbs-Merrill, 1965. Cited by page number, occasionally by section (§) number.

TL   *Metaphysik der Sitten* (1797): Tugendlehre, *GS 6.*

The Doctrine of Virtue, translated by Mary J. Gregor. New York: Harper & Row, 1964. Cited by page number.

TP   *Über den Gemeinspruch: Das mag in der Theorie richtig sein, taugt aber nicht für die Praxis* (1793), *GS 8.*

"On the Common Saying: This May Be True in Theory, But It Does Not Apply in Practice," translated by H. B. Nisbet, in *Kant's Political Writings*.

VE   *Eine Vorlesung über Ethik* (1780), edited by Paul Menzer. Berlin: Rolf Heise, 1924. Reprinted in *GS 28.1.*

Lectures on Ethics, translated by Louis Infield. New York: Harper, 1963. Cited by page number.

Writings of J. G. Fichte (1762–1814)

FW   *Fichtes Werke*, edited by I. H. Fichte. Berlin: W. de Gruyter, 1971.

GNR   *Grundlage des Naturrechts* (1796), *FW 3.*

Science of Rights, translated by A. E. Kroeger. London: Truebner, 1889. Cited by page number, occasionally also by section (§) number.

SL   *System der Sittenlehre* (1798), *FW 4*.

       The Science of Ethics, translated by A. E. Kroeger. London: Kegan Paul, Trench, Truebner, 1897.

W   *Wissenschaftslehre* (*1794*), including the two Introductions (1797), *FW 1*.

       The Science of Knowledge, translated by Peter Heath and John Lachs. Cambridge: Cambridge University Press, 1983. Cited by page number.

Writings of J. F. Fries (1773–1843)

GDJ   *Über die Gefährdung des Wohlstandes und Charakters der Deutschen durch die Juden.* ["On the Danger to the German Well-Being and Character Posed by the Jews."] Heidelberg: Mohr und Winter, 1816. Cited by page number.

HPP   *Handbuch der praktischen Philosophie, 1. Teil: Ethik.* ["Manual of Practical Philosophy. Part One: Ethics."] Heidelberg: Mohr und Winter, 1818. Cited by page number.

JE   *Julius und Evagoras, oder: Schönheit der Seele. Ein philosophischer Roman.* ["Julius and Evagoras, or: Beauty of Soul. A Philosophical Novel."] Heidelberg: Christian Friedrich Winter, 1822. (Revised and expanded from first edition of 1813.)

       Dialogues on Morality and Religion, translated by David Walford. Totowa, NJ: Barnes and Noble, 1982. Cited by page number.

NKV   *Neue Kritik der Vernunft.* ["New Critique of Reason."] Heidelberg: Mohr und Zimmer, 1807. (New edition of 1838 under the title: *Anthropologische Kritik der Vernunft.* ["Anthropological Critique of Reason."]) Cited by volume and page number.

Introduction

1. Hegel as speculative philosopher

Hegel holds that philosophy is a wholly unique discipline, which deals with unique objects and employs a unique method (*EL* §§ 1–4). Philosophy is distinguished both from everyday common sense and from the empirical sciences by the way it abstracts from their concerns, and grasps in their purity the "determinations of thought" which, unnoticed, provide everyday life and inquiry with their genuine content (*EL* § 5; *WL* 5: 38/45). In Hegel's view, the foundation of all philosophy is the self-evolving system of these abstract thought-determinations, presented in the purely philosophical discipline of speculative logic.

Hegel sees traditional Aristotelian logic as an empty, formal discipline; he intends speculative logic to transform it into a science with profound metaphysical content (*EL* § 24). Speculative logic will thereby provide a metaphysical key to the a priori comprehension of all reality, enabling philosophy to encompass and systematize the results of empirical science and give to them an a priori character (*EL* § 12). In so doing, it will overcome the alien, accidental, and objective form taken by these facts in the modern empirical sciences (*EL* § 7), exhibiting the inner essence of the objective world as at one with our own freedom as thinkers (*EL* § 23).[1] Hegel thus regards his own philosophical achievement as fundamentally a contribution to metaphysics or "first philosophy."

Hegel is the most methodologically self-conscious of all philosophers in the Western tradition. There is no modern philosopher, not even excepting Descartes, Kant, and Husserl, who displays greater originality in laying the methodological foundations of a philosophical system. This is Hegel's main project during his Jena period, culminating in the *Phenomenology of Spirit* of 1807. It is a side of Hegel seldom appreciated, because Hegel's methodological reflections are a response to the problems of ancient Pyrrhonistic skepticism, rather than to the skeptical worries of the post-Cartesian tradition, which Hegel always esteemed less highly than he did the ancient skeptical tradition.[2]

2. Dialectical logic

The lifeblood of Hegel's system of speculative logic is the famous Hegelian dialectic. Hegel's dialectic may be viewed as a highly novel theory of philosophical paradoxes: where and why philosophical thought runs into them, what they mean, how to deal with them. Kant argues that when human reason attempts to extend its cognition beyond the bounds of possible experience, it not only is tempted to make unwarranted claims to knowledge, but also is in danger of falling into contradictions (antinomies); the only way to avoid them is by carefully observing the proper limits of its cognitive powers. The part of this account Hegel retains is the idea that our thinking has an inherent tendency to go beyond every limit, and thus to undermine or overthrow itself. He associates this idea with the human self's tendency to change, develop, and progress through a process involving a stage of self-conflict followed by its resolution.[3]

Hegel holds that a thought determination is what it is because it is determined (or limited) in a definite way. But each such thought has an inherent tendency to push beyond its limit and turn into its opposite, resulting in a contradiction. This "dialectic" of thought determinations, as Hegel calls it, is a cause of consternation to the "understanding" – that analytical disposition of thought which tries to grasp thought determinations in their determinacy, keeping them clearly and distinctly separated from one another. For the understanding, dialectic is a source of scandal and paradox, something to avoid at all costs. But the understanding's efforts are to no avail, because thought itself is dynamic, self-transcending, fundamentally dialectical. Kant realized that thoughts obey the understanding's rules only so long as they remain within their proper bounds. Hegel hastens to add that they have an inherent tendency not to remain confined, a tendency that is as much a part of their nature as the neat analytical definitions within which the understanding wants to confine them. Dialectical paradoxes cannot be avoided, done away with, or treated as mere illusions, as the understanding would wish. They are real, unavoidable, virtually omnipresent.

Hegel argues that the proper way to resolve dialectical paradoxes is not to suppress them, but to systematize them. If you become master of them, they can do positive philosophical work for you. Just as thought inevitably gives rise to contradictions, so it also inevitably reconciles them in a higher unity, as a human self that grows through self-conflict proves its growth by emerging from the conflict into a higher self-harmony. For example, Kant's Second Antinomy opposes the infinite divisibility of the real in space to the indivisibility of its smallest parts ($A434/B462$). Hegel thinks the antinomy can be resolved by recognizing that the concept of quantity contains within itself both of the opposed determinations, discreteness and continuity (WL 5: 216–227/190–199; cf. EL § 100). Kant resolves the antinomy by saying that as a mere appearance, matter is *neither* infinitely divisible nor composed of simples ($A502–507/B530–53$ 6); Hegel resolves it by saying that matter is *both* at once. It can be both because our thought may legitimately employ both conceptions involving discreteness and conceptions involving continuity in its theorizing about matter.

In effect, Hegel resolves philosophical paradoxes such as the Second Antinomy by relying on an idealist or constructivist picture of the relation of theory to reality. If reality is constituted by our thought about it, and that thought systematically involves contrasting (even contradictory) aspects or moments, then reality itself must embody the same contradictions. Contradictory thinking about reality is tolerable if we are capable (via the understanding) of distinguishing clearly between the contradictory aspects of our thought, and also (via speculative reason) of reconciling the contradictions in a higher theoretical conception.

We might compare Hegel's treatment of philosophical paradoxes with the later Wittgenstein's. Wittgenstein held that contradictions or paradoxes do not "make our language less usable" because, once we "know our way about" and become clear about exactly where and why they arise, we can "seal them off"; we need not view a contradiction as "the local symptom of a sickness of the whole body."[4] For Wittgenstein contradictions can be tolerated because they are marginal and we can keep them sequestered from the rest of our thinking; for Hegel, they arise systematically in the course of philosophical thought, but they do no harm so long as a system of speculative logic can keep them in their proper place, refusing them admittance to those contexts in which they would do harm. Thus Hegel claims that the old-fashioned logic of the understanding is just a limiting case of speculative logic, which we obtain simply by omitting the dialectical element in thought (*EL* § 82).

The guarantee that contradictions need not ultimately disrupt thinking is provided by the higher unity, in which the opposites are reconciled and the proper place of each is simultaneously determined. For example, the opposition between continuous quantity and discrete quantity leads to a contradiction when we don't realize that the concept of quantity contains both (*WL* 5: 229/200). Their difference is overcome in the concept of a determinate quantity or a quantum. This concept sets limits to simple continuity, and hence supersedes *(aufhebt)* the opposition between continuous and discrete quantity (*WL* 5: 230/201).

Hegel has a broader and a narrower conception of dialectic. Sometimes he includes the "positive reason" that "grasps opposites in their unity" within "dialectic" (*WL* 5: 52/56), but sometimes he calls this stage "speculation" or "positive reason," in contrast to "dialectic" or "negative reason" (*EL* § 82). Negative reason is the activity of reason that drives thought determinations beyond themselves and engenders the contradictions that so plague the understanding; speculation or positive reason reconciles contradictions in a higher unity, enabling them to be included in a rational system. In the system of speculative logic, each thought determination leads to another that opposes it, and that opposition leads in turn to a new determination in which the opposition is overcome.

(The regrettable tradition of expounding this theme in the Hegelian dialectic through the grotesque jargon of "thesis," "antithesis," and "synthesis" began in 1837 with Heinrich Moritz Chalybäus, a bowdlerizer of German idealist philosophy, whose ridiculous expository devices should have been forgotten along with his name.[5] This triad of terms is used by both Fichte and Schelling, though never to express the Hegelian ideas we have just been examining; to my knowledge, it is never used by Hegel, not even once, for this purpose or for any other. The use of Chalybäus's terminology to expound the Hegelian dialectic is nearly always an unwitting confession that the expositor has little or no firsthand knowledge of Hegel.)

Hegel's speculative logic attempts to run through all basic determinations of thought in a systematic way, assigning each its proper place within the development. At the pinnacle of the system is the "Idea" – thought's tendency to actualize itself by going outside itself. Hegel associates the Idea with the ontological proof for God's existence, since the Idea exhibits the capacity of the highest thought directly to demonstrate its own existence (*EL* § 64). But the Idea also represents, in religious terms, God's creation of the world. The Idea is thought's proceeding beyond itself to give itself immediate reality in finite, sensuous nature (*EL* § 244). Hegel's system, comprising the philosophy of nature and philosophy of spirit, attempts to develop the structure of the world of nature and the world of the human mind, using the categories and movement of the system of speculative logic as its key. Nature is thought going outside itself; mind or spirit is its return to itself. As a natural being, the human being, through its awareness of itself as thought, transcends the merely natural to the level of the spiritual. "Spirit" embraces not only "subjective spirit" (or individual psychology), but also "objective spirit" (society or culture, culminating in the political state), and finally "absolute spirit," the realms of art, religion, and philosophy – those forms of higher human culture in which spirit becomes aware of itself as absolute, or the ultimate reality.

3. Speculative logic is dead; but Hegel's thought is not

We must admire the boldness of Hegel's methodological conception in the *Phenomenology*, but we must also admit that Hegel's hopelessly ambitious project proves utterly unconvincing in its execution. Even Hegel himself perhaps tacitly abandoned the *Phenomenology* as the foundation of his system in the Heidelberg *Encyclopedia* (1817), where he relegated the contents of *PhG* Chapters 1–5 to a subordinate part of the philosophy of spirit. The Berlin *Encyclopedia* (1827, 1830) includes a new introduction to the system (*EL* §§ 1–83). This introduction expresses reservations about the *Phenomenology*'s procedure as a starting point, at the same time candidly confessing itself encumbered with the identical defects to an even greater extent (*EL* § 25R).

Viewed from a late twentieth-century perspective, it is evident that Hegel totally failed in his attempt to canonize speculative logic as the only proper form of philosophical thinking. Many of the philosophical paradoxes Hegel needs in order to make his system work are based on shallow sophistries; the resolution to paradoxes supplied by his system is often artificial and unilluminating. When the theory of logic actually was revolutionized in the late nineteenth and early twentieth centuries, the new theory was built upon precisely those features of traditional logic that Hegel thought most dispensable. In light of it, philosophical sanity now usually judges that the most promising way to deal with the paradoxes that plague philosophy is the understanding's way. Hegel's system of dialectical logic has never won acceptance outside an isolated and dwindling tradition of incorrigible enthusiasts.

Of course, the history of philosophy is a history of spectacular failures. Descartes failed to put the sciences on an absolutely indubitable basis in his first philosophy. Kant also failed to establish metaphysics as the forever closed and finished science of the transcendental forms of empirical knowledge. Yet Hegel's failure was essentially more final and unredeemable than theirs, since even the problems of Hegel's logic remain alien and artificial to us in ways that the problems of Cartesian and Kantian philosophy do not. As one recent scholar of Hegel's method confesses, the short answer to the question "What is living in the logic of Hegel?" is: "Nothing."[6]

Because Hegel regards speculative logic as the foundation of his system, we might conclude from its failure that nothing in his philosophy could any longer be deserving of our interest. But that would be quite wrong. The fact is rather that Hegel's great positive achievements as a philosopher do not lie where he thought they did, in his system of speculative logic, but in quite a different realm, in his reflections on the social and spiritual predicament of modern Western European culture. Like no one before, and perhaps no one since, Hegel's thought explores the self-conception of modern human beings, the ambivalent relation of modern European culture to its Hebraic–Hellenic heritage, its quest in the modern world for a new image of nature and society, its hopes and self-doubts, its needs and aspirations.

Soon after his death, the influence of Hegel's philosophy began to decline rapidly. Hegel was held in quite low esteem during the latter half of the nineteenth century and the first few decades of the present one. Hegel's contribution to the "human sciences" *(Geisteswissenschaften)* was always acknowledged even during those periods, however, at least in the German tradition.[7] It was also this side of Hegel's thought that since the 1930s has led to a remarkable resurgence of interest in his philosophy. The situation was already quite clear to Ernst Cassirer nearly a half century ago:

[Hegel's] logic and metaphysics were at first regarded as the strongest bulwarks of his system; yet it was precisely from this side that the system was open to the most violent and dangerous attacks. And after a short struggle they seemed to have been successful. Yet Hegelianism has had a rebirth not in the field of logical or metaphysical thought, but in the field of political thought. There has hardly been a single great political system that has resisted its influence. All our modern political ideologies show us the strength, the durability and permanence of the principles that were first introduced and defended in Hegel's philosophy of right and his philosophy of history.[8]

The living traditions that derive from Hegel's thought – the traditions of Marxist social theory and existential philosophy – are distinctly antimetaphysical in their orientation. The Hegel who still lives and speaks to us is not a speculative logician and idealist metaphysician but a philosophical historian, a political and social theorist, a philosopher of our ethical concerns and cultural identity crises.

4. Speculative philosophy and modern society

This is not necessarily to contradict the assertion that we cannot understand Hegel's social and political concerns without reference to his speculative metaphysics.[9] But we are likely to miss the connection between the two if (with Hegel) we suppose that Hegelian social thought is *grounded* in Hegelian metaphysics, and conclude that speculative logic is a propaedeutic to Hegel's theory of modern society. In fact, the relation between the two may be very nearly the reverse of this; often Hegel's treatment of metaphysical issues is best viewed as an attempt to interpret these issues as an expression of cultural and existential concerns. The most influential recent interpretation of Hegel's philosophy, that of Charles Taylor's *Hegel* (1975), understands Hegel's metaphysics essentially as an "expressivist" vision of human agency and its products, viewing Hegel's entire philosophy as a response to the cultural predicament of the post-Enlightenment.[10] If Hegel understood his philosophy as the activity of pure thought-thinking itself, its legacy has rather been that of enabling us to understand how all human thought expresses its concrete social and cultural context.

Even Hegel's own conception of his task speaks in favor of regarding his philosophy as fundamentally occupied with cultural self-understanding and practical self-concern. In 1801, Hegel opens his first piece of published writing with a meditation on "the need of philosophy" in the present age. He sees this need as arising at a time when the unreflective harmony of human individuals with themselves and their world has been rent by a culture based on reflection; and he assigns philosophy the task of reestablishing this harmony at a higher level through reason (*D* 20–21/89–91). In his last published work, the *Philosophy of Right* (1821), Hegel assigns to philosophy essentially the same function: reconciling reflective individuals with the world, and above all with the social world, through a speculative cognition of the actual in its rationality (*PR* Preface 27).[11] If an understanding of Hegel's thinking about human selfhood and society refers us to his metaphysics, it is because the principal aim of Hegel's metaphysics is to address the predicament of modern humanity in modern society.

Georg Lukacs acknowledges this point when he says: "The entire Hegelian philosophy is essentially oriented to the knowledge of society and history. Hence its categories are by their very nature adapted to this sphere of being."[12] But once again it is not as though Hegel's social philosophy drives us constantly back to the categories of his metaphysics as to some source of esoteric wisdom. The point is rather that Hegel sees his metaphysics as the foundation of a philosophy that deals with the modern predicament because his own deepest response to the modern predicament is a response on the level of metaphysics or speculative philosophy. Hegel's response to the alienation of modern life is not (like Schiller's or Schelling's) aesthetic, nor (like

Schleiermacher's) religious. Still less does Hegel respond (like Kant and Fichte) by turning the struggle inward to the individual's moral life, nor (like Marx) does he turn it outward to social revolution. Hegel seeks to overcome alienation by rationally reconciling us to the world, comprehending a divine reason, akin to our own, immanent in it.

Hegel makes many extravagant claims for his philosophy, even to the point of arrogating the terms "philosophy" and "science" as nicknames for his own system. But in view of the fact that Hegel's language and ideas often strike us as bewilderingly novel and unfamiliar, it is especially noteworthy that one distinction he never claims for it is *originality*. Hegel sees himself rather as a synthetic, encyclopedic thinker whose task is to reconcile the wisdom of ancient Greek metaphysics with the faith of the Christian religion, reinterpreting both in terms of the modern claims of free subjectivity and Enlightenment reason. Thus in *The Science of Logic* Hegel conceives his task not as that of "building a new city in a wasteland" but rather as "remodeling an ancient city, solidly built, and maintained in continuous possession and occupation" (*WL* 6: 243/575). Hegel does not see himself as the architect of a new system or method like Descartes, still less as the destroyer of a tradition like Nietzsche or Heidegger. He is rather the restorer of an ancient building in need of repair; his original contribution, such as it is, consists in buttressing it through the use of recently acquired materials and engineering techniques, so that it may once again be a sound structure in which to live.

It is this modest and ingenuous self-conception that leads Hegel to speak of his own system simply as "science" or "philosophy." He is as far as possible in this regard from his Romantic contemporaries who thought of both philosophy and art as products of individual genius, monuments to the idiosyncrasy of their self-celebrating creators. For Hegel, a sound philosophical system is not anyone's personal creation at all. In his view, the content of his system is merely the Western philosophical tradition, appropriated by the reflective spirit of modernity. The aim of philosophy is to vindicate *die Sache selbst*, and it can do this only if it owes as little as possible to the unique personality of the individual who happens to formulate it.

In contrast with his misestimate of himself as primarily a metaphysician and speculative logician, Hegel's self-understanding on this point seems to me to contain a good deal of truth, especially regarding ethical topics. In the area of moral philosophy, Hegel's thought represents an attempt, in many ways strikingly successful, to remodel classical ethical theory, exhibiting its fundamental soundness by investing it with the style, and adapting it to the content, of a modern self-understanding. Like Goethe's poetry, Hegel's ethical thought is an attempt to marry the classical ideal with the modern, to unite the harmony of Greek culture with the reflective spirit of the Enlightenment, so as to conceive the modern social order as one in which Faustian aspirations can reach fulfillment without violating the requirements of classical form.

Hegel's achievement lies in his sensitivity to the diverse aspirations of modern humanity, his ability to relate these aspirations to their historical roots

7

and their focus in social institutions, and his success in integrating these aspirations into a single conception of the modern spirit. Hegel's *Philosophy of Right* articulates our deepest human needs and is sensitive to their diversity and the destructive possibilities that such diversity presents. It points the way to a society in which reflective, rational, and self-integrated individuals can satisfy all of their needs simultaneously, without the regret of lost alternatives or tragic choices between incompatible and incommensurable goods.

For Hegel, of course, its chief significance is philosophical or speculative: to exhibit the social world and one's role in it as rationally satisfying because it is the actualization of reason, the work of divine providence, manifest to the philosopher even in the most worldly aspects of life. Few of Hegel's readers today find it natural to adopt rational theodicy as their fundamental relation to their cultural predicament. Accordingly, they should be more willing than he was to consider Hegel's conception of the vocation of modern individuals and its fulfillment in the modern state in their practical meaning – as a project in rational ethics. To read Hegel in this way is, admittedly, to read him in some measure against his own self-understanding; it is nevertheless the only way in which most of us, if we are honest with ourselves, can read him seriously at all. Such a reading requires that we first look closely at Hegel's own conception of his philosophical project, so that we may see clearly where it leaves room for the possibility of a Hegelian ethical theory.

5. Does Hegel have an ethics?

It is sometimes said, by Hegel's sympathizers as well as his detractors, that Hegel's system contains no "ethics" at all, that for Hegel moral philosophy is "dissolved in sociology" or "absorbed in political philosophy".[13] Such remarks are misleading exaggerations, but there is some truth in them if they are understood in the right way.

Hegel's philosophy is fundamentally a speculative metaphysics whose aim is to overcome, through philosophical insight, the alienation of the modern mind from itself, nature, and society. Because of this, in Hegel's mature system even "practical philosophy" is treated from a contemplative perspective – as a stage in spirit's self-knowledge (*EG* §§ 469–552). Thus Hegel treats "the will" not from the perspective of the volitional agent engaging in practical deliberation, but from the perspective of the speculative philosopher contemplating the will and its mode of actualization. Likewise, the avowed aim of the *Philosophy of Right* is not to tell the state how it ought to be, but rather to provide us with a rational theodicy of modern social life, by exhibiting the actuality of divine reason and the rationality of the social world it has created (*PR* Preface 24–28).

It is simply false to say that Hegel's philosophy aims at justifying the social and political status quo. On the contrary, Hegel insists that every existing state, standing as it does in the sphere of transitoriness and contingency, is disfigured to some extent by error and wickedness, and fails to be wholly rational, because it fails to be wholly actual (*PR* § 258A). The *Philosophy of*

Right clearly leaves room for rational criticism of what exists, and also for practical efforts to improve the existing state by actualizing it, bringing it more into harmony with its own rational essence or concept.

Hegel does deny, however, that such criticism belongs among the tasks of *philosophy:*

> For who is not clever enough to see much in his environment that is not in fact as it ought to be? But this cleverness is wrong to imagine that such objects and their "ought" have any place within the interests of philosophical science. For science has to do only with the Idea, which is not so impotent that it only ought to be without actually being; hence philosophy has to do with an actuality of which those objects, institutions, conditions, etc. are only the superficial outside. (*EL* § 6; cf. *PR* Preface 25)

The rhetorical question that introduces this passage is in effect a declaration that no one (least of all Hegel) is so stupid as to claim that the status quo is always as it ought to be. Yet the passage contains two other controversial ideas which, though they do not deny that much in the world is not as it ought to be, nevertheless tend to denigrate the importance often attached to this obvious truth by partisans of the "understanding." The first is an idea about the scope and aim of philosophy. Hegel claims that although it may often be correct to say that social institutions and conditions are not as they should be, it is always wrong to regard such assertions (even where they are correct) as of interest to "philosophical science." For the task of philosophy (conceived here in 1830 very much as it was in the *Differenzschrift* of 1801) is to heal the division or bifurcation *(Entzweiung)* which the modern principle of reflection has opened between our minds and the world; it effects this healing by exhibiting to our reason the world's own deep inner rationality.

We might take Hegel to be agreeing with Aristotle that the highest end of reason is philosophical contemplation and not the ends of practice in the narrower sense (*VGP* 2: 167/151). But Hegel opposes speculative cognition both to theory and to practice, treating it as a higher unity in which both are contained. The absolute Idea lies beyond both the Idea of cognition and the Idea of the good (*EL* § 236), just as the realm of absolute spirit transcends both theoretical and practical spirit (*EG* § 553). Hegel's view seems to be that speculative wisdom belongs equally in contemplation of the reason that shows itself in the world, and in practice that actualizes reason in the world – just as art, religion, and philosophy nourish the human spirit equally in its cognition and its action.

This conception of philosophy rests on a second controversial idea: that although there is much in the contingent, transitory world of existence and appearance that is not as it ought to be, nevertheless the inner essence of things, viewed by speculative reason in its necessity, is inevitably seen to be fully rational and hence spiritually satisfying. Because of this there can be a genuine "science" of speculative logic, which deals entirely with the "thought determinations" that constitute the conceptual essence of the world, and display themselves in external reality. This science is philosophy proper, and its object is solely the "Idea" – the self-realizing rational concept, or the "ab-

9

solute unity of the concept and objectivity" (*EL* § 213). In the "real" part of philosophical science, the outward forms taken by thought in the worlds of nature and human society can be reappropriated by the human spirit through our cognition of them. Hegel is convinced that once we have tasted of this purely philosophical science and its truth, we will want to distinguish it from all other standpoints on the world, including the practical one, and to treat them all as essentially inferior.

6. Rationality and actuality

This is the point of Hegel's saying, "The rational is actual, and the actual is rational." In his own exegesis of the saying, Hegel is at pains to distinguish what is "actual" from what merely "exists." The "actual," he says, includes only those existents that fully express and correspond to their essence (*EL* §§ 6, 142). Such an existent Hegel calls an "appearance" or "phenomenon" *(Erscheinung)* (*EL* § 131). The transitory existents that we encounter in everyday life (including societies and states) often fail to be "actual," fail to be "appearances" of their "essence." In them the outer expression is inadequate to the inner essence; and an existent that is imperfect in this way Hegel calls "illusion" or "show" *(Schein)* (*WL 6*: 17/394; *EL* § 131A). (Hegel's use of the term *Schein* is likely to mislead, since "illusions" in this sense – e.g., evil or sick human beings, badly organized or unjust states – certainly *exist* every bit as much as "actualities" do.)

> What is actual is rational. But one must know, distinguish, what is in fact actual. In common life all is actual, but [in philosophy] there is a distinction between the world of appearance and actuality. The actual has also an external existence, which displays arbitrariness and contingency. . . . Men will always be wicked and depraved, but this is not the Idea. On the surface passions wrestle everywhere, but that is not the actuality of substance. The temporal and transitory certainly exists, and may cause us enough distress; but in spite of that it, along with the particularity of the subject and its wishes and inclinations, is no true actuality. (*VGP 2*: 110–111/95–96)

Hegel distinguishes between the rational "essence," whose adequate appearance is the "actual," and the "transitory, contingent, superficial exterior," which this essence wears in the sphere of finitude. In effect, this is Hegel's way of drawing the distinction between God and creation; God is the "rational essence" of things, whereas creation is their "superficial exterior" (*WL 5*; 44/50). Because "philosophy is the true theodicy" (*VGP 3*: 455/ 546; *VPG* 28/15), the only true subject matter of philosophy is God, and philosophy proper occupies itself with the finite world only to the extent that the divine presence is immanent in it – that is, only to the extent that the finite is "actual." The defects of finitude exist, but they are superficial contingencies, justified by the fact that contingency itself is a necessary factor in God's self-manifestation (*WL 6*: 180/542–553; *EL* § 145A).[14]

Hegel's philosophy of the state justifies not the status quo, but God; it hallows not the political order but the divine revealing itself in the spiritual realm of the state, just as it does in the lower realm of nature (*PR* Preface

15). The task of philosophy is to contemplate the divine or "affirmative" factor that necessarily reveals itself to speculative reason in even the most defective state, just as the rational essence of humanity displays itself even in the ugliest, most deformed or most corrupt human beings (*PR* § 258A). Philosophy can neither justify nor condemn any existing state, since it is not the task of philosophy to pass judgment on how well or badly any given state has actualized its rational essence.

This restriction on the scope of "philosophy" or "philosophical science" does appear to entail that for Hegel "philosophy," taking the word in the strict sense, cannot contain an ethics; in other words, in the strict sense of the word there can be no such thing as a "practical *philosophy*." For philosophy concerns itself with what exists only to the extent that it manifests the divine; and in respect of existents that do, there can be no distinction between what they are and what they ought to be.

Yet Hegel's position clearly commits him to hold (and he often explicitly affirms) that reason *is* practical. Reason constantly works changes in the world through human actions, actualizing itself in what exists. The only ground Hegel has for excluding the practical use of reason from "philosophy" is a jealous reservation of the term to speculative contemplation, the supreme activity of thought divinely thinking only itself. Abandoning these strictures, however, Hegel occasionally regards his philosophy of objective spirit (especially in the *Philosophy of Right*) as a "practical philosophy" (*PR* § 4A).[15]

Hegel's ambivalence on this point is reflected in the ambiguity of the term "objective spirit" itself. It refers both to the objective *world* which spirit has made for itself in the form of the rational social order, and to the objective *validity* of the duties, laws, and institutions constituting the world. It is "objective" in the sense that it stands over against the subject as an existing world, and also in the very different (even opposite) sense that it lays claim on the subject's will through its own concept and vocation (*PR* § 26). The Berlin *Encyclopedia* thus defines "objective spirit" as a world not only "brought forth" by spirit but also "to be brought forth" by it (*EG* § 385).

Accordingly, the *Philosophy of Right* must be looked at simultaneously in two ways: (1) as "philosophical science" in the strict sense of *EL* § 6, an exercise in speculative theodicy; and (2) as "practical philosophy," an ethical and political theory on the basis of which conclusions can be drawn about how the world should be, including how social institutions and conditions should be changed. Some things Hegel says in the *Philosophy of Right* are no doubt intended as "philosophical science" in the strict sense; but many, many others make sense only as pieces of practical ethics or political theory, and cannot be comfortably fit into Hegel's official project of speculative theodicy.

7. Hegel's practical philosophy

Hegel's thesis that the actual is rational not only leaves room for practical philosophy; it also helps to define the method of Hegel's practical philosophy. It implies that we are mistaken if we think the right way to go about practical philosophy is first to formulate "ideals" and then to look around for some way in which the errant world might be brought into conformity with them. Reason's actuality in the world consists in the exercise of the capacities of existing things, the fulfillment of essential tendencies in them. Such tendencies toward rationality do not inevitably prevail in a world of transitoriness and contingency, but we can learn about them through the actual behavior of things, and what we learn in this way is indispensable to ethical knowledge. This means that practical reason is not autonomous in the sense that it is cut off from the world to which it is to be applied. Rather, it consists in working with the essential tendencies in the existent to actualize the rationality that is there. Hegel's ethical thought thus turns out to represent a rather Aristotelian variety of ethical naturalism.

It is in this light that we should interpret Hegel's frequent, emphatic, yet cryptic and sometimes paradoxical remarks disparaging "the ought" (*PhG* §§ 249, 425, 619; *WL* 6 : 544/820; *EL* §§ 6, 234) and criticizing those who want to "teach the world how it ought to be" (*PR* Preface 27). "The true ideal," says Hegel, "is not what ought to be actual but what is actual, and the only actuality. If an ideal is held to be too good to exist, there must be some fault in the ideal itself, since actuality is too good for it" (*VGP* 2 : 110/95). An ideal is defective if it is not founded on the rational essence of that to which it is applied. Where practical recommendations do have such a basis, there will be an essential tendency in the existence to actualize it. But an ideal to which no such tendency corresponds is an ideal alien to the *Bestimmung* – the nature, destiny, or vocation, of those to whom it is addressed. Because of this, it will forever remain an "ought" without actuality, and for their sake it is just as well that it remain so.

Hegel's polemics against the "ought" are criticisms of the view, present in Kant and exaggerated by Fichte, that practical reason has primacy over theoretical reason, and that this entails that the only truly rational order is an ideal one, entirely independent of what is, eternally confronting it as its "ought-to-be." From the Aristotelian perspective Hegel adopts, it makes good sense to reject such ideals.

Largely on the basis of the Preface to the *Philosophy of Right*, Hegel acquired a reputation among his liberal critics as the "Prussian State philosopher," a philosophical apologist for the Prussian restoration. There can be little doubt that in 1820 Hegel intended the Preface to be understood as a pledge of allegiance by the Prussian authorities who employed him. Yet it is noteworthy that in the same paragraph where Hegel insists that the task of philosophy is to "apprehend the present and the actual, not to erect a beyond," he goes on immediately to argue that Plato's *Republic* represents political philosophy in the truest sense because it "grasped nothing but the nature of Greek ethical life" (*PR* Preface 24). Together with a long tradition of Hegel's detractors, the Prussian censors seem to have been too dull to draw the plain inference that as far as Hegel's protestations in its Preface are concerned, the *Philosophy of Right* might just as easily be the same sort of apology for Prussian absolutism as Plato's *Republic* was for Athenian democracy.

The rational state described in the *Philosophy of Right* does closely resemble Prussia; not as it ever was, but Prussia as it was to have become under the reform ministry led by Chancellor Karl August von Hardenberg, with the advice of Interior Minister Wilhelm von Humboldt (who had established the professorship Hegel occupied) and Minister of Education Karl von Altenstein (who had arranged for Hegel's appointment to it). In May of 1815, King Friedrich Wilhelm III had issued a proclamation promising that Prussia would be given a written constitution providing for the regular convening of an estates assembly (or parliament). Early in 1819, Hardenberg and Humboldt both drafted plans for such a constitution. The rational state described in the *Philosophy of Right* bears a striking resemblance to these plans. They would have converted Prussia from an absolute monarchy into a constitutional monarchy (*PR* § 273,R) and would have established a bicameral estates assembly, with an upper house drawn from the hereditary nobility, and a lower house comprised of representatives drawn from municipal and professional corporations (*PR* §§ 300–316).[16]

In some of his early lectures on the *Philosophy of Right,* prior to its publication in 1820, we get a very different picture of the political implications of his philosophy from the one given in the Preface.[17] For instance, in 1819, Hegel puts his famous thesis in a slightly different way: "What is actual becomes rational, and the rational becomes actual" (*VPR19* : 51). Here the relation between rationality and actuality is a dynamic one, asserting not the rationality of the status quo but rather the rationality of social change. This harmonizes well with Hegel's sympathy with the Reform Era, expressing Hegel's confidence that the Prussian state was evolving toward rationality, becoming more and more like the "actual" or "rational" constitutional monarchy of the *Philosophy of Right*. This same optimism is also expressed in a statement of Hegel's thesis about the rationality of the actual from his Heidelberg lectures of 1817–1818: "What is rational must happen, since on the whole the constitution is only its development" (*VPR17* : 157).

The Reform Era was brought to a sudden end by events of the summer of 1819. Internal foes of reform, such as Fürst Wittgenstein, and its external foes, such as Metternich, prevailed over Chancellor Hardenberg; Humboldt was forced to resign from the ministry, and thus ended the prospects for constitutional reform in Prussia. In order to reconcile Hegel's statements in the Preface with the actual contents of the book, one would have to argue that, owing to human error, wickedness, and other unfortunate contingencies, the Prussian state in its existence never achieved full actuality, but always remained defective in relation to the Idea of the modern state. We have seen that Hegel's conceptions of actuality, existence, and contingency do allow for this possibility.

Critics of Hegel such as Søren Kierkegaard have often charged that he masquerades as a Christian apologist while actually defending a philosophy of rationalist humanism which is wholly at odds with the spirit of Christian faith. In view of Hegel's penetrating critique of the otherworldly "unhappy consciousness" and his rationalistic reinterpretation of such Christian doctrines as the Incarnation and the Trinity, there is evidently some truth in these charges. The same complaint might be brought with equal justice against Hegel's attempt (in the Preface to the *Philosophy of Right*) to appease the censors by portraying himself as a defender of the Prussian state against its enemies. The reactionary King Friedrich Wilhelm IV, who came to the throne in 1840, certainly regarded Hegelian philosophy in all its forms as either a false friend or an open enemy.[18]

Hegel's thesis that "the rational is actual, and the actual is rational" has both a speculative meaning and a practical one. The speculative meaning is that philosophical wisdom consists in contemplating the inner rational essence of things rather than dwelling on their contingent appearances. The practical meaning is that rational action proceeds not from ideals or principles set up in independence of what is, but rather from a rational comprehension of what is. The thesis in its speculative meaning gives some support to the thesis in its practical meaning, by providing a metaphysical rationale for the Aristotelian assumptions of an ethical theory of self-actualization. But it is possible to accept the thesis in its practical meaning while repudiating it in its speculative meaning, if we are prepared to give a conception of human self-actualization some other basis (e.g., an empirical, historical analysis of the nature of human beings in modern Western culture). In neither meaning does the thesis deny that there may be defects in what exists. In its speculative meaning it does imply that the business of philosophical science involves a principled direction of one's attention away from these defects, in order to obtain a purer insight into God's immanence in the world. In its practical meaning the thesis is controversial, since it involves a variety of ethical naturalism and an Aristotelian self-actualization theory of the human good. But it has no more tendency to sanctify whatever happens to exist than most other versions of Aristotelian naturalism.

I
Hegelian ethical theory

I
Self-actualization

1. Ethical theory and self-awareness

If there is any hope for ethics as a branch of rational inquiry, it lies in showing how ethical conceptions and a theory of the human good can be grounded in human self-understanding.[1] Ethics must be grounded in a knowledge of human beings that enables us to say that some modes of life are suited to our nature, whereas others are not. In that sense, ethical theories generally may be regarded as theories of human self-actualization. Plato grounds his ethics in psychology, and Aristotle identifies the human good with a life actualizing the human essence in accordance with its proper excellences. Even the ethical theories of modern times rest on some identifiable conception of human beings, Kantian theories conceiving human nature as finite rational will, and utilitarian theories identifying human beings with bundles of desires, preferences, or affective states.

The common pitfall of ethical theories in this respect is that their conceptions of human nature are too thin, one-sided, and abstract, or else too much dictated by the needs of some convenient theoretical program. Hegel's ethical theory is based on a complex conception of human nature, which systematizes a number of different human self-images. Hegel grounds this conception in his theory of history, which attempts to show how the different elements arose through a process of cultural development. Hegel's ethical theory is therefore culturally and historically specific in ways that most ethical theories are not. At the same time, it tries to avoid cultural relativism by defending its conception of human nature as the outcome of a process in which human beings have acquired a measure of genuine human self-*knowledge*.

Hegel's account of the historical process through which this self-knowledge has been acquired is grounded in a theory of human selfhood and self-awareness. This theory owes much to the thought of his two principal predecessors, Kant and Fichte. Kant treated theoretical self-awareness not as the awareness of a soul-thing underlying our psychic states (in the Cartesian tradition), or even the passive perception of relations of continuity and causal connectedness between these states (in the Lockean and Humean tradition) but rather as the awareness of the activity of synthesizing or combining them (*B* 131–133). Self-awareness is therefore essentially practical; it is not so much an awareness of our various urges and desires as it is the awareness of a system of abiding concerns and projects with which we actively identify.

17

General self-concerns modify or inhibit our desires, give rise to new desires, and serve as a basis for rational judgments about what is for our own good or about what we have best reason to do on the whole.

Thus Kant identifies the will (the practical self) with practical reason (*G* 412/29). Concernful awareness of oneself is indispensable for a sense of one's *identity*, in two related senses: that which ties together all one's mental states as the states of a single person, and that which determines the content of one's self-interest and self-worth. Like Derek Parfit, Kant and his idealist followers regard the identity of a person as a rational construct. Contrary to Parfit, however, they think this enhances rather than diminishes the importance of individual selfhood. For it makes us our own work and our own task; our fundamental vocation is to make ourselves into what we are.[2]

Fichte's way of expressing this idea is to say that the self "posits itself" (*W* 98/99), and that the self is "not a being but a doing" (*W* 495/66). The self is the object of an awareness, but this awareness is not a detached contemplation. Fichte interprets self-awareness as an activity of reflection on another activity already given; this is practical activity or will (*W* 264/232–233, *GNR* 20/36). Self-awareness reflects on will, intuits its own identity with that will, and at the same time forms a concept of it (*W* 463–464/38–39). Thus self-awareness is always *self-concern*, involving issues of self-interest and self-worth. It is self-awareness, in fact, that turns given desires into concerns for self-interest and self-worth. To be a self is always simultaneously to *be aware of* something and to *do* something. It is to "posit" what one is by deciding or positing what one is to be. A self-conception involves simultaneously what one is and what one is striving to become.

These Fichtean ideas are taken up into Hegel's theory of self-awareness, through the thesis that the will's "individuality" results from its own activity of self-determination, proceeding from "universality" through "particularity" (*PR* §§ 5–7). One can speak of a self at all only in relation to an actively willed system of practical concerns, but these concerns have a dimension that goes beyond my "particularity" – the traits, desires, and other qualities that distinguish me from other people. It is not merely a result of the philosopher's peculiar craving for generality that ethical theories focus on the *human* good rather than on the good of this or that individual.

Fichte's way of expressing this is by developing a theory not of the self-awareness of this or that individual but a theory of *das Ich*, of *the I* or *the self*. The Fichtean "I" is not some metaphysical entity distinct from your self and mine, but a transcendental structure or type necessarily exemplified by any particular self. Hegel makes the same point by insisting that one "moment" of the will, that which enables me to apply the word "I" to myself at all, is the moment of "universality," in which I identify myself with what is common to all beings capable of calling themselves "I" (*PR* § 5; *EG* § 381A). But self-concern for Hegel is always socially and culturally situated. An individual self is an expression of its culture's historically developed understanding of human nature and its practical possibilities. Self-concern is universal concern, but it is a socially and historically situated concern, expressing a collective practical project of fashioning a human world (*VG* 54–56/47–48).

The practical project of being a self does not leave either the self or its self-knowledge unaltered. In carrying out the practical project through which they define themselves and their humanity, people acquire a deeper knowledge of themselves and so develop the human nature which it is their project to actualize. In this way, people alter not only their conception of themselves but also the goals involved in this conception. Because this alteration comes about through an alteration of their striving itself, we may even say that people shape or create their own goals and aspirations. Because of this constant interplay of self-understanding, self-actualization, and self-alteration, Hegel refers to the process of creative self-development as a "dialectical" process, to which he gives the name "experience" (*PhG* ¶ 86).

The dialectical project of self-understanding and self-actualization is one in which individual human beings participate through the forms shaped by a cultural tradition. Any individual's project of self-actualization must be understood in its social and historical meaning. Hegel thinks that the strivings of individuals can themselves be understood as cumulative and collective, as aspects of a collective striving of humanity itself for an understanding of its essence and for the proper objective shape in which that essence may be actualized.

2. Spirit

Hegel's adventurous claim is that the various strivings of individual human selves may be gathered together and understood as expressions of a single historical tendency or movement with an intelligibility of its own. He calls the collective subject of this striving "mind" or "spirit" *(Geist)*. The whole of humanity constitutes such a collective subject, and so do the peoples or "national spirits" of particular cultures.

The Hegelian concept of spirit is often ridiculed as a belief in "group minds." This is easiest to do when one thinks of a mind in the Cartesian way, as a nonspatial interior place where immaterial items (called by such names as "thoughts," "ideas," or "representations") enact a microcosmic drama before an audience that, as a matter of logical necessity, is limited to a single spectator. Hegel, however, has a more Aristotelian conception of mentality. For him, mind is a kind of form or organization exhibited by a body in its structure and behavior. This enables us to hypothesize that the collective behavior of human beings might display an organization analogous to the mentality exhibited by the behavior of human individuals. When it is not founded on methodological dogmatism, our resistance to Hegel's talk of national spirits and the world spirit probably derives from a sense that such talk grossly exaggerates the extent of the organization and functional interdependence displayed by the thoughts and activities of nations (and of humanity as a whole). That need not prevent us from treating Hegel's conception of spirit as something to which the reality of society and history may approximate, even if there really is no such entity as the "world spirit."

For Hegel, spirit's self-awareness or "self-relation" is what Hegel calls "subjective spirit" (*EG* § 385). In other words, it is nothing over and above the consciousness that individuals have of spirit's activity. Insofar as human beings give spirit's strivings after self-actualization the external, substantial shape of a functioning social order, Hegel calls this social order "objective spirit" (*EG* §§ 385, 483; cf. *PR* § 27). But the deeds of spirit are also nothing over and above the deeds that individuals do in spirit's behalf. It is only in individuals that the powers of spirit become conscious and actual (*PR* § 145).

Hegel's practical philosophy in the *Philosophy of Right* presents a system of objective spirit for modern culture, the latest and the deepest form in which spirit has attained to knowledge of its essence and expressed that essence in a social world. Like the classical ethical theories of Plato, Aristotle, and the Stoics, Hegel's practical philosophy is based on a conception of an encompassing human good which is *objective* in the sense that it is not reducible to the contingent desires and preferences of particular human beings. Those desires and preferences are in a general way directed toward the good, but they can be based on false beliefs about what it is.

The life that actualizes me, of course, may not be the same as what actualizes you; the good of one person differs from the good of another. But these differences themselves are not merely accidental. They can be understood at least partly in terms of the needs and values pertaining to the individuals' differing social and historical circumstances. The good of a particular individual is a determinate form of the good of spirit, and it can be understood in terms of the good of spirit.

In the classical tradition, the final human good is called "happiness" *(eudaemonia)*. It is conceived as the perfection or self-actualization of human nature, which was identified with the rational element or capacity of the human soul. We will see in § 9 of this chapter that Hegel's ethical theory differs significantly in form from these classical theories, at least if they are interpreted as teleological theories, founded on a final human end or purpose. Hegel's theory is based instead on a conception of human nature – on what Hegel calls the "determination" *(Bestimmung)* or "fundamental determination" *(Grundbestimmung)* of spirit – where *Bestimmung* signifies simultaneously the nature of spirit and its vocation, just as human self-awareness itself is simultaneously an awareness of what I am and of what I strive to do and to be.

It also differs significantly from them in content. For Hegel, as for the classical theorists, the human essence or vocation is related closely to the exercise of our rational powers, both theoretical and practical. Hegel's name for the human determination, however, is not "happiness" but "freedom" (*PR* § 4; *VG* 54/47; *VPR 4*: 101; *EG* § 382). In Chapter 2, we will take a closer look at what Hegel means by "freedom." In Chapter 3, we will investigate his reasons for regarding freedom rather than happiness as the final human good. In the remainder of the present chapter, we will try to see how Hegel articulates the self-understanding of human beings in modern society, and how he attempts to use this self-understanding to develop a distinctive ethical theory.

3. Modern self-understanding

We often hear that Hegel's ethical thought is oriented more toward society than toward the individual. There is a foundation in reality for saying this. Hegel's *Philosophy of Right* belongs to "objective" rather than "subjective" spirit: Hegel's ethical system is a theory of rational social life rather than a theory of individual conduct. But probably its chief foundation is Hegel's belief that rational individuals actualize their freedom most fully when they participate in a state (*PR* § 258). Like utilitarianism, Hegel's ethical theory tells individuals to devote themselves to the good of society, not solely to their own private good. But utilitarianism treats the social good as a simple sum of individual goods; Hegel thinks of it in terms of a certain institutional structure that is a "universal end," valuable in itself and not merely as a means to the good of individuals. That is doubtless one reason why Hegel's ethical theory culminates in the description of a rational social order, and not in an account of the good life for an individual or a doctrine of duties for the regulation of our private lives.

Nevertheless, the developmental structure of the theory presented in the *Philosophy of Right* is dictated not by collective ends but by a certain conception of the modern human individual – or, more accurately, a system or developing series of such conceptions. It is this system of self-images, together with the necessary forms of activity corresponding to it, that founds the complex system of social institutions constituting the Hegelian rational state. The rational state is an end in itself only because the highest stage of *individual* self-actualization consists in participating in the state and recognizing it as such an end. This means that Hegel's ethical theory is after all founded on a conception of individual human beings and their self-actualization. Even the state's rationality is grounded on the fact that the individual will is actualized through participating in it and contributing to it as a universal end. In that sense, Hegel's ethical thought is oriented to the individual, not the collective.

We can see this in Hegel's procedure in the *Philosophy of Right*. This book is a fuller version of the science of "objective spirit," part of the third volume of Hegel's *Encyclopedia of Philosophical Sciences* (*EG* §§ 483–552). As in the *Encyclopedia*, the Introduction to the *Philosophy of Right* presents a philosophical propaedeutic to objective spirit (*PR* § 2) drawn from Hegel's treatment of the will or "practical spirit" (*EG* §§ 469–482), which is the final stage in the development of "subjective spirit," of individual psychology (*EG* §§ 387, 440). Hegel's discussion of "the free will" in the Introduction deals with the human individual as a rational agent whose freedom is to be actualized.

Hegel tells us that of the three principal parts of the *Philosophy of Right*

(Abstract Right, Morality, Ethical Life), only the third deals with human beings in their concreteness; Abstract Right and Morality are "abstract moments" (*PR* § 33). Their images of the individual are one-sided, and the truth contained in these images is best appreciated when we see how they are actualized in social institutions belonging to ethical life (*PR* § 141R; cf. *PR* §§ 207, 209). But both images are very important, because they are characteristically modern, representing a deeper human self-awareness than was available to any premodern culture. The following sections (§§ 4–7) of this chapter will briefly examine the system of human self-images that belong to this modern self-understanding, and so constitute the elements of Hegel's ethical theory.

4. Abstract right

Abstract right is based on a distinctive human self-image: the *person*, a being capable of arbitrary free choice (*PR* § 35,R) and demanding respect for this capacity in the form of an external sphere within which to exercise it (*PR* § 41). This makes a person a property owner, a subject of dominion over part of the external world (*PR* § 44). Property in this sense of course prominently includes the right of possession over external things, but even more basically it includes the possession of one's own body and life (*PR* §§ 47–48). Hegel's view on this point is anticipated by Locke, for whom the right of "property" includes not only the right over one's "estate," but also – and more fundamentally – the rights to life and liberty.[3] A person is therefore a subject of *rights* (*PR* § 36) – the sort of rights that the tradition calls "natural rights" and today usually go by the name of "human rights."

Hegel thinks that the concept of a person in this sense first came to exercise an important social influence at the time of Imperial Rome (*PR* § 357; cf. *PhG* ¶¶ 477–483; *VPG* 380–385/314–318). The earlier ethical life of Greece, which preceded the development of personality in this sense, consisted in a beautiful immediate harmony. This was a harmony between humanity and nature and also a social harmony. It was a harmony between individuals, and within each individual it was a harmony between the individual's "universality" and "particularity," between an individual's proper selfhood and her social role. Individuals simply identified their self-interest and self-worth with their excellences as members of the community.

Reflection inevitably distinguished these two sides of the individual's life from each other, and this led to the dissolution of the beautiful harmony of classical Greek life. Individuals came to see themselves as needing social protection against others and against the whole. Hegel interprets Roman culture, with its emphasis on the legal rights and privileges of individuals, as the heir to this socially alienated and self-protective attitude. Contrary to most liberal theory, Hegel thinks that such a culture fosters political autocracy, because the universal that was once shared by individuals tends to take up residence in a single seat of political power, the imperial lord:

Just as when a physical body is corrupted, each point wins a life of its own for itself, which however is only the wretched life of worms, so here the state organism is dissolved into the atoms of private persons. Such a condition is the life of Rome: on the one side fate and the abstract universality of [imperial] lordship, on the other the individual abstraction, the person, which contains the determination that the individual is something in itself not through its life, or its fulfilled individuality, but as an abstract individual. (*VPG* 384/317)

In pagan Rome, some had the right of personality, but some were excluded from it by their status as slaves. Hegel thinks it was Christianity that first laid a foundation for the idea *every* individual is a person, and it is only in the modern world that this Christian idea had found its way systematically into social reality: "It is over a millennium and a half since the *freedom of the person* has begun through Christianity to blossom and become a universal principle among a small part of the human race" (*PR* § 62R). "The Orientals knew only that *one* is free, the Greek and Roman world that *some* are free. Only the Germanic nations in Christianity have come to the consciousness that the human being as human is free" (*VG* 62–63/54). This process of self-knowledge was associated with the rise of another important modern self-image: the moral subject.

5. Morality

The *subject* is the "reflection of the [free] will into itself and its identity for itself over against being in itself and immediacy" (*PR* § 105). As a subject I attend to my own willing and the way in which my external actions can be judged as expressions of it. Thus morality is concerned not only with my assertion of my right to act freely within a proper sphere, but also with the worth of my actions as measured by the goodness or badness of my will (*PR* §§ 131–133). Moral will is essentially a striving to overcome the gap between the objective and the subjective, and to give itself a real expression in the objective world (*PR* §§ 8–9, 109). Thus morality is inevitably concerned with the scope of my moral responsibility for what happens in the world (*PR* §§ 115–120). It is respect for people as subjects that makes us place value on what Hegel calls "subjective freedom," action from reasons that the agents approve on the basis of their own conscience and their individual thinking (*PR* §§ 132, 136–138, 228R, 274).

Hegel is known as a *critic* of the moral standpoint, especially as it is represented in the ethical thought of Kant and Fichte. But at least after his Jena period, subjective freedom and morality play an important role in Hegel's own ethical thought:

The substance of spirit is freedom. Its end in the historical process is given along with this: it is the freedom of the subject to have its own conscience and morality, to have its own universal ends for itself and to make them valid; the subject must have infinite value and also come to consciousness of this extremity. What is substantial in the world spirit's end is reached through the freedom of each individual. (*VG* 64/55)

Hegel thinks that morality, the conception of the self as a subject, is the most distinctive feature of Christianized modernity. The dissolution of ancient ethical life under the Roman empire led to a culture in which individuals were alienated from their common social life. Their own social essence assumed the form of the emperor, a supreme person with all the legal person's tyrannical arbitrariness (*PhG* ¶ 481; *VPG* 380–385/314–318). The spiritual life of individuals, alienated from the real social world, turned inward (*PR* § 138R). Their self-loss became the suffering and unhappiness of the self-alienated individual (*PhG* ¶¶ 207–210, 483–484, 751–752; *VPG* 388/320). In this crisis the ancient world naturally turned to a religion of Hebraic origin because Hebrew religious culture, with its spirit of submission to the law of a single jealous God, alien to both nature and humanity, had long been a veritable school of self-alienation (*PR* § 358; cf. *VPG* 241–245/195–198; *TJ* 274–297/*ETW* 182–205). Christianity began as an expression of self-alienation, in the practical forms of self-chastisement (*Zucht*) and culture (*Bildung*) (*VPG* 388/320). But its vocation was equally to overcome alienation, at least on the plane of religious thought: "Spirit thrust back into itself in the extreme of its absolute *negativity* grasps the turning point in and for itself, the *infinite positivity* of this, its inwardness, the principle of the unity of divine and human nature, reconciliation" (*PR* § 358).

Hegel thinks that the most significant impact of Christian discipline and reconciliation was not their reception by the cultured peoples of classical antiquity. Instead, it was their influence on the European barbarians whose cultural history was to contribute to the creation of a new world order on the basis of Christianity. These "Germanic" peoples (*germanische Völker*) (a term Hegel uses in a very broad sense, encompassing all the Christianized nations of Europe)[4] had as their most noteworthy characteristic "the sensation of natural totality," to which Hegel gives the name *Gemüt* or *Gemütlichkeit*. These are difficult words to translate: The meaning of *gemütlich* includes friendly, good-natured, cosy, hearty, jovial, convivial, easy-going. In one place, *Gemüt* is equated with "heart" (*Herz*) (*VPG* 424/353). Hegel describes (*Gemüt*) as "this enclosed, indeterminate totality of spirit, in which a human being has just as universal and indeterminate a satisfaction in himself" (*VPG* 423/350). *Gemüt* is opposed to "character," which asserts itself through a determinate form of the will and in behalf of a determinate interest, such as wealth or honor. *Gemüt* has no determinate end, no particular content. It is "formal will" or "subjective freedom as willfulness (*Eigensinn*)" (*VPG* 423/350–351).

Hegel relates the *Gemüt* of the Germanic barbarians to the spirit of individual freedom and personal independence that showed itself in their social institutions. "This element of freedom, when it is carried over into a social relation, can posit nothing but popular communities, so that these communities comprise the whole and every member of the community, as such is a free man. Murder can be atoned for by a monetary payment, because the free man is valid and remains so, whatever he might have done" (*VPG* 425/353). Among Germanic peoples, social bonds were formed not through laws or principles of right, nor even through a collective aim to be achieved, but rather on the basis of personal "fidelity" (*Treue*): "Individuals attached themselves to other individuals through free choice or arbitrariness (*mit freier Willkür*) and their associations were confederations of private compacts and arbitrary private rights" (*VPG* 425–426/353–354).

To this Germanic spirit Christianity brought two things. First, it gave depth to the Germanic self by supplying it with an object of concern adequate to engage its whole selfhood: "*Gemüt* has no particular content; but Christianity deals precisely with the Thing (*Sache*), with the content as object. . . . The indeterminate as substance, objectively, is the wholly universal – God; but the other moment in Christianity is concrete unity, that the individual will is taken up by God in grace. . . . The subject must now also win objective form, i.e., unfold itself as object" (*VPG* 423/351). Second, Christianity infected the Germanic peoples with self-alienation, the separation of sacred and secular, and the self-loss of the individual self in the forsaken world of actuality. Out of this, the "hardness" of the Germanic "heart" was "broken and mellowed by the frightful chastisement of the middle ages" (*VPG* 487/407). The human body was put in bondage by feudal serfdom, and the soul was in servitude to the church. Germanic self-will became something evil, deserving of this chastisement, while at the same time the individual self was identified with the absolute object, with God.

The result of this process was a division within the self, an internalization of the outward servitude, and the emergence of a new kind of self, one that regards itself as free only when it sees itself as its own master. To this self, liberation consists in bringing the particular self-will into conformity with the universal. Hegel has a special name for this task of liberation through a self-discipline: He calls it *Bildung* – "culture," "education," or (self-)formation. It is out of the discipline of *Bildung* that there emerges the true volitional "subject" or moral self (*PhG* ¶¶ 488–489; *VG* 65–66/56–57).

In morality, the primitive Germanic respect for the integrity of the individual self is preserved, yet the self is now identified not with its passing fancy or arbitrary self-will, but with the "universal will" or "will in itself" which it is the task of the subject to actualize (*PR* § 106, R). Individual freedom is valued because it is required for this task, and not merely out of primitive Germanic stubbornness. This is the moral way of thinking, which has come to be an important part of modern culture and common sense, and distinguishes modernity decisively from earlier stages of the human spirit. More than anything else, it is what gives modern European culture a deeper understanding of human nature than non-European cultures, and deeper than earlier stages of itself (*VG* 56/48, 61–63/54–55).

6. Modern ethical life

The person and the subject are abstractions, incomplete or one-sided images of the individual human self, which are overcome only when individuals are considered in relation to "ethical life" (*Sittlichkeit*). Hegel identifies ethical life with "the objective ethical order" (*PR* § 144), the "ethical substance," to which particular individuals relate as "accidents" (PR § 145). It is above all in his conception of ethical life that Hegel seems to assert the primacy of the social over the individual. But we have just seen that free subjectivity itself is the distinctive principle of modern ethical life. Ethical life is more concrete than abstract right and morality not because it emphasizes the collective over the individual, but because the ethical image of the individual is a more concrete one. It addresses every side of the individual self, and situates the self in a living social order.

What is most basic or primitive to a self, its first need, is *love*, "spirit's feeling of its own unity." It finds its ethical place in the *family*, where one has "the self-consciousness of [one's] individuality *in this unity* as an essentiality in and for itself, so that in it one is not a person for oneself but a *member*" (PR § 158). Hegel thinks that family life satisfies a fundamental human need for love or unity with others at the level of feeling. He accords such importance to the family that he believes that half the human race (the female sex) must restrict its sphere of activity to family life (PR § 166; see Chapter 14, §§ 5–6). But Hegel rejects the view of some of his Romantic contemporaries, who saw the familial principle as the basis of social life generally. On the contrary, in the modern world, where individuals are free persons, Hegel thinks that this principle must be kept carefully circumscribed. In modern society, for instance, the family can mean only a nuclear family; an extended family or clan (*Stamm*) has no status in modern society because it would compromise the free personality of the clan's adult members (PR §§ 172, 177, 180R).

Hegel restricts the scope of the family as a form of economic organization in order to make room for the distinctively modern social institution: "civil society" (*bürgerliche Gesellschaft*). Civil society is the system of social relationships in which individuals participate when they interact economically as free, independent persons. One of Hegel's most original contributions to social theory is his conception of the modern market economy as a social institution distinct from both the family and the political state.[5] Hegel acknowledges his debt to the political economists, who studied the market system and its laws (PR § 189R); but his original contribution is to see civil society not merely as the natural result of the interaction of private persons – a conception Hegel ridicules, calling it the "spiritual animal kingdom" (PhG ¶¶ 397–418) – but as a social *institution,* a distinctively modern form of human community, indispensable for the self-actualization of the modern self (see Chapter 14, §§ 1–2).

Civil society is a social institution, a form of ethical life, grounded on the self-image of modern individuals, on a far richer and more complex image of the individual self than that which grounds the family. It is only within civil society that the self as person gains concreteness, through the economic relation of private property owners (PR § 182) recognized by the system of legal justice (PR §§ 209–229). It is also chiefly in the contingent interactions of private persons afforded by civil society that moral subjectivity finds free scope for its activity (PR §§ 207, 242). The human self-images of person and subject become concrete only in one's self-image as a "burgher" (*Bürger*), a member of civil society (*bürgerliche Gesellschaft*). [In this context, Hegel insists that *Bürger* does not mean "citizen" (French: *citoyen*), a member of the political state, but is equivalent to the French *bourgeois* (*PR* § 190R; cf. *VPR17*: 108).]

It is in his exposition of civil society that Hegel makes most explicit the fact that it is a series of self-images of the individual human being that structures his theory of objective spirit: "In [abstract] right, the object is the *person*, in the moral standpoint it is the *subject*, and in the family it is the *family member*, in civil society in general it is the burgher (as *bourgeois*); here at the standpoint of need it is the concretum formed by *conception* which we call a *human being (Mensch)*" (*PR* § 190R). We understand ourselves as "human beings" when we think of ourselves as beings with "needs" – both animal needs and needs engendered by social life (*PR* § 190). Thus Hegel characterizes a "human being" as "a concrete whole of many powers" whose "end" is its own "particular subjectivity" (*VPR17*: 109–110). We might say that our conception of ourselves as "human beings" is our conception of ourselves simply as *consumers* of what civil society produces. As "human beings" we are concerned with our own welfare (cf. *PR* §§ 190R, 123), and we are induced to participate in civil society simply in order to satisfy our needs and advance our welfare (*PR* § 196).

It is not true, however, to say that "civil society, for Hegel, is essentially the market and its legal framework."[6] The *bourgeois* is not simply the self-interested *homo oeconomicus*. Once human beings are drawn into the life and labor of civil society, Hegel thinks that they receive through it both a theoretical and practical education (*Bildung*) (*PR* § 197). Individuals participate in civil society as part of a particular "estate" (*Stand*), which gives them a definite social "standing" or "position" (*Stand*) in civil society (*PR* § 201). Their image of themselves comes to be bound up with the honor or dignity of their estate (*Standesehre*), through which they gain recognition both in their own eyes and in the eyes of others (*PR* § 207). At the same time they acquire ethical dispositions, values, and interests in common with others in their estate, and this leads to a sense of solidarity with these others, institutionalized in corporation membership (*PR* § 251; see Chapter 14, §§ 3–4). A burgher thus becomes a "man with a trade or profession" (*Gewerbsmann*), whose sense of dignity and self-worth is bound up with the skill and ethical rectitude (*Rechtschaffenheit*) which he displays in his work (*PR* § 253R). Finally, the burgher's concerns as a professional man and a corporation member prominently include concerns about the welfare of others and about the common good of civil society as a whole. In this way, the individual's participation in civil society passes over naturally into the universal life of the state (*PR* § 256).

7. The modern state

Hegel regards the state as the highest actualization of the individual's freedom (*PR* § 257). In relation to the state, the individual is a *citizen* (*PR* §§

261R, 265A), a *Bürger als citoyen* (*VPR17* : 94). As such, however, individuals are also *members* of the state (*PR* §§ 258R, 261R), parts of a whole as members of a family are. In this respect, the state is unlike civil society, where the differentiation or separation of individuals is the fundamental determinant of their relationship to one another (*PR* §§ 181, 184, 186, 263R).

Membership in the state is also fundamentally different from membership in the family: "The family is also ethical, only the end is not a conscious one . . . but [in the state] the ground, the final truth, is spirit, which is [the state's] universal end and conscious object" (*PR* § 263A). In the family, the social whole is not a conscious end; the individual's commitment to this institution is always experienced as an immediate feeling of love for other particular individuals. But citizens devote themselves to the state *as* an institution, with an explicit political constitution. Their participation in the state takes the form not of immediate feeling but of rational thought (*PR* § 257R).

The state is an "end in itself" (*PR* § 257): "*Unification* as such is itself the [state's] true content and end, and the individual's vocation is to lead a universal life" (*PR* § 257R). Hegel has often been criticized for holding that participation in the state gives to individuals a *universal* end, over and above the particular well-being of its individual members. He certainly does hold this. But it is a serious distortion of Hegel's meaning to think that the good of individuals is supposed to be swallowed up in, or sacrificed to, some quite different end. Hegel maintains that the modern state works only because the universal life of the state provides for the subjective freedom and particular happiness of its members. The "rationality" of the modern state consists in the "thoroughgoing unity of universality and individuality" (*PR* § 257R). "The principle of modern states has this tremendous strength and depth, that it lets the principle of subjectivity complete itself in the *independent extreme* of personal particularity, and simultaneously *brings it back to substantial unity*" (*PR* § 260).

Hegel rejects the common view that patriotism is the readiness to make sacrifices for the sake of one's country. He insists that it is rather "the disposition that habitually knows the community as the substantial foundation and end in the usual conditions and relationships of life" (*PR* § 268R). Far from being a disposition to sacrifice oneself for the state, patriotism is closely allied to "trust," the sense that one's own particular self-interest is "contained and preserved in another's: whereby this other is immediately no other for me, and in this consciousness I am free" (*PR* § 268).

Hegel does hold that all particular interests must give way to the universal interest of the state in time of war (*PR* §§ 323–325). But he does so precisely because he takes war to be the extreme case in which the universal interest can (for once) be clearly distinguished from the particular. The state has "stability" only insofar as the universal end is "identical" with particular ends (*PR* § 265A); war strengthens the state only in the sense that it poses a threat to its stability, and a healthy state grows stronger for overcoming the threat.

Hegel asks explicitly whether the state exists for the sake of its citizens, or whether the state is an end and they are its instruments. He replies by denying both alternatives, because the state is an organic unity in which no member is end and none is means (*VG* 112/95). Elsewhere he insists that "the end of the state is the happiness of the citizens" (*PR* § 265A). Hegel's view at this point is not, after all, so very different from that of John Stuart Mill, who holds that an individual's life has meaning only when devoted to a social or collective good, a "good to the aggregate of all persons," which is pursued in concert with others.[7] For the content of this end, neither Mill nor Hegel can conceive of anything except the well-being of individuals who comprise the collective.

But there is an important difference in the way in which the two philosophers think of individual well-being, and so of the collective human end. Because an individual for Hegel is always a product of a determinate social order, he conceives of the human good not abstractly, as the maximizing of pleasures, but as an ethical life providing for the individual's self-actualization as person, subject, family member, burgher, and citizen. This structure reaches its highest point in the political state, because there the structure of social life is consciously known and willed for the sake of its rationality.

The state is an institution in which human beings make rational collective decisions about the form of their life together. In the family, such decisions are very limited, not only in scope but also through the fact that the family is held together by feelings of love rather than by rational thought. In civil society, the common mode of life is the result of rational choices, but of isolated individual choices and not collective ones. For this reason, civil society can be apprehended as a rational form of social life only from the higher standpoint of the state, and Hegel describes the rationality of civil society as an illusion or "show" (*Schein*) (*PR* § 189). In the state, Hegel thinks that social life based on rational choice is no longer a mere appearance but a living institutional reality.

The term "state" for Hegel has a broader and a narrower meaning: "State" refers to the whole organized existence of a people, including its family life and its civil society; but it also refers, more narrowly to a set of political institutions (*PR* § 267; *VG* 114–115/96–97). The two meanings are connected, because it is only in the political state that the form of social life becomes an object of rational human choice: Only there is it true that "the state *knows* what it wills, and knows it in its *universality,* as something *thought*" (*PR* § 270).

Hegel has other reasons for regarding the political state as the highest actualization of freedom (*PR* § 257). He regards the state as the only social institution that can claim genuine independence. Modern family life is economically dependent on the life of civil society; both the family and civil society depend on the political state and are subordinate to it. The state, however, is sovereign, dependent on nothing larger. Unlike "humanity" at large or the Kantian "realm of ends" composed ideally of all rational beings, it is not a mere mental construct or a creation of the cosmopolitan moralist's wishful imagination. The state has an institutional reality; it is in fact the supreme human power on earth.

The state is an actual reality only because it is has "individuality, as exclusive being for itself, [which] appears *as a relation to other states*" (*PR* § 322). Hegel thinks that human beings unite for the accomplishment of great ends (even ends of universal or cosmopolitan worth) only when they form a determinate social unity, distinct from – at least implicitly in opposition to – others. Hegel believes that states are the unities that make history, just as Marx later thought classes were.[8]

States are therefore the "material" of world history, the concrete agents of world-historical development (*VG* 111–112/93–94). Thus it is through my relation to my state that I as an individual acquire a genuine and positive relation to the process of world history (*PR* § 348). Hegel's insistence that each individual's supreme duty is to be a member of the state (*PR* § 258) is therefore *not* a rejection of the idea that the individual should aspire to play a role in the universal life of the human race. On the contrary, Hegel thinks that it is only through participation in the state that individuals can realistically hope that their actions will gain such a universal significance.

Hegel's picture of the state has lost a good deal of its credibility in our century. The political states we know have long been divided into great world empires; the political processes of even the most powerful states are at the mercy of multinational corporations and other geopolitical social and economic influences. State sovereignty is sometimes a just demand, sometimes an unconvincing ploy (sometimes both at once), sometimes an approximation, seldom a full reality. If the most powerful states may still claim to be the greatest powers on earth, even they have credible competitors in the form of international political or religious movements, as well as drug cartels and other multinational corporations.

For these reasons, it is only too evident to us that the political state cannot play the role, whether in the life of the individual or in the collective life of the human race, which Hegel tried to assign it. But it doesn't follow that we as rational beings don't have the needs that the Hegelian state was supposed to fulfill. Hegel's theory of the state may still teach us a great deal about ourselves and our aspirations, even if the lesson cannot have the joyful effect on us Hegel intended it to have (*PR* Preface 27).

8. A self-actualization theory

In §§ 4–7 of this chapter, we have taken a brief look at the human self-images that form the elements of Hegel's ethical theory. This has led us to the social institutions within which Hegel thinks the modern self can be actualized. Now it is time to ask ourselves what sort of an ethical theory this might be.

The two commonest models for ethical theory are the *deontological* and the *teleological*. Deontological theories are based on a law or principle that tells us what to do and what not to do, an ultimate imperative or set of imperatives that we are supposed to obey. This theory selects the actions to be performed by their conformity to the relevant set of commandments. Biblical ethics is deontological, as is Kantian ethics. Teleological theories are based on a conception of some end or set of ends that is to be realized in action. They select actions as instruments to the end. Utilitarianism is a teleological theory, as are the various forms of egoistic eudaemonism found in classical Greek ethics.

Hegel's ethical theory does not fit either model very comfortably. Like Kantian ethics, it is based on the value of freedom or rational selfhood. But Hegel eschews the term "autonomy" and the image of moral self-legislation, because he wants to avoid the idea of the rational self as one in which one part of the self constrains or coerces another part. Hegelian ethics incorporates one imperative, the "commandment of right": "Be a person and respect others as persons" (*PR* § 36). This imperative belongs only to the most abstract branch of Hegel's theory; it is essentially incomplete, and its whole content is negative (*PR* §§ 37–38).

It might seem more appropriate to treat Hegel's theory as teleological. The theory does have a role for an idea of the good – "freedom realized, the absolutely final end of the world" (*PR* § 129). But this good is not introduced until Part Two, Section Three of the *Philosophy of Right,* and even then it is not given what Hegel regards as a satisfactory content (*PR* §§ 134–135). Surely in a teleological theory, the first order of business is to specify the good, so as to be in a position to select the actions most conducive to achieving it. Hegel, on the contrary, has specified some of the main categories of actions that actualize freedom (those regarding rights, those pursuing the moral good) before defining their ends in any satisfactory way. In Hegel's theory, the good is given determinate content along with a more determinate account of the actions that actualize it.

Hegel's *self-actualization* theory represents a distinctive type of ethical theory, different from both deontological and teleological theories.[9] It begins neither with an imperative, law, or principle to be followed nor with the idea of an end to be achieved. Its starting point is the conception of a certain self or identity to be exercised or actualized, to be embodied and expressed in action. The theory selects the actions to be performed and the ends to be pursued because they are the actions and ends of that kind of self. In such a theory, laws and commandments owe their force to the fact that they turn out to be principles which the right sort of self would follow. Ends owe their desirability to the fact that they turn out to be the ends which that sort of self would pursue.

In such a theory, it is misleading to consider "self-actualization" as the *end* or *goal* of the self. If the self is successful, it does actualize itself in doing the right things and pursuing the right ends; but the content of this "self-actualization" cannot be specified independently of those actions and ends. In a theory like Hegel's, "self-actualization" is not to begin with an end with a specifiable content to which such a self directs its efforts. From one point of view, self-actualization is simply a by-product of acting in certain ways, following certain principles and successfully pursuing other ends. But it has the appearance of an end because for a self-actualization theory, these ends have their value and these principles their force because they are the ends and principles of a certain sort of self.[10]

The starting point of a self-actualization theory is a certain concept of what human beings *are* – a concept that cannot ultimately be divorced from the practical self-concern that belongs necessarily to being a self. Hegel sees this as the point of the classical injunction *Gnothi seauton* ("Know thyself") (*EG* § 377). In seeking the knowledge demanded by this injunction, it is bound to be inappropriate to try to draw any ultimate distinction between "facts" and "values," or between theoretical and practical rationality. Asking with self-concern what it is to be human is the same thing as asking what sort of human being one is to be; it is asking about what Hegel calls one's *Bestimmung* – about one's nature and simultaneously about one's vocation.

This is the reason Hegel's own account of "subjective spirit" (of the human individual) in the *Encyclopedia* moves from a discussion of embodiment (*EG* §§ 388–412) through consciousness and reason (*EG* §§ 413–439) to theoretical spirit (*EG* §§ 440–468) and ends with practical spirit (*EG* §§ 469–480) defining itself as free spirit (*EG* §§ 481–482). Hegel tells us that what have traditionally been thought of as the self's different "faculties" are not so much diverse capacities or activities, as different (and more or less adequate) conceptions of mind or spirit itself and as a whole, or stages in its development toward self-knowledge (*EG* §§ 379,A, 380). The "practical spirit" or "will" therefore includes the theoretical, because the basis of theoretical concern is practical concern, concern with what I am and am to be (*PR* § 4A). And the outcome of this concern is the awareness that what I am is freedom, that is, a being whose vocation is to know itself and actualize its knowledge of itself (*EG* § 481).

It is the development of this simultaneously theoretical and practical self-concept of the human individual in the *Philosophy of Right* which we have sketched in §§ 5–8 of this chapter. We have seen that the scaffolding of the *Philosophy of Right* is the developing image of the free will or self-knowing and self-concerned human agent, conceiving of itself successively, ever more concretely and adequately, first as a "person" possessing abstract rights, then as a "subject" with a moral vocation, then in the concrete spheres of ethical life as a family member, then a burgher, and finally as a citizen.

To each of these self-images there correspond determinate activities, principles to be followed, and ends to be pursued and achieved, either individually (as in the "abstract" spheres of abstract right and morality) or together with others in the context of determinate social institutions (as in the sphere of ethical life, in the family, civil society, and the state). The principles and ends, however, are seen as binding and valuable because they are ways in which the free will actualizes the various aspects or moments of its self-knowledge or identity. That is what Hegel means when he calls the system of "right" a system in which "freedom is its own object" and describes Idea or self-actualized free will as "the free will that wills the free will" (*PR* § 27). Chapter 2 will take up the concept of freedom that figures in these claims.

9. Historicized naturalism

As a normative ethical theory, we have characterized Hegel's theory as a self-actualization theory. On the metaethical level, it is a variety of ethical realism or naturalism. Hegel's ethical theory is founded on a conception of human nature that has implications for what human beings need, what is good for them, what fulfills or actualizes them. In this respect, it may be compared with the *classical naturalism* found in the ethical theories of Plato and Aristotle. Plato's theory says that the human soul actualizes itself when each part fulfills its proper function. Aristotle's ethical theory holds that the human good consists in the actualization of rational capacities, especially the capacities for practical reason and philosophical contemplation, and it provides a theory about the other things (such as external goods and friends) that people need in order to lead the good life. The basis for classical naturalism is a psychological theory, about the functions of the soul, the relation among its different parts or faculties, and its needs, desires, and natural ends.

Hegel's theory, in contrast, might be called a dialectical or *historicized naturalism*. It views the human nature to be actualized as a historical product, the result of a dialectical process of experience involving the acquisition of self-knowledge, the struggle to actualize the self, and an interaction between these activities, which modifies the self that is known and actualized. Historicized naturalism provides for a variable and malleable notion of the human good in a way that classical naturalism does not. The element of truth in the misleading claim that Marx's social critique is not based on any idea of "human nature" is that Marx's conception of the human good, like its Hegelian predecessor, is based on a historicized rather than a classical version of ethical naturalism.

Both classical and historicized naturalism are an embarrassment to some contemporary ethical naturalists, because they are so unashamedly part of a philosophical tradition of grand theorizing about human nature and history. Easily embarrassed naturalists would rather start with people's conscious desires and preferences, yielding a theory that looks more like empirical social science than old fashioned philosophy. But conscious desires and preferences are sometimes the result of misinformation, pathology, ideology, and other distorting processes, whose effects it is one of the tasks of a theory of the good to expose and correct. Thus ethical naturalists such as Richard Brandt and Peter Railton prefer what we might call *idealized preference naturalism*: A person's good is to be identified not with what that person in fact desires or prefers, but with what the person *would* desire or prefer if fully informed about and lucidly aware of all the relevant facts.[11] Although they describe themselves as "stark raving moral realists," idealized preference naturalists seem to regard even hypothetical subjective preferences as more real than ordinary objective goodness and badness.

Idealized preference naturalism depends on a set of rather speculative counterfactual claims. It is doubtful that, at least in the interesting and controversial cases, they are any easier to justify than the central claims of grand

33

theory naturalism (whether classical or historicized). Perhaps they would even benefit from a grand theory to back them up. Idealized preference naturalism suffers from a further defect when we come to issues about how children are to be raised and educated.[12] It makes no sense to inquire about a newborn infant's idealized preferences unless we mean to ask about the preferences it might have as an adult, after it has fully formed capacities to absorb information and deliberate on the basis of it. The way we raise an infant, however, will partly determine its fully informed and lucid preferences as an adult. An important question about raising children is, How shall we influence these preferences? Idealized preference naturalism has no theory of the newborn child's good that is independent of what its idealized preferences will be once it is mature enough to have idealized preferences. It seems that idealized preference naturalism has nothing to say to us about how to form the people whose idealized preferences are to be the sole indicators of their good. By extension, idealized preference naturalism will also have trouble determining the good of people belonging to future generations.

Classical naturalism, on the other hand, has a general conception of the human good, and it can choose the childrearing practices that will maximize that. Historicized naturalism has no general conception of the human good, but for any infant it will be born into a determinate social and historical situation, inheriting from its culture a determinate human self-understanding. Historicized naturalism tells us to choose the childrearing practices that will actualize the self of the newborn child on that understanding.

Historicized naturalism does face a problem of indeterminacy when it comes to the good of future generations, which classical naturalism does not. Some things about people's needs and the conditions of their self-actualization will, no doubt, remain the same; and some changes might even be predictable. Yet if human self-understanding is always growing, and if the action based on it is always modifying and deepening the nature of human beings, then the historicized naturalist must confess that our present self-conception is inadequate, in ways we can never hope to repair, for deciding the good of future human beings.

Hegel is clearly aware of this limitation, and resigned to it. That is why he tells us that every individual is a child of his own time, which he can no more overleap than he can jump over Rhodes; that the Owl of Minerva begins its flight only at dusk (PR Preface 25–26). The same is true of Marx. For he insists that communists have no recipes for the cookshops of the future, and no ideals to realize beyond setting free the new society through participating in a historical process that will "transform both circumstances and men."[13] It is easier to live with these limitations than with those that idealized preference naturalism would impose on us. We may comfortably leave some issues about the good of future human beings to be settled by them. But we cannot ignore issues about our own children's good to the extent that it depends on our childrearing practices. Those issues have to be settled by us if they are going to be settled by anybody.

It might be objected that historicized naturalism, because it is based on a culturally inherited conception of human nature, has an inherently conservative bias. If this charge means that historicized naturalism has to be socially conservative in its *results,* then it is easy to see that this is not so. A historicized naturalist might very well conclude that the good of human beings, as they now understand themselves and as they have made themselves through history, can be actualized only in a radically new form of society. (This is exactly what Marx's historicized naturalism does conclude.) On the other hand, the objection may be that whatever its results, the *process* of ethical reasoning according to historicized naturalism has an inherent bias toward conservatism simply because its conception of human nature is a historical product. This objection only reminds us of the unavoidable limits on our knowledge about the good of future human beings mentioned in the previous paragraph. It should begin to worry historicized naturalists only when someone brings forward a knowledge of human nature that is not subject to those limits.

2
Freedom

1. Hegel and freedom

In Hegel's self-actualization theory, the essence of the self to be actualized goes by the name of "freedom." What does Hegel mean by "freedom"?

In the liberal tradition, "freedom" usually refers to a sphere of privacy in which individuals may do as they please, immune from the interference of others – especially of the state. For liberals, to value "freedom" means to insist that there are definite limits to legitimate interference with individuals; the main issues about freedom have to do with where these limits are to be set. Hegel also believes that the state's power over individuals should be limited, and takes the existence of such limits to be a distinctive feature of modern ethical life (*PR* §§ 41, 185R, 206,R, 262A, 299R). He criticizes Fichte for advocating too much state regulation of people's lives – he is particularly outraged by Fichte's suggestion that citizens should be required to carry around identification passbooks with their pictures in them (*VPR 4*: 617; *PR* Preface 25; *VPR17*: 139; cf. *GNR* 291–303/374–387). Hegel insists that the police should not be permitted to enter private residences without a special order, and he says of the British use of "police spies" to detect and prevent crime that this practice opens the way to "the greatest abyss of corruption" (*VPR17*: 139).

Nevertheless, Hegel does not see issues about freedom as liberals see them, and his agenda regarding freedom is not the liberal one. He is not averse to state paternalism toward those whose improvidence brings economic ruin upon themselves and their families (*PR* § 240). He thinks that the normal limits of state interference with individual liberty do not apply in times of war or other national emergency, when the state's very survival is at stake (*PR* § 323; *VPR 3*: 694). Even more symptomatic of Hegel's distance from the liberal tradition is the fact that though he holds that there are limits on the state's legitimate regulation of individual conduct, he refuses to specify these limits precisely, on the ground that this simply cannot be done (*PR* §§ 234,A, 319R). Hegel does not share the liberal's fear that the state will inevitably encroach on our private sphere unless we guard it with vigilance and zeal. As we saw in Chapter 1, § 4, he thinks that a society [such as ancient Rome, or Fichte's police state (*NR* 517–519/122–124)] that is too preoccupied with personal rights is likely to destroy the very ethical values that preserve individual freedom. In Hegel's view, the whole strength of the modern state lies in the fact that its unity depends on its preservation of subjective freedom (*PR* § 260). Why should we fear that the state will want to undermine its own foundation?

Though Hegel's theory is ostensibly founded on "freedom," liberals are often outraged to find that Hegel does not mean by this word what most people mean by it. "No doubt Hegel professed (as who does not?) and even persuaded himself (as who cannot?) that he was an admirer of freedom. And he managed this by giving the word a peculiar meaning of his own."[1] This is quite right; indeed, it is something Hegel himself asserts emphatically and repeatedly (*PR* §§ 15R, 22R, 149A, 206R, 319R; *EL* § 145A; *EG* § 482; *VGP 1* : 45/26). Of course it does not follow that Hegel does *not* admire freedom in the ordinary sense; it follows only that the freedom which grounds his ethical theory is something different.

2. Freedom as possibility and freedom as actuality

In ordinary speech, "free" often means pretty much the same as "without."[2] A foodstuff is free of additives when it has none, a freestanding building is one without supports or attachments, and a free lunch is a lunch with no charge. The freedom of people or their actions usually refers to a more specific lack: the lack of obstacles or hindrances to their doing something.[3] By extension, the freedom to act sometimes refers to the positive presence of capacities, enabling conditions or entitlements to act. Freedom of speech is not only the absence of hindrances or threats, but also the presence of positive guarantees and protections. "Freedom of the will" is a capacity, such as the ability to cause your actions, or the ability to do either one thing or another as you choose. In any case, freedom of people or actions in the ordinary sense always refers to *possibilities*. We do not call people "free" on account of the specific use they make of their possibilities, but simply on account of the fact that they have them.

Hegel uses the term "formal freedom" to refer to one kind of freedom as possibility. The freedom that is "formally" the essence of spirit consists in the fact that a spiritual being "*can* abstract from everything external and from its own externality, even from its existence itself; it can endure the negation of its individual immediacy, or infinite *pain;* i.e., it can preserve itself in this negativity and be for itself identical" (*EG* § 382). "Formal freedom" is the capacity to "abstract" from our desires. Hegel holds that every spiritual being is formally free. Such a being, he thinks, is always able to detach itself from all its desires, drives, wishes, and so forth, and act contrary to them (*PR* § 5,R).[4] His view is that though our desires may determine what we *in fact* do, they in no way limit what we *can* do. That is why he flatly denies that the free will can be coerced at all. When we speak of the coercion of a free will, Hegel thinks, we must be talking about a case in which the will itself has been identified by its own choice with something external to the will itself, such as the body of the person whose will it is, or some object which the will has made its property. What we call the "coercion" of the free will consists in a wrongful violation of the will's right over that external object (*PR* § 91; cf. *NR* 447–449/89–92).

For Hegel, formal freedom is the "foundation" (*Grundlage*) of the freedom of spirit" (*EG* § 382A), but it is not spirit's freedom itself. The freedom on which Hegel bases his ethical theory is instead called "absolute freedom" (*PR* §§ 21–24). Hegel explicitly contrasts absolute freedom with the mere "capacity for freedom," which (he says) is what most people mean by the word "freedom" (*PR* § 22R). Closely related to "absolute freedom" in Hegel's vocabulary are the terms "substantive freedom" (*PR* §§ 145A, 149, 257), "concrete freedom" (*PR* §§ 7A, 260), "freedom for itself" (*PR* § 10A), and "positive" or "affirmative" freedom (*VG* 57/50; *PR* 149A). To these various aspects of "absolute freedom," Hegel sets up a series of contrasts: "substantive" with "formal freedom" (*PR* §§ 123, 187), "concrete" with "abstract freedom" (*PR* §§ 7A, 123, 149,A), and "freedom for itself" with "freedom in itself" (*PR* § 10A). With the single exception of "formal freedom," the latter term of each contrast refers not to a possibility but to a *way of acting* that falls short of "absolute freedom" because it is immature, arbitrary, the result of accidental inclinations, or otherwise lacking in full rationality.

Isaiah Berlin coins the term "negative freedom" to designate freedom as the absence of external interferences to acting as we please.[5] Hegel uses the same term to mean something very different. For him negative freedom is a particular (misguided) sort of action. It is the practice of those who regard all forms of "particularity" (such as determinate desires, traits, or social roles) as alien to their true selfhood, and who therefore "flee from every content as a restriction." Hegel perceives such an irrational flight in the religious world, where Oriental mystics seek liberation by emptying their minds of all content and activity. He sees it also in the social world, where French revolutionaries failed because they identified freedom with the destruction of every "particularization of organizations and individuals" (*PR* § 5R).

Hegel also occasionally uses the terms "personal" freedom (*VPR 4*: 593), and "civil" or "bourgeois" (*bürgerliche*) freedom (*VPR17*: 140) to refer to the absence of external interference (e.g., state interference) in the lives of individuals. The former term alludes to the fact that such freedoms belong to the abstract right of a person; the latter indicates that their proper home is the sphere of civil society, where individual burghers act as independent economic agents. Hegel thus distinguishes the "civil freedom" guaranteed through the administration of the legal system, from "political freedom," or "public freedom," which pertains to the individual as a participant (directly or through representatives) in the political state (*VPR17*: 140; *PR* § 301R).

The kind of freedom Hegel discusses most often in the *Philosophy of Right* is "subjective freedom." This term alludes indirectly to noninterference, but what it directly refers to is a kind of *action*, one that is reflective, conscious, explicitly chosen by the agent, as opposed to actions performed unthinkingly, habitually, or from coercion (*PR* §§ 185R, 228R, 258R, 270R, 273R, 274, 301, 316; cf. *PR* §§ 132, 138, 140R). Subjective freedom also includes actions that satisfy the agent's particular needs or interests, especially the agent's reflective interest in seeing our chosen plans and projects carried successfully to completion (*PR* §§ 121, 185R,A, 258R, 299R).

Sometimes "subjective freedom" is equated with the less rational forms of

38

action, such as "arbitrariness" (*PR* §§ 185R, 206R, 262A, 299A), and contrasted with absolute freedom. It would be a serious mistake to think that Hegel is opposed to subjective freedom even in these cases, since at other times Hegel makes it clear that he regards "subjective freedom" – even the element of arbitrariness it involves – as one side of absolute freedom. In fact, Hegel argues that personal or civil freedoms are essential to the modern state just because they are necessary for subjective freedom (*PR* §§ 185R, 206R, 260).

3. Freedom and autonomy

Hegelian "absolute freedom" obviously means something like Kantian "autonomy." It refers to a way of acting in which our will is determined through itself alone, and is not at all determined by alien influences. For Kant, we act autonomously only when our will is determined solely through pure reason or respect for the moral law. Just for this reason, Kant does not think that freedom and autonomy are quite the same thing. Rather, freedom is related to autonomy as potency to act. Kant defines "freedom" as "that property of [the will's] causality by which it *can* be effective independently of foreign causes" (*G* 446/64, emphasis added), or again as "the power (*Vermögen*) of pure reason to be of itself practical" (*TL* 213–124/10). For Kant, we are free whenever we have the capacity to be autonomous, whether or not we *exercise* our freedom by acting autonomously. Thus Kant preserves the idea that freedom consists in possibilities or capacities rather than in any particular way in which they may be exercised or actualized.[6]

A similar distinction is drawn by Fichte. He gives the name "formal freedom" to the power to act independently of natural determination and to be effective on the objective world (*SL* 135/141, 276/292). Fichte distinguishes "formal freedom" from "material freedom" or "absolute freedom," in which the self uses its formal freedom to determine itself solely through itself, acting "solely for the sake of freedom" (*SL* 139/145, 149/157). Whereas Kant consistently preserves the ordinary sense of freedom as possibility, Fichte departs decisively from ordinary usage and treats autonomy itself as a kind of freedom, even the highest or truest kind.

Hegel follows Fichte rather than Kant. For him, too, absolute freedom is not a possibility or capacity but a determinate way of acting. Thus in an addition to the Berlin *Encyclopedia*, Hegel subtly turns ostensible praise for Kant's concept of freedom into praise for the Fichtean–Hegelian concept of freedom as actuality:

> Kant expressly recognized the positive infinity of practical reason when he ascribed to the *will* the capacity to determine itself in a universal way, i.e. *thinkingly*. Of course the will does possess this capacity, and it is of great importance to know that the human being is free only insofar as he possesses it *and avails himself of it in action*. (*El* § 54A; final italics added)

The main puzzles concerning Hegel's concept of freedom can be formulated in terms of this revision of the meaning of the word. Why does Hegel permit himself so radical an alteration in the meaning of the word "freedom"– an alteration as radical as the difference between potentiality and actuality? What connection is there between "freedom" in the ordinary sense and "freedom" in Hegel's sense? Does Hegel's insistence that "freedom" in the ordinary sense is not true freedom entail that Hegel is indifferent or hostile to freedom in the ordinary sense?

4. Freedom as a good

One idea behind Hegel's revision of the idea of freedom is that properly speaking, freedom must be something good. The reasoning is simple. Hegel thinks that the primary human good consists in an actuality, more specifically, in absolute freedom. Freedom as possibility is good chiefly or even solely because it is a necessary condition for absolute freedom. If freedom is a good, then naturally the name "freedom" belongs more properly to what is good in itself than it does to something whose goodness consists in being a necessary condition for what is good in itself.

The idea that freedom must be something good usually belongs among the connotations of "free" in the ordinary sense of the word, even when it is not used in connection with human agency. I say that my basement is free of rodents and mildew because we all understand that rodents and mildew are noxious; I won't describe it as "free of storage space" unless I think storage space is undesirable, and I won't say that it is "free of heat" if that means the water pipes might burst in the winter. When you describe a foodstuff as free of additives, you imply that additives are something it would be better for food to be without; it would be difficult to make sense, except as irony, of the remark that a certain food is "free of nutrients" or "free of flavor." Analogously, it is arguable that we use the word "freedom" to describe the absence of hindrances to action only because we think of such hindrances as bad and the absence of them as good. Usually this is true.

There are exceptional cases, though. Odysseus had his sailors lash him to the mast of his ship so that he would not be seduced to his death by the sirens' song. We choose to surround ourselves in everyday life with gentler hindrances whose purpose is analogous: alarm clocks, guardrails on steep paths, automatic payroll savings plans, strings tied around the little finger. We are reluctant to describe their absence as increasing our freedom, because we regard them as desirable. We may even see them as increasing our freedom, to the extent that they enable us to do certain things (listen to the sirens, climb the path in safety, get to work on time, save money).

The idea that freedom is necessarily something good plays an important role in the thinking of many modern philosophers, including some whose standing in the liberal tradition is unimpeachable. They distinguish between "liberty" and "license," including in the latter category those possibilities for action that would destroy our happiness or violate the rights of others. John Locke says:

Freedom then is not what Sir Robert Filmer tells us, "a liberty for everyone to do what he lists, to live as he pleases, and not to be tied to any laws"; but freedom of men under government is to have a standing rule to live by, . . . a liberty to follow my own will in all things where the rule prescribes not.[7]

Locke's point is endorsed by Montesquieu, Kant, and the 1789 Declaration of the Rights of Man and Citizen.[8] It is the *only* idea expressed in Rousseau's notorious (because notoriously misunderstood) remark that when we are compelled to obey the general will we are only being "forced to be free."[9] John Stuart Mill subscribes to the same idea when he says that "the only freedom which deserves the name, is that of pursuing our own good in our own way, *so long as we do not attempt to deprive others of theirs, or impede their efforts to obtain it.*"[10] All these philosophers agree that we are not deprived of freedom by laws that restrain us from doing harm or injustice to others, because freedom must be something good, and the ability to do harm or injustice is not good.

The contrary view is asserted by Isaiah Berlin, following Jeremy Bentham (and Sir Robert Filmer).[11] Bentham says: "A law by which nobody is bound, a law by which nobody is coerced, a law by which nobody's liberty is curtailed, all these phrases which come to the same thing would be so many contradictions in terms."[12] Bentham and Berlin might have a point if they mean that the ability to do evil can sometimes be something good. But they are mistaken if they think that ordinary usage supports the false idea that "freedom" refers to the absence of any and every hindrance to action, whether good or bad. Worse yet, they proceed inconsistently if they intend first to say that "freedom" includes any and every possibility of action, and then later to invoke the presupposition of ordinary speech that all freedom is something good in support of the erroneous view that any and every absence of hindrances is (considered in itself) something good and every legal hindrance to action constitutes some (perhaps necessary) evil. Generally speaking, hindrances are bad and their absence is good; but there are exceptions, which no philosophical theory (or lack of one) can get rid of.

5. Does positive freedom lead to totalitarianism?

It should be self-evident that an ethical theory based on the idea of positive freedom or autonomy must give high priority to securing a considerable degree of freedom in the ordinary sense (Hegel's "personal" or "civil" freedom). To be autonomous, you must act not only rationally, but also according to your *own* reason; in Hegel's terms, you have to be "subjectively" free. You can't have positive freedom unless you have enough choices open to you that it makes a significant difference whether your choices are rational or not. Thus a Hegelian has reasons for valuing personal or civil freedom that some others (Platonists, Hobbesian egoists, hedonistic utilitarians) do not have.

Against this, Isaiah Berlin has famously argued that the idea of "positive freedom" leads naturally down the primrose path to totalitarianism. Berlin may not have intended this specifically as a criticism of Hegel, but anyone who finds Berlin's arguments convincing probably thinks that Hegel's views on freedom are seriously damaged by them. Berlin clearly realizes that it would be paradoxical if a political theory based on the idea of freedom (in *any* sense) were *thereby* disposed to defend a political system that is hostile to individual liberty. He admits that the steps from an ethics of positive freedom to totalitarian conclusions may not be "logically valid," but insists that they are nevertheless "psychologically and historically intelligible."[13]

In his attempt to make them so, Berlin finds it necessary to ascribe to his totalitarians several beliefs quite independent of their ethics of positive freedom: They are convinced that there is only one answer to any practical question that a rational person could even entertain; they think that on every question *they* are infallibly in possession of the right answer; and they are sure that no one else will ever arrive at the right answer unless led to it through their own enlightened and benevolent coercion.[14] It would be disastrous if political power fell into the hands of people with these beliefs, no matter what their other convictions might be.

If people with these beliefs also happened to espouse an ethics of positive freedom, that would at least provide them with a countervailing reason for wanting people to take the rational course by their own rational choice rather than being coerced into it. Hence Berlin has to make his positive freedom fanatics extremely absent minded as well as paranoid: They see no advantage in education over coercion except that education is an easier way of controlling people.[15] Berlin's positive freedom totalitarians have to be so *distrait* that they forget their fundamental aim with every step they take to achieve it.

Perhaps Berlin's only point is that *any* idea (however true and noble) may be perverted into its virtual opposite if it falls into the hands of people who are sufficiently deranged, self-deceiving, or opportunistic. The fact that *even* an ethics of positive freedom might conceivably be used to rationalize a totalitarian system is a rather extreme illustration of this quite general point. We completely miss the point if we see this as a defect in the idea of positive freedom.

The general point is one we would all do well to heed. During our lifetime, the liberal individualism Berlin advocates has been used regularly in English-speaking countries to justify suppressing political dissent and limiting individual freedom – all in the name of protecting the "free world" against its "totalitarian" enemies. It is *that* abuse of the idea of freedom, not Berlin's bizarre tale of totalitarianism based on positive freedom, which should have *for us* the greatest "psychological and historical intelligibility."

6. Absolute self-activity

Hegel's identification of freedom with rational choice can be motivated by the idea that freedom is a good. There is another line of thinking, even more intimately connected with Hegel's philosophical roots, which leads to the same conclusion. It starts with Spinoza's idea that you are free when the source of your actions is *in* you, and unfree when the source is *outside* you.[16]

Accordingly, any external cause of an action may be regarded as a hindrance – not (of course) to the particular action that it causes, but to the independence of the agent. Perfect freedom is the condition in which your actions are caused only internally, not at all externally.

This idea is present in Kant's conception of the autonomous will, which acts solely from respect for a self-given law rather than from natural inclinations, which Kant takes to lie outside the rational agent's real self. The philosopher in whom this thought is most prominent, explicit, and fully developed is Fichte. It is no exaggeration to say that Fichte's entire philosophy is nothing but the attempt to work out completely the idea of a self that strives to be entirely its own work. For Fichte, the essence of selfhood is a drive toward freedom, a tendency which he variously calls the "tendency to absolute self-activity" (SL 39/44), or to "self-sufficiency" (Selbständigkeit) (SL 57/61) – or just "the absolute tendency to the absolute" (SL 28/33).

The same idea is present in Hegel's conception of spirit's freedom:

> Thus spirit is purely with itself and hence free. For freedom is just this: to be with oneself in the other, to depend on oneself, to be self-determining. (EL § 24A)
>
> Spirit is being with itself, and this is freedom. For if I am dependent, then I am related to an other which I am not, and I cannot be without this other. I am free when I am with myself. (VG 55/48)

The Introduction of the *Philosophy of Right* begins by developing the concept of a free will whose vocation is to achieve *absolute* freedom, whose absoluteness consists in the fact that it "refers to nothing other than its own self, so that every relation of *dependence* on something other falls away" (PR § 23).

Hegel understands the idea of complete self-sufficiency to mean that the will must have nothing outside itself, not even as an object or end. "[The free will] has universality, itself as the infinite form, for its content, object and end" (PR § 21). "The will in and for itself is *truly infinite* because its object is itself, and so not an *other* or a *limit*" (PR § 22). Just as Fichte's "tendency to absolute self-activity" belongs to a will that wills "freedom solely for the sake of freedom" (SL 139/145), so Hegel's absolutely free will is "the free will that wills the free will" (PR § 27). "The will is free only insofar as it wills nothing other, external, alien, for then it would be dependent, but wills only itself – wills the will. The absolute will is this: willing to be free" (VPG 524/442).

This conception of freedom surely must strike many of us as hopelessly extravagant and metaphysical. But in the age of German idealism, its social and political significance was vivid and immediate. It was a philosophical expression of the bourgeoisie's struggle against feudal economic and political forms, and the Enlightenment's demand that we should think for ourselves, in defiance of the "positivity" of traditional morality and religious authority. The modern spirit, according to Hegel, is one that claims "an absolute title for subjective self-consciousness to know *within itself* and *from itself* what duty and right is, and to recognize nothing except what it knows as the good" (PR § 137R).

43

The idea of absolute activity was *supposed* to sound extreme: It gave expression to the spirit of a revolutionary age, for which there can ultimately be no compromise between the aspiration to freedom and the forces of unfreedom.[17] Marx still appeals to the revolutionary connotations of the term "self-activity" when he uses it prominently to characterize the emancipation and actualization of the human self in postcapitalist society.[18] The fact that the idea of positive freedom still has the capacity to terrify people indicates that it has retained some of its original force. It expresses the sense that we are still in need of a radical liberation whose content cannot become clear to us until we have been liberated; at the same time, it suggests a radically open future which frightens those who imagine the ways in which the uncompromising demand for freedom may go disastrously astray.

Critics of the modern revolutionary impulse have often charged that it is doomed to failure because its goals are metaphysical rather than practical, or even that they are misconceived, impossible in principle to actualize; the only possible effect of pursuing them is the vengeance wrought against the real world by misbegotten hopes when they encounter their inevitable frustration.[19] Hegel was perhaps the first to formulate this critique of radical revolution (*PhG* ¶¶ 367–380, 582–595). That makes him simultaneously a proponent and a critic of the radical Fichtean idea of freedom as "absolute self-activity." Hegel's notion of absolute freedom may be viewed as an attempt to reconceptualize and deradicalize this idea so that it can be seen as something more than a pretext for Romantic yearning and the terror of destruction. Hegel wants to convince us that absolute freedom is something we can have here and now, through rationally comprehending how the reason in the objective world does not limit but actualizes the reason in ourselves.

7. Self-activity and otherness

Whether it is possible to attain absolute self-activity of course depends on what counts as oneself and what counts as other. Fichte identifies the self with reason, so freedom is acting from one's own reason rather than according to the authority of someone else (*SL* 175–177/185–187). Following Kant, he identifies the self more properly with *pure* reason, so mere nature is also other, including one's empirical desires and natural inclinations. To be absolutely self-active is to act solely from duty or respect for the moral law given by pure reason. British idealist ethics (especially Bradley and Bosanquet) carried on the Fichtean tradition, identifying freedom with the triumph of the active or rational self over the supine, empirical, or irrational self. Because the British idealists are supposed to be "Hegelians," Hegel's name has sometimes been associated with such views in English-speaking philosophy. In fact, Hegel rejects this entire conception of autonomy along with the conception of self and other on which it rests.

Hegel thinks the Kantian–Fichtean view involves an exactly wrong way of dealing with otherness, a strategy of escape or self-withdrawal, akin to what Berlin calls the "retreat to the inner citadel."[20] It resembles the Stoic idea, popularized by Epictetus, of independence through self-withdrawal and ceasing to care about what lies outside oneself.[21] Kant and Fichte don't tell us not to *care* about what is other than the self, but they do draw a sharp distinction between the rational self and everything empirical, and they regard the freedom of the self as compromised by any motive reflecting the self's relation to empirical otherness.

Hegel follows Fichte in holding that a self is its own self-positing activity. But he regards the self as the outcome of this activity; its identity is determined dialectically through experience, through the interaction of self-awareness, self-actualization, and self-alteration. Because self-identity is not fixed but self-made, the same is true of the self's relation to otherness. For a self, otherness is always relative, and it can be overcome. It follows that we do not achieve true self-sufficiency in relation to an other by escaping it or separating ourselves from it – as by Stoical aloofness from our external condition, or Kantian detachment from empirical motives. Such a strategy is self-defeating, like the strategy of the neurotic personality that avoids the trauma of failure by precluding from the outset any possibility of success. True independence in relation to an other is achieved rather by struggling with otherness, overcoming it, and making it our own. "The freedom of spirit is an independence from the other that is won not merely outside the other but in the other. It comes to actuality not by fleeing before the other but by overcoming it" (*EG* § 482A; cf. *EL* § 38A).

8. "Being with oneself"

About the time he begins lecturing on the philosophy of right in Berlin, Hegel coins his own special technical term for absolute freedom or absolute self-activity. To be free in this special way, he says, is to be *bei sich selbst*, "with oneself" (*PR* § 23).[22] In ordinary German, *bei sich* has two principal meanings when applied to human persons: It means to be awake or conscious, and it means to be in control of oneself. Freedom as *Beisichselbstsein* refers to the human capacities for self-awareness and self-mastery, but its meaning is still richer. The primary sense of the German preposition *bei* is to express spatial proximity, contact, or belonging. This suggests that a self "with itself" is unified, coherent, well integrated; its parts, elements, or aspects belong to and fit well into one another. The spatial metaphor also suggests that the free self has "arrived at" itself, that it has actualized or perfected itself, made itself its end and then attained this end – which is nothing external to itself.

Beisichselbstsein does not refer merely to a state of myself. "Being with myself" is always a *relation* between me and an "object" or "other" whose difference or otherness has, however, been overcome. Freedom is always *Beisichselbstsein in einem Andern*, "being with oneself in an other." This is the way "being with oneself" gives expression to Hegel's new conception of the relation between self and other, and so to his reconceptualization of absolute self-activity. It also entails that absolute freedom is not merely a state of the self or its action, but also involves a relation between the self and its circumstances.

Hegel's first authentic use of the concept *bei sich . . . in einem Andern* emphasizes the idea that "being with oneself" is a conception of freedom as self-activity: "The free will wills only itself, wills nothing but to be free; it receives only its freedom as intuition. The will determines itself, it puts itself into an object; but this object is the will itself, the will is *with itself in* its object" (*VPR17* : 216; *italics added*). The very same emphasis is present in one of Hegel's last expressions of the same idea in the *Philosophy of History* lectures of 1830: "Spirit is being with itself, and this is freedom. For if I am dependent, then I am related to an other which I am not, and I cannot be without this other. I am free when I am with myself" (*VG* 55/48).

Hegel uses a number of additional expressions to capture the relation "with oneself in," which obtains between the free self and its other. Some of these expressions convey the idea that the object is something over which I have power, dominion, or control: He speaks of the object as "mine" or as "posited by me" (*VPR 4*: 105, 146). Other expressions suggest that the object manifests my agency and mirrors my nature back to me: I am "present" (*präsent*) in it (*VPR 4*: 124); still others emphasize the overcoming of self-alienation: I am also said to be "at home" (*zu Hause*) in my object (*VPR 4*: 102), and to stand in a relation to it similar to Adam's relation to Eve when he said: "Thou art flesh of my flesh and bone of my bone" (*PR* § 4A).

"Being with oneself in an other" is a paradox. It speaks of something that is different from or other than myself and yet at the same time not different or other at all, because I am "with myself" in it. The central paradoxes in Hegel's philosophy need not scandalize us once their point is properly understood (and we do not need a new system of "dialectical logic" in order to understand them). The paradox of "being with oneself in an other" should not surprise us, since freedom is the essence of spirit, and the paradox of freedom as "being with oneself in an other" is also the central paradox in Hegel's concept of spirit. Spirit is "self-restoring sameness" (*PhG* ¶ 18), just as spirit's self-consciousness is "consciousness of itself in its otherness" (*PhG* ¶ 164). For Hegel, to be a spiritual self or a subject is a "movement of positing oneself, or the mediation of becoming other to oneself with itself" (*PhG* ¶ 18).

Hegel's spirit is a model of human agency. According to it, the agent creates or "posits" an external "object." This object is not merely the external shadow of an internal intention that was fully actual and self-complete within itself, but something through which I discover myself.[23] A spiritual being actualizes itself only through the process of producing or "positing" such objects and then "mediating" this otherness with the self that posited it. I learn what I am through the interpretation, by myself and by others, of what I have done. As a spiritual being, I do not exist fully and actually except through these contrary and complementary movements of "becoming other" and "mediating otherness," that is, through the activities of self-expression and self-interpretation.[24]

Freedom for Hegel is a relational property. It involves a self, an object (in the widest sense of that term), and a rational project of the self. Any object, simply as object, is an "other" to the self whose object it is. But because a self is actual by identifying itself with a set of rational projects involving objects, the otherness of an object can be overcome when the object is integrated into the self's rational projects. A self is with itself or free in an object with respect to a rational project if that object belongs to that project, becoming a part of that self.

9. Freedom in my determinations

In his first systematic application of the concept of freedom as "being with oneself in another," Hegel seems to add to the paradox inherent in that formula the further paradox that the "other" in which I am free is my own "determinations" – a term that appears to cover all my mental states and characteristics, but especially my drives, desires, and inclinations (*PR* §§ 5–23). Hegel not only wants us to think that we can be "with ourselves in" objects external to us, but also that we can treat our own mental states as something "other" with which we must somehow reconcile ourselves if we are to be free.

The identity of a human person is usually focused on the person's body and psychic states. But personal identity can without metaphor or hyperbole be either extended beyond that or contracted within it. This is especially true if we accept Fichte's idea that I am not a being but a doing, and that what fundamentally constitutes the unity of my person is but the activity that unifies a system of plans and projects. On this view, what enables me to identify myself with a physical body or a set of mental states is the fact that this body is the "external sphere" in which my agency is expressed, and that these mental states are unified by the projects which identify me (*GNR* 56–61/87–94). The limits of my self are the limits of my activity, and, conversely, I extend as far as the activity extends. My freedom is limited only by what resists or interrupts the activity with which I identify myself; whatever resists is "other."

Even my own desires are sometimes experienced as alien or different or other, not a part of *me*, when they interfere with my activity. Recalcitrant desires are different from or other than myself, and hinder my freedom or self-activity, because they are in disharmony with the practical system with which I actively identify.[25] This is what enables Kant and Fichte to treat their inclinations and empirical desires as something coming to them from outside, threatening to interfere with their freedom of self-activity. Because they identify self-activity solely with the activity of the pure rational legislative self, they regard all contents present in them through empirical inclinations as alien to their self-activity or freedom.

The limits of my self-activity can be regarded as the limits of my identity, and this makes it possible for me to play with these limits, at least in imagination. It is even possible, at least in a kind of fantasy, to withdraw myself

47

from everything that I am or have been and to treat that as something with which I do not choose to identify myself. Fichte interprets the act of self-reflection as one that originates in the "wavering" or "floating" (*schweben*) of the imagination between opposed possibilities, and that ends with the "fixing" or "stabilizing" (*fixieren*) of a determinate boundary between the ego and the real world opposing it (W 226–227/202, 232–233/206–207). The Fichtean "pure ego" is "that which remains over after all objects have been eliminated by the absolute power of abstraction" (W 244/216). Hegel is thinking of this experience of imaginative self-withdrawal from all my determinations when he describes the capacity of "formal freedom" which we encountered in § 2 of this chapter. Hegel also calls this the "universal" moment of the will, "the pure *thinking* of oneself," which is "the element of pure indeterminacy or pure reflection of the I into itself" where "every limitation and every content . . . is dissolved" (PR § 5). He thinks that I can objectify any of my needs, desires, or drives, treating it as alien or other. He interprets this as the free agent's capacity to act contrary to any of her desires, or even all of them at once: "I am the absolute possibility of being able to *abstract* from every determination" (PR § 5R), "I can do anything, omit anything" (VPR 3: 111; VPR 4: 112). Hegel thinks it is an illusion to identify the ego with this power of abstraction, as Fichte seems to. For this may lead us perversely to equate absolute freedom with "the flight from every content as from a restriction" (PR § 5R). This is the misguided conception to which Hegel gives the name "negative freedom."

True freedom consists instead in choosing one's determinacies, actively identifying oneself with them. This, Hegel says, is "*self-determination* of the I, positing oneself in a negative of oneself, that is, positing oneself as *determined, limited,* and remaining with oneself (*bei sich*)" (PR § 7; cf. EG § 469). "Being with oneself in one's determinacies" is a reinterpretation of the Kantian conception of autonomy. In this new version, my self includes empirical desires and inclinations if I have identified myself with them and I am "with myself" in them. Self-activity does not exclude activity motivated by such inclinations, as it does with Kant and Fichte.

More is required for me to be "with myself" in a desire than merely some choice on my part to "identify" with it. This is the point of Hegel's denial that freedom consists in "arbitrariness" (*Willkür*). By "arbitrariness," Hegel means a choice that, operating by "free reflection, abstracting from everything," seizes on some contingent content "given internally or externally" (PR § 15). An arbitrary choice is made with the consciousness of my ability to take any of several options presented to me, but without concern for the way in which this choice might relate to my other values, goals, or projects. I may think of such a choice as free because it is at the mercy of my momentary whim and not constrained by anything else. But, Hegel argues, arbitrariness involves a dependency I have overlooked. "It is contained in arbitrariness that the content is determined as mine not through the nature of my will, but through contingency. Thus I am dependent on this content, and this is the contradiction that lies in arbitrariness" (PR § 15A).

Following the Kantian tradition in which Hegel stands, to be *self*-aware is to be aware of an activity that unifies a content distinct from it. If the limits of the self, or at least of its positive freedom, are the limits of this activity, then the self's free content is whatever its self-activity successfully unites. The object of an arbitrary choice has not been properly made a part of the self that chooses it, since it bears only a contingent relation to the self's needs, desires, and other choices. In this respect, the content of such a choice is not something in which I am "with myself," and so an arbitrary choice is "unfree." It does not manifest only the self-activity of the self that makes it, but includes an additional content which is alien to this self because it is related only accidentally to its other contents. "The ordinary man believes he is free when he is permitted to act arbitrarily, but in this very arbitrariness lies the fact that he is unfree" (*PR* § 15A). A choice is absolutely free only when I am "with myself" in it. This requires that it be specifically characteristic of me, integrated reflectively into my other choices, and standing in a rational relation to my desires, traits, projects, and my total situation. I am free or "with myself" in my "contents" or "determinations" – my desires and my choices – when they harmonize with the practical system constituting my self-identity as an agent – with the "rational system of volitional determination" which I am (*PR* § 19).

10. A system of objective freedom

Hegel's concept of spirit is based on the idea that I can be free or "with myself" in something external, which can count as a manifestation of my freedom or self-activity. There is room for the relation "with myself in" wherever there is a self engaged in some rational project and there is an object that plays some positive role in that project, either as a product or an intended result, or else as a means or an enabling condition.

Hegel views the whole of the *Philosophy of Right* as a "system of objective freedom" – a system of objects in which the will is "with itself" (*PR* § 28), or the "Idea" of the will as "the free will that wills the free will" (*PR* § 27). In chapter 1, we looked at the structure of the *Philosophy of Right* as a developing system of self-images, all of which belong to the self-understanding of modern humanity. To look at the *Philosophy of Right* in this way is to look at it "subjectively," from the side of the subject whose freedom is in question. But we might equally well look at the same system "objectively," from the side of the objects in which the free will actualizes itself, or, as we have now learned to express it, the kinds of objects "in" which the free will is "with itself."

In the course of the *Philosophy of Right,* Hegel considers four basic types of entities in which the self or free will can be "with itself":

1. The will's own determinations
2. External objects or "things" (*Sachen*)
3. The will's external actions and doings, including their consequences

4. The social institutions that define the will's situation

In effect, this also reproduces the structure of Hegel's system of objective spirit; (1) is treated in the *PR,* Introduction; (2) is Abstract Right; (3) is Morality; and (4) is Ethical Life.

In Abstract Right, Hegel takes up objective freedom in the form of the external objects or things that are the property of the *person,* and hence in which I as person am "with myself": "As free will I am object to myself in what I possess, and only thus am I an actual will. This side constitutes what is true and rightful, the determination of property" (*PR* § 45). Morality deals with the freedom of the *subject,* the will's being with itself in its own willing, in its actions and their ends (*PR* § 109), and in the results it brings about in the objective world, for which it regards itself as morally responsible (*PR* § 117; *EG* § 503). In Ethical Life the will comes to be free or "with itself" in the social institutions of the rational state. The state's interests and mine are not in reality opposed, and to the extent that I become conscious of this fact "just this [other, i.e., the state] is immediately not an other for me, and in this consciousness I am free" (*PR* § 268).

Hegel's most striking claim in this regard is that my duties as a member of the rational social order do not really constrain me, but instead liberate me (*PR* § 149). This claim may seem to go a step beyond paradox, passing over into doublethink. But it makes perfectly good sense, if we keep in mind what Hegel's concept of freedom is, and if we grant the strong claims he makes on behalf of the institutions of the modern ethical order. These institutions mark out for me a certain role, or a set of roles, in society – as a family member, as a professional in civil society, as a citizen of a state (*PR* § 157). Hegel claims that our social roles in the modern state are indispensable to the fulfillment or actualization of ourselves as rational beings. It follows that ethical duties liberate us because only by fulfilling them can we actualize ourselves as part of this rational system of cooperation. Without them, my will would contain only natural impulses and striving after vaguely defined moral goals. I could have neither a concrete self-image, nor a determinate plan of action, nor any confidence that what I think ought to happen actually will happen. When I fulfill my role in a rational social order, on the other hand, I define myself through my action, and my action is part of a larger social process that systematically achieves the good. Duties count as enabling conditions for us, and when we see this, we come to be "with ourselves" or free in performing them.

> [In ethical life] the individual is not limited but rather freed. What the individual is, his essential will, is not an other toward which he relates himself. He finds himself confined, oppressed only insofar as he stands in his particularity, only insofar as he has a particular "ought" and "may be"; what presses on him is only his own subjectivity. Insofar as he relates to himself as something ethical, he liberates himself. The ethical living together of human beings is their liberation; in it they come to an intuition of themselves. (*VPR19* : 125)
>
> It is my own objectivity, in the true sense, which I fulfill in doing my duty: in doing my duty, I am with myself and free. (*PR* § 133A)

Of course, Hegel does not think that we are free *only* in doing our duties. Unlike Fichte, he does not maintain fanatically that even our bodily survival should have "no other purpose than to live and to be an effective tool for the promotion of the end of reason" (*SL* 268/284). He insists that subjective freedom and particular self-satisfaction are the foundation of morality, and that ethical duties liberate us only because we fulfill our particularity through them (*PR* §§ 121–124, 152–154, 162,R, 185–189, 260; cf. *EG* § 475). By the same token, it is clearly not Hegel's view that we could be "liberated" by being compelled to perform our duties (whether through police power or, more subtly, through social pressure). We are with ourselves in our duties only if we have rational knowledge of or insight into the worth of what we do (*PR* § 132,R); the chief avowed purpose of the *Philosophy of Right* is to provide this knowledge (*PR* Preface 13).

Finally, duty does not liberate us unless it is *true* that we actualize ourselves through fulfilling our duties. Duty is liberation only because fulfilling duty is a "coming to the essence, to the truth of the will" (*VPR 3*: 490; cf. *PR* §§ 24, 149A). Our best reason for resisting Hegel's assertion that "duty liberates" is a healthy skepticism concerning Hegel's view that the fulfillment of our duties in a modern social order really contributes to a concretely free and rational life. We may even come to take for granted that to think independently and critically is necessarily to take a conscientiously detached view of society and one's place in it which precludes being "with oneself" in one's duties.[26] Even if this is right, Hegel may still be correct in thinking that we have a fundamental need for rational, reflective identification with a social role, and that modern individuals cannot be truly free until they create a social order in which this is possible. Surely the most wretched unfreedom of all would be to lose the ability even to conceive of what it would be like to have the freedom we lack, and so dismiss even the aspiration to freedom as something wicked and dangerous.

11. Hegelian freedom and ordinary freedom

Hegel's concept of absolute freedom is not the ordinary one, but we are now in a position to see how a Hegelian ethical theory based on absolute freedom will provide for freedom in the ordinary sense. To be free we must be with ourselves in our actions. As modern individuals, our self-image prominently includes the conception of ourselves as subjects, directing our lives through our own choices and finding satisfaction in our deeds as expressions of our subjectivity (*PR* § 121). In other words, we cannot be with ourselves in our actions unless we achieve subjective freedom. We cannot be subjectively free unless we have personal freedom and civil freedom. As persons we require an external sphere in which to exercise our free choice (*PR* § 41). We cannot fulfill ourselves as subjects unless we belong to civil society, and enjoy the freedom from state interference necessary to build our lives and livelihoods on our own work (*PR* § 189). We cannot actualize subjective freedom as citizens of the state unless we can participate in the formation of public opinion through the give and take of free discussion (*PR* § 319). Thus in Hegel's ethical theory, freedom in the ordinary sense turns out to be required as a necessary condition for subjective freedom, which is one aspect of absolute freedom. The value of freedom in the ordinary sense is subordinate to and conditional on other values, but it is important just the same.

Isaiah Berlin, along with many other writers in the liberal tradition, warns us against identifying freedom (in the ordinary sense) with some other good, such as self-actualization. To do this, they think, is to run the risk of losing sight of the special value of freedom, perhaps sacrificing it in our pursuit of other goals. One Hegelian response to this is that unless we view freedom in the ordinary sense as subordinate to other goals, we cannot properly estimate its value, or have full insight into its importance, since that is best appreciated when it is seen in light of the larger human good it serves. For Hegel, as for John Stuart Mill, freedom in the ordinary sense is a very important good, but its value is conditional on the specific conditions of human self-actualization in modern society. We will not do a better job of protecting freedom by pretending it has a more exalted place in the scheme of things than it really has.

The other Hegelian reply to such liberal arguments is that they beg the question in supposing that freedom, properly speaking, is a different good from self-actualization. Hegel's theory identifies freedom as the *Bestimmung* of human beings, the essence of the self to be actualized. We have already seen that Hegel has a theoretical basis for claiming that human self-actualization is freedom, and freedom is not really the ability to do as you please, but absolute self-activity, or being with yourself.

This may seem like a mere dispute about the meaning of a word, but in some cases words matter a lot. In modern society, the demand for liberation, emancipation, freedom, occupies a very important place. If Hegel is right, then this demand may not mean what liberals think it does. If you think that freedom is nothing beyond the ability to do as you please, then you will say that if a society provides lavishly for that ability, it must be a free society. If critics claim that it is still not a free society, because people cannot rationally identify with their roles in that society, or because there is no meaning in any of the choices it provides people, then you will dismiss such claims as confused, or reinterpret them as demands for something other than freedom. Of course, it would be nice to have those other things, you think, and maybe someday we will find a way to get them; in the meantime we should at least be glad that we are living in a free society. But you might be all wrong; the critics may be saying exactly what they mean, and you may simply be failing to understand them.

3
Happiness

1. Happiness: ancient and modern

The classical Greek tradition in ethics from Socrates to the Stoics is concerned with one very simple and fundamental question: What sort of life should one live? This inquiry is focused on the pursuit of *eudaemonia,* or "happiness." Happiness consists in that sort of life in which a human being does and has what is most fitting to human nature. The happy life is the life of human self-actualization.

Hegel shares with classical ethics the idea that practical philosophy is focused on a single encompassing human good, consisting in the self-actualization of human beings as rational agents. His theory differs from classical theories in two main ways. First, as we saw in Chapter 1, § 8, it is misleading in Hegel's theory to think of this good as an *end,* because it is a self-actualization theory rather than a teleological theory. Second, Hegel's name for the final human good is not "happiness" but "freedom." To appreciate the significance of this second difference we need to take a look at the way classical ethics thought about happiness, and then at the way the concept has changed in modern ethics.

Aristotle reports that some think happiness consists in pleasure, or wealth, or honor, whereas others hold that it consists in virtue, or the exercise of virtue, or philosophical knowledge.[1] Aristotle apparently thinks that everyone in his society would agree that happiness is the comprehensive good, the good including all other goods worth having. In Plato, too, the question "How should I live?" was apparently taken to be equivalent to the question "How can I achieve happiness?"[2]

Classical ethics thereby takes two other things for granted as well: first, the *objectivity* of happiness; second, the *egoistic* orientation of ethics. Both have been brought into question by modern ethical thought.

2. The issue of objectivity

It is agreed by Socrates, Plato, Aristotle, and the Stoics that the constitution of an individual's happiness is an objective matter, not dependent on what the individual thinks or believes about it. If a certain sort of life constitutes my happiness, then that is an objective fact about me, independent of my actual desires, preferences, or beliefs about what my happiness consists in. Suppose I believe that happiness consists in bodily pleasures, and, following this belief, I succeed in enjoying a life of bodily pleasure. I have a life that contents me, and I believe it to be a happy life. Nevertheless, classical ethical theorists (even the Epicureans) deny that happiness for any human being consists in a life of bodily pleasures. On this ground, they deny not only that I know what my good is, but also that I am really happy. In the classical view, if people's values and priorities are sufficiently at odds with the objectively correct ones, they can be wretched without knowing it; their thoughts and feelings to the contrary count for nothing.

It is characteristic of modern ethical thought to regard happiness as a much more subjective matter than this. Many modern thinkers regard happiness as consisting simply of pleasure and the absence of pain, whereas most others maintain that whether I am happy depends on whether I satisfy the desires I actually have. This change appears to have begun with Hobbes. Descartes, for example, still espouses the Stoic view, identifying happiness with virtue.[3] Hobbes, however, considers happiness to be not a state of the person, but a transition from desire unsatisfied to desire satisfied:

> I put for a general inclination of all mankind a perpetual and restless desire of power after power that ceases only in death. . . . The felicity of this life, consisteth not in the repose of a mind satisfied. For there is no such *finus ultimus,* utmost aim, nor *summum bonum,* greatest good, as is spoken of in the books of the old moral philosophers. Nor can a man any more live, whose desires are at an end, than he, whose senses and imagination are at a stand. Felicity is continual progress of the desire, from one object to another; the attaining of the former, being still but the way to the latter.[4]

By the late seventeenth century, it was common to identify happiness not merely with the satisfaction of desire, but with a determinate subjective state: pleasure. Malebranche and Arnauld, for example, argue over whether happiness is pleasure in general or pleasures of the intellect only; but they agree that happiness consists in pleasure (a position that had been roundly rejected by St. Thomas Aquinas and most other Scholastics).[5]

John Locke agrees with Arnauld and Malebranche about this, and takes two further steps toward subjectivizing the idea of happiness.[6] First, Locke recognizes that what may give pleasure to one person may not give it to another, and concludes that happiness is subjective not only in the sense that it consist in a subjective state, but also in the further sense that the happy life varies from person to person.[7] (Thus it is a step backward, in the direction of ancient objectivism about happiness, when Shaftesbury claims – and when Mill later repeats the claim – that mental pleasures are more conducive to happiness than bodily ones on the ground that those who know both pleasures systematically prefer the former.)[8] Second, Locke makes the interesting claim that we are moved to desire and pursue what we consider good only insofar as we regard that good under the guise of our happiness:

> Yet all good, even seen, and confessed to be so, does not necessarily move every particular man's *desire;* but only that part, or so much of it, as is consider'd, and taken to make a necessary part of his happiness. All other good however great in

reality, or appearance, excites not a man's *desires,* who looks not on it to make a part of that happiness.[9]

As it stands, of course, this flies in the face of the familiar fact that people sometimes desire and pursue something (such as another person's affection) while realizing that such striving will be destructive of their happiness. But Locke's claim is interesting because it gives special emphasis to the role played by an individual's *conception* of happiness in that individual's desires and choices. As we shall see, the same thought is central to Kant's and Hegel's reflections on the idea of happiness, even though (unlike Locke) they do not identify happiness with pleasure and they recognize that people may desire things not included in their notion of what will make them happy.

There are three quite different senses in which Locke's conception of happiness is more "subjective" than the classical conceptions of Plato, Aristotle, and the Stoics:

SC *Subjectivity of content:* Happiness consists in a subjective state of mind, such as pleasure or satisfaction, not in extramental states or achievements (such as having a just soul, or acting virtuously).
SV *Subjective variability:* The content of happiness may differ from person to person; what makes me happy may be quite different from what makes you happy.
SD *Subjective determination:* The content of a person's happiness is at least in part up to that person; at least to some extent, what counts as my happiness depends on what I think will count as my happiness.

Of the three, SD is by far the greatest departure from classical ethics. It is arguable that SV is already part of classical ethics itself, since Plato seems to hold that a happy life for a member of one class in the ideal state will differ in content from a happy life for a member of another class; and at least on some interpretations, Aristotle recognizes that some people can be happy by devoting their lives to political activity, whereas others are happy by devoting their lives to philosophical contemplation. Aristotle rejects SC, but reports it as a common opinion in his day, and SC was held by some ancient philosophers, such as Epicurus and Eudoxus.[10] But all ancient ethical theories, even the most hedonistic of them, seem to hold that what my happiness consists in is a matter of fact entirely independent of my beliefs about it. In contrast, Locke and later modern thinkers such as Kant and Hegel hold that my conception of happiness has an irreducible role to play in determining the actual content of my happiness.

Because the modern conception of happiness differs so much from the ancient one, it is sometimes alleged that "happiness" is not a correct translation of *eudaemonia.* In modern languages, however, there is no other word that is more suitable, and the alternative translations of *eudaemonia* that have been proposed (such as "flourishing") have a distinctly artificial ring to them. The problem is not one of lexicography or translation. Both *eudaemonia* and "happiness" can perfectly well be used to refer to an individual's total good, to the unrestricted whole of what is in that individual's interests,

55

benefits that individual, or makes that individual well off. If *eudaemonia* in classical ethics is used differently from "happiness" and its modern equivalents, the most natural explanation is that there is a systematic and substantive disagreement between classical and modern ethical thought concerning what an individual's good *is,* and especially over the extent to which my conscious desires and my beliefs about my good determine the content of my good.

Richard Kraut has suggested that our modern conception of happiness is less "objective" and more "subjective" than the ancient one because the ancients were more confident than we are that they knew what the human good consists in.[11] He may be right that we are less confident about this than Aristotle was, but Aristotle's own report of common opinion indicates that there was considerable disagreement among the ancients, and that suggests that there might have been a good deal of uncertainty as well. But even if we are less confident than the ancients that we know the content of the human good, that still does not explain why we relate an individual's happiness more closely than they did to that individual's beliefs, desires, and preferences. If one physician feels less confident than her colleagues that she knows the real nature of a certain disease, that would not explain her concluding that the nature of the disease varies from patient to patient; still less would it account for her adopting the bizarre theory that for each individual patient the nature of the disease is whatever that patient happens to think it is. The modern tendency to subjectivize happiness or the good cannot be explained by anyone's degree of confidence in their knowledge about what happiness consists in. What needs explanation is the fact that we moderns *are* so confident that a person's good depends on the satisfaction of that person's actual desires and conception of the good.

3. The issue of egoism

A person's happiness is the sum of that person's good, that person's *self-interested* good. By posing the question as it does, the classical ethical tradition takes for granted that the answer to questions about how one should live must ultimately be *egoistic* answers. Of course it is true that ancient ethical thought often stresses the role of non–self-interested pursuits in the happy life. Sometimes ancient moral philosophers even insist that such pursuits are indispensable to happiness, as when Plato makes happiness consist in justice, and Aristotle treats friendship as an indispensable condition for happiness. Classical ethical theories all hold that one cannot be happy unless one possesses certain virtues the practice of which involves non–self-interested behavior toward others. But in classical ethics the ultimate rationale for my having non–self-interested concerns is that having them is required for my own happiness, necessary to my own good.

Hegel realizes that we totally miss the point of ancient egoism if we think it reflects the attitude we moderns call "selfishness." According to Hegel's interpretation of classical ethics, ancient Greek culture was originally one in which individual self-interest was basically in harmony with the interests of the community, in which people experienced no serious division between their own welfare and the demands of social life. There was no sense in which self-interest was perceived as conflicting with any other important values. My good is simply my share in *the* good. Until the rise of the subversive idea of subjective freedom in fifth-century Athens, the distinction between different interests, as something that might be mutually opposed, was not a natural one to draw for people living in the naive harmony of Greek culture. Hegel thinks that the awareness of social conflict – that the claims of the family and the state might conflict, or that individual self-interest might diverge from the common good – was extremely traumatic for the Greeks, and so became the main focus of their tragedies (cf. *PhG* ¶¶ 464–476).

If we think ancient egoism represents "selfishness," then we should be surprised that the classical egoism was not immediately called into question by Christian philosophy. Christianity places very strong emphasis on *agape,* self-denial and service to others; but such thinkers as St. Augustine and St. Thomas Aquinas continue to pose the questions of ethics from an egoistic standpoint. They modify the classical position only by identifying our final happiness with an afterworldly beatific vision of God. Sin is viewed as the assertion of individual self-*will,* but not of individual self-*interest;* this always consists in conforming our will to God's. In Christian ethics, classical objectivism and egoism both remain unquestioned. This continuity between pagan and Christian ethics becomes intelligible if we realize that classical ethics is egoistic simply because the ancients did not yet clearly differentiate clearly between the good of the individual self and the good of the social or cosmic whole to which the self belongs. The pantheism of Stoic ethics was a natural transition from pagan to Christian ethical thought, retaining the egoistic presuppositions of classical ethics.

Hegel thinks that modern ethics has abandoned ancient egoism only because we moderns have come to see ourselves as individual subjects, with self-determined lives to lead distinct from the life of the state, the order of nature, and the life of God. Thus we come to regard our subjective self-satisfaction as a good distinct from, and possibly in conflict with, the private good of others, the public good of the community, and the divine order of the universe. This modern spirit for Hegel gives rise to the deepest corruption, but at the same time to the idea of absolute freedom – the modern spirit's fundamental vocation (*PR* §§ 138–139). The reconciliation of universal and particular good in the modern state is thus a reconciliation of genuine opposites, a true return out of otherness (*PR* § 260).

It is not until Kant that modern ethics decisively challenges classical egoism. Kant demotes happiness to second place among goods, making the rational value of happiness dependent on the possession of moral virtue, the condition even of the worthiness to be happy (*G* 393/9). A Hegelian explanation of this is that with the rise of modern subjective self-consciousness, the concept of individual good had to be subjectivized; consequently, individual happiness no longer necessarily shares in the universal good, or in its absolute

claims upon us. If individual good arises through individual desire and preference, it can fundamentally oppose the good of others, the common good
of society, the moral law of God. Therefore, ethics must depose happiness
from its position as the first principle of practical philosophy.

4. The natural will, resolve, and choice

On both issues, objectivity and egoism, Hegel sides with the moderns. Hegel
is no hedonist, so he rejects SC; but his concept of happiness is subjectivistic
in respect of both SV and SD. Hegel identifies my happiness with the satisfaction of my desires – in fact, with the attainment of a good whose content
is subjectively determined by me. Hegel thinks of happiness, my subjective
or self-interested good, as only one part of the larger good for which I have
good reason to strive in actualizing my freedom. As we shall see in the next
section, Hegel's conception of happiness is very close to Kant's. Although
Hegel's ethical theory takes a more favorable attitude toward the pursuit of
happiness than Kant's does, it still treats happiness as a conditioned good,
not as the final aim of all action.

The Introduction to the *Philosophy of Right* derives the concept of happiness, in the course of developing the concept of the free will. It also argues
that absolute freedom rather than happiness is the final good of the free will.
Hegel's aim is not to show that freedom as such must be people's conscious
end. Because his ethical theory is a self-actualization theory rather than a
teleological theory, he begins not with an identification of the conscious goal
of action, but with a conception of the agent to be actualized, and he derives
freedom as the objective content of the goals that such a will sets for itself.
In other words, he tries to show that the characteristic ways of reasoning and
deciding point to a tacit acknowledgment of the evaluative priority of freedom over happiness, even by people who do not explicitly recognize the value
of freedom.

Hegel proceeds by considering some characteristic ways in which people
make decisions about what they want and employ their reason in making
such decisions. He thinks that insofar as these ways of deciding are carried
out with full self-awareness, they involve – or at least approximate to – an
explicit recognition of freedom as the final human good. The argument involves three grades or levels of the free will, a hierarchy of different ways of
exercising agency. It begins with the "immediate or natural will" (*PR* § 11).
This is, so to speak, the will simply as it comes from nature, the will considered prior to (that is, in abstraction from) any exercise of free agency. The
"content" of this will is a "medley and manifold of drives (*Triebe*)," each of
which is "something universal and indeterminate, having many modes and
objects of satisfaction" (*PR* § 12). Hegel appears to include among such
drives not only sensuous drives, such as hunger and thirst, but also drives of
a "spiritual nature," such as "sympathy" and the drives for "honor" and
"fame" (*VPR* 2: 135). Hegel's theory holds first, that these drives are just
found in us, or immediately "given"; second, that there are an indeterminate

multiplicity of them; and third, that each is a drive for a general kind of thing, and not a desire for a specific object.

The first task of the free will consists in "resolving" (*Beschliessen*), "canceling the indeterminacy" of these natural drives. To resolve is to convert one's general and indefinite drives into desires for more or less definite objects. This is what I do, for instance, when I feel hungry and decide that what I want to eat is enchiladas rather than lamb curry, or steak, or scampi. Of course, it is not often that we first feel hungry in general and then subsequently, after a conscious process of "resolving," decide what food we are hungry for. Usually our hunger presents itself to us directly as a desire for a specific food. But it is open to Hegel to claim that there can be resolving even in cases where no explicit mental process of this sort takes place. His theory of our volition treats our basic or immediate desires as indeterminate drives, and assigns to our will the function of converting these drives into desires for determinate objects. Resolving is sometimes an explicit and conscious process of deciding, but sometimes it is performed tacitly or unconsciously. Hence the theory can appeal to the fact that sometimes resolving is an explicit and conscious process of deciding what we desire, but it is not refuted by the fact that this does not always occur.

Once the will has "resolved," its desires take the form of wants directed at determinate objects. Then it is in a position to move on to its second task, which Hegel calls "choosing" (*Wählen*). When we "choose," we select which of our determinate desires we will count as most properly our own. In Chapter 2, we saw that there is a sense in which it is not a trivial truth that all the desires I find in myself are mine, or a part of me. There are important differences between my desires in respect of the extent to which I regard them as truly mine, or expressive of myself. As some recent philosophers have emphasized, most of us have second-order desires, desires concerned with other desires. About some of my desires I form the second-order desire that I should continue to have them, whereas about others I desire not to have them at all. Some desires are affirmed through my choice, or "chosen" (in Hegel's sense) as part of me. I identify with these desires, I regard them as part of me; the desires that I desire not to have remain, by contrast, "external" to me, they fall outside what I regard as my real self.

Choosing is a function of what Hegel calls the "reflective will" (*EG* §§ 476–477; *PR* § 20), because in choosing, the will detaches itself, as it were, from its particular desires so as to choose between them. As choice, the content of the will is "for the reflection of the *self* into itself only a possible [content], it may be mine or not, and the self is the *possibility* of determining myself to this or that other, of *choosing* among these determinations, which are external for the self on this side" (*PR* § 14). If I am to be free or with myself in my actions, they must proceed from desires that are truly mine, desires with which I have chosen to identify. When it makes such a choice, Hegel says, the reflective will "closes with" its desire (*sich mit ihr zusammenschliesst*) and thereby makes the desire really "its own" (*seinige*) (*EG* § 477).

As in the case of resolving, choosing is sometimes done by an explicit, conscious process, sometimes not. I sometimes identify with a desire through a process of explicitly deciding to, but choosing can also occur through spontaneous self-directed attitudes, such as pride or shame. The ritual act of consciously deciding to identify with a desire will mean little if it is not ratified by these attitudes. As before, Hegel's theory assigns the identification with a desire not to our natural constitution but to our free agency, to the "reflective will," whatever the degree of consciousness with which the identification process has been carried out.

As choosing, the will is also called "arbitrariness" (*Willkür*) – or, as we might also translate the term in this context, "option." Choosing is a function of the will that can be exercised indifferently in either of two or more ways. For example, I might desire great wealth and power, but also desire not to be burdened with the cares and responsibilities that wealth and power inevitably bring with them. It is up to me which of these conflicting desires I identify with and count as most truly mine. Choosing does not have the power to create new desires, or to destroy desires that are already there. But it makes a great deal of difference whether I think of my greed and ambition as warping my life, or think of my childish irresponsibility as standing in the way of success. My self-definition is at stake, along with the content of my freedom.

The term *Willkür* also suggests, however, that such choices can be arbitrary, accidental, at the mercy of whims and caprices. As we have seen, Hegel denies that absolute freedom is present in arbitrary choices. He considers arbitrariness as one technique for overcoming the will's "finitude," the fact that its has some determinate, naturally given desire as its content (*PR* § 6). Through its capacity to identify arbitrarily with one content and reject another, the will seeks "infinitude" (*PR* § 5). Hegel sees such a quest among some of his Romantic contemporaries, such as Friedrich Schlegel, who try to vindicate their infinite freedom through an attitude of ironic detachment toward all finite aspects of life. Another illustration of it, later but perhaps better known to us, is found in Kierkegaard's "aesthetic man" in *Either/Or*.[12] We saw in Chapter 2 that Hegel regards this Romantic quest for freedom as a deception. Instead of being everything, the arbitrary will is nothing determinate at all, hence just as one-sided as the finite determinacy it is trying to avoid (*PR* § 16). As Kierkegaard was later to put it, this self falls into the "despair of infinitude."[13]

Arbitrariness does not get the will beyond the "dialectic" of different drives and inclinations, getting in the way of one another and pulling the will in different directions (*PR* § 17). In order to overcome this dialectic, the will must move on to a third stage beyond both "resolve" and "choice." It reflects on its drives and tries to harmonize them both with one another and with the practical means of their satisfaction, so that they form a consistent whole, a "sum of satisfaction." The idea of this whole is what Hegel calls "happiness" (*PR* § 20).

5. Kant's idea of happiness

This notion of happiness is quite close to the one developed in Kant's ethical writings. Kant identifies happiness with the "well-being" (*Wohl*) of a finite rational being (G 395/11), its total and lasting advantage (G 416n/33n), which consists in the satisfaction of its natural desires or inclinations. But happiness is also an "idea," in which "all inclinations are summed up" (G 399/15); to pursue happiness is to pursue an "absolute whole or maximum of well-being" (G 418/35). To be happy is to be in that state where these inclinations are maximally satisfied, so that happiness consists in a total "contentment with one's condition" (G 393/9).

Happiness is the maximal satisfaction of one's inclinations, but inclinations are heterogeneous, lacking any common measure in themselves (*PR* § 17). There are no desires whose satisfaction counts as *my* satisfaction apart from my choice to "close with" a given desire found in me; and there are not even any desires for determinate objects apart from my act of "resolve" which gives determinacy to an indeterminate a natural drive. Likewise, both Kant and Hegel think that the notion of a "total" or "maximal" satisfaction makes sense only in terms of an idea devised by the individual whose good it is supposed to be. My agency is involved in deciding which combination of satisfactions will count as my "total" or "maximal"satisfaction.

In framing this idea of a greatest "sum of satisfaction," I may consider not only the relative strength of my desires, but also the resources available and consequences of applying these resources in various ways (*PR* § 21). As Hegel puts it:

> The result, the ideal of this sphere is happiness, satisfaction of drives. But drives contradict each other, their means and consequences complicate and contradict each other. Through reflection, conception (*Vorstellung*) makes a whole out of this bundle, a universal satisfaction of drives, but in such a way that they do not contradict each other, they are posited in harmony and subordinated to one another. (*VPR 4*: 135)

I am *satisfied* (or content) at a given time if whatever desires I happen to have at that time are satisfied. But that is not sufficient for *happiness*. I can be called happy only by means of a *conception* of happiness that I have framed for myself, an idea of a life in which all my inclinations will achieve maximal and balanced satisfaction. The content of my happiness depends in part on my *decision* about what my happiness is going to consist in. Kant puts this point most explicitly in a fragment from his *Nachlass* (dated about 1775): "Happiness is not something sensed but something thought. Nor is it a thought that can be taken from experience but a thought that only makes its experience possible. [It is] not as if one had to know happiness in all its elements, but the a priori condition by which alone one can be capable of happiness."[14]

Happiness for Kant requires not only empirical desires and their satisfaction, but also an interpretation of these desires in terms of a conception of myself – a comprehensive set of aims, and a plan in terms of which I imagine these aims fulfilled. Only a conception of the sort of life I regard as making me happy "makes the experience of happiness possible." To be happy (as opposed to being merely pleased or contented at the moment) requires reflection on oneself and one's life. It also requires what Hegel has called a "choice" of one's desires, and it means that this choice has been made in a systematic way, so that the pursuit and satisfaction of the desires chosen constitute a coherent whole.

No one has a "conception of happiness" in the sense of a well worked out picture, complete and consistent down to the last detail, of how life is supposed to go. What people have at any given time is a set of goals, desires, and preferences, perhaps to some extent inchoate or inconsistent, and a picture, more or less vague, of how they would like various issues in their life to turn out. Moreover, the standard against which I measure my life may alter as it goes along. I may think that happiness for me consists in becoming a lawyer, but when I fail at that or become dissatisfied with the practice of law, I might decide that what I really want is to be a novelist. In both these ways, Kant's conception of happiness is an idealization when it speaks of our having an "idea" of happiness. The same idealization is involved in talking about our having "standards" for our life. But these are idealizations of something real. When we judge ourselves happy or unhappy, we do not merely express pleassure or displeasure with our momentary state; we are pleased or displeased with our life, because it measures up to our standards for a happy life.

Most people's conception of happiness will presumably include the normal satisfaction of their physical needs and desires; for many, happiness also requires such things as sufficient wealth, professional success, social status, a good marriage, and a satisfactory family life. Each individual's idea of happiness will probably also include goals characteristic of that individual, based on that individual's particular circumstances, talents, opportunities, and aspirations. Happiness is subjective in the sense of SV, partly just because it is subjective in the sense of SD. What my happiness consists in will differ from what yours consists in not only because you and I are different, but also because we have *chosen* to identify our happiness with different things.

Kant's conception of happiness, however, undeniably contains objectivist elements as well. To be happy, I must objectively succeed in getting what I think will make me happy. If I identify my happiness with making a million dollars or winning a Pulitzer Prize, then in order for me to have a happy life, I must actually have made a million dollars, or actually have won a Pulitzer Prize. These achievements are not subjective states of my mind.

It is not plausible to argue that I would be equally happy if I had not actually made a million dollars but only mistakenly believed I had, since the subjective satisfaction derived would be the same either way. This would be all right if we were working with a hedonistic conception of happiness that is subjective in the sense of SC. But a hedonist must hold that my happiness consists in subjective pleasure or satisfaction even if I believe that it consists instead in objective accomplishments. Hence a hedonistic conception of happiness necessarily betrays subjectivism in the more important sense of SD. From the standpoint of SD, if you feel good about your life only because

62

you falsely believe that you have a million dollars, then you aren't really happy, but only think you are. One could of course say that in such a case the person *feels* happy, but one could equally say that the person *feels* rich. On a conception of happiness, like Kant's, which is subjectivist in the sense of SD, perhaps the distinction between feeling and being happy is very similar to the distinction between feeling and being rich.

There is still a valid point to be made by insisting on the role of felt satisfaction in happiness, for a happy person must not only have a life that objectively meets self-devised standards for happiness, but also feel satisfaction in life when it objectively meets those standards. This entails, for one thing, that in order to be happy, the person who has met self-devised standards must also know (or at least believe truly) that the standards have been met. It also means that the person must actually feel satisfaction in that life – which, as we know, all too frequently does not happen. This points to the subjectivity of happiness in the sense of SC, but also it shows how the subjectivity of happiness in the sense of SD must be qualified. It always remains an objective fact, not up to me, whether I will feel satisfied with my life once it has met my self-devised standards.

6. The indeterminacy of happiness

Kant and Hegel agree on the conception of happiness we have been examining. They also agree that happiness, so conceived, is not the final human end or chief human good. Two distinct lines of argument for this appear in their writings. The first, present in Hegel but more explicit in Kant, is what I will call "the indeterminacy argument." The second, clear enough in Hegel but not to be found at all in Kant, I will call "the priority argument." This section will be devoted to the indeterminacy argument; §§ 7–8 will focus on the priority argument.

Hegel contrasts the desire for happiness with specific empirical desires by saying that the idea of happiness gives the form of "universality" to "particular" desires (*VPR 4*: 137). But this "universality," Hegel tells us, is "abstract," and so there is no "contradiction" in it between "form" and "content" (*PR* § 21; *VPR 3*: 145; *VPR 4*: 137–138). In putting the point this way, Hegel is trying to see it as an instance of one of the principles of his speculative logic. In *The Science of Logic*, Hegel rejects the conception of a universal concept as capturing merely something "common," a "similarity" between particulars, which are thought of as the substrata in which the common feature inheres. This, he says, is the merely "abstract universal" or the universal as it is grasped by the "understanding" (*WL 6*: 257–258/587). The true universal is rather "self-determining" or "self-specifying": It is the ultimately real, the ground of its individual instances, and it is at home with itself in them (*WL 6*:260/589; *EL* § 163,A). Hegel is an extreme realist about universals: The truly real and self-subsistent is the universal; particular instances are merely a derivative phase of the universal's existence, the medium through which it actualizes itself.

In these terms, happiness corresponds to the universal as conceived by the understanding. The idea of happiness is defective because it is a universal end that merely harmonizes and organizes empirical ends given external to it, not a universal end that generates from within itself the particulars it systematizes. The true end of reason must be a true universal, self-subsistent and self-determining:

> Happiness has two moments, [universality and particularity]. Now we have the first moment in happiness, but the second is only in the drives. These drives ought to be subordinated to each other, and their determinacy is therefore a contingency. Hence a universality is demanded which has determinacy in itself, [since] the determinacy of drives does not correspond to universality. What is thus demanded is a universality, and what is contained but not realized in it is a determining that corresponds to it, and hence a free universal determining, a real determining. (*VPR 4*: 139)

In this passage, Hegel presents not only the objection based on his speculative critique of abstract universality, but also – entwined with it – another idea that does not depend on speculative logic or Hegelian realism about universals. He claims that the determinacy of the empirical drives "does not correspond to universality." That is, so long as the end of action is concocted on the basis of empirical drives, it cannot have the "determinacy" required for a genuinely "universal end."

Happiness is an end of action in which rational agents represent to themselves the maximum attainable satisfaction of their empirical desires. The point of framing such an end for oneself is to provide rational guidance to action, to provide determinate principles of action. The burden of Hegel's objection is that no ideal of happiness can do an adequate job of providing such principles, because in the ideal of happiness, the different drives are related to one another only contingently or arbitrarily. There is no standard or measure with which to compare them, and so the only practical principles that can be given using the idea of happiness will be vague and platitudinous: "We aren't helped by a subordination of drives, such as the understanding usually comes to, because no measure for the ordering is to be found here, and thus the demand usually ends up with boring generalizations" (*PR* § 17).

Hegel seems to derive this conclusion merely from the fact that the components of happiness are empirical in nature (*EG* § 479; *VPR* 3: 145). But it is not immediately clear why an end fashioned from empirical drives must be indeterminate, incapable of yielding principles of action. On this point Kant is more informative. He claims that the idea of happiness can never give us valid hypothetical imperatives of the sort that can generally be given in the case of more determinate ends (*G* 418/35–36). A valid imperative is one that might rationally constrain the will of every rational being (*G* 413/30). In the case of a technical imperative, what the imperative says is that any rational being who wills a given end ought to take a certain action. For example, such an imperative might say that if I seek to construct a circle of radius r, I should rotate a straight line of length r around one of its endpoints; likewise, if I want to heal a certain disease, I should administer such and such medication in a specified amount (*G* 415/32). Though not all rational agents may

64

happen to have the end mentioned in these imperatives, they are universal because it is true universally that any agent who does have that end ought rationally to act as the imperatives direct.

Kant calls an imperative not "hypothetical" but "assertoric" if it presupposes an end that any rational agent necessarily has. Kant holds that happiness is the one empirical end that every rational being necessarily has. Nevertheless, he denies that there are any valid assertoric imperatives, because such imperatives depend on a definition of the end (happiness), and "it is a misfortune that the concept of happiness is so indeterminate that although every person wishes to attain it, he can never determinately and self-consistently state what it is he really wishes and wills" (G 418/35). "The reason for this," Kant says – agreeing with Hegel – "is that all elements which belong to the concept of happiness are empirical, . . . while for the idea of happiness an absolute whole, a maximum, of well-being is needed in my present and in every future condition" (G 418/35).

Unlike Hegel, Kant elaborates on this reason. The elements of happiness are empirical desires, whose objects are desirable to us solely because of the pleasure or satisfaction we expect to experience when we have gotten them. But, Kant contends, human nature is such that we can never be sure that the objects we desire will fulfill their promise of satisfaction. Some may disappoint us, whereas others may have side effects that altogether cancel out the satisfaction we expected. We desire wealth, for instance, but the life of the wealthy often looks more attractive from a distance than it does up close, and riches often bring with them a host of cares, anxieties, and complications, which deprive the wealthy of the contentment they hoped for. If we want knowledge and vision, they may only show us evils of which we might otherwise have remained blissfully ignorant. Even long life, which almost all people desire, may turn out to be only long misery (G 41/35–36).

This systematic gap between empirical desire and satisfaction has two potentially devastating effects on our attempt to form a determinate idea of our happiness. First, our inability to envision all the noxious by-products of what we desire makes it impossible for us to weigh with accuracy the costs and benefits of pursuing different objects. This in turn makes it impossible for us to give determinate shape to the idea of a harmonious whole of satisfaction. Second, in extreme cases it might even make it impossible for us to frame any self-consistent idea of happiness at all. Suppose I have a desire (e.g., a passionate desire to be united with "her") that is so urgent and ineradicable that I will necessarily be unhappy unless it is satisfied; at the same time, it turns out that the satisfaction of this desire will leave me bitterly disappointed and miserable (our characters are so ill-suited that we can only make a hell of each other's lives). In such a case, I can never state "determinately and self-consistently" what would make me happy, because no self-consistent conception of happiness is possible for me. No matter what happens to me, I am doomed to be unhappy.

This is *not* the Schopenhaurian thesis that all desire is inherently insatiable and delusive, so that happiness is always a tantalizing illusion. Kant does not think that everyone is in a hopeless condition, only that some people may be. His point is that we can never be so certain of where our satisfaction will lie as to formulate universally valid imperatives that specify the means to happiness unfailingly (as Kant thinks we can for many imperatives of geometrical construction, and some imperatives of medical art). "The task of determining infallibly and universally what action will promote the happiness of a rational being is completely unsolvable" (*G* 418/36).

What we do have to guide us in pursuing happiness, Kant thinks, are rules of prudence ("of diet, economy, courtesy, restraint, etc."). These rules are not true imperatives, commanding actions that are practically necessary to the given end; they are only "counsels" indicating conduct that is "shown by experience best to promote welfare on the average" (*G* 418/36). Thus most people cannot attain happiness if they become addicted to alcohol or cocaine, if they systematically spend more money than they make, or if they habitually treat those around them with arrogance and ingratitude. But these rules are never without exceptions. Superstars of screen or playing field are often loved and admired for conduct that would bring enmity and ostracism on you and me; the most wanton profligacy does not destroy happiness for Charles Surface in Sheridan's play, or for U.S. Government-insured financiers in real life; and, if we can take the word of Charles Bukowski (or of Rosin the Bow in the old Irish folk song), there are even some people for whom happiness consists in a life of alcohol addiction.

7. Why do we care about happiness?

The indeterminacy argument depends on contingent (perhaps disputable) claims about the actual constitution of human desires and what will produce satisfaction in human beings. Further, its conclusion is restricted to claiming that happiness is defective as the final human good because it cannot provide us with determinate universal principles. This conclusion, even if true, provides us with no rationale for the claim that freedom (or anything else) is a better candidate for the final human good than happiness is. The indeterminacy argument, even if sound, leaves us free to conclude either that there is no final good, or else that happiness is the final good but there are no determinate universal principles of practical reason.

The same limitations do not attach to another line of thinking, presented by Hegel. The best way to approach this argument is to ask, Why do we pursue happiness? But perhaps this isn't quite the right question. For it is sometimes argued that many people don't actually pursue happiness as an end, and that those who do are less likely to be happy than those who don't. But even those who don't actually make their happiness their end usually desire it, care about it, treat it as a measure of their life. So let us ask, more generally, Why does it matter to us whether we are happy? The answer to such questions is not at all obvious. Hegel thinks that the best answer points toward freedom rather than happiness as the final good.

Kant insists that all of us necessarily have a desire for our own happiness.

66

Happiness is not an arbitrary or merely possible end, but an end that we "can assume a priori for everyone" because it "belongs to our nature" (*G* 415–416/33). "All human beings have the strongest and deepest inclination to happiness, because in this idea all inclinations are summed up" (*G* 399/15). This account is not satisfactory. The mere fact that the idea of happiness is the idea of a sum of satisfactions does not entail that we necessarily desire happiness. It is one thing to have a desire, and another thing to have the desire that this first desire be fulfilled. (For instance, I may have a desire to go to bed with my neighbor's spouse, but desire even more strongly not to satisfy this first desire, because I can foresee the inevitable complications.) The desire for happiness essentially includes a second-order desire for the fulfillment of the desires whose objects are included in our idea of a sum of satisfaction. The fact that I have the first-order desires of which happiness is composed does not entail that I have the second-order desire to satisfy the whole which they constitute. If all of us do in fact have a desire for a "sum of satisfactions" either in general or as specified according to some particular idea of what my happiness consists in, then this fact needs an explanation.

Perhaps our desire for happiness can be treated simply as a primitive desire, like the desires for food, sex, or a comfortable surrounding temperature.[15] This suggestion seems implausible, however. The desire for happiness essentially involves a second-order desire to satisfy other desires whose nature is variable and partly at the mercy of our choices; it is unlikely that a desire of this kind should be present in us as a natural instinct. For that matter, Kant may even be wrong in saying that everyone has a desire for happiness. Hegel suggests that the idea of happiness is the product of a certain kind of culture, requiring a certain degree of reflectiveness and naturally mild mores, so that it could not have arisen in a culture less cultivated than that of Greek ethical life (*PR* § 123R; *VPR* 3: 145). Any idea of happiness essentially arises through reflective deliberation, and it seems likely that the desire for happiness is also based on reasoning. What we need to make explicit is the rationale behind our desire for happiness.

The need for such a rationale is further indicated by the fact that pursuing happiness sometimes requires us to forego the satisfaction of our immediate desires, which (Hegel says) "come to be sacrificed partly to each other on behalf of [happiness], and partly to [happiness] itself directly" (*EG* § 479). This fact makes it even plainer than before that the idea of happiness must have some appeal to us over and above the satisfaction of the particular desires that comprise it. It won't do to say that I desire happiness for the sake of my particular desires, adding that the desire for happiness is merely the desire that the pursuit of one desire should not unnecessarily hinder the pursuit of others. To achieve this unity among desires, I would not need the idea of a "whole of satisfaction" consisting in the satisfaction of many mutually limiting desires. I could accomplish it much more simply by what we might call a policy of "monomania," concentrating all my energy on satisfying just one of my desires, and sacrificing all my other desires to that one. Of course, I do not take the option of monomania seriously in practice, because I take it for granted that I want to satisfy a variety of different desires, and so I require some plan of mutual limitation. But why do I want to satisfy a variety of desires?

One influential answer to this question is to say that I want to *maximize* my satisfaction, so I desire a whole composed of different desires because this strategy leads to greater total satisfaction than any policy of monomania could do. There is, so the fairytale goes, a declining marginal utility in the satisfaction of any single desire, and so the maximum total utility will be achieved through a strategy of equalizing the marginal utility to be gotten from each separate satisfaction. Hegel uncompromisingly rejects this answer, and his theory of the will gives him very good reasons for doing so. As we have seen, Hegel denies that any particular drive contains a "measure" by which it could be compared to other, qualitatively different drives (PR § 17,A). This is why Hegel thinks that the will needs to "resolve," to convert indeterminate drives into desires for definite objects, and then "choose" among these desires, thereby establishing for the first time some definite order of priority among them. There is, of course, a sense in which we experience our desires "passively," and this passivity may play some role in deciding what we call their relative "strength"; but our agency also plays a role large enough that it is quite artificial to represent the relative weight we give to our satisfaction of different desires as something we could simply record as passive observers of our feelings.

Hegel need not deny that for certain theoretical purposes the pattern of a person's preferences might usefully be described by adopting the fiction that there is some quantity that the agent is trying to maximize. The description might even be more than a fiction if we are talking about one of our particular desires that aims at a maximum of something that is literally quantifiable – for example, our desire for money. But if Hegel is right, the existence of anything like a "utility function," assigning determinate (cardinal or ordinal) values to the objects of different desires, cannot be represented as a simple psychic given. My utility function has to be the result of my resolving, choosing, and forming an idea of happiness; to suppose the existence of such a function is simply to presuppose that we have chosen to order our desires and to assign relative priorities to them according to the idea of a sum of satisfaction. The idea of maximizing utility thus already takes for granted the activity of forming an idea of happiness, and presupposes that we have a desire to maximize satisfaction in accordance with such an idea. Hence it cannot be used to explain why we would trouble ourselves to form an idea of happiness and to sacrifice the satisfaction of particular desires to it. Like Kant, utility theory takes for granted the desire for happiness as a simple natural fact, whereas we have seen that it is unlikely to be anything of the sort.[16]

It might be suggested that the reason we guide our conduct by an idea of happiness rather than by following a policy of monomania is that it is simply a natural fact about us that we have many desires that we cannot get rid of or limit to the degree that any policy of monomania would require. This explanation may be true as far as it goes, but it is still inadequate because it does not account for the fact that we often tolerate (or even cultivate) dispensable desires whose pursuit complicates the problem of satisfying desires we cannot get rid of. An individual's idea of happiness very often includes the satisfaction (even the expansion of) such desires. People of modest means sometimes cultivate a taste in opera and fine wines, even though the trouble and expense of seeking out good vintages or traveling to see La Scala or the Wiener Staatsoper make it harder for them to keep up with the mortgage.

8. The priority of freedom over happiness

What this suggests is that our desire for happiness cannot be explained merely in terms of conduct instrumental to achieving the satisfactions of which happiness consists. The fact that we even count as part of our happiness the cultivation of desires, including those that make it harder to satisfy our desires as a whole, strongly suggests that we form the idea of happiness not so much to facilitate the satisfaction of our desires, as to give our desires themselves a determinate shape and content.

Hegel follows up on this suggestion when he tells us quite explicitly why he thinks we form an idea of happiness rather than adopting a policy of monomania: "If I place myself merely in one [of my drives], disregarding all others, then I find myself in a destructive state of limitedness, for I have given up my universality, which is a system of all drives" (*PR* § 17A). Hegel holds that we best make sense of our desire for happiness by supposing that our final good is the assertion of our "universality" or selfhood, which requires us to express ourselves through a coherent system of desires.

This same aspiration to selfhood can already be seen in the activities of resolving and choosing which we looked at earlier. Anticipating Heidegger, Hegel notes that an equivalent expression for "resolve" (*beschliessen*) is *sich entschliessen* – etymologically, "unclosing oneself" (*PR* § 12).[17] When I resolve, converting my indeterminate drives into desires for determinate objects, I am in effect transforming general human needs into the desires of this individual person. I am expressing, or even defining, my self. As Hegel puts it: "Through resolving, the will posits itself as the will of a determinate individual" (*PR* § 13). Likewise, in reflecting on and choosing between my determinate desires, the point is to define myself by deciding which desires I will identify as truly mine. Human desires are not just brute givens for consciousness; they become my desires by being defined through resolve and by being posited as mine through choice. This is true because it is the function of human desires to express the self whose desires they are.

But this self, Hegel insists, is something "universal"; it is the function of forming an idea of happiness to vindicate this universality. This claim might seem paradoxical at first, since it might seem that the point of defining my self through resolve and choice is to do away with what is universal about my aims, vindicating my particularity. But the universal Hegel is thinking of here is not merely what I have in common with all other selves or human beings (this conception of universality, we should recall, is what Hegel attributes to the "dead understanding"). Hegel is thinking of the *self* as a true or rational universal, in relation to the various elements (desires, traits, acts, states of consciousness) that constitute it. A true Hegelian universal, like a Platonic or Aristotelian universal, exhibits itself in the different particulars that participate in it, determining each of them in a specific way by its presence. A self for Hegel is a universal because it is something that manifests itself in each of its determinate desires and acts by connecting them. A self is defined and expressed in its desires when it relates to them as a universal relates to its particular instances – that is, when these desires have to be the determinate desires they are, and when they have to be such because they are the desires of this determinate self. My self attains to this universality when its desires form a whole that is coherent, not only in the sense that it involves few conflicts, but even more in the sense that my various desires systematically support, explain, and justify one another, perhaps analogously to the concepts and propositions of a well-constituted theoretical system.

What lies behind the desire for happiness, then, is the desire to manifest my "universality, as a system of all drives" (*PR* § 17A). We form the idea of happiness not so much in order to get the satisfactions that constitute it as in order to bring it about that our desires are adequate expressions of our universal self. For this reason, Hegel says that the true function of the idea of happiness is one of "educating" and "purifying" our drives, "freeing them from their *form* as immediate natural determinatenesses, and from the subjectivity and contingency of their *content*," transforming them into "the rational system of volitional determination" (*das vernünftige System der Willensbestimmung*) (*PR* § 19).

"The rational system of volitional determination" is nothing but absolute freedom: being with myself in my desires or determinations. Thus Hegel says that the "truth" of happiness is freedom of the will, "the free will that wills the free will" (*EG* § 480; *PR* § 27). He further insists that it is only freedom, and not happiness or well-being, that deserves to be called the human *good* (*PR* § 123A). If "eudaemonism" is the view that our own happiness is the good (*VPR 4*: 135–136), then Hegel is arguing that eudaemonism, when reduced to its basis, is self-refuting, because the best rationale for guiding one's conduct by the idea of happiness is one that implicitly recognizes the priority of freedom over happiness as a human good.

In contrast to Kant, Hegel sees happiness and freedom as intimately connected. Kantian autonomy consists in the will's subjecting itself to an a priori supernatural legislation, and limiting its natural or empirical desires in accordance with the law. Hegel attacks Kant for seeing dichotomies in the self between freedom and nature, reason and sense, where he ought to have seen freedom as actualizing nature and reason as fulfilling itself through sense. Absolute freedom includes the desire for happiness, since the idea of happiness is the idea of a rational system of desires in which the will is with itself or free; indeed, freedom even includes achieving happiness or satisfaction, since in achieving happiness the will actualizes itself in the external world, comes to be with itself in relation to that world.

It still makes sense to distinguish happiness from of freedom, and to treat freedom as the prior good, because the desire for happiness is only one side of freedom. Happiness or individual well-being is the whole of satisfaction relating to only some of our desires: those arising from our immediate natural drives and belonging to the will's "particularity" (*PR* §§ 122–125). The *Philosophy of Right* describes a whole system of rational volition. Much of this system involves volitions that do not have my own natural needs as their source and do not aim at my particular satisfaction. These include non–self-interested desires, arising from the claims of abstract right, morality, and ethical duties arising within the family, civil society, and the state. My happiness is a self-interested good, and it forms one indispensable part of my self-actualization as a rational agent. Because the sphere of abstract right abstracts from the particularity of the agent (*PR* § 37), there is no concern with happiness in that sphere. But my own happiness is systematically integrated into the spheres of both morality (*PR* §§ 123–125, 130) and ethical life (*PR* §§ 163A, 183–187, 241–242, 253,R, 260, 263–264, 268,R). Even so, the rights and welfare of others and the good of the community are goods not reducible to my happiness or self-interest. They lay claim to me not because I desire happiness, but because my final good is freedom.

Hegel even suggests that insofar as I am a self-consciously free individual, my desire for my own happiness should not be seen as an instance of "selfishness" (*Selbstsucht*), which Hegel defines as "preferring the particular to the objective content" of an action (*EG* § 475A). Selfishness consists in pursuing our aims, even those that belong to a fully rational or autonomous system of desires, solely for the sake of particular satisfactions (*EL* § 54A). If I am a eudaemonist, someone who pursues my own happiness as the final and encompassing end of my action, then I seek my own happiness for the sake of the particular satisfactions of which it consists; that makes me a selfish person. But not all desire for my happiness need be selfish. If I am absolutely free, then I will want to be happy because my happiness is one object of a free and rational system of desires that includes the rights and welfare of others and the good of the community. In that case, I cannot be called selfish even in the pursuit of my own happiness.

9. Right in general

The aim of the *Philosophy of Right* is to develop the Idea of right, that is, to expound the concept of right and present its full actualization (*PR* § 1). In Hegel's vocabulary, "right" is a technical term, whose broadest meaning is explained as follows: "Right is: that existence which is in any way an existence of the free will" (*PR* § 29). "Existence" (*Dasein*) here means something objective, something "immediately external" to the will (*PR* § 26). Thus in Hegel's technical usage "right" refers to a thing or object, something that counts as other than the will. But it is an other in which the free will is with itself. A right is a thing in which the free will has successfully actualized itself or accomplished its ends. "Right" means "freedom objectified," or (as Hegel also puts it) "freedom as Idea" (*PR* § 29).

The system of right is the system of objects in which the will is free or with itself. The first form of right Hegel takes up is abstract right, the right we have in the form of external objects, our property, including our own body and life. These are, according to Hegel's technical usage of the term, "rights" in the most straightforward sense, since they are external objects in which our free will has immediate existence (*PR* §§ 33, 40). Later on, Hegel will extend the term "right" to other, less immediate kinds of objects. The free will receives *moral* existence in the form of a subjective will and its acts in the world in which it expresses itself, and it has *ethical* existence in the form of the institutions of a rational society (*PR* § 33).

Obviously, this is a highly unusual way to use the term "right." Normally, we do not refer to a thing we own as a right, but say instead that we have a right *to* it, meaning at least that we do nothing contrary to obligation in using it as we see fit, and perhaps also that we have valid claims against others with regard to its use. We speak of right action, but if we say of an action itself that it is *a right,* this would be an elliptical way of saying something quite different from what Hegel means, namely that we have a right to perform it. We might think of social institutions as being *right* (or *just*), but we wouldn't speak of a just institution itself as *a right.*

Recht has an equivalent in other European languages, but not in English (Latin *ius,* French *droit,* Italian *diritto,* Spanish *derecho,* Hungarian *jog,* Polish *prawo,* etc.). It means "right" or "justice," and also refers to the whole body and foundation of the law, as distinct from specific legal statutes, to which a different word is applied (*Gesetz, lex, loi, legge,* etc.). Most of the time, Hegel uses *Recht* in ways that apparently conform more to this common usage than to his technical one as expounded in *PR* § 29. We may better understand both Hegel's theory of right and his general philosophical procedures if we see how this apparent gap between technical and ordinary usage might be bridged.

Hegel makes it plain that for philosophical purposes, the technical meaning should always be primary. Hegel takes himself to be engaging in the uniquely philosophical task of deducing or developing categories or thought-determinations out of one another. He believes that the system of philosophical categories is in fact "stored in language," and hence (perhaps to our astonishment) Hegel denies that philosophy needs any special terminology (*WL* 5: 20/31–32). At the same time, he realizes that ordinary language reflects ordinary thinking, which is often confused, shallow, and erroneous, in need of philosophical correction. Appeals to ordinary usage are therefore entirely out of place in philosophy. "Rather the main thing in philosophical cognition is the *necessity* of the concept, and the process of having come to be as a *result* [is] its proof and deduction. Since the *content* is necessary *for itself,* the second thing is to look around for what corresponds to it in [ordinary] conceptions and language" (*PR* § 2R).

Recht seems to Hegel the best word in ordinary language to capture the concept of an existence that is the existence of the free will. Both the law and the rights of persons are regarded as something sacred, deserving of our veneration and respect. Hegel's ethical theory attempts to account for this by showing how they are existences of the free will, since freedom of the will is shown by Hegel's theory to be the final human good (*PR* § 30). In order to do this, Hegel needs to connect his technical meaning of "right" more closely with the ordinary one(s). He attempts the connection in his lectures: "*Right* in general expresses a relation, constituted by the freedom of the will and its realization *(Realisation). Duty* is such a relation insofar as it is essentially valid for me, insofar as I have to recognize or respect or produce it" (*VPR17* : 40; cf. *PR* § 260R, *VPR 1* : 249).

Hegel's technical definition of "right" in *PR* § 29 says that right is an "existence" of the free will, and this is presumably equivalent to some object in which my freedom is "realized," in which it takes the form of a thing or object. But here Hegel says that right is a *relation* between the free will and such an object. More specifically, it is the relation that I bear to something in which the freedom of my will exists, insofar as that thing "realizes" my freedom. Let us give these two Hegelian uses of "right" two different names, calling right as the existence itself *existent right,* and right as the relation I bear to this existence *relative right.*

10. Hegel's institutionalism

Prominent among existent rights are the institutions of a rational society. Hegel also says that "the true and proper ground in which freedom is existent [is] the relation of will to will" (*PR* § 71). Property rights become actual and recognized only within legal institutions where they can be specified and enforced (*PR* § 217). Even the moral rights of the subjective will, such as its right to be judged according to its knowledge and conviction of the consequences and worth of its acts (*PR* §§ 117, 120, 132R) are actual rights only within a community that recognizes such rights and treats subjects accordingly. An existent right for Hegel seems always to involve (explicitly or implicitly) a social institution, whose external functioning realizes my freedom. As we have seen, Hegel holds that only the institutions of ethical life provide a concrete foundation for the rights found in the spheres of abstract right and morality. For Hegel, existent rights of other kinds seem to have their foundation in social institutions that are the fundamental or concrete existent rights.

Accordingly, we may view a relative right as my relation to an *institution* that is an existent right (i.e., that realizes my freedom). As Hegel indicates, relative rights are very closely related to duties. For a duty is also my relation to an existent right, to an institution that realizes freedom. But the relation is a different one: It is the relation of having to recognize, respect, or produce the existent right in question. Thus when I have a right, the claims that I have over against others are simply their duties in relation to the same existent right that realizes my freedom.

Some are disturbed by the central role of social institutions in Hegel's theory of right. For Hegel, individuals have claims on one another, but solely by virtue of institutions founded in the ethical life in which they participate. They have no claims on others, or on these institutions, based on anything except the institutions. Dieter Henrich finds it especially disquieting that individuals have no rights *against* institutions themselves, a feature of Hegel's theory which he calls "strong institutionalism."[18]

What exactly is supposed to be missing in Hegel's theory? What sort of rights ought I to be able to claim which Hegel's theory will not let me claim? I may demand that others behave according to their duties under the actual institutions. I may also demand of the institutions themselves that they operate according to their own rational nature, since this is what makes these institutions existent rights in the first place. Thus there certainly is room in Hegel's theory for appealing beyond the contingent and possibly wicked wills of the individuals who administer social institutions, and whose arbitrariness might turn their rationality to unreason, their freedom to oppression. We would do this precisely in appealing to the *actuality* of the institution, as distinct from its contingent existence; in such appeals we have "what is universally recognized and valid" on our side (*PR* Preface 15). Finally, Hegel thinks that living under rational institutions (an *actual* ethical order) is also the right of individuals, since such institutions give existence to their free will: "The *right of individuals* to their *subjective determination to freedom* has its fulfillment when they belong to ethical actuality" (*PR* § 153).

The only thing Hegel will not give us is a certain moralistic picture of what it is to demand one's right against social institutions. He rejects the idea that in making such demands we might be appealing to something beyond the actual essence of the institutions themselves – to a set of subjective moral sentiments with no basis in the actual ethical order, or to a divine providence which so utterly transcends human history as to leave it utterly godforsaken. The only rights Hegel's theory denies us are rights we could never exercise anyway, and shouldn't exercise even if we could.

II
Abstract right

4
Recognition

1. The right to abstract freedom

In Hegel's ethical theory, the final good is not happiness but freedom. One consequence of this is the importance of the right of persons in Hegel's theory. Personal rights set limits to what may be done to a person in the name of interests, whether that person's own interests or the interests of others. If rights are there in order to override eudaemonistic considerations generally, then we might expect them to be ascribed to persons independently of those considerations. Hegel's theory meets this expectation, since "abstract" right is so called precisely because it abstracts from all considerations of well-being or happiness: In abstract right "it is not a matter of particular interests, my utility or my well-being" (*PR* § 37). Instead, it is a matter of securing the abstract freedom of a "person."

As we saw in Chapter 2, § 2, Hegel holds that every human being has "formal freedom," the capacity to abstract from all particular determinations, desires, and interests. This capacity is what makes someone a person, "a self-consciousness of itself as a perfectly abstract I, in which all concrete limitedness and validity is negated and invalid" (*PR* § 35R). As persons, all human beings are equal (*VPR19* : 67–68). Even though the exercise of this capacity to abstract (as in negative freedom or arbitrariness) is not freedom in its most proper sense, Hegel holds just the same that it is essential to guarantee individuals in the modern state adequate room for the exercise of arbitrariness (Chapter 2, §§ 2, 5, and 11). This is the point of abstract right.

"A person must give its freedom an external sphere in order to exist as Idea" (*PR* § 41). "Idea" for Hegel refers to a rational concept when it expresses or embodies itself in something real (*WL 6* : 462–469/755–760; *EL* §§ 213–215; *PR* § 1); a spiritual being "exists as Idea" when it actualizes itself appropriately in the objective world. I "exist as Idea" when my personality, my capacity to make abstract choices, is given adequate scope to actualize itself, and in Hegel's view this happens when I have a sufficient "external sphere" subject to my arbitrary choice.

2. Fichte's theory of recognition

To justify the claim that human beings have abstract rights, what Hegel must show us is why formally free agents ought to guarantee one another exclusive spheres of arbitrary activity. Hegel's argument on this point is developed in

77

his Jena period lectures and shows up again in the *Encyclopedia* (1817, final version 1830) (*EG* §§ 430–436). Much of it is merely presupposed in the *Philosophy of Right*, since that work deals with objective spirit, whereas the argument in question belongs to the *Encyclopedia's* discussion of subjective spirit. Hegel's argument is based on the concept of "recognition" (*Anerkennung*), or mutual awareness. The gist of Hegel's position is that I can have an adequate consciousness of myself only if I am recognized by others, and recognition can be adequate only if it is fully mutual. Much in Hegel's discussion of recognition is novel and provocative, but both the concept of recognition and its use as the basis of a theory of natural right are derived from Fichte's *Foundations of Natural Right (GNR)* (1796). It will enhance our understanding of Hegel's theory of recognition and the rights of persons if we are aware of the Fichtean theory he adopts and modifies.

Fichte's entire philosophy is transcendentally deduced from the possibility of self-consciousness, the consciousness of an object that is identical to the subject of the same consciousness. For Fichte, the self defines itself through its own activity; but it is nevertheless limited or finite, distinguishable from other objects. This means that the self's activity must be limited by a not-self, an objective world different from and opposed to the self. From this Fichte infers that the activity of which we are aware in self-awareness must be practical activity or volition, concerned with altering an outside world (*GNR* 17–20/31–33). Hence our awareness of this activity as limited must be the awareness of an external object that checks or resists it (*GNR* 23–24/40). A self's practical activity is related to some possible change in the objective world, through which the self brings about a state of the world contrasting with a previous state. In this way, self-awareness involves the awareness of time (*GNR* 29/48). The external object that checks the self's activity must be represented as *already* existing for the self at a moment in time prior to that of the self-awareness we are setting out to explain (*GNR* 28/47).

Fichte argues that this threatens us with a vicious regress (or, alternatively, a vicious circularity). At every moment we presuppose the previous consciousness of an object for the self, and along with it the very self-consciousness that was to be accounted for (*GNR* 31/49). Fichte proposes to avoid the regress (or circularity) by thinking of the self as related not only to an external world, but at the same time also to a different sort of object: one in which an activity of the self is already combined with a limitation of this same activity, all within a single temporal moment (*GNR* 32/51). The concept that answers to this description, Fichte says, is that of a "requirement" or "demand" (*Aufforderung*) that the subject should manifest its free activity, but in a determinate way (*GNR* 32–33/52).

More precisely, Fichte argues, self-consciousness presupposes the consciousness of an object that is the *ground* of such a demand, or – as he also puts it – an object that "addresses a demand" to the subject (*GNR* 36/57). This must be an object of a very special kind, one whose influence on the subject is to cause the subject not only to act in a determinate way, but also to set itself an end, which means that this subject must bring about in itself

78

a cognition of the object it intends to produce (*GNR* 37/58). Fichte now argues that an object whose essential influence on us is to produce such a cognition in us must itself be a conscious being, one that possesses the conceptions both of free activity and of the capacity to manifest it according to a concept (*GNR* 37–38/58–59):

> The rational being cannot posit itself as such, without its happening that there is a requirement that it act freely. But if such a requirement to act happens to it, then it must necessarily posit a rational being outside it as the cause of the requirement, and so in general it must posit a rational being outside itself. (*GNR* 39/60)

Fichte understands this to presuppose that a self-conscious being must actually have been affected by another self-conscious being: "It has been shown that if a rational being is to come to self-consciousness, then necessarily another must have had an effect on it, as on one capable of reason" (*GNR* 87/129). In fact, Fichte claims, the two must stand in a relation of "free reciprocal effect" of each on the other "through concepts and according to concepts" (*GNR* 39/61). This mutual relation, which Fichte regards as the "proper characteristic of humanity," is "recognition" (*Anerkennung*).

3. "A human being becomes human only among others"

Fichte's transcendental argument is riddled with difficulties. Suppose we grant that awareness of a determinate self presupposes awareness of already existing external objects that condition and resist one's activity. It is far from clear that there is any vicious circularity or regress in this. There would be if the presupposition raised precisely the same problem that it was invoked to solve, but this is far from evident. If there is a problem involved in presupposing that every moment of self-awareness is conditioned by a previously existing moment, that is only the familiar problem of Kant's First Antinomy. It is arbitrary to invoke the notion of a "demand" to solve *that* problem; and hopeless besides. For if there were a problem about an endless regressive series of objective awarenesses, how would it be a solution to introduce a *different* sort of object that does not raise the problem? It might do so if we were going to *replace* the presupposition of an external world with the presupposition of a demand, but that is evidently not Fichte's intention.

Fichte immediately follows this unsuccessful argument with a "corollary" defending the same conclusion less transcendentally but more persuasively. "A human being," he claims, "becomes human only among others" (*GNR* 39/60).[1] To be a rational self, you have to be "educated"; the demand by one human being that another manifest free activity is the original meaning of "education" (*Erziehung*) (*GNR* 39/61). Self-awareness, according to Fichte, has genetic as well as transcendental conditions. My awareness of the demands of others on my conduct is one of these genetic conditions.

To be self-aware as a rational agent, it is not enough to distinguish myself from external objects; I must also be able to address requirements to myself based on my conception of myself. That is, I must be able to distinguish, within the practical options open to me, between those that manifest my proper selfhood and those that do not. I must have the capacity to act not only on immediate desires or impulses, but also on relatively stable principles expressing who I am. My identity as an agent consists not only of momentary mental states, but also of enduring projects and practical commitments. My selfhood would be impoverished if I lacked these features, and my self-awareness would be impoverished if I lacked the capacity to become aware of them.

Developmental psychologists tell us that children acquire these capacities only by internalizing demands that others (chiefly their parents) have made on them.[2] Fichte anticipates the same point when he insists that I become a self only by being "educated" through the demands of others. My awareness of external demands is a genetic condition for my full selfhood as a rational agent. Fichte concludes that a human self-consciousness is possible only on the assumption of a plurality of human beings; the concept of humanity is not the concept of a single individual, but instead the concept of a species or kind (*Gattung*) (*GNR* 39/61). The most basic relation between human beings is recognition, the making of demands on others and understanding their demands on you. Recognition in this sense is indispensable to being human.

When they recognize others, free beings distinguish themselves from the others. They do this, according to Fichte, through each one's assigning to itself a limited "external sphere" in which to exercise its free activity and recognizing a similar sphere for every other. Originally a person's external sphere is to be identified with that person's body (*GNR* 59/91), but it is eventually supposed to encompass the entire external realm which is subject to a rational being's free choices. In Fichte's theory, it is the function of a certain sort of social contract (the "property contract") to give public recognition to these determinate external spheres (*GNR* 195/213; cf. 197/215).

Thus far we have considered only Fichte's argument that self-awareness requires the awareness of another's demand on me to manifest my free activity in a determinate way. But he also thinks that these demands have a determinable content. When free beings recognize each other, the fundamental demand that they address to each other is the demand to respect each other's external spheres. The determinate action I demand is that you not encroach on my external sphere (*GNR* 43/66). Presumably Fichte thinks that this is so because self-awareness is fundamentally an awareness of the will to act freely in the external world. As soon as I become aware of other free beings, this volition naturally leads to a desire that others should not prevent me from doing what I fundamentally will to do, hence it expresses itself as the demand that others should respect my external sphere of freedom. Naturally, the demand is reciprocal, addressed by each rational being to every other. When I make such a demand, I am also reciprocally recognizing the other's demand upon me.

Fichte insists that these mutual demands must not remain mere expressions of will; they must also manifest themselves in action. "No [free being] can recognize another unless both reciprocally recognize each other; and neither can treat the other as a free being unless both so treat each other recipro-cally" (*GNR* 44/67). To treat another as a free rational being is to grant to the other an external sphere, and also to claim such a sphere for oneself. This relation of mutual self-restriction constitutes the "relation of right" (*Rechts-verhältnis*) (*GNR* 41/63).

4. The relation of right

Fichte claims that to recognize another is to stand in a "relation of right" to that other. It is to stand with the other under the "principle of right": "So limit your freedom that others besides you can also be free" (*GNR* 89/131; cf. 52/78). Individuals who stand in a relation of right demand of one another that they comply with this principle, and they recognize a like demand on the part of others. "Recognizing" the demand involves more than the aware-ness that it has been made; it involves also a "confession" (*Geständniss*) or "declaration" (*Declaration*) that I will for the future respect the other's sphere (*GNR* 47/72, 130/182).

Fichte understands these demands we make on one another not to be *moral* imperatives, but something much more primitive and fundamental than that. To begin with, the demands involved in the relation of right have to do only with external actions, not with the internal intentions that are (for Fichte, as for Kant) the essential thing in morality. More importantly, Fichte insists that it is not in the name of morality, but merely in the name of consistency (*Conzequenz*), that I demand the other to respect my rights (*GNR* 49–50/75).[3] Whether inconsistency in this matter involves an act of moral wrongdo-ing is for Fichte entirely irrelevant to the theory of right. He thinks right can be founded, independently of morality, merely on a *logical* principle (*GNR* 13/23, 50/76, 54/80).

Of course, it is one thing to say that I contradict myself by invading the other's external sphere, and quite another thing to say that I have a *reason* not to invade it. If I stand to benefit from contradicting myself, then so much the better for self-contradiction. So we might argue that unless Fichte's theory appeals to morality (or some other consideration beyond logical con-sistency), it gives no one any reason for respecting the rights of others, and hence it can provide no guarantee that anyone's rights will be respected.

Fichte accepts this argument in full. According to him, the relation of right is a presupposition of self-consciousness, but a reason to respect others' rights is not. That is why Fichte goes on to discuss the "law of compulsion" through which the relation of right may be enforced; the aim of this dis-cussion is to provide a transcendental deduction of the social arrangements necessary to enforce it. He argues that free persons must undertake by mutual agreement to guarantee that each of them will have reason to be-have consistently and respect the rights of others (*GNR* 145–146/200), and this in turn will require the establishment of a community or state (*GNR* 150/205).

A more serious problem for Fichte's theory is that there seems to be a

81

fallacy in the argument that recognizing another requires me to treat that other as a person with rights, in the sense of granting the other a sphere of free activity with which I refrain from interference. To recognize another as a free being may very well involve acknowledging that this other is capable of making free choices; this may even commit me to the admission that there is in fact some sphere of external reality determined by the other's choices. But it is hard to see how it involves anything like a declaration on my part that I will sustain this sphere by restricting my own actions. Suppose we grant Fichte that in recognizing and being recognized by another, I have addressed to the other a demand to respect my external sphere of freedom, and I have become aware of a like demand on the part of the other. Even so, no reason has yet been given for me to comply with the other's demand, or even for me to agree or declare, in actions, words, or even in thoughts, that I will comply with it. If that is right, then I am involved in no inconsistency when I infringe on the other's sphere of activity.

We might try to reply to this objection on the basis of the fact that Fichte's theory of self-awareness involves the attribution to everyone of a desire to exercise a causal influence freely over the external world. From this we could argue in Fichte's behalf that since I want the other to comply with my demand to respect my external sphere of freedom, I might be willing to respect the other's sphere in return. This could be the basis for a mutual declaration that we will respect each other's external spheres. Such an argument would treat our reciprocal declarations as the result of a mutually advantageous contract or agreement. But the argument is surely just as hopeless as the agreement would be pointless, for there is supposed to be no reason to comply with the other's demands, and hence no guarantee that either of us will have a reason to comply with them. So what point could there be in declaring that we will comply, or in inducing the other to make such a declaration? Since it will be advantageous to contradict such declarations whenever we feel like it, and since both of us know this, no one has anything to gain from making them or getting others to make them.

Fichte's own argument on the point has nothing in common with this contractarian one. He treats mutual recognition and the relation of right as the *basis* of contracts or agreements, not as a *result* of any contract or agreement. Fichte asserts that when you and I recognize each other, we employ a concept of human individuality that is a "reciprocal concept, which can be thought only in reference to another's thought, . . . a common concept, in which two consciousnesses are united into one" (*GRN* 47–48/72). What Fichte wants to claim is that my awareness of myself as rational being involves a conception of a free rational individual, which I must ascribe to others as well as to myself. In laying claim to a sphere of freedom for myself, I lay claim simultaneously on the other's behalf to a sphere of freedom for the other. Because I am aware of both myself and the other as rational beings, I am recognizing the other's right to a like sphere of external freedom in the very act of demanding of the other a sphere of freedom for myself.

In light of this, it is more promising to interpret Fichte's theory of recognition as an account of an ideal socialization process for individuals in a culture in which values such as individual freedom and autonomy hold an important place. In teaching people to think of themselves as rational beings, we teach them to think of themselves as having the right to an external sphere for free action, and we teach them to employ the same conception in thinking of other rational beings. Fichte himself suggests this reading not only in his references to the education of human beings but also when he stresses that the self-consciousness of rational agents is something that can develop only through its social cultivation (*GNR* 79–80/118–119).[4] If individuals were socialized in some such way, that would explain both why they want to make the demands involved in relations of right, and why they are prepared to recognize the reciprocal demands of others. But they still might not be motivated to behave consistently with this recognition; thus it does not obviate Fichte's argument that a law of compulsion is also necessary.

On this reading, the problem with Fichte's theory is that he has not defended the claim that this sort of socialization is better suited to the concept of rational nature than various others might be. Human selves may desire external freedom, but it does not follow that they must educate one another to demand a determinate sphere of external freedom and to respect a like demand on the part of every other. Individuals whose fundamental desire is to exercise causality freely over the external world might decide to educate one another in accordance with Fichte's theory. But they might also be socialized to think of one another as seeking to appropriate the entire external world, killing or enslaving as many of their competitors as they can. It is not enough for Fichte's purposes to show that it would be *advantageous* if people thought of themselves and others as having rights to external spheres of action; the theory requires that such thinking should be *correct,* that the conception of a subject of rights should be somehow connected to the concept of a rational being as such.

We may see Hegel as attempting to supply this deficiency in Fichte's theory. Hegel does not treat recognition as a transcendental condition for the possibility of self-consciousness. He understands it instead as a "process," beginning with a "struggle to the death," and passing through an asymmetrical "master–servant" relation in which one self is recognized by the other without having to recognize the other in turn. In the course of this process, the selves acquire a deeper conception of what it is to be a free self, and the rational outcome of the process is the mutual awareness of free self-conscious beings as persons with abstract rights. Hegel's model involves a philosophical argument, but it also has historical applications. It attempts to say something about the difference between (modern) societies, which recognize every human being as a person with abstract rights, and (premodern) societies, which do not. Hegel tries to show that people have a deeper knowledge of their human nature in societies that respect the right of persons than in societies that do not.

5. The desire for self-certainty

Earlier we saw that Hegel locates the origin of the concept of a person in ancient Rome. He credits Christianity with extending this status in principle to all, and he finds the worldly application of this Christian view only in the modern state. But Hegel's discussion of recognition, in both his Jena period and his later philosophy of spirit, is not so much an historical account as a rational reconstruction of the process through which the mutual recognition of persons might have developed out of simpler forms of self-consciousness.[5]

We might think of social contract theories of the state as one analogy for Hegel's procedure, since they, too, are rational reconstructions of the way in which an existing institution might have come about. We would do better, however, to think of the peculiar form of social contract theory found in Rousseau's *Discourse on the Origin of Inequality*. Hegel's reconstruction, like Rousseau's, does not try to show how individuals might construct a social institution in order to satisfy given ends using given resources. Instead, it attempts to understand how the mutual interaction of individuals fundamentally alters their knowledge of themselves, thereby changing their ends, resources, and their human nature itself.

In the Berlin *Encyclopedia,* Hegel divides the development of "self-consciousness" into three distinct stages: (1) desire (*EG* §§ 426–429), (2) recognition (*EG* §§ 430–435), and (3) universal self-consciousness or reason (*EG* §§ 436–439). Hegel's model begins with human individuals conceived simply as living things possessing "self-consciousness" or "will" (*PhG* ¶ 165; *JR* 194/ 99; *EG* § 426). Hegel follows Fichte in regarding the human self as fundamentally a striving of the "I" against the "not-I," of self against otherness, an impulse to overcome all otherness (*W* 262/231). Hegel expresses this by saying that self-consciousness is "desire." More specifically, it is a desire to achieve "self-certainty" through overcoming an object or "other." Self-consciousness seeks to destroy the independence or "self-sufficiency" (*Selbständigkeit*) of the object, in order to establish its own self-standing independence.

> Certain of the nothingness of this other, it posits this nothingness *for itself* as the truth of the other; it negates the independent object and thereby gives itself self-certainty, as *true* certainty as such, which has become so for it *in an objective way.* (*PhG* ¶ 174)

It is in this "nothingness" of the object or other that the desire of self-consciousness finds its "satisfaction" (*PhG* ¶ 175).

For Hegel, the "object" of a desire is never merely a subjective mental state, such as pleasure or the absence of pain. Hegel interprets desire as a function of self-conscious, spiritual being – an embodied being situated in a world of *external* objects toward which its desires are directed. Further, Hegel interprets this desire in accordance with his theory of spirit as self-actualization through the overcoming of otherness. The fundamental desire that Hegel attributes to self-consciousness is a desire for self-worth or "self-certainty." As spirit, the self engages in an activity of positing an object and then interpreting itself in terms of it. Self-certainty is gained only through

84

something external, which is brought into harmony with the self, an objectivity whose independence is done away with or "negated." This negation of the object refers to my using it up or consuming it (as when I literally eat it up), but also includes my shaping or forming it. Even more broadly, it covers any sort of integration of it into my plans and projects. In the most abstract form, it occurs when I assert my dominion over the object in the social forms suitable to property ownership (*PR* §§ 54–70).

The attempt to achieve self-certainty through the appropriation of things proves inadequate. Satisfaction taken in external objects merely leads to a new desire for a new object. This result only points to the fact that the desiring self-consciousness is always dependent on a new object, whereas its aim was rather to establish its own independence, and the nothingness of the object (*EG* § 428). What self-consciousness needs is an object that brings about this negation within itself without ceasing to be an object. But only a self-consciousness is able to endure the "contradiction" of negating itself or being its own other (*PhG* ¶ 162). In other words, "self-consciousness reaches its satisfaction only in another self-consciousness" (*PhG* ¶ 175).

From the standpoint of self-certainty, the fundamental problem with non-human objects of desire is that they can contribute to my self-worth only secondarily or indirectly, by confirming an image of myself that I already have independently of them. Even animals, which are living and conscious objects, cannot provide me directly with a sense of my self-worth, since they possess no conception of a free self, and so I can never find in them a confirming perspective on myself. The only "other" that can form a conception of me as a free self is another free self. Self-consciousness can find satisfaction for its desire for self-certainty only when it comes "outside itself," so that its object becomes "another self" (*PhG* ¶ 179; *EG* § 429,A). "Self-consciousness has an existence only through being recognized by another self-consciousness" (*NP* 78); "Self-consciousness is *in* and *for itself* insofar and through the fact that it is in and for itself for another, i.e., it is only as something recognized" (*PhG* ¶ 178).

When I see my free selfhood reflected back to me out of another self, I actualize my self-consciousness in the form of "spirit," as a "self-restoring sameness." It is only in relation to another free self that I can be truly free, "with myself in another" as regards my self-certainty. Thus the full actualization of spirit is possible only through the relation between selves that recognize each other. This is why Hegel even goes so far as to say that the essence of spirit itself lies in recognition, in a community of selves, "the I that is a we and the we that is an I" (*PhG* ¶ 177; cf. *EG* § 436).

6. The struggle for recognition

The first stage in the development of self-consciousness is desire in general. The second stage comes when desire becomes a desire for recognition (*EG* § 430A). "Each *wills* to be valid for the other; it is the end of each to look upon *itself* in the other" (*JR* 210/116).

I am "recognized" by another when the other self-conscious being has an image of me as a being self-conscious like itself, and I am aware of it as having this image. Hence to be recognized, I must also recognize the other. At this point, we might see a certain mutuality, equality, even an identity of my desire and interest with that of the other. Hegel suggests this by saying (both hyperbolically and paradoxically) that the other of which I am aware *is* myself – myself as other (*PhG* ¶ 180; *JR* 204/110; *EG* § 430). The point of the hyperbole is that at this stage we are abstracting from all our particular properties, and so simply as free self-consciousnesses we are exactly alike. There is nothing to distinguish one of us from another except my awareness of you (and your awareness of me) *as other*.

This sort of equality or identity, instead of creating a common interest between us, leads immediately to a *struggle,* for our characteristic conduct as desiring beings confronted with an other is simply to "negate" or "do away with" the other. Each of us wants recognition from the other, but sees no reason to recognize the other. My recognition would only attest to the other's independent existence (or "immediacy"), and that would be a threat to my self-certainty. Each of us therefore tries to do away with (*aufheben*) the other's immediacy, that is, with its bodily life (*EG* § 431). The struggle for recognition becomes a struggle to the death.

Hegel suggests another reason for regarding the struggle as a battle of life and death. Since each is a "pure abstraction of self-consciousness" attempting to vindicate its freedom or independence, its self-certainty consists in "showing that it is connected to no determinate *existence,* not at all to the universal individually of existence, that it is not connected to life" (*PhG* ¶ 187). The deeper meaning of the struggle for recognition is not the need to seek the other's death, but the need to risk my own life. "To him as consciousness it appears that it is a question of the *death* of the other; but it is really a question of his own" (*JR* 211/117).

Whether the life and death struggle ends in your death or mine, neither of us can get out of it what we desire. The one who dies is no longer there to be recognized, and the one who lives no longer has an other to provide recognition. Thus self-certainty through recognition is unattainable under these conditions. If it is ever going to be attainable, something in our aims and desires will have to change. Specifically, what seems to be needed is a form of self-consciousness that will recognize without demanding recognition in return. At this point, self-certainty appears attainable only through being recognized by such a self-consciousness.

7. Master and servant

Hegel imagines this form of self-consciousness arising out of the struggle, when one combatant, faced with death at the hands of the other, chooses to live at the cost of renouncing its claim on the other's recognition. "One of those involved in the struggle prefers life, preserves himself as a single self-consciousness, but gives up being recognized, while the other holds [fast] to its reference to itself

86

and is recognized by the first, who is his subject (*Unterworfenen*): the relation of master and servant" (*EG* § 433). The master-consciousness apparently gets precisely what it wants. It is recognized by its other, but does not have to recognize the other. Conversely, the servant-consciousness is utterly non–self-sufficient (*unselbständig*): "Its essence is life or being for another" (*PhG* ¶ 189). The servant also takes over the dependent side of the master's relation to external things, laboring on them without satisfaction, whereas the master gets the enjoyment without laboring (*PhG* ¶ 190).

As Hegel describes it, the master–servant relation has much in common with Hobbes's account of "despotical dominion":

> Dominion acquired by conquest or victory in war is that which some writers call DESPOTICAL from *despotes*, which signifies a *lord* or *master* – and is the dominion of the master over his servant. And this dominion is then acquired to the victor when the vanquished, to avoid the present stroke of death, covenants . . . that, so long as his life and the liberty of his body is allowed him, the victor shall have the use of it at his pleasure.[6]

Hegel's servant, like Hobbes's, is put in bondage through the desire to save his life; and he is put in bondage not by mere force, but by his own consent to the arrangement: "Nor is he obliged because he is conquered – that is to say, beaten and taken, or put to flight – but because he comes in and submits to the victor."[7]

There are two significant differences between Hobbes's account and Hegel's, both consequences of the fact that the Hegelian master–servant relation arises in the course of the struggle for recognition, as part of the drive for self-certainty. First, for Hobbes the servant is nothing but a tool to satisfy the master's other desires; the humanity of the servant is at best a circumstantial advantage – a human servant might be able to perform tasks to which a machine or an animal would be unequal. For Hegel's master, however, the servant is essentially a self-conscious being, since he is primarily a means to the master's self-certainty. This also means that for the master, the relation is to be judged primarily by how well it procures self-certainty.

Second, when Hobbes's servant saves his life at all costs, he merely behaves consistently with his fundamental drive, self-preservation; but Hegel's servant abandons – or at least modifies – his fundamental desire, the desire for self-sufficient self-certainty. The servant claims no validity for his particular self, and not even over against the world of external objects. The servant's life is devoted entirely to the transient process of "negating" external things for the master's sake, while the servant's own enjoyment of the object is indefinitely postponed. Thus Hegel describes the servant's labor as "desire *restrained*, disappearance *delayed*" (*PhG* ¶ 195). In other words, the servant's labor is "labor according to an alien will" (*NP* 82).

For the master, the earlier impasse in the struggle for recognition has apparently been overcome. He gets the one-sided recognition that self-consciousness has been wanting. Hegel argues, however, that the master's apparent success is an illusion, that the master's condition is in fact the very opposite of what he was trying to achieve: "This object does not correspond to its concept; rather, that in which the master has fulfilled himself has become something wholly other than a self-sufficient consciousness" (*PhG* ¶ 192). It is through the servant's recognition that the master achieves the status he dignifies by the name of self-sufficiency; the servant's activity rather than the master's is the one shaping and dominating external things.

Hegel even goes so far as to say that it is the servant's consciousness rather than the master's that has achieved self-sufficiency: "The truth of the self-sufficient consciousness is the servant's consciousness" (*PhG* ¶ 193); it is the servant's consciousness, not the master's, that suffices to itself and does not depend on another. The fear of death, which made the servant willing to labor for an alien will, has also set the servant-consciousness on the path to a more complete self-sufficiency than any that self-consciousness has known, or even imagined. Hegel quotes ironically the Biblical proverb: "The fear of the lord is the beginning of wisdom" (*PhG* ¶ 195; cf. *Proverbs 1*: 7; 9: 10).

Hegel does not mean that the servant-consciousness *as such* is a self-sufficient self-consciousness. "But just as domination showed that its essence is the inversion of what it wants to be, so servitude will in its completion become the opposite of what it immediately is; as a *repressed* consciousness it will go into itself and convert itself into true self-sufficiency" (*PhG* ¶ 193). True self-sufficiency or "freedom" is reached when the servant-consciousness becomes conscious of what servitude has won for it (*PhG* ¶ 197).

Hegel sees the servant's subjection to an alien will as a preparation for the self-discipline of a rational life and membership in a community of free persons. The servant's self-consciousness "labors off its particular will and its self-will, supersedes (*hebt . . . auf*) the inner immediacy of desire, and, in this alienation and fear of the lord – the beginning of wisdom – it makes the transition to *universal self-consciousness*" (*EG* § 435; cf. *PhG* ¶ 196). Servitude to an alien will makes possible the disciplining of particular whims and desires, so that they may be brought under the sway of one's own rational or universal will. "This subjection of the servant's selfishness forms the *beginning* of true human freedom, . . . a necessary moment in the formative education (*Bildung*) of every human being" (*EG* § 435A).

8. Universal self-consciousness

In this last point, there seem to be two distinct ideas at work. One is nothing but a doubtful platitude of authoritarian pedagogy: You learn to command by learning to obey, and acquire self-discipline by having your will forcibly broken by another's will. The other idea is more Kantian: Genuine freedom and self-worth are available only to those who are capable of detaching themselves from their particular desires and adopting a universal or rational standpoint that respects equally the freedom of others. It is through the second idea that we may pass from the second stage of self-consciousness (recognition) to the third and final stage (universal self-consciousness).

What matters about the education of servitude is not the breaking of self-will, but the dawning conviction that what is important for self-worth is not the gratification of desire but the dignity of formally free agency. Thus being recognized consists not in the domination of another self-consciousness, but in the mutual relation of different self-consciousnesses who identify their dignity with the freedom they have in common.

> Universal self-consciousness is the affirmative knowing of oneself in another self, so that each self has *absolute self-sufficiency* as free individuality; . . . each is thus universal [self-consciousness] and objective, and has real universality as reciprocity, in such a way that it knows itself as recognized in the free other, and knows this other insofar as it recognizes it and knows it as free. (*EG* § 436)

I win freedom for myself not by subjugating others but by liberating them, granting them the same free status I claim for myself. "The master standing over against the servant was still not truly free, for he still did not thoroughly look on himself in the other. Consequently, it is only through the liberation of the servant that the master, too, becomes perfectly free" (*EG* § 436A).

Hegel's point might be viewed as an instance of the general truth that if I want to acquire worth in my own eyes on the basis of another's esteem, I can do it only to the extent that I esteem the other as a judge of my worth. An author will add nothing to her self-esteem by reading favorable critical notices of her work if she despises the opinion of all the critics. Only a free being has the capacity to recognize another as free. Hence if I want self-certainty as a free being through recognition, then I can get it only from a being I regard as free. The master's attempt to achieve recognition through dominion over another is necessarily a failure, because it demands the impossible: that the other be free and independent, and yet do away with this very freedom and independence in the act of giving recognition. To provide self-certainty for self-consciousness, recognition must be reciprocal.

The deeper source of the master's failure is that he has an inadequate concept of self. He is trying to claim self-sufficiency for the merely particular self, distinguished from others by its selfish desires and special traits. The attempt to win self-certainty through recognition for that self leads to the strategy of domination, which necessarily fails for the reasons we have just seen. The recognition I need from others requires a different self-image, that of an abstractly free person participating equally with others in a "universal self-consciousness." By providing an argument that "universal self-consciousness" is the only solution to the problem of self-certainty, Hegel succeeds in vindicating Fichte's claim that the correct concept of a rational nature must be a "reciprocal concept" or a "common concept," which I can apply to myself only by applying it in the same way to others, and granting to others the same rights I claim for myself.

"Universal self-consciousness" means more for Hegel than the mutual relation of persons having abstract rights. He insists that "it forms the substance of ethical life" generally, and is "the form of consciousness of the *substance* of every essential spirituality, whether of family, fatherland, state, or of all virtues – love, friendship, courage, honor, fame" (*EG* § 436,A). That is why

Hegel says that the master–servant relation pertains to "the transition from the natural state of humanity to a truly ethical condition" (*PR* § 57A). Beyond this, universal self-consciousness is for Hegel the foundation of reason generally, regarded as the human mind's highest capacity (*EG* § 437; *NP* 82–85). For Hegel, rational thought in general is possible for a human mind only as part of a community of minds that mutually recognize each other's rationality.

Nevertheless, the most immediate application of universal self-consciousness is to the abstract right of persons. In the Jena lectures, Hegel states quite directly the connection between personal right and the universal self-consciousness arising from genuine recognition.

> The knowing will is now *universal*. It is *recognition*. Put opposite itself in the form of universality it is being, actuality in general, and the individual, the subject, is the *person*. The will of individuals is the universal and the universal is individual; it is ethical life in general, but immediately it is right. (*JR* 212/118)

In the *Phenomenology of Spirit* the connection is indicated less directly, but still quite clearly. Hegel identifies Stoicism as the form of self-consciousness that emerges from servitude, and indicates that a society founded on persons and their rights is one that corresponds to Stoical self-consciousness (*PhG* ¶ 479). The dependence of abstract right on the dialectic of recognition is stated quite directly in the *Philosophy of Right*: "Contract presupposes that those who enter into it *recognize* each other as persons and property owners; since it is a relation of objective spirit, the moment of recognition is already contained and presupposed in it" (*PR* § 71; cf. *VPR***17**: 56–57).

9. Hegel's dialectic of recognition

Hegel's account of the self's development through recognition and the master–servant dialectic may look more like an abstract fable than a philosophical argument. It may help us to see the point of the account if we consider things differently, by focusing on five main theses which ground Hegel's defense of the concept of a person and the ethical sphere of abstract right.

1. *Selfhood involves the desire for self-certainty.* Hegel's argument begins with his view of human beings as spiritual beings, whose fundamental desires include the desire to establish their self-worth through self-positing and self-interpretation.
2. *Self-certainty requires recognition.* Self-positing through nonhuman objects is inadequate for a human being's sense of self-worth. What I need is an object capable of reflecting back to me my conception of myself as a free self, and that object can be only another free self. Self-worth requires recognition by others.
3. *One-sided recognition cannot succeed.* If I want self-certainty only for my particular self, then I will want recognition through dominating the other, just as I might dominate nonhuman objects. But this form of recognition will not give me what I need, because it denies to the other the freedom

it must have if its recognition is to confirm my self-worth. Consequently, if recognition is to provide us with self-certainty, it must be mutual.

4. *Mutual recognition requires universal self-consciousness.* Mutual recognition is possible only if I deepen my conception of myself. I must view myself as a rational being, capable of independence in relation to my particular desires, and capable of acting on principles that are universally valid for all selves.

5. *Recognition through universal self-consciousness requires a community of persons, standing in mutual relations of abstract right.* Universal self-consciousness arises only under certain social conditions. Individuals must belong to a community in which they are socialized mutually to claim and grant to each other the right to exercise their freedom within a limited external sphere.

Hegel's conclusion is virtually identical to Fichte's, but his route to the conclusion is very different. It is not a transcendental argument from the conditions for self-consciousness, but an argument about the conditions under which human beings can gain a sense of freedom and self-worth through their relations with others. It rests not on the conditions for self-awareness in general, but on the assumption that we have a fundamental desire to vindicate our self-worth, and on a theory about the conditions under which it is possible for us to satisfy that desire.

Hegel's argument remedies the most important defect we found in Fichte's. It makes explicit our reasons not only for addressing to others the demand for a sphere of freedom, but also for recognizing and accepting a like demand on the part of others. It justifies the self-conception of ourselves as rational beings which might be made the basis of a socialization of people as free and equal members of a community that respects the rights of every rational being.

The argument might be compared to Hobbes's argument for the "laws of nature" which bid us to seek peace, to make and keep covenants with others, and in general to accommodate ourselves to a social condition.[8] Both arguments aim to show that recognizing the rights of others is the only way in which we can achieve something we ourselves deeply need and want. An important difference is that Hegel's argument is not an egoistic argument in the way that Hobbes's is. The desire for survival on which Hobbes's argument rests is an obviously egoistic desire, but the desire for self-certainty is not necessarily egoistic. In fact, we might describe Hegel's argument as showing that the desire for self-sufficiency and self-worth cannot be adequately satisfied as long as it is treated as a purely egoistic desire – a desire for wants based on my particularity, as distinct from wants that express my universal rationality. The conclusion of Hegel's argument is that the desire to vindicate my self-worth can be satisfied only if I locate my fundamental worth in something I share with other free beings and respect in them as well.

Hegel is arguing for a certain conception of the self as universal self-consciousness. His argument is *practical* in the sense that it defends this conception by saying that the self can satisfy its basic desire for self-certainty only if it has this conception. But the conclusion nonetheless is supposed to be a piece of self-*knowledge*. We might say that the argument presupposes that if a certain self-conception enables the self to achieve its basic desires, that is a sign that this self-conception is correct. But since having a certain self-conception is part of what makes a self what it is, it might be more accurate to put it another way: A self actualizes itself when it makes itself into what it needs to be in order to satisfy its desire for self-certainty. It turns out that in order to do this, a self must become a free person, through participating in a community of recognition or universal self-consciousness, and becoming aware of itself as a free person. When it has done this, its conception of itself as a free person will be correct, and constitute knowledge of itself.

10. The reality of oppression

It will also clarify Hegel's argument to mention two important *limitations* on what it proves.

First, Hegel's argument does not show (it does not even claim) that there cannot be good reasons for wanting to dominate others, exploit them, reduce them to a condition of servitude. Dominion promotes the master's freedom (in the ordinary sense), since it adds to his capacities and removes obstacles to satisfying his desires. Hegel's argument shows only that dominating others is not the way to achieve self-certainty as a free being. Hegel's argument gives me no reason for respecting the rights of others if I happen to prefer freedom in the ordinary sense to self-certainty or absolute freedom in the Hegelian sense. Dominion may even provide me with a semblance of self-certainty if my conception of free selfhood is sufficiently undeveloped that I still confuse the dominion over others with self-certainty afforded me through recognition by others. Hegel cannot say about me what Hobbes could say about those who fail to seek peace – that they do not know the right way to get what they most want.

What Hegel can say instead is that what I want in this case, or at least the priority among my wants, is based on an inadequate conception of myself as a human being. Hegel thinks that such an inadequate self-conception was characteristic of pre-Christian and premodern societies, where social institutions such as slavery still prevailed. He seems convinced that normal mature individuals in modern society do implicitly recognize others as persons with rights. As we shall see in Chapter 6, this conviction plays a crucial role in his theory of punishment.

It is easy to reconcile Hegel's argument with the obvious fact that many people prefer dominion over others to living on equal terms with them. It is especially easy to see how one might have this preference in a social order where the recognition of at least some is only formal, nominal, or a mere sham (see Chapter 14, §§ 8–10). If there is in fact a division between oppressors and oppressed, our most natural desire is to prevent ourselves from falling into the latter category, probably by securing our position as best we can in the former one. Hegel's argument helps to explain the fact that in modern societies people prefer to conceal from themselves their dominion over others, by sequestering the others in different parts of town or in distant lands, or by representing the others as formally free and equal to themselves. In these ways, people enjoy simultaneously the (real) advantages of oppressing others and the (at least pretended) self-certainty that only a society of free and equal persons can offer.

Hegel's argument is subject to a *second* limitation, which points in the same direction. Hegel's argument shows that I cannot achieve self-certainty except as a member of a community of free persons who mutually recognize one another's rights. Hegel claims that in modern (post-Christian) society we regard all human beings as persons with rights, but his dialectic of recognition does not establish that self-certainty requires me to recognize everyone as a person. Consistently with Hegel's argument, I might find self-certainty in the parochial society constituted by a privileged race, caste, or class, whose members mutually recognize one another as persons but treat outsiders as nonpersons. Hegel's argument proves that I could not achieve self-certainty through my relations with these nonpersons; but if I have already achieved it through membership in my privileged group, I will have nothing to lose and perhaps much to gain from ignoring the supposed rights of those who do not belong to it.

Of course, such a distinction between persons and nonpersons could not be drawn arbitrarily. If members of the outgroup have the same capacity to participate in universal consciousness as members of the ingroup, then Hegel's argument requires that both be recognized alike. In practice, however, this presents little difficulty because people prove to be very ingenious in discovering (or inventing) differences on which to base the exclusion of others from rights which they recognize for themselves and their own kind. Some of Hegel's own remarks – about women (*PR* § 166A), or African peoples (*VPG* 120–129/91–102), or societies not organized as European nation-states are (PR § 331R) – could, without a forced interpretation, be used in precisely this way. Some rebuttal to the common rationales for restricting human rights in practice is necessary if we are to provide a thoroughgoing Hegelian defense of the idea that all human beings are free and equal persons.

5
Persons, property, law

1. Persons and their abstract right to things

English-speaking philosophy recognizes a distinction between "legal" and "moral" rights, the former established by positive law, the latter with a foundation in morality. Along with other German philosophers of the same period, Hegel maps the ethical landscape differently. For him, the fundamental distinction is between right (*Recht*) and ethics or morality (*Sitte, Moral, Ethik*). As we saw in Chapter 3, § 9, *Recht* (the whole body of law, constitutional, criminal or civil, or the rational foundation of law and the state) contrasts with *Gesetz* (particular positive legal statutes). Right (*Recht*) is capable of codification in positive law, but it has a rational foundation independent of positive law. Right is also independent of morality – of virtue, goodness of will, and the proper ends of conduct.

Hegel also has a technical sense of *Recht* that is even broader than this: "Right" refers to any existent that is the existence of the free will, any object in which the free will is with itself (*PR* § 29). In this sense, "right" refers to the whole realm of objective freedom, including morality and ethical life, and the whole of modern social organization. Hegel also uses "right" in the traditional sense, contrasting it with ethics or morality and referring to the sphere of people's rights that are subject to protection by coercive positive laws. For this purpose he uses the term "abstract right."

Abstract right has to do with the proper safeguarding of a sphere of arbitrary choices. Morality is concerned with which actions we ought to perform; abstract right deals only with what is possible or permissible for us in the special juridical (*rechtlich*) sense. "Right is only a *possibility,* and hence only a *permission (Erlaubnis)* or *warrant (Befugnis)*" (*PR* § 38).

The two terms do not mean quite the same thing: " 'Permitted' means possible according to right" (*VPR17* : 45); "that is permitted which does not violate my free will; a warrant is that others have to recognize this" (*VPR 1* : 255). I have the right to plant a tree in my backyard. This right involves a *permission:* in planting the tree, I do nothing contrary to right, nothing that violates the external sphere of any free will. It also involves a *warrant:* Others are required to recognize my right; they must not interfere with my planting activities or harm the tree I have planted.[1]

"The commandment of right is: 'Be a person and respect others as persons' " (*PR* § 36). We respect others as persons when we refrain from infringing on their sphere of abstract or arbitrary freedom. Thus Hegel also states

94

the commandment of right as: "Respect the abstract freedom of others" (*VPR19*: 68). Hegel also thinks that we have a positive duty to assert our own personality, to exercise our own freedom within its proper sphere. We do this through property ownership; and this is what is meant by the imperative "Be a person": "It is a *duty* to possess things as property, i.e., to be as a person" (*EG* § 486). To recognize a person is always to recognize the person as free in relation to a "thing" (*Sache*), which counts as the "*Repräsentant* or embodiment of [the person's] freedom" (*VPR 4*: 151).

Fichte says that the right of property includes the "external sphere" for each person's exercise of freedom (*GNR* 41ff/63ff), and that the extent of one's right to property is determined by the extent of this sphere (*GNR* 210/289–290). In Hegel's theory, too, the rationale for property right is that a person "exists as Idea" when personality is given a sufficient "external sphere" in which to exercise its abstract or arbitrary freedom (*PR* § 41). A person's "property" thus consists in that part of the external world that falls within that person's sphere of arbitrary choice.

A piece of property is a "thing." A thing is "immediately different from free spirit, something external in general . . . unfree, unpersonal and without right" (*PR* § 42). Hegel thinks that natural things have no end or destination except to serve the will of rational beings:

> As a person, I have the right of putting my will into every thing, which thereby becomes *mine,* and giving it its substantial end; for it has no such end in itself, but receives through my will its destination (*Bestimmung*) and soul – the absolute *right of appropriation* human beings have over all things. (*PR* § 44)

My appropriation of a thing is actualized when I use the thing (*PR* § 59R); when a thing is consumed by its possessor, "its nature as 'selfless' is revealed, and thus its destination is fulfilled" (*PR* § 59).

"Thing" refers primarily to natural objects given immediately through the senses. "The deciding and *immediate* individuality of the person is related to a nature confronting it," which the personality seeks to claim as "its own" (*PR* § 39). But what is "not at first immediate" can "become so through the mediation of spirit, which reduces what is inner to immediacy and externality" (*PR* § 43R). It is in this way that not only external, sensible things, but even such things as a person's mental and spiritual skills, knowledge, and arts can be treated as "things," can be bought and sold or made the object of contractual agreements, just as if they were external and directly sensible things. Hegel does insist that the category of "things" cannot include persons themselves, and he repeatedly castigates Roman law for treating children as the property of their parents (*PR* §§ 3R, 43R, 175,R). But beyond this, there are apparently no limits at all to what might in principle be regarded as a "thing" and made the subject of property right.

Locke bases property right on labor.[2] Hegel bases it on something more abstract: on will. The act of will that makes something our property is called "taking possession" (*Besitznahme*) (*PR* § 54); it can consist in a direct, bodily grasping of the thing (*PR* § 55), or (more abstractly) in laboring on the thing and forming it (*PR* § 56), or (most abstractly of all) in marking the thing as ours (*PR* § 58). To appropriate something is to "put one's will into it" in one of these three ways. Ownership also gives me three distinguishable rights over the thing: (1) the right to use the thing (*PR* § 59), (2) the right to alienate it – to transfer ownership to another (*PR* § 65), and (3) the right to make it the object of a contract with others by stipulating will which the parties share as their common will (*PR* § 75).

When the object is regarded under the aspect of its use, it can be compared with other objects that satisfy a similar need, and equated with other objects; thereby it is assigned a "value" (*PR* § 63). I can thus be regarded as the owner not merely of the particular object, but also of its value, which can be recovered in case of breached contracts or other infringements on my right (*PR* § 77). Through the process of abstraction, the right of property thus goes far beyond the physical possession of external objects, and involves a complex set of claims that I may have on others, and that they may have on me.[3]

2. Property as the fundamental right

Hegel treats all abstract right as a right of property, even the right to our own life and body, the right over our inner life and conscience, and the right to a social status as free persons. "Only *personality* gives a right to *things,* and hence personal right is essentially a *right to things* – things in the universal sense as what is external to freedom, and even my life and body belong to this" (*PR* § 40R). Hegel's theory involves what G. A. Cohen aptly calls "self-ownership"; it conceives of all one's personal rights as consequences of self-ownership.[4]

We might think that such a theory would inevitably overvalue our right to external and alienable things and underestimate the human rights we care most about. Hegel disagrees. In his Nuremberg lectures, he distinguishes three degrees in which violence can be done to me as a person. The first and most serious is the "robbery of my freedom through *imprisonment* or slavery", the second degree consists in injuries to my body and life; and the third, and least serious, consists in the theft of my external property (*NP* 243–244). At this point, Hegel is close to Locke, who treats "life, liberty, and estate" as three different forms that my "property" can take.[5]

I have a right to my life and body only because they are paradigmatically my property, things external to my freedom, which I possess by putting my will into them: "As a person, I have *my life and body,* like other things, only *insofar as it is my will*" (*PR* § 47). Hegel even argues that people do not have personality or right until they actually take possession of their personality through willing it (*PR* § 57,R). "Individuals and peoples still have no personality insofar as they have not yet come to this pure thinking and knowing of themselves [as thinking raised into simple infinity]" (*PR* § 35R).

People take possession of themselves through "education" (*Bildung*) (*PR* § 43R, 57, R). *Bildung* is acquisition of the capacity to subordinate the particular to the universal (*PhG* ¶ 488; *PR* § 20), or, in other words, the capacity needed in order to enter into mutual recognition of others as persons (*EG* § 436). We have taken possession of ourselves when we have acquired the capacity to think of ourselves as persons by regarding ourselves as members of a community of persons, a "universal self-consciousness." Hegel's dialectic of recognition thus specifies the circumstances under which individuals have taken possession of themselves as persons.

Whatever his words occasionally seem to imply, Hegel does not hold that I acquire the status of a person only after some contingent act of "self-appropriation" on my part. He insists that if I am a human being, then there is a presumption from the standpoint of others that I am a person, even if I have not yet actually educated myself to the standpoint where I have made myself my own property. "*For others* I am essentially a free being in my body, just as I possess it immediately" (*PR* § 48). Hegel's view is apparently that in a society that recognizes human beings as persons, we ought to recognize the right of children, mental incompetents, and others who have not actually taken possession of their bodies, lives, and free status by education or through determinate acts of self-appropriation. Strictly speaking, it would seem, such individuals are not persons on Hegel's theory; but they should nevertheless be treated as if they were.

Hegel faces a problem here, which is common to all theories that base human rights on the possession of determinate human faculties that some members of the human species may either temporarily or permanently lack. Kant, for instance, regards human beings as ends in themselves, possessing dignity and entitled to respect, only insofar as they are rational agents, capable of setting ends through reason and thus of regarding their ends as objectively good (*G* 428–429/46–47).[6] John Rawls treats as "moral persons" only those who have a conception of their own good and a sense of justice.[7] No more than Hegel's can such theories regard all human beings literally as persons with rights. Without some supplement, they cannot justify ascribing the status of ends in themselves to small children or the severely mentally incapacitated (or to fetuses). Hegel's strategy in defending the rights of the problematic individuals seems to be to argue that we have good and powerful reasons for treating certain individuals *as if* they were persons with rights even though strictly speaking they are not. It is hard to see how there could be an alternative for any theory that bases human rights on empirically observable properties of individuals, since all the natural candidates for such properties are such that some human beings do not actually have them. Few, however, seem willing to face up to the consequence that some human beings do not literally have rights, and that it requires some special argument to show that we should treat them as if they did.

3. Self-appropriation and slavery

Hegel's theory is not supposed to have the consequence that we are to grant more rights to mature, intelligent, or educated individuals than to others.

But Hegel does seem willing to distinguish between different cultures and epochs insofar as abstract right is concerned. As long as an entire culture lacks awareness of human beings as persons, there is a sense in which its members do not yet have the right of persons. We have seen that even ancient Greek and Roman culture lacked the awareness that all are persons (*VG* 61–62/54). For Hegel, there is a sense in which slavery, which we recognize to be a fundamental injustice at all times and places, was nevertheless "valid" in those cultures. To be sure, for Hegel the struggle against slavery is always a struggle to "achieve recognition of eternal human rights" (*EG* § 433A). Slaves always have the "absolute right" to free themselves (*PR* § 66A). But some cultures are so far from having a developed conception of humanity that even the slaves accept slavery as their natural condition. Where this is so, human beings still have not taken possession of themselves as persons, and we find ourselves "in a world where an injustice is still right. Here the injustice *is valid* and so finds itself necessarily in place" (*PR* § 57A).

Slavery ought not to be, since according to the concept of the thing it is unjust in and for itself. This *ought* expresses something subjective, which as such is not historical. What is lacking to the ought is the substantial ethical life of a state. Slavery is not present in rational states, but before there are such states, the true idea is present in some aspects only as an ought, and there slavery is still necessary: it is a moment of the transition to a higher stage. (*VG* 226/184)

Hegel's emphasis on *Sittlichkeit* ("customary morality") as the basis of all specific ethical duties has sometimes led his readers to interpret him as a cultural relativist about morality (see Chapter 11, § 6). The views just cited about slavery might be understood in a similar vein; and we might read the passage just quoted as denying that slavery was always wrong.[8] That would be a serious misunderstanding. We have already seen that Hegel grants slaves an "absolute right" to free themselves, and regards their struggle against slavery as a struggle for "eternal human rights" (*PR* § 66A; *EG* § 433A).

In *PR* § 57R Hegel tries to resolve the "antinomy" between this argument that slavery is not wrong where it is not contrary to custom, and the contrary argument that slavery is always unjust simply because the human being is spirit and hence "in itself free." Though he grants that the latter view is superior in having a more correct starting point, he still regards both arguments as "one-sided." The proslavery argument ignores what human beings essentially are, but the antislavery argument ignores the fact that in some cultures, the human essence is still not actual. People come into their right as free persons only in a rational state that recognizes and guarantees these rights publicly. Where such a state does not yet exist, Hegel says that the obligation not to hold slaves is a mere "ought." Even when human beings do not understand themselves as persons, there is still a moral (*moralisch*) imperative not to treat them as slaves, but there is no obligation of abstract right: "To make no one into a slave is not a demand of right but a moral demand. The claim of right refers only to freedom, where the latter shows itself in existence, and so falls away where freedom does not show itself in existence. – Only in the state is the recognition of freedom complete" (VPR*19* : 74). Even where the institutions of the state do not recognize all as free persons, morally insightful and well-disposed individuals will treat them as persons.

4. The right to personality itself

Hegel regards part of our right – the right over our own body, the right to inner life and conscience, the right to free status and property ownership – as special, because it is the right over our own personality itself (PR §§ 40R, 66, 70). Hegel regards this right as both "inalienable" (we cannot give or barter it away) and "imprescriptible" (we cannot lose it through disuse or the passage of time) (PR § 66). Hegel's position is that this is a property right consequent in some way on our having taken possession of our own personality through an act of knowledge and will. But when he comes to speak of the inalienability and imprescriptibility of the right to personality itself, he appears to give quite a different account.

In general, abstract right for Hegel is a claim we have over something "immediately external" to our free volition, or which can at least be treated as external, as our property. But of my status as a free person, my rationality, and my moral and religious feelings, Hegel says that these are not external to my freedom, but are rather "substantial determinations" that "constitute my ownmost person and the universal essence of my self-consciousness"; consequently, the right to them is not a right over externals but over "the act by which I take possession of my personality" (PR § 66). The alienation of such a right (as in slavery, superstition, and limits on property ownership) is possible only through ignorance of the real nature of human personality (PR § 66R). In reality, a right is inalienable and imprescriptible because it is impossible for me to alienate my personality, or to have it separated from me by the passage of time or by anything else. There is a "contradiction" in supposedly having given into the possession of others "my capacity for right, my ethical life, my religiosity, what I myself did not possess and what, as soon as I possess it, exists essentially only as mine and not as something external" (PR § 66R).

This is not a good argument. Surely it is quite possible to conceive without contradiction that I have bartered away my personality, even bartered away my capacity to barter any more. This would be the last transaction I would have made (at least until my personality had somehow been restored) but that does not show that there is any contradiction in supposing that I have made it; the same is true of bartering or giving away my own body or conscience. In this argument Hegel seems to confuse what (logically or naturally) *cannot* be violated with what (by right) *must not* be violated.

In a different context, Hegel argues that "the moral side and moral commands, which have to do with the will in its ownmost subjectivity and particularity, cannot be the object of positive law-giving" (PR § 213). This might be interpreted either of two ways:

99

1. Morality should not be legislated, because it is wrong or inappropriate for positive laws to trespass on what is subjective and particular.
2. Morality cannot be legislated, because what is moral belongs to an aspect of the human personality that is inaccessible to legal coercion.

Interpreted as (2), the claim seems to be notoriously false, and in any case gives the state no reason at all for refraining from the attempt to legislate morality (as far as it is able to); it asserts only that the state's capacity to coerce people has certain (perhaps regrettable) limitations. To be relevant to determining the proper limits of legislation, what we need to argue for is (1) rather than (2). But then the argument is incomplete, for we need to be told more about which matters are too subjective and particular to be the object of positive legislation, and also why it is wrong to legislate in matters that are subjective and particular.

The same problem affects Hegel's attempt to argue for the inalienability of rights to personality in *PR* § 66. If these rights are inalienable in the sense that they literally cannot be alienated, then the claim that they are inalienable sets no limits at all on what people may rightfully do to deprive others of their free status, inner liberty, and bodily integrity. If some rights are supposed to be inalienable in the sense that people *must* not deprive others of these rights (even when they are able to do so), then we need a further argument to show why they must not.

Hegel would have done better simply to hold consistently to his "self-ownership" theory, treating personal right as a case (even a paradigmatic case) of the right of property in externals. What we want protected by such rights is always our access to some external thing (since this includes our own body), or our freedom from external interference with our bodily movement or private thought processes. Our right to free status is a right to do things and to own things; our right to our own moral or religious conscience is a right to form our thoughts and feelings and express them through words and actions without harassment or fear of reprisal. It is in these externals that our rights over personality can be violated, and it is precisely there that they need protection. The inalienability and imprescriptibility of rights to personality can be defended by treating a person's life, body, conscience, and free status as pieces of property so central and essential to the external sphere which defines the person that treating rights to them as something alienable or prescriptible would amount to a failure to recognize the individual in question as a person at all.

In passages other than *PR* § 66, Hegel follows the line I have just recommended. He unhesitatingly rejects the "sophistry" (put forward by August von Rehberg, whose criticisms of the French Revolution were the object of Fichte's attacks) that one cannot violate a person's inner soul or free will by attacking the body (*PR* § 48R).[9] Later, Hegel bases the invalidity of contracts disposing of inalienable goods on the Roman legal principle of *laesio enormis* (excessive damage), which Hegel seems to interpret as saying that a contract is voidable if the values exchanged are so unequal that one party will be excessively harmed by the exchange. Hegel insists that to alienate personality itself is to incur a damage that is not merely excessive, but infinite (*PR* § 77R). This account is not merely different from *PR* § 66 but inconsistent with it; § 66 says that no contract at all can be formulated concerning inalienables, whereas § 77 says that but for the principle of *laesio enormis*, people who barter away their conscience or free status would have succeeded in alienating their personality.

If the property rights over our own person and free status are regarded as inalienable and imprescriptible in this way, then we need have no fear that these rights will be misconstrued or undervalued if we treat them as a species of property right. If it still strikes us as somehow inappropriate to treat the lives and bodies of human beings simply as pieces of property (even their own property), then that ought simply to underscore the inherent limitations of the sphere of abstract right itself.

5. The limits of abstract right

Hegel's theory moves from "abstract" to "concrete." Abstract right and morality are founded on abstract images of the human being, as "person" and as moral "subject." These images contain important truths about human nature which have been fully appreciated in practice only in the modern state, but they remain abstractions, which are integrated into the concrete life of human beings only in the sphere of ethical life, where they can be embodied in social institutions. Within ethical life, too, Hegel's theory moves from the abstract toward the concrete, from the more incomplete and dependent social institutions of the family and civil society to the state, which is their foundation and also their end (*PR* §§ 157, 261).

Abstract right and morality reach concreteness by being embodied in specific social institutions – in both cases, in the sphere of civil society. The person with abstract right becomes concrete like the self-interested economic agent (*PR* § 182) whose right is determined and guaranteed through the system of legal justice (*PR* § 209); morality finds its place in the reflection of individuals on the duties of their trade or profession, and the relation of their mode of life and their choices in it to their own happiness and that of others (*PR* § 207).

One conclusion which Hegel draws from this structural feature of his theory is that what is more "concrete" has a kind of priority over what is more "abstract." In a number of contexts, Hegel puts forward the thesis that something that is more concrete has a "higher right" than something that is more abstract, with the effect that the claims of the more abstract sphere are to be overriden by the claims of the more concrete one. Especially conspicuous are Hegel's assertions that the right of the state is "absolute" in relation to all the lower spheres (*PR* §§ 258, 261–262, 323) and that the world spirit operating in history takes precedence even over the right of states, so that its right is "supreme" (*PR* §§ 33, 340).

Since abstract right is the "lowest" and most "abstract" object of Hegel's theory, its claims ought therefore to be the most limited and the most easily overridden. But this seems to yield a paradox if we think that it is precisely the function of rights to serve as "trumps" that protect persons by overriding claims of other kinds, especially those derived from the public good and the interests of the state.[10] For then Hegel's thesis that the right of the state is "higher" than the abstract rights of persons, even "absolute" in relation to them, appears to reduce people's rights to a sham.

What does Hegel mean when he claims that the state's right (for instance) is "higher" than abstract right? In part, I think, Hegel's point is an antireductionist one: "Higher" spheres of right, such as the family and the state, are not to be analyzed into lower ones, such as property and contract, as happens in Kant's theory of the marriage relation (RL § 24, PR § 75R), in the absolutist notion that the state is the monarch's property (PR § 258R), or in contract theories of the state (PR §§ 75R, 100R, 258R). Hobbes, for example, wants to reduce most social obligations to contractual ones, and to found all obligations whatever on a few fundamental "laws of nature" dictating to each of us the conduct that is most advantageous.[11] The claim that the right of the state is "higher" than abstract right is in part a denial that it can be adequately accounted for by a theory of that type.

But doesn't Hegel's claim commit him to say that the state's right *overrides* that of the lower spheres? The general answer is: No.

For Hegel, the "higher right" of the state (or of other spheres) in comparison with abstract right does not consist in the state's (or any other sphere's) having the prerogative of ignoring people's abstract right.[12] Rather, it consists in certain determinate ways in which considerations of abstract right need to be adjusted to considerations arising from those higher spheres. Abstract right is, for instance, limited by morality, whose primary end, Hegel maintains, is the particular welfare or happiness of individuals. Because abstract right is supposed to abstract from all particular needs and wants, there is no abstract right to the means of subsistence; the abstract right to life is no abstract right to the means of subsistence; the abstract right to life consists only in the right not to be wrongfully deprived of life through force (PR § 49R). Hegel argues, however, that when what is at stake is a person's particular interests as a whole, in the form of personal existence or life, that life deserves to prevail against the property rights of someone else.

> If, for instance, [life] can be prolonged through stealing a loaf of bread, then the property of a human being is thereby violated, but it would be unjust to consider this action as a common theft. (PR § 127R)
> There are moral points of view that limit abstract right, e.g., if a debtor would be ruined by paying, then the strict right of the creditor is limited from this standpoint; the manual laborer must be left his tools; thus abstract right recognizes morality, and strict, formal right is not treated as holy. To this extent, moral right is more concrete than abstract strict right. (VPR17: 41)

For such cases Hegel uses the traditional term "right of necessity" (*Notrecht, ius necessitatis*) (PR § 127).

Hegel also holds that abstract right is limited and modified by the state.

Hegel believes that strictly speaking, all property should be private property; it should belong to individual persons, or at least to families, since a family constitutes a single juridical person (*PR* §§ 169–171). But "the organism of the state" can require that collectives – partnerships or limited liability corporations – be treated as persons and property owners (*PR* § 46R,A). We saw in Chapter 1, § 7, that in time of war the state has the right to demand that its members risk or sacrifice their property and even their lives for its sake (PR § 324). Hegel's statements on this point are (and are intended to be) hard sayings:

> This is the [state's] highest *ownmost* moment – its actual infinity as the ideality of everything finite in it – the side in which substance, as the absolute power against everything individual and particular, against life, property and their rights, as against the further circles, brings their nullity to existence and consciousness. (*PR* § 323)

This power belongs to the state only in the most extreme circumstances, when its survival is at stake. Of course, we Americans are all too familiar with the way "national security" is used to justify endless imperial expansion, as well as with cases in which rulers appeal to their "emergency powers" as a pretext for any violation of their citizens' rights which they deem expedient. But if we read Hegel as countenancing such fraud and abuse, then we misinterpret his doctrine in a way that precisely parallels the injustice practiced in the abuses themselves.

6. Abstract right and positive law

Perhaps Hegel provides the clearest explanation of his claim that the right of the state is "higher" than abstract right when he remarks that the state "has a much higher right than abstract right, and so private right (*Privatrecht*) is limited by constitutional law (*Staatsrecht*)" (*VPR17* : 41). The actual content of the rights of persons has to be determined in relation to the entire legal and political structure of the state. The content of those rights cannot be determined in abstraction from a concrete social order, but must be conceived so as to harmonize with the ethical life of a people and the constitution of a state. This is a controversial position to the extent that it implies that the content of individual right should be a function of the state's political constitution. Many would surely want to insist that the constitution of a state must adjust itself to the human rights of its citizens, rather than the other way round.

But to see matters in this way is to put oneself in a vicious circle Hegel wants to avoid. It forces us to define the structure of the state in terms of rights whose precise content can be specified (Hegel thinks) only in light of the state's structure. It is true that a constitution that ignores the abstract right of persons is not the constitution of a modern state; but it is equally true that apart from a concrete social context as defined by a rational system of law, it is not possible to say determinately what it means to respect the right of persons. In Hegel's view, those who give laws and codify them have the vocation of specifying the content of right precisely. Through positive legislation, right (*Recht*) is posited (*gesetzt*) as law (*Gesetz*) (*PR* § 211). The law regulates people's behavior. But its more important function is to give an explicitly rational form to what is right. Only through positive law do people come to *know* in concrete terms what their abstract rights are. "Only when it becomes law does what is right first receive not only the *form* of its universality but also its true determinacy"; the most important aspect of legislation is not the laying down of rules but the "cognition of [their] content in its determinate universality," that is, as rational and right (*PR* § 211R).

Hegel's high opinion of the calling of legal codification puts him at odds with his great Berlin colleague Karl Friedrich von Savigny, founder of the historical school of German jurisprudence. The historical school, reacting against the legal rationalism of the Enlightenment, emphasized the value of historical tradition in law, and criticized the attempt to provide systematization and codification to legal traditions, which they thought would distort the traditional meaning of laws by forcing them into the framework of modern, artificial ideas. Their views exhibit a laudable respect for the empirical history of law, but also a Romantic reaction against all attempts to place reason ahead of tradition in the ordering of social and political life. The historical school's hostility to legal codification was also an expression of German nationalist sentiments. The principal model of codified law was of course the Napoleonic Code; many Germans in Hegel's day (including those who were at opposite poles of the political spectrum on most other issues) resented the imposition of French institutions on their political life, and the historical jurists viewed attempts to codify German law in that light.

Hegel's attitude toward legal codification is very different:

> To deny to an educated nation or its professional jurists the capacity to frame a legal code would be the greatest insult that could be offered to a nation or to that profession. For it cannot be a matter of making a system of *new* laws as regards their *content,* but rather of cognizing the present content of laws in its determinate universality, i.e., grasping it *thinkingly,* with a view to its application to the particular. (*PR* § 211R)

Hegel does not despise national traditions, but he does subordinate their claims to those of universal reason. He sees a legal code as the opportunity to bring national tradition into harmony with reason. Its essence lies in explicating the rational core in the products of a nation's history, and at the same time bringing tradition before the bar of reason and making it prove its worth.

If it is the function of positive law to give determinate content to abstract right, Hegel also sees the authority of such laws as resting on their successful performance of their function. In general, Hegel conceives of "natural right" (what is "in itself right") not as something to be contrasted with positive law, but rather something to be made determinate by it (*PR* § 3R). It can happen that what is posited as the law can differ from what is "right in itself"; in such a case, the law lacks bindingness or obligatoriness (*Verbindlichkeit*). "In the identity of *being in itself* and *being posited (Gesetztseins)*, only what is *law (Gesetz)* has obligatoriness as *right*" (*PR* § 212). Hegel holds that to be "obligatory as right," a command or precept must be both "posited" and "right in itself." Thus what is right in itself is not obligatory as right unless it has been laid down in positive law; equally, a positive law is not binding as right unless it is also right in itself. Hegel emphasizes that positive laws are sometimes at serious variance with what is right in itself (*PR* §§ 3R, 180A, 212). Those laws are not binding on us as right.

It seems to be commonly thought that Hegel, with his habitual reverence for the state and the law, must naturally take a very hard line concerning our obligation to obey the law. As one recent writer puts it, Hegel's views "seem to lead in the uncongenial direction of absolute obedience."[13] As we have just seen, however, Hegel's position in fact has much in common with that strand of the natural law tradition which says that "an unjust law is no law." It is true that Hegel never actually advocates that we disobey unjust laws. As far as I know, he is completely silent on the question of what we should do when we are confronted with an unjust law which the authorities expect us to obey. It would be *consistent* with his views to adopt a *policy* of absolute obedience even to unjust laws, on the ground that by and large the state and the legal system are rational and so we should avoid doing anything that might tend to undermine them. (Of course, this argument tends to lose its force in proportion to the number and gravity of the injustices with which we are dealing.) Such a policy, however, is neither articulated by Hegel nor required by any of his views. On the other hand, it is positively *inconsistent* with Hegel's explicit account of legal obligation to maintain that we are *obligated by right* to obey unjust laws. In this respect, Hegel's view represents a significant departure from traditional Lutheran doctrines of absolute obedience to the powers that be, which were staunchly defended by Kant (*RL* 318–323/ 84–88).

At this point, we may still wonder whether Hegel has avoided the vicious circle after all. How can Hegel think that there might be a difference between positive law and what is "in itself right" if he also thinks that abstract right acquires a determinate content only through positive law? Part of the answer is that he would regard positive laws as contrary to right if they sanctioned plain violations of abstract right, if they forbade individuals to hold property, or required individuals to participate in religious observances contrary to their conscience, or regulated a system of slaveholding, which is fundamentally contrary to what is right in itself (*VPR4*: 458). More generally, Hegel's position seems to be that the conception of individuals as persons provides modern society with an ethical spirit, with which the letter of positive law can either harmonize or clash (*VPR19*: 175). Obviously what some people want at this point is something more than an "ethical spirit" with which to compare the letter of the law; they want a rational decision procedure that settles disputes about which laws are just and unjust, and provides us with a systematic justification for judgments about this in particular cases. It seems to be Hegel's position, however, that they won't get what they want;

questions of this kind must be considered in their particular historical and social context, and it is competent legislators and jurists who are most likely to give wise and reasoned answers to them. Such answers can always be subjected to rational scrutiny, and sometimes we can see them to be the wrong answers; but no general theory will help us to do any better.

7. Private property

For Hegel, the fundamental social institution that concretizes the abstract rights of persons is private property. The fundamental commandment of abstract right – "Be a person" – imposes on us an obligation to own property (*EG* § 486). But a person, Hegel tells us, is an *individual* will, and this makes private property the fundamental form of ownership (*PR* § 46). "The idea of the Platonic state," he says, "contains as a universal principle the injustice against persons that they are ineligible for private property" (*PR* § 46R).[14]

Hegel himself introduces one significant restriction on private property with his doctrine that the partners in a marriage are not individual persons but together constitute a single person (*PR* §§, 158, 168). He thinks that the resources of a nuclear family are held by its members in common. "No member of a family has particular property, but each has a right in what is common" (*PR* § 171). The normal administrator of this common property is the husband and father, but according to Hegel he is no more a private proprietor in his own right than anyone else in the family (*PR* § 171).[15] One consequence Hegel draws from this is that there are limits on a father's right to dispose of the family property at his death. Thus Hegel opposes both primogeniture and the exclusion of daughters from inheritance (*PR* § 180R); he holds that the father has no right to bequeath property outside the nuclear family (*PR* § 179R).

We will see later (Chapter 14, § 7) that Hegel is sensitive to the ways in which a market economy founded on the right of private property may sometimes lead to irrational and inhuman results (*PR* §§ 241–244; *JR I* : 321/247). He regards the gaps between rich and poor, educated and uneducated, not merely as misfortunes, but as wrongs (*PR* §§ 241, 244A). Hegel charges the state with the responsibility of dealing with these problems (*PR* § 242), but he is downright pessimistic about the prospects of a solution to them (*PR* § 245,R).

Hegel treats these issues in the context of his idea that abstract right must accommodate itself to the higher right of more concrete spheres, such as civil society and the state. He sees it as a problem of adjusting the abstract strict right of private property to more concrete considerations arising out of people's particular needs, from which we must abstract when we take the standpoint of property rights. From the standpoint of right itself, he thinks, the formal equality of persons has no implications for the different amounts of property that individual persons may own (*PR* § 49R).

Because he thinks we can resort to considerations arising out of the spheres of morality and ethical life to deal with such problems, Hegel recognizes nothing like the so-called Lockean proviso that one person can appropriate things from the common stock of nature only as long as "there is enough and as good left in common for others."[16] Wealth and poverty are one thing, the rights of persons are another. Questions about the distribution of property are relevant in the context of morality and civil society, but irrelevant in the sphere of abstract right. "That all human beings should have enough subsistence for their needs is partly a moral . . . *wish,* but partly, subsistence is something other than *possession,* and belongs to another sphere, that of civil society" (*PR* § 49R).

It is not clear that Hegel can remain consistent in holding to the centrality of private property within his own conception of abstract rights, while ignoring (or at any rate abstracting from) the actual effects of the institution of private property. The fundamental idea in abstract right is that every person, as an abstractly free will, has a claim on an external sphere in which to exercise and actualize this abstract freedom (*PR* § 41). Private property is supposed to provide this sphere, and consequent to this thought, Hegel does make one distributive proviso concerning private property: The equality of persons does require that each of them should own *some* property (*PR* § 49A).

But it is difficult to see how Hegel's theory could provide any reason for insisting that each person must own *some* property, that is not also a reason for insisting that each person own *enough* property (and the right sort of property) to guarantee an external sphere of freedom sufficient to fulfill the individual's free personality. It seems arguable that I have not been provided with such a sphere if I own no more (for instance) than a few items of clothing and the supply of food that I must consume each day if I am to stay alive. This is especially true if others' ownership over land and other means of production puts me in a position where I must virtually enslave myself to them if I am to acquire even the miserable share of property I have. To defend the centrality of the institution of private property in actualizing the abstract rights of persons, Hegel needs to show that *in its actual consequences* this institution is compatible with a social order in which the status of a free person is not a mere sham for many members of society.

Hegel would have a hard time showing this. The social history of modern capitalism, with its systematic impoverishment, exploitation, and dehumanization of working classes and poorer nations, strongly suggests that the institution of private property, far from providing for the actualization of the personality of all, is fundamentally *incompatible* with a social order in which all individuals recognize each other as free persons. Moreover, Hegel himself seems at certain points to be aware of this (see Chapter 14, §§ 9–10). If in its actual social consequences the institution of private property destroys the sphere of personal freedom for some as it provides that sphere for others, then this poses the problem of devising alternative social arrangements that do guarantee to all individuals an adequate external sphere for the exercise of abstract freedom or arbitrary choice. What is fundamental to Hegel's conception of abstract right is the insistence that social arrangements should make ample provision for this side of human self-actualization.

6
Punishment

1. Retributivism

Punishment is the social practice of inflicting evil (pain or harm) as a response to wrongdoing. To be punished is to have an evil inflicted on you by a duly constituted authority simply because it is an evil and because that authority ostensibly believes you have done something wrong. It is still punishment – *unjust* punishment – if the authority's belief is false, or even shammed. It is not punishment at all to inflict evil on a person who is not even alleged to have done wrong. Nor do you punish a person when your reason for inflicting the evil is that it is a means to or a by-product of some good (as in a painful medical treatment or annoying educational process). You have to choose it *as* an evil, and your reason for inflicting it has to be that the person has supposedly done something wrong.

In that sense, the very conception of punishment is retributive. Borrowing Rawls's terminology, we could say that it is essential to punishment as an institution that particular acts of punishment should be justified by reference to the general practice of punishment; and the general practice is *conceived* in an essentially retributive way.[1]

It is an altogether different issue how the practice itself is to be justified. Here people often appeal to good consequences of various kinds: to the supposedly beneficial effects of punishment on wrongdoers themselves, or its deterrent effect on people generally, or to the part punishment might play in moral education, or to the way in which punishing wrongdoers gives satisfaction to the public's vengeful feelings toward them. Those who offer such consequentialist justifications for the practice of punishment should not be called "retributivists," even if they acknowledge that punishment itself is an inherently retributive practice in the sense described in the last two paragraphs.[2] True retributivists are those who hold a distinctive view about how the practice of punishment is to be justified. They think that the practice is sufficiently justified merely by the fact that justice demands that some proportionate evil should be visited on a person guilty of wrongdoing. Retributivists do not necessarily deny that punishment has good consequences, but they do deny that we need to appeal to them in justifying the practice of punishment. Rather, they say that the essential point in the justification of punishment is that it is inherently just to inflict some evil on those who have done wrong.

Hegel is a genuine retributivist. He rejects as "superficial" all theories that try to justify punishment by the "good" which is supposed to come of it. To him, what matters is "that crime is to be canceled, not as the production of an evil, but as the violation of the right as right"; punishment, as the "cancellation" (*Aufhebung*) or "annulment" (*Vernichtung*) of crime is justified merely because it is "in and for itself just" (*PR* § 99R).[3] This position agrees with Kant, whose commitment to retributivism is clear, but whose defense of it remains at best embryonic (*RL* 331–337/99–107). Equally, it is a response to Fichte's scornful rejection of retributivism as a nonsensical theory based on an "inscrutable categorical imperative" (*GNR* 283/372).[4]

Hegel's theory of punishment belongs to the sphere of abstract right because punishment is a response to crime as a "wrong" or "injustice" (*Unrecht*), which is a violation of abstract right (*PR* § 81). A crime is an act of "coercion"; it violates the free will in its external existence, as in the body or property of a person (*PR* § 92). Further, crime violates the free will knowingly and intentionally; it "violates the right as right" (*PR* § 95). Such a violation, Hegel declares, has a "positive, external existence, but *within itself* it is null (*nichtig*). The *manifestation* of its nullity is the annulment of that violation, which also steps into existence – the actuality of right" (*PR* § 97). Crime, "null within itself," thus calls forth its own "annulment" in the form of "justice" (*Gerechtigkeit*), an external act of "retribution" which "violates the violation" (*PR* § 101).

When an act of just retribution is carried out by a private person, it is an act of "revenge." Revenge is "just in its content," but "in form" only a new violation of right (*PR* § 102). From the standpoint of the wrongdoer who suffers the just revenge, the private act of vengeance is just. But if the avenger is only a private person, from the avenger's standpoint the act of vengeance is merely a new crime, which calls for its own annulment. Hence Hegel argues that revenge leads naturally to an endless series of wrongs, perpetuating itself from generation to generation (*PR* § 102). Final justice can be done only when crime is annulled not by a private will but by the universal will, the public authority of the state, in the form of the court of justice (*PR* §§ 219–220). Only this authoritative annulment of crime is "punishment" strictly so-called (*PR* § 103).

The retributivist intent of Hegel's theory is clear enough, but its central claims are shrouded in obscure metaphors. What does it mean to say that a crime is "null within itself"? How does this "nullity" call for punishment as its proper "manifestation"?

Even before we try to answer these questions, however, we can appreciate one distinctive feature of Hegel's theory of punishment. Just as Hegel conceives of crime as the intentional violation of the right, so he conceives of punishment (or the "annulment" of crime) as "the violation of a violation." The punishment of a criminal takes the form of inflicting a distinctive kind of evil. To punish a criminal is to do something that would normally count as the violation of the criminal's own right – typically, the right to property, or liberty, or life. To justify punishment is to show how the state can be justified in doing things to criminals which, but for their commission of crimes, no one could ever have the right to do to them.

2. Punishment as the restoration of right

One interpretation of Hegel's theory begins with Hegel's assertion that crime must be punished because otherwise the crime would be "valid"; hence punishment "restores the right" (*PR* § 99).[5] This theme in Hegel's defense of punishment is clearly related to the idea (defended by Joel Feinberg) that one important function of punishment is simply to express society's strong condemnation of criminal acts.[6] By violating the right of another, the criminal is in effect asserting that this right has no validity. By punishing the criminal, the state effectively contradicts this assertion, demonstrating in practical terms that people do have rights, that their rights count for something.

Hegel finds in this theme some affinity to his own metaphysics, in which something displays true actuality when it is capable of enduring otherness and contradiction, and returning to itself even from its own opposite. If crime, wrongdoing, or injustice (*Unrecht*) is the negation of right (*Recht*), punishment is the actuality of right; it is (as the participial form of the noun might suggest) "wrong righted," or "justice" (*Gerechtigkeit*). Punishment is "the negation of the negation. Actual right is the canceling of the violation [of right], which thus shows its validity and preserves itself as a necessary, mediated existence" (*PR* § 97A). Punishment asserts the actuality of the right even in the face of wrong or injustice; like spirit itself, right proves its actuality by vindicating itself even in its own opposite.

We run into some problems if we try to use this theme in interpreting Hegel's theory of punishment. One is that it is not clear how such an interpretation will save the retributivist intent of the theory. The righting of wrong and the doing of justice, of course, do look like paradigmatically retributivist reasons for punishing. But the state's intention to *reassert* the validity of right in the face of wrong looks like an intention not to do justice as such, but to promote a good end, namely the *public recognition* of the validity of right. If there is room for doubt about this, that is largely because the precise nature of the end is rather mysterious. Why is it important for the state to *assert* the validity of right, to *express* its disapproval of crime? Is there any reason for it to do this apart from its devotion to such consequentialist ends as preventing future crimes and reassuring people that their rights are being protected?

A deeper problem with Hegel's theory on this interpretation is that it seems to presuppose a justification of punishment rather than to supply one. Whatever the state's reasons for expressing its disapproval of crime, it still remains to be shown why the state is justified in making such assertions in the way punishment does, at the expense of the person punished.

David Cooper attempts to fill these gaps by attributing to Hegel the following "conceptual thesis":

CT: It is a *conceptual* truth that the violation of a person's right calls forth punishment as its proper response.

I do not actually have rights, Cooper argues, unless society is prepared to punish the violation of my rights; hence "the justification of punishment is the same as the justification of the rights the crimes violate."[7] He thinks the criminal act involves the assertion that the victim of the crime has no rights. This assertion is "null" in the sense that it is false, since the victim does have rights, and this gets manifested when the criminal is punished.[8]

On Cooper's interpretation, Hegel's justification of punishment turns on CT. Unfortunately, we look in vain for any explicit statements of CT in Hegel's writings. Even worse, on its own CT is far from compelling. It may be true (even tautologous) that the existence of (socially guaranteed) rights requires that society be prepared to protect them in some way. But why must this protection take the specific form of punishing their violation? Suppose there were a society in which the authorities have devised fairly effective ways of protecting (what we would otherwise call) people's rights, but without the use of punishment – as by making it difficult to violate rights, or by educating people so that violations of right will not be common. Suppose that despite these precautions people's rights are sometimes violated in this society (though less often, let us say, than people's rights are violated in our society); still, their violation is never punished. Cooper must claim, purely on conceptual grounds, that the people in that society have no rights at all, that if we speak of rights in that society, we must be using some new or odd concept of right. I find such claims extremely dubious.

Even if CT were correct, however, that would not provide any justification for the practice of punishment. It would instead place the burden of argument on substantiating the claim that people have (or ought to have) rights (in the sense in which people's having rights requires that the violation of their rights will be punished). To make good that claim, we would have to justify the institution of punishment – from scratch. It is one thing to say that people are entitled to freedom of speech or proprietorship over parts of the earth, even that they are entitled to having their freedom or property protected by the state. It is another thing to say that they are entitled to have these things protected in a certain way, by the state's inflicting evil on those who interfere with freedom or property. If Cooper's interpretation is correct, Hegel's theory of abstract right ought to concentrate on defending this last claim.

Hegel proceeds in no such way. In the theory of abstract right developed in *PR* §§ 34–80, he regards abstract right as conferring on persons both a permission and a warrant to exercise arbitrary choice within a limited sphere (*PR* §§ 38, 41). Only later does he focus attention on the claim that others should respect this sphere (cf. *PR* § 49R), and nowhere before *PR* § 81 does he intimate what might happen if they do not respect it. Hegel's procedure strongly suggests that either his defense of punishment rests on a fundamental confusion or else CT plays no role in his thinking about punishment.

Even if an argument could be given for CT, there is no reason to think that the resulting justification for punishment would be retributivist. Once we ask why CT's concept of right ought to be instantiated, it is open to consequentialists to cite the benefits to be gained by granting people such rights and punishing their violation. If Hegel is correctly interpreted as resting his justification of punishment on CT, then he is confused if he thinks this lends any support to his preference for retributivism. In the absence of any explicit textual warrant for it, we should not ascribe to Hegel such a confused and underargued position.

3. The nullity of the criminal will

Central to Hegel's theory of punishment is the baffling claim that the criminal act is "null within itself." Hegel's hints at the meaning of this claim point in a disturbing variety of directions.

1. As we have just seen, Cooper says that the nullity of the criminal will consists in the falsity of its implied assertion that the victim has no rights. Hegel nowhere directly supports this interpretation; but he does suggest that the criminal will is "null" because it *attempts to do what cannot be done*. Some texts say that the criminal will is null because it tries to coerce the free will, which, qua free, cannot be coerced (*VPR17*: 69: cf. *PR* § 91). Others say that it is null because it tries to violate the universal will (the "will in itself") which, having no external existence as such, is, in principle, inviolable (*PR* § 99). These suggestions are both unpromising. Even granted (what is far from evident) that these things are impossible and that the criminal *will* tries to do them, the main question still remains: Why should anyone be punished for attempting the impossible?

2. Hegel sometimes implies that the criminal act is "null" because it is inherently self-destructive. Thus Hegel says that coercion is "in its very conception directly self-destructive because it is an expression of a will that annuls the expression of determinate existence of a will" (*PR* § 92). This is nothing but an impudent sophistry. When I coerce you or violate your right, *my* will annuls the expression or determinate existence of *your* will; there is nothing self-destructive in that.

3. "Nullity" is also associated with Hegel's notion that injustice or wrong is a kind of "show" (*Schein*), not in the usual sense of an illusion (something that only seems to exist) but in the technical Hegelian sense of an act whose outer existence is somehow at odds with its inner nature or concept.[9] Punishment manifests the nullity of the criminal act by reasserting the right, thus revealing the truth of this show (*PR* § 82). Such an account raises many more questions than it answers. Perhaps a crime is in some sense a free act whose outer existence is at odds with its essence. But how

is the inadequacy of the act manifested by the state's inflicting evil on the agent? Even if it does provide such a manifestation, how does that fact *justify* the inflicting of evil?

4. Sometimes Hegel speaks of the "nullity" not of the criminal act, but of the criminal's *will*. It, too, is called "self-destructive" or even "self-contradictory" (*PR* § 92). "The right of freedom in respect of coercion is that, as the contradictory of itself, it destroys itself. The manifestation of this is that coercion is canceled through coercion" (*VPR19* : 85). These remarks do at last suggest a way in which the "nullity" of the criminal will might call forth punishment as its "manifestation." If the criminal's will can be seen as somehow *willing* its own frustration, then punishment might be seen as the carrying out of this volition, and thus manifesting the latent self-contradiction. In that case, the criminal's will is "null" in the sense that, when it wills the violation of the victim's right, it also wills the violation of its own right, and this violation is carried out when the criminal is punished.

If this is what Hegel means by the "nullity" of crime, then it dovetails with another line of thinking about the criminal act on which Hegel lays considerable stress. Hegel insists that when I have committed a crime, punishment is my "right," because it is something that I myself have willed. Not only is punishment "in itself just," he says, but "it is also a *right posited in the criminal* himself, in his existing will, in his action. For it lies in his action, as *rational,* that something universal is set up, a law that he has recognized for himself and under which he thus may be subsumed as under *his own* right" (*PR* § 100).

More specifically, Hegel claims that my act of violating another's right sets up the law, which is valid for me, that my own right may be violated: "The criminal has set up a universal law: 'It is right to violate freedom' " (*VPR17* : 70; cf. *VPR 3*: 316). Moreover, the specific law established by the criminal corresponds to the specific crime committed, the specific right violated:

When he kills, he declares as a universal law that killing is allowed. (*VPR17* 70)

As a murderer he sets up the law that life is not to be respected; he expresses this universal in his deed; but thereby he pronounces his own death sentence. (*VPR 3*: 318)

Insofar as the agent is a rational being, it lies in his action that it is something universal. If you steal from another, then you steal from yourself! If you kill someone, then you kill everybody, and even yourself! The action is a law that you set up and that through your action you have recognized in and for yourself. (*NP* 244)[10]

When I commit a crime, do I thereby will that the same crime should be committed against me? Clearly murderers do not typically desire to be killed, nor thieves to be stolen from. Sometimes, however, we ascribe volition to people not on the basis of what they desire, but on the basis of their expressions of intent (in word or action). The clearest case is probably a contractual agreement. Suppose I agree to shovel your walk next winter if you mow my lawn this summer. When winter comes and I am due to perform my part of the bargain, it can be said on the basis of this agreement that I shovel your walk in accordance with my own will. This is true even if the shoveling is something I do not want to do, even if it is something I hate doing and wish that I had never agreed to do.

Hegel explicitly rejects Cesare Beccaria's contractarian theory of punishment (PR § 100R). But he does accept Beccaria's claim that punishment is based on the criminal's consent to be punished: "What *Beccaria* demands, that a man must give his consent to be punished, is quite right; but the criminal already gives his consent through his deed. It is the nature of the crime and the criminal's own will that the violation proceeding from him should be canceled" (PR § 100A). Hegel even insists that the criminal's consent to be punished is explicit rather than tacit (VPR 4: 291).

4. Consenting to be punished

Beccaria holds that when I consent to the social contract, I conditionally alienate the rights and liberties that the law takes from me when I am punished.[11] In effect, I consent in advance to be punished in the event that I should commit a crime.[12] Hegel's theory is different, but analogous. He says that when I commit a crime, I set up a law making it permissible for others to violate my right to the same extent that my crime violates the right of its victim. "The same right that is violated in another through a crime is lost to the criminal. . . . His deed becomes universal, and the right that he has canceled is also cancelled for him" (TJ 388–339/ETW 225–226). Punishment is justified because the right infringed by the state in punishing me is one that I have explicitly renounced.

Why does Hegel think that my commission of a crime involves my consent to be punished for it? Perhaps his theory of recognition and abstract right puts him in a position to defend such a thought. To belong to the ethical life of modern society is to participate in its "universal self-consciousness," to see oneself as a person among persons, each of us entitled to an external sphere for the exercise of our freedom. To understand oneself as a person is to claim this free status for oneself, and since modern recognition is inherently reciprocal in character, it is simultaneously to claim the same status for all other persons. When I commit a crime, my act revokes my own claim on the right that I violate. If a right is the enjoyment of a determinate sphere of freedom in connection with a person's body or property, then by invading another's sphere of freedom I declare by my action that I no longer recognize that right as inviolable. My declaration applies most directly not to the other's right (since the other has not joined in the declaration), but rather to my own right. In effect, my crime is an act of consent to someone else's invasion of my own sphere of freedom to the same extent that I have invaded the sphere of my victim. This consent is the source of what Hegel calls the "law" that I lay down, declaring that it is allowed to do to me what I have done to the other.[13] Of course, neither my victim nor anyone else has renounced the right I violate. Hence my renunciation of right applies – ironically – only to me: The law expressed in the criminal's act, Hegel says, is "recognized for himself" (*PR* § 100); it is "a principle valid only for him" (*EG* § 500). "The criminal's law is a universal, but only he has recognized it" (*VPR17* : 70); hence it is "valid *only for the agent,* because only he through his action has recognized it, not the others" (NP 244).

This law is simply carried out on me when I am punished, and my own will is thereby fulfilled. That is why Hegel insists that in being punished, I am not being treated as a mere means to someone else's ends, or as a dangerous animal that must be rendered harmless; I am being "honored as a rational being" (*PR* § 100R). Since "right," in Hegel's technical sense, refers to any existence that is the existence of a free will (*PR* § 29), my punishment can also be called my "right" – for it gives existence to the *rational* volition expressed in my criminal act (*PR* § 100).

The criminal's consent to punishment enables us to interpret Hegel's insistence on the "nullity" of the criminal will in the sense of its self-destructiveness. My criminal act is self-destructive in the sense that the right it actually revokes is not my victim's, but only my own. Punishment manifests this nullity, since it takes from me (by my own consent) the very right that I have tried to take from another.

5. The incompleteness of Hegel's theory

As we should expect from a retributivist, Hegel's theory of punishment tries to show that punishment is justified because it is inherently just. In effect, Hegel's theory of the annulment of crime is a theory of the forfeiture of rights. The theory says that when I commit a crime, I forfeit the same right that is threatened by my criminal act; the mechanism of this forfeiture is a renunciation of the right, contained in my criminal act. This is a well-conceived theory of the forfeiture of rights, founded on the theory of abstract right which proceeds from Hegel's theory of recognition and rational personality. But the theory is also subject to several serious limitations. In the remainder of this chapter, I intend to explore them.

First, Hegel's theory has one important assumption that may seriously limit its capacity to justify the institution of legal punishment as it actually exists. Hegel usually takes for granted that those who are to be punished do in fact regard themselves as persons with abstract rights, and also recognize their victims as persons equal to themselves. Without that assumption, it cannot be inferred that my criminal act lays down a universal law that I may be treated as I treat my victim. Occasionally, however, Hegel observes that social conditions in modern civil society tend to produce a whole class of people (the poor or "the rabble") who have neither rights nor duties, and tend to be altogether lacking in a sense of right (*PR* § 244; see Chapter 14, §§ 9–10). If there are people who fail to share the conception of themselves as persons, as part of a system of mutual recognition, then we cannot attribute to their actions a universal law founded on a universal self-consciousness that recognizes everyone as a person. Hegel's theory provides no guidance on the treatment of such people when they violate the rights of others. Hegel is troubled by the existence of an underclass that is effectively excluded from the ethical life of modern civil society. The inability of his theory of punishment to deal with such people is one good reason, among others, why he should be troubled.

Hegel's theory suffers from a second serious limitation, regarded as a defense of retributivism. We might ask two different questions about the justification of punishment. First, we might ask *by what right* the state punishes the criminal. This is the question on which a retributivist theory of punishment tends to focus. Second, we might ask for a *positive reason* why the state should actually inflict punishment. That is, granting that punishment does no injustice, we might still ask if there is any good reason for the state to punish.

Hegel's theory answers the first question by showing how criminals have renounced or forfeited the rights they violate. Hegel appears to want to answer the second question in the same way, by appealing to the idea that punishment is the criminal's right, the fulfillment of the criminal's rational will. But it is not clear that the second question can be satisfactorily answered in this way. If I renounce my right to something, then it follows that you are not obligated or required to give it to me; if you choose not to give it to me, you cite my renunciation in support of the claim that your refusal to give it to me is in accordance with my will. But it does not follow from this that you *must* not give it to me, or that you are doing anything wrong if you go ahead and give it to me anyway. If I have contracted to shovel your walk in the winter, then you have the right to that service, and I have an obligation to perform it. But our contractual arrangement gives you no positive reason to insist that I perform the service for you; and you do no wrong if you choose not to exact the service.

If criminals will their own punishment, as Hegel's theory says, then it follows that the state violates no right of theirs by punishing them; they are punished in accordance with their own rational will. It does not follow, however, that the state has acquired any positive reason to punish them. In particular, it does not follow that the state in any sense fails to honor a criminal's rational will if it chooses not to punish the criminal.

Perhaps Hegel's thought is that since criminals will the actual violation of the other's right, they are committed to willing the actual violation of their own right. That thought is mistaken, or at least without foundation in Hegel's theory. Criminals do not typically desire the violation of the other's right for its own sake; often they regard it only as a regrettable means to their end. Even where criminals do desire the violation of right for its own sake, it is not clear that Hegel's theory of abstract right entitles us to say that the criminal act commits the criminal to positively willing that anyone else's rights should be violated. Abstract right, according to Hegel, deals entirely with permissions. It grounds positive actions only when they can be interpreted as cases of standing aside and allowing persons to exercise freedom within their proper external sphere (*PR* § 38). It seems inconsistent with the spirit of Hegel's theory to suppose that the criminal act has the effect of going beyond the granting of a permission. Hegel's own language reflects this, when he describes the criminal as "consenting" to punishment, as having declared that "it is right to violate freedom" and that it is "allowed" to violate the right he is violating (*VPR17* : 70). To say that I consent to or allow something is to say that I permit it, but not that I positively demand it.

Occasionally, it is true, criminals do positively desire to be punished, and do not feel properly reconciled with themselves until they have undergone punishment. Hegel, like Dostoyevsky, might find such sentiments appropriate and want to encourage them. There is nothing in Hegel's theory, however, that explains the desire of wrongdoers to be punished or lends any support to it. If criminals want to be punished, that might provide the state with a reason for punishing them; but it would be a consequentialist, not a retributivist reason.

Of course, there are a number of other reasons often given for the state's actually doing what Hegel's theory says it has the right to do. A criminal's incarceration or death protects society against that criminal, temporarily or permanently; the general knowledge that crimes are punished deters other potential criminals, expresses social disapproval of their acts, and satisfies society's vengeful feelings; appropriate punishments might educate or reform criminals; and so forth. None of these reasons is retributivist in character. All are reasons to which the retributivist Hegel proudly and consistently refuses to appeal (*PR* §§ 99–100).

Hegel's theory that criminals will their own punishment thus provides no positive reason at all for punishing them. It stands in need of supplement by additional, nonretributivist considerations if it is to provide a complete rational justification for the practice of punishment. Hegel might try to obtain a retributivist justification for punishing from his other claim, that punishment is required because it is "in itself just" owing to the fact that the criminal act is "null within itself." But I have confessed defeat in the attempt to render that claim defensible (or even fully intelligible). My conclusion must be that nothing defensible in Hegel's theory of punishment is capable of providing a retributivist reason why criminals should actually be punished.

This by no means entails that Hegel's theory is a total failure. It answers the basic question it sets out to answer: Why is it just to punish criminals? It shows how the practice of punishment might be rendered consistent, exclusively on retributivist grounds, with the abstract right of persons. Further, the theory provides a rationale for deciding what it is permissible for the state to do in response to crime. It says that the state may deprive the criminal of the same right which the criminal act was attempting to violate, and it implies that the state may not do more than this in its attempts to protect the public, or appease its feelings, or to advance its projects of educating or reforming the criminals themselves. If Hegel's retributivist theory stands in need of supplement by consequentialist considerations, it nevertheless provides a framework, independent of such considerations, for deciding questions about the justice of punishment. It is doubtful that any consequentialist theory of punishment is capable of answering these questions satisfactorily.

6. Violations of right and violations of law

Hegel's theory of crime and its annulment belongs to the sphere of abstract right. This theory conceives of crime simply as "coercion" – the violation of the abstract right of one or more individual persons. Crime is perhaps more conventionally thought of in another way: as the violation of criminal *law*. Hegel attempts to reconceive crime as the violation of law later in the *Philosophy of Right* when he comes to his treatment of punishment proper, the annulment of crime by the state through the courts (*PR* §§ 219–228). Punishment, he says, is "objectively regarded, the reconciliation of the self-restoring and hence actually valid law with itself through the annulment of crime" (*PR* § 220). In effect, Hegel simply transfers to the law the attributes of self-restoration and actual validity which he earlier ascribed to abstract right in its annulment of crime. Perhaps he feels entitled to do this because his philosophy of law takes the basic function of positive criminal law itself to be that of making abstract right determinate and hence enforceable by the state.

It is not true, however, that the only function of criminal law is to determine and enforce the abstract right of persons. Along with acts that are inherently wrong (so-called *mala in se*), the law also finds it expedient to forbid acts that are not inherently wrong, and that violate no individual's rights. Such acts (so-called *mala prohibita*) include counterfeiting, smuggling, drug-dealing, insider stock-trading, driving on the wrong side of the road, etc. – acts not wrong in themselves whose prohibition nevertheless serves some legitimate legislative end. The law also forbids some acts that are usually considered wrong in themselves, not because they violate the right of a person but because they directly attack the *state:* for example, rebellion and treason. As with *mala prohibita,* on Hegel's theory, it is not clear how the state can be warranted in punishing such acts.

Hegel plainly intends *all* violations of criminal law to count as crimes under his theory. Prominent among the crimes he mentions are examples of crimes against the state or the judicial process ("perjury, treason") and examples of *mala prohibita* ("forgery, coining") (*PR* § 95R). But it is not clear how his theory is going to justify the punishment of either class of crimes. That theory argues that the state is entitled to take the criminal's liberty, property, or life because the criminal has renounced or forfeited the right to what is taken through the attempt to deprive some other person of the same right. Unless an act that violates the law also counts as an attempt to deprive a person of an abstract right, the theory provides no account of how such a renunciation or forfeiture can take place, and hence provides no justification for the state's act of punishing the lawbreaker. Hegel the renowned statist seems to have no justification for punishing crimes against the state.

Hegel might try to bring such acts under his theory either by arguing from the incidental harm that such lawless acts may do to persons, or else by ap-

pealing somehow to the (perhaps indirect) way in which the laws that pro-
hibit them serve the basic purpose of law, protecting the rights of persons.
Hegel shows no sign of employing such strategies, and they do not look very
promising. Even if they work, there might still be a problem about some
violations of right themselves. There are sometimes rights – even rights recognized under the law – for which the law provides no mechanism of enforcement (e.g., certain civil rights in the United States before the Civil Rights
Act of 1964).[14] Hegel may intend to address this point when he claims that
abstract right becomes "recognized" and "determinate" only through positive
law (PR § 217). But that claim does a much better job of explaining the
rationale for laws against violating the right of persons than of explaining
why the violation of the right of persons is punishable only when it takes the
form of violating the law.

In his Jena period, Hegel adumbrates an alternative theory of punishment
focusing on crime as the violation of the universal will of the community.
Here crime is described as "the individual will to *power,* to validity, to being
recognized. [The criminal] wills *to be something* . . . to carry out *his* will in
spite of the universal will" (*JR* 224/130–131). In response the universal will
becomes active, "canceling the individual. *Punishment* is this reversal. It is
retaliation as the universal will. Its essence does not rest on any contract, or
on the deterrence of others, or on the betterment of the criminal. Rather its
essence, its concept, is this transition, this reversal of the injured universal
recognition" (*JR* 224/131).

These remarks make clear the retributivist intent of Hegel's theory, but
leave virtually everything else in hopeless obscurity. They provide no justification for punishment, because they do not tell us why or under what circumstances the "universal" has a right to "cancel" the "individual." Hegel
admits that "even the state may not do what is not right in itself (*für sich*)"
(*VPR17*: 70–71). It is the greatest strength of his mature theory of punishment that it addresses itself to the problem of showing how the state may
punish a criminal without violating the criminal's right. Hegel simply has no
theory that solves this problem and also justifies the punishment of everything he regards as a crime.

7. The measure of punishment

Retributivist theories of punishment usually hold that punishment should
"equal" the crime. This feature of retributivism often gives rise to difficult
questions about how punishments are to be meted out. Consequentialist theories tell us to choose those punishments that have the best results, but retributivist theories appear to mandate punishments completely irrespective of
the results. They threaten to require punishments we regard as too severe,
or too lenient, or counterproductive to the social good.[15] Sometimes the requirement that punishment should "equal" the crime has seemed to objectors
too metaphorical to yield any determinate policy at all.

Hegel's theory seems to involve some fairly precise conclusions about the measure of punishment. It says that the criminal has violated or attempted to violate a determinate right and in so doing he has renounced or forfeited the *very same* right; consequently, it seems to imply that his punishment should consist in the violation of the very same right. Taken literally that seems to mean that if I break into your house and steal $100,[16] then the state should break into my house and steal $100 from me; if I assault you and break your arm, then I should be assaulted and have my arm broken; if I steal your car and wreck it, then I should have my own car stolen and wrecked. Clearly this is not always going to yield a workable measure of punishment. The punishments sometimes appear to be too lenient, sometimes cruel. What, for instance, is to be done to me in the last case if I do not happen to own a car? Hegel himself wonders how the Biblical injunction "an eye for an eye and a tooth for a tooth" (Exodus 21 : 24) is supposed to apply to a criminal who has only one eye or no teeth (*PR* § 101R).

Hegel's response to these difficulties is to say that when I commit a crime, what I forfeit is not the very same right I violate, but only an *equivalent* right. On this ground, he even denies that punishment should be conceived as a *talion* (*VPR17* : 72). Crime and punishment should be regarded as equivalent in a more abstract sense, in their "value" (*PR* § 101). Perhaps when we regard crimes in terms of their value, we can treat a monetary fine as equivalent to an assault, and a period of incarceration as equivalent to a theft. Hegel insists that such equivalences must be possible, since they are employed in civil law: Money is awarded, for instance, for damages that may not have taken the form of a pecuniary loss (*VPR17* : 72). Hegel argues that the violation of right can have a value in this sense simply because abstract right concerns a free will that has entered into something external, "into the sphere of quantitative extent and qualitative determination" (*PR* § 96). To determine the value of a crime, it is necessary to consider the violation of rights in relation to people's needs and expectations, which vary from place to place and time to time. For this reason, Hegel regards criminal codes as a matter for changing positive legislation, not for abstract philosophical reflection: "How each crime is to be punished cannot be decided by thoughts. Positive laws are necessary" (*PR* § 96A); "a criminal code belongs chiefly to its time, and to the conditions of civil society in its time" (*PR* § 218).

We may wonder how far this account remains faithful to Hegel's purely retributivist intentions. When legislators get their hands on a penal code, what guarantee is there that they will not be influenced by consequentialist as well as retributivist considerations unless our retributivist theory puts them under fairly precise constraints? Of course, if our argument in § 5 was correct, then the only function of a retributivist theory with respect to the measure of punishment is to set upward limits to the state's right to punish. That leaves room for penal legislators to be consequentialists within those limits, but it is also a significant modification of retributivism.

We may also question whether the notion of "value" is appropriate for measuring violations of right. Hegel understands "value" as a function of the needs satisfied by a thing, and people's dispositions to substitute different need satisfactions for one another (*PR* § § 63,A, 77; cf. *VPR19* : 162). In a civil suit, monetary damages are appropriate because the injured party is seeking compensation for something measurable by market standards. But crime is an invasion of my personality. It would be demeaning to regard any market price as an acceptable equivalent for that. Perhaps there is such a thing as an equality between crimes and punishments, in the form of the forfeiture of an equivalent though different right. The fundamentally economic notion of "value," however, does not seem to capture it.

8. The death penalty

Cesare Beccaria argues against the death penalty on the basis of social contract theory. He contends that the state's right over the individual consists only in what individuals have granted to the state for the purpose of protecting their own interests. Individuals cannot be supposed under any circumstances to grant others the right to kill them, since life is the greatest of all the goods to be protected. Consequently, there can be no right of the state to employ the punishment of death.[17]

Hegel rejects both the argument and its conclusion. He spurns the contract theory of the state, insisting that the state is an end in itself, and a higher end than the private good of its individual members (*PR* § 100R). Hegel approves of the fact that the death penalty is imposed less often than it used to be, and he thinks there are very few offenses to which it is appropriate (*PR* § 100A). But he regards death as a legitimate punishment in some cases, and he thinks that it is the only just punishment for the crime of murder (*PR* § 101A).

As we have seen, Hegel's theory of punishment has in common with Beccaria's the feature that it proposes to justify punishment on the basis of the criminal's consent. Hegel's theory of punishment is a theory of the forfeiture of rights, and the mechanism of forfeiture is the criminal's renunciation of a right through the giving of consent to renounce it. A Hegelian defense of the death penalty therefore requires us to maintain that murderers have, through their capital offense, divested themselves of the right not to be killed.

It is questionable whether Hegel can consistently hold that people may do this. If I forfeit a right only through consenting to its violation, then it follows that I can forfeit only those rights that it is in my power to alienate through my consent. Following Hegel's theory, then, an inalienable right would be immune to forfeiture. It is perhaps noteworthy that Hegel never explicitly includes the right not to be killed among inalienable rights. But he does say that a right is inalienable and imprescriptible if it is a right constituting personality itself (*PR* § 66), and he denies that I have a right to kill myself on the ground that my life is not external to my personality (*PR* § 70). This seems to commit him to regarding the right not to be killed as inalienable. Hegel insists that I have not only the right but even the duty to sacrifice my life for the state in time of war (*PR* § 70). But it certainly seems inconsistent with his view to suppose that I might validly contract to permit someone else to kill me outright.[18] Consequently, Hegel's views appear to commit him to the position that I cannot forfeit my right not to be killed.

Perhaps Hegel thinks that the death penalty is the only just punishment for murder because he thinks that the act of taking another's life involves the violation of a right that is at once very sacred and highly specific, so that the equivalent punishment is equally extreme and equally precise. Yet an analogous line of reasoning in the case of other inalienable rights would be unconvincing, to say the least. No decent person would regard it as appropriate to punish rapists by raping them, or to punish those who enslave others by making them into slaves. If an inquisitor forces others to worship against their religious conscience, it would not be a fit punishment to force him to worship gods in which he does not believe. Opponents of the death penalty are often motivated by the idea that capital punishment is a barbaric and degrading practice, as wrong and demeaning as are the crimes to which people want to apply it.[19] It is interesting that Hegel's retributivist theory of punishment tends (even against Hegel's intentions) to support this opinion.

Most people who believe that murder should not be punished by death believe that it is at least permissible to punish it with life imprisonment (this is Beccaria's view, for instance).[20] Hegel also seems to regard life imprisonment as permissible in cases of murder where the death penalty is inappropriate (*VPR 4*: 285). On the other hand, if the death penalty is illegitimate because the right not to be killed is immune to forfeiture, then we ought also to ask whether I can alienate or forfeit my liberty for the whole of my life. Free status is explicitly included among inalienable rights (*PR* § 66). Hegel regards the alienation of one's free activity for the whole future as impermissible, since it is equivalent to the alienation of one's free status (*PR* § 67). From this it follows that life imprisonment is just as illegitimate a punishment as death. Hegel himself appears to endorse this argument at least in his lectures:

I cannot give over to another what is inward to me, but I can give over to someone only my services as limited by time and particularity. In the same way, I cannot give over my capacity to hold property along with my property. A criminal who comes into the penitentiary can lose his freedom only for a determinate time, a limited time. (*VPR17*: 56)

9. Should we expect an ethical justification of punishment?

People sometimes do such monstrous things to one another that we cannot decently do anything to them that might plausibly be regarded as "equal" to what they have done. Torture, rape, and enslavement are examples of such egregious acts; some think that murder is as well. Retributivism may have a bad name partly because it seems to imply that we are morally required to requite every evil with an equal evil, even in such cases. But the most distinctive feature of retributivism is its concern with the criminal's right. As Hegel's theory illustrates, a retributivist theory sets limits to what it is permissible to do to criminals in ways that no consequentialist theory can.

Egregious crimes pose a problem for retributivism because they threaten a conflict between this side of retributivist theories and the retributivist idea that punishment is just only if it is equal to the crime. If (on this conception of justice) we respond "justly" to egregious crimes, then we cease to behave with minimal moral decency; we violate rights that must not be violated under any circumstances. Perhaps in these cases no just response to crime is open to us.

A different, but in some ways analogous problem is faced by consequentialist theories that view prevention of crime as the aim of punishment. The state threatens to punish crimes, and it tries – with imperfect success – to carry out the threat. No doubt there are fewer crimes than there would be if the state tried less hard, but if we are rational consequentialists, then we should be interested not only in reaching our ends, but also in reaching them in a cost-effective way. As a method of preventing crime in modern society, punishment is extremely expensive in proportion to its results. Not only is the criminal justice system very costly to operate, but it is plainly counterproductive in many cases, since punishment typically renders criminals more rather than less likely to commit future crimes. (It is false to the point of obscenity to suggest that what society actually does to criminals under the name of punishment can be justified on the ground that it benefits them by providing them with moral education.)[21] Social and economic measures to reduce the incentives to commit crimes would obviously work much better at much lower social cost, but they are rejected for moral and political reasons.

Probably nothing we could do would come anywhere near to eliminating crime in modern society as it is presently organized. Hegel is aware that ethical corruption is one of the side effects of the subjective freedom fostered by modern civil society, and he realizes that the workings of its market system tend to produce a class of people who are especially prone to commit crimes (*PR* § 244, see Chapter 14, § 9). If the problem for retributivism is that sometimes no just response to crime is available to us, the problem for consequentialists concerned with preventing crime is that as a means of protecting people's rights in modern society punishment is so hideously expensive and so utterly ineffective as to be hopelessly irrational.

Philosophers who try to justify punishment are sometimes taken to task for giving the impression that this is difficult to do, that it is even hard to make rational sense of the institution of punishment.[22] There are, however, good reasons for thinking that the philosophers may not be to blame. Generally speaking, people are not at their best when they have suffered wrong and are under attack. Whether you measure their conduct by standards of morality or those of rational self-interest, they tend to behave very badly. Moreover, there seems to be no reason to expect their collective behavior to be essentially better than their individual behavior in this regard. If the institution of punishment, as it actually exists, represents people's collective response to attacks on their rights, then we should not be too surprised to find it less than rational and less than admirable. Hence we might expect to be unable to make rational sense of punishment or to provide a satisfactory ethical justification for it. Perhaps the most we should expect philosophical theories to prove is that society's behavior toward criminals is not as senseless and outrageous as criminals' behavior toward their victims. If we begin to wonder whether that is enough, maybe philosophy is just doing its job.

III
Morality

7
The concept of morality

1. Development of the concept of morality: Tübigen and Bern (1793–1796)

Perhaps the most well-known feature of Hegel's ethical thought is his distinction between "morality" (*Moralität*) and "ethical life" (*Sittlichkeit*). But is the distinction well understood? One common interpretation is the following: "Morality" for Hegel means Kant's moral philosophy; it represents what is reflective, critical, and individualistic in the moral life. Hegel identifies "ethical life" with ancient Greek society; it stands for an attitude of unthinking, pious devotion to the traditional laws and customs of one's people. Hegel is a partisan of ethical life and an opponent of morality. He favors social conformism and moral traditionalism, and is an opponent of individualism and critical moral thinking.

There is some truth in each of the elements of this picture, but in every case that truth is seriously oversimplified. The picture as a whole (summed up in the last two sentences of the previous paragraph) is a hopeless distortion. The picture comes closest to describing Hegel's views during his Jena period (1801–1806). But Hegel's views about morality and ethical life underwent quite radical changes in the course of his philosophical development, and during the Jena period itself Hegel's conception of morality presents us with a moving target. The best way to begin a discussion of this conception is with a brief account of its evolution.

Hegel's earliest manuscripts, composed while he was a student in Tübingen (1793) and a private tutor in Bern (1794–1796), are ostensibly concerned with religion and its history. Recent scholarship argues that they are Hegel's attempt to sketch an ambitious program of religious and social reform for the age.[1] Hegel's manuscripts exhibit the powerful influence of Kant's moral philosophy, and especially of his newly published *Religion Within the Bounds of Unaided Reason* (1793–1794). Like Kant, Hegel holds that "the essence of all true religion, including our [Christian] religion, is human morality" (*TJ* 105/*ETW* 68). Along with Kant, he is interested in the complex relation of the pure moral religion of reason and freedom to the historical traditions of "statutory faith" (or "positive" religion), which serves as the necessary vehicle of pure moral religion, but against whose superstition and spiritual bondage pure religion has also waged a continual struggle.

In the writings of the young Hegel, the combat between rational religion and positive religion is given a historical dramatis personae. The main protagonists are the beautiful and loving pagan "folk religion" of ancient Greece, the slavish positive religion of Hebrew monotheism, and Jesus' attempt to revolutionize the latter through the introduction of a pure moral religion. Hegel views Greek and Hebrew religion as expressive of radically different social orders. The naïve spiritual self-harmony of the Greeks gives rise to political freedom and to a religion that is simple in its tenets, but powerful in its sensuous imagery and in its public cult, admirably suited to instill in the human heart an enthusiasm for moral virtue. By contrast, the authoritarianism and self-alienation of Hebrew culture show themselves in an utterly positive religion, a cult of servile devotion to a single divine tyrant external to both nature and the human world.

In such a milieu, the religious reform attempted by Jesus could not be the creation of a genuine folk religion in which the individual and the social, the rational and the sensuous, are happily united. Instead, the religion of Jesus is a private, other-worldly moral religion suited to the needs of isolated individuals who have no conception of a free earthly social order. "A folk religion, which produces and nourishes great dispositions, goes hand in hand with freedom. But our [Christian] religion wants to educate human beings to be citizens of heaven, their gaze always directed upward, where human feelings become alien to them" (*TJ* 41–42/*TE* 56).

Hegel is ostensibly writing about the distant historical past, but it is not difficult to recognize, behind their historical masks, the real actors in Hegel's own world whose struggle is his actual concern: the positive, alienated society of the *ancien régime*, the moral individualism of Enlightenment (especially Kantian) philosophy, and the new society of the young Hegel's hopes, free and unified, modeled on his image of a lost Hellenic greatness.

2. Beyond morality: Frankfurt (1796–1800)

In 1796, Hegel moved to a new tutoring position in Frankfurt. At about the same time, his thought about morality took a new turn. "The Spirit of Christianity and Its Fate" (1798–1799) begins with a polemic against the positivity and self-alienation of Hebrew religion, but then directs the same criticisms against Kantian morality. Between the victim of positive religion and the Kantian moralist, he says, "the difference is not that the former makes himself into a servant while the latter is free; instead it is that the former carries his master outside himself, while the latter carries his master within himself and is in bondage to himself" (*TJ* 323/*ETW* 211).

In Kantian morality, the self is never present in its wholeness. Its law is never the law of the whole self, hence never a real autonomy of the will. Kantian morality overcomes the positivity of an external law, but internalizes bondage rather than abolishing it. The empirical self is supposed to respect the law given by reason, but this law is not its own law. It is the a priori law of a supernatural self, dwelling in a supersensible beyond. Consequently, Kantian morality contains within it an "indestructible positivity" which "fills us with indignation" because it pretends to be self-legislation but is really a legislation alien to the empirical self which is expected to obey it (*TJ* 323/ *ETW* 211–212).

For the Frankfurt Hegel, Jesus' teaching is no longer a version of Kantian morality. Now it is an antinomian religion of love that goes *beyond* morality. Jesus preaches not obedience to the moral law but "fulfillment" (*plerōma*) of the law (*TJ* 309, 326/*ETW* 214), a fulfillment that "abolishes [the moral law] as law" and "takes from the laws their lawfulness, their form of law" (*TJ* 324/ *ETW* 212). The spirit of Jesus is "the extinguishing of law and duty in love" (*TJ* 334/*ETW* 223).

In Tübingen and Bern, Hegel still agrees with Kant that "the sole moral incentive is respect for the moral law" (*TJ* 189/*ETW* 144). He regards love as a sensuous principle, hence in itself devoid of moral worth (*TJ* 30/*TE* 46). Love is instrumental to morality only because it inhibits evil inclinations and helps to bring our sensuous nature into harmony with the moral law (*TJ* 12–14/*TE* 32–34; *TJ* 30/*TE* 47). In Frankfurt, however, love is no longer a harmony between the law and inclination, but a state of the soul that transcends and even abolishes their opposition. Love is now "the relation [of law and inclination] as indifferents to one another. . . . Subject and object have lost their opposition, law loses its universality and the subject its particularity" so that "all duties fall away" (*TJ* 325–327/*ETW* 213–215). Love no longer serves morality; it is "a spirit elevated above morality" (*TJ* 324/*ETW* 212).

"The Spirit of Christianity" indicates a hierarchy of spiritual levels. In each we become cognizant of the limits of the previous one, and thereby "cancel" or "supersede" (*aufheben*) it (*TJ* 302, 307–308). The four stages are:

1. Positivity
2. Morality
3. Love
4. Religion

The lowest level is the "positivity" of statutory or ceremonial religion. Kantian morality replaces this unreflective subjection of the mind to something external with the subjection of the senses to the rational command of duty. Love "fulfills" morality through the identity (or "indifference") of reason's law and the desire of sense. Love is "a divine spirit," but it is also limited because it is merely subjective feeling, which requires to be united with the "objective." Love is therefore "fulfilled" by the final stage: "religion . . . the supreme need of the spirit" (*TJ* 406/*ETW* 289). "Religion" in the Frankfurt period anticipates Hegel's later conception of speculative thought, whose function is similarly to provide a supreme reconciliation of subjective and objective, sense and intellect.

In "The Spirit of Christianity" Hegel first articulates some of his most characteristic criticisms of morality:

1. He charges, as we have seen, that morality involves an alienated relation of reason to sense, and in consequence an internalized "positivity," an *unfreedom* (*TJ* 323/*ETW* 211).

2. This leads directly to a second contention, that morality is *impotent* to accomplish the good it intends. Really to do the good, Hegel says, the whole self must be involved, not only abstract reason but also determinate sensuous drives. But morality commands us to act only from respect for the law; for morality, the good will is present "only in the idea, in representation"; the determinate will to do good "is not *actual* in the passive man"; consequently, "the idea of their willing is the opposite of the will; its end is not to will" (*TJ* 300). From this Hegel concludes that morality cannot act, cannot accomplish its ends: It can only judge and condemn (*TJ* 234/*ETW* 222–223). Morality tells us only what "ought to be," whereas love is a "being' (*TJ* 324/*ETW* 212), a unity of sense and reason that actually achieves the good.

3. Hegel brings a third charge against morality: He says that it has an inherent tendency to *hypocrisy*. The good is truly achieved only through the spirit of love; but love does the good freely, spontaneously, without reflection or compulsion. Kantian morality identifies the moral worth of acts with the motive of duty, with a reflection on the act which represents it as something that is done under constraint. But if the pure spirit is the spirit of love, then Kantian morality puts action in a perspective that necessarily renders it impure, and that gives credit for doing the good not to the spontaneous loving disposition but to the subsequent reflection on the action as a "duty." Instead of thinking spontaneously of the good to be done, morality makes us think about our own doings. It concentrates our attention on the reflective apprehension of what we do as something "to be done from duty." The spirit of morality is therefore the hypocritical spirit, the spirit of Pharisaism (*TJ* 332–333/*ETW* 220–221). As Hegel was to put the point several years later in Jena: "Virtue, in transforming itself into morality, becomes necessarily the knowledge of one's own virtue, or in other words, it becomes Pharisaism" (*GW* 426/184).

4. Finally, Hegel also criticizes morality for ignoring, or even suppressing, in favor of this subjective reflection, the healthy relations and social forms within which good actions are done freely and habitually. In place of the rich emotional fabric of social life, with the manifold claims of loyalty and affection they make on us, morality puts a single formal principle, to which we are to be bound by the single abstract motive of duty:

> On account of its form of universality, [duty] makes the hardest pretentions for its one-sidedness. Woe to those human relations that are not found directly in the concept of duty! For because it is not merely the empty thought of universality but must display itself in action, this concept excludes or dominates all other relations. (*TJ* 323/*ETW* 212)

5. Conspicuously absent from the early writings is any explicit statement of what is perhaps Hegel's best known criticism of Kantian morality: the charge that it is an "empty formalism" incapable of providing any "immanent doctrine of duties." Morality's principle has no content; it is incapable of providing any criterion at all for what is morally right and wrong,

and even the most despicable conduct is capable of being reconciled with it. These accusation plainly have an affinity with some of the charges Hegel does make – for instance, with the charge that morality is hypocritical and the charge that morality is "positive" because the motive of duty is separated both from sensuousness and from healthy social relations (*TJ* 323/*ETW* 212). But the "emptiness charge" (as I shall call it) is not actually articulated until Hegel's Jena writings (1801–1802). We will leave aside the emptiness charge for now, since Chapter 9 will be devoted entirely to it.

3. Morality versus ethical life: Jena (1801–1806)

In 1799, Fichte was dismissed from his professorship at Jena on the grounds of "atheism." Hegel's friend Schelling (whose religious views were, if anything, even less orthodox than Fichte's) was appointed to replace him, at the astonishingly early age of 24. The following year, Schelling helped Hegel (then age 30) to gain a post at Jena as *Privatdozent*. In a letter to Schelling of November 2, 1800, Hegel describes how his intellectual development has moved away from "the more subordinate needs of men" and toward speculative metaphysics: "I was driven inevitably toward science, and the ideal of youth had to take the form of reflection and so too of a system" (*B 1* : 59/64). Along with his construction of a speculative system, Hegel's views on morality continued to develop, chiefly in reaction to the ethical writings Fichte produced during his own Jena period (1794–1799).

Hegel's first published essay was *The Difference Between Fichte's and Schelling's System of Philosophy* (1801). In it he makes Fichte the object of his continuing attacks on morality. Here he first articulates the emptiness charge. Its target is Fichte's version of Kantian autonomy. "[For Fichte] 'We obey ourselves' means 'our natural inclination obeys our ethical law' "; Hegel regards this conception of autonomy as "deformed, anxious, oppressed, ugly" (*D* 92–93/153–154). To the "polarity of nature and freedom," and the "unnatural self-suppression" of Fichtean morality, Hegel now opposes not "love" but "an identity as character" – which, he says, is to be found in "the beauty of the soul and of the [art] work" as well as in "the complete and living community of individuals in a congregation (*Gemeinde*)" (*D* 88–90/150–151).

In *Faith and Knowledge* (1802), Hegel coins a new term for this "identity as character," or – as he puts it there – the "true identity of universal and particular, of matter and form." The term is "ethical life" (*Sittlichkeit*) (*GW* 426/183).[2] For the rest of the Jena period, Hegel's ethical thought focuses on the contrast between morality and ethical life. The latter concept is further developed in the essay *On the Ways of Treating Natural Right Scientifically* (1802), in the unpublished fragment *System of Ethical Life* (1802–1803), and in Hegel's lectures of the period (1803–1804, 1805–1806). At the same time, Hegel also refines his concept of morality. He comes to recognize morality as a form of consciousness characteristic of modern social life, best articulated in the moral philosophy of Kant and Fichte.

Ethical life is the "living shape of organic totality" of a community (*NR* 499/108); at the same time, it is the "essence of the individual"; consequently, "the nature of absolute ethical life" includes "the relation of the *individual's* ethical life to *real absolute* ethical life" (*NR* 504/112). (These two sides of ethical life will be discussed, respectively, in Chapters 11 and 12). Considered as the ethical life of a society, it is a totality of social relationships between the occupants of different social and economic roles, forming an interdependent whole.

"Morality" (*Moralität*) is defined as "the *formal* positing, in mutual indifference, of the specific terms of the relation" (*NR* 506/114). The moral standpoint considers an individual's role in ethical life in abstraction from the whole of which it is a part. Moral theories "make being-for-self and individuality into a principle" (*NR* 504/112); they consider everything from the standpoint of the abstracted individual. Though this standpoint should not simply be denied, Hegel insists that it is "inferior" and "one-sided," and cannot be "the absolute standpoint" (*NR* 458–459/74–75, 504/112).

Hegel locates the moral standpoint within the ethical life of modern society. He regards it as "the ethical life of the *bourgeois* or private individual for whom the difference of relations is fixed and who depends on them and is in them" (*NR* 506/114). For Hegel in 1802, the modern bourgeoisie participates in a "universal private life." Its ethical life is not "free" because it is limited to private self-seeking (*NR* 492–493/102–103). In contrast, Hegel regards the nobility as the free estate because its political position relieves it from the need to provide for its own needs, and gives it the vocation for public service as military officers and high government officials. Its ethical life is therefore "a universal life bound up with the public interest" (*NR* 490/100).

The "science" of morality (in Kantian and Fichtean moral theory) is a science of ethical life, viewed from the standpoint of private individuals. It fails to appreciate the specificity of the social relationships because private individuals see these relationships only as a natural expression of their contingent, particular volition. Moral theory involves an awareness of specific ethical relations, but it does not understand them as organic parts of a social whole. Instead, it treats them as something absolute, depending only on the isolated individual. Duties and virtues that belong to determinate bourgeois social roles are "fixed" (a later Marxist jargon would say "reified") and treated as universally binding.

Hegel holds that the real bond of moral duty depends on the way in which duties bear on people's social roles and relationships in the ethical life of a rational social order. The standpoint of morality, however, considers these duties in abstraction from such a system of relationships. Consequently, it is tempted to see them as merely "contingent," yet it must also try to give them the form of "absoluteness" appropriate to a moral demand. This it does by associating them with the formal principle of the absolute self (*NR* 507/114). This is the light in which Hegel interprets the moral fanaticism of Fichte's ethical theory. It is also his diagnosis of the harsh, mechanistic character of

Fichte's conception of the state. Where the vision of a fluid, organic ethical life has been lost, there is nothing left for political philosophy except the abstract opposition of private and public, leading to a "lifeless" (or, as we might now put it, a totalitarian) conception of the state – to a "police state" (*NR* 517–518/124; cf. Fichte *GNR* 291–303/374–387).[3]

In the *Natural Right* essay, Hegel's nascent conception of ethical life is modeled on the classical political theories of Plato and Aristotle. The "free" estate corresponds to the public classes in those theories, to Plato's guardians and Aristotle's free ruling citizenry; the modern bourgeoisie is seen in light of the unfree class of artisans or producers who play no role in the political deliberations of the community (*NR* 489–494/99–104). There is as yet little sign that Hegel sees anything in the bourgeoisie's "universal private life" except a necessary evil, little evidence that he appreciates the positive historical significance of bourgeois subjectivity (cf. *NR* 492/103).

4. The *Phenomenology of Spirit* (1807)

Things have changed again by the end of Hegel's Jena period. Chapter 6 of the *Phenomenology of Spirit,* which attempts to depict a history of spirit's development from ancient Greek culture to Hegel's own time, is structured around the opposition between ethical life and morality, beginning with the "ethical substance" of Greek society and ending with the "moral world-view." Here "morality" is no longer merely a false or one-sided theory of ethical life, nor even an experience of ethical life from a limited (and unfree) social perspective within it. Hegel now sees morality as a standpoint that is characteristic of the modern spirit, in contrast with the noble naïveté of ancient ethical life. More specifically, Hegel describes morality as a spirit that has overcome the self-alienation of the world of Christian faith and undergone the "culture" (*Bildung*) of the early modern period, achieving an awareness of the individual self as identical with the universal law of reason.

> [Morality is] *absolute mediation,* like the consciousnesses of culture and faith; for it is essentially the movement of the self to supersede the abstraction of *immediate existence* and to become universal for itself – but neither through a pure alienation and disruption of itself and actuality nor through a flight. Instead it is *present* to itself *immediately* in its substance, for this substance is its knowledge, it is the intuited pure certainty of itself. (*PhG* ¶ 597)

In the *Phenomenology,* Hegel plainly sees modern morality as an advance on ancient ethical life; but he has still not abandoned his earlier view that morality is at the same time a one-sided view of ethical life. This leaves an unresolved tension in Hegel's ethical thought: the *systematic* superiority of ethical life versus the *historical* superiority of morality. Instead of resolving the tension, Hegel provides a critique of the moral standpoint, exhibiting the limitations of finite spirit as a whole and pointing to the awareness of absolute spirit in religious consciousness. It is not until Hegel's return to university teaching a decade later that he attempts to present a picture of modern ethical life with which moral consciousness has been fully and positively reconciled.

5. Subjectivity

Hegel's Jena writings tell us that morality is a standpoint characteristic of the modern world. The moral standpoint is limited, but not false. These writings make no real attempt, however, to show how morality is a *positive* (if limited) aspect of ethical life. Nor do they provide an account of a specifically modern ethical life in which morality is supposed to play a decisive role. Both these tasks are left to Hegel's mature ethical writings, beginning with the Heidelberg *Encyclopedia* and culminating in the *Philosophy of Right*.

It is no accident that Hegel begins to provide a more positive account of morality exactly when he starts to provide a theory of civil society. Already in the *Natural Right* essay, Hegel identified morality as the ethical life of the bourgeois. What is new in the ethical writings after 1816 is Hegel's awareness that the bourgeois moral attitude represents something unique to modern ethical life that constitutes the essential superiority of modern European culture (the "Germanic world"). In Hegel's mature writings, there are still recognizably Kantian and Fichtean elements in the presentation of morality, but they are reworked to give an account of a moral standpoint which, within its proper sphere, Hegel is prepared fully to endorse.

The distinguishing characteristic of modern social life is "subjectivity"; the moral standpoint is the standpoint of the "subject." This standpoint may be difficult for us to grasp in its specificity, because it may be hard for us to see how there could be any real alternatives to it. Subjectivity is simply the standpoint of any individual agent. The will of the subject, as Hegel says, is just "the form of all willing" (*PR* § 108). Yet Hegel thinks that consciousness of myself as a subject is something distinctive, culturally specific, and historically recent. Like the awareness of myself as a person, it requires abstraction. To take the moral standpoint seriously, as Hegel thinks we do in the modern world, we must regard our subjectivity as vitally important to our identity.

Subjectivity is abstract, but less so than personality. Personality, which includes only my formal or abstract freedom, excludes those very features that make up the content of my self-consciousness as this determinate rational agent. In contrast, subjectivity is "the reflection of the will into itself and its identity for itself" (*PR* § 105). To be a subject is to be aware of oneself as the particular, contingent individual that one is, but at the same time to relate all the particular things one happens to be to one's capacities as a free and rational being, and to regard one's exercise of these capacities as the core or foundation of one's identity as a self.

Hegel makes this point by describing subjectivity as a reflective identity of universality and particularity. More precisely, subjectivity is the "movement" by which these universal and particular sides of the self are made identical, experienced as harmonious aspects of the same self. Subjectivity is the task of "working this ground of freedom," transforming "abstract" subjectivity into "concrete" subjectivity by making it "objective" and "equal to its concept" (*PR* § 106R). As a subject, I am, on the one side, a free agent in the abstract, whose will falls under the universally valid standards of practical rationality. On the other side, I am this particular individual, with needs and desires peculiarly my own. I actualize myself as a subject when I bring these two sides together by making my particular volitions rational and by giving my abstract rationality a determinate individual content by turning its universal principles into my particular ends and actions.

The task of subjectivity is thus the (Kantian) project of bringing my willing into conformity with a universal rational principle, so that it "accords with the will in itself" or has "the objectivity of the concept" (*PR* § 111). The universal side of subjectivity thus takes the form of an "ought" (*PR* §§ 108, 113), legislating to the particular side. For all we have seen thus far, however, this "ought" might consist only in the regulation of my will by rational self-interest. Principles of prudence are "universal" and "objective" in the sense that they are binding on any and every subject whose self-interest is in question: They have what we may call a *universality of applicability*. There is nothing "universal" about the scope of the interests such principles promote: These interests are solely mine. They do not involve what we might call a *universality of concern*. If the universal "ought" belonging to subjectivity is to be a recognizably *moral* ought, then it must be shown to have universality of concern, not merely universality of applicability.

6. The moral ought and objectivity

Hegel moves from universality of applicability to universality of concern through the idea that the subjective will seeks to make itself "objective," seeking to bring about external states of affairs. Like all stages in the development of right, morality involves the will's giving "existence" to itself or "being with itself in an other." Where the person's existence-in-otherness is existence in an external thing, Hegel (apparently piling paradox on paradox) describes the moral will as one that "is to have itself for its existence" (*VPR19* : 91). In other words, the "other" in which the will is to be "with itself" is supposed to be just its own inner willing.

Willing itself, Hegel insists, is a process of "translating the subjective end into objectivity" (*PR* § 8). The self as subject is not just a bundle of desires, or even a clearinghouse for selecting actions to satisfy desires. The task of the subject is to bring about objective results that manifest its subjectivity, and thereby confirm its own freedom or being with itself. The ends of the subject are never merely "subjective"; they always reach out into the objective world. Although we judge our actions morally as expressions of our subjectivity, our subjectivity itself exists only by showing itself in actions with external results (*PR* §§ 108–110).

This point leads us from subjectivity to universality of concern. To embody my subjectivity in an external object is to "supersede the immediacy of this subjectivity, along with its character as my individual subjectivity"; it is therefore to posit at the same time "an external subjectivity which is identical with me," or, in other words, "the will of others. . . . The carrying out of my end thus has in itself the identity of my will and another's will – it has a *positive* reference to the will of others" (*PR* § 112). "The external existence of the subject is essentially the will of another" (*VPR* 2 : 397).

Hegel's argument here is terse and obscure. It may even seem sophistical, a mere play on words – as if "my subjective will externalized" (i.e., expressed in something external) meant the same as "an external subjective will" (the subjective will of another). The substantial idea behind it is that since my end as a subject is not merely subjective satisfaction but an external result, it follows that my rational concern as a subject is essentially about external or public objects. Such objects are there for others as well as for myself. These others are subjects, too, with desires and interests of their own. Because my subjectivity is actualized only in what is present for these others, the universality (or rationality) of what I do must take account of the interests of others as well as my interests. Their standpoint on the rationality of what I do is equal to my standpoint. Hence the universal concept of subjectivity which serves as an ought must include a universality of concern as well as a universality of applicability.

Hegel distinguishes three related senses in which the moral subject seeks "objectivity." He makes this threefold distinction explicitly, and at some length (*PR* §§ 110–112, 112R, 113). First, the subject seeks an "external existence" in which its subjective end becomes a real object. Second, it seeks objectivity in the sense of that which is universally binding or adequate to the universal concept of the subject (what I have called "universality of applicability"). Third, it seeks objectivity or universality in the sense of something that involves the will of others, of all subjects ("universality of concern"). Hegel goes on to infer that the moral good, whose content is the satisfaction of particularity or "well-being" (*Wohl*), must not be considered only as the subject's own well-being, but it must be thought of ("though quite emptily") as "the well-being of all" (*PR* § 125) or "universal well-being" (*PR* § 130).

None of this settles any questions about how far rational universality requires me to weigh the interests of others against my own interests. It tells us nothing about the degree to which one moral subject ought to contribute to the well-being of others, and is minimally consistent with the supposition that, all things considered, each subject ought to provide exclusively for her own well-being and take no thought for that of the others. Hegel's argument provides for a universality of concern only in the minimal sense that it removes the presumption that subjectivity concerns solely the subject's own well-being. Beyond that, Hegel thinks that morality leaves indeterminate how we are to weigh the interests of different subjects against one another.

This limited conclusion of Hegel's argument accords perfectly with his intentions. It is Hegel's position that the moral standpoint provides us with no determinate criteria of action, no determinate concept of the moral good. These are supplied only by the more concrete social relationships of ethical life. It is Hegel's habit to apply the term "moral" to those cases of other-concern which are not determinately structured by the relations of ethical life – for example, contingent acts of private charity toward the needy (cf. *PR* §§ 207, 242). From the standpoint of morality, the only important thing is that the *possibility* of concern for others' well-being should be recognized as integral to the project of actualizing the moral subject's freedom.

7. Subjectivity and action

"The identity of inner and outer" is one of the principles of Hegelian speculative logic (*WL 6* : 179–185/523–528; *EL* § 138). As applied to morality, Hegel interprets this principle as saying that the inwardness of willing must be judged by outer actions:

> What a human being is externally, i.e. in his actions . . ., he is inwardly, and if he is virtuous, moral, etc. *only* inwardly, i.e. *only* in his intentions or dispositions and his externality is not identical with this, then the one is as hollow and empty as the other. (*EL* § 140)
> What the subject is, is the series of his actions. If these are a series of worthless productions, then the subjectivity of his willing is just as worthless. But if the series of his deeds is of a substantial nature, then so it is also with the will of the individual. (*PR* § 124)

Hegel does not deny that people can conceal their intentions (*VG* 66/57), or that in particular cases they may fail to achieve what they intend, owing to unfavorable circumstances (*EL* § 140A). This means only that we should judge an individual's inner willing by the *overall* pattern of outward deeds, just as these deeds are always to be interpreted as the expression of a determinate inner volition: "What a man does is to be considered not in its immediacy but only as mediated through his inwardness and as a manifestation of his inwardness. Only here we must not overlook the fact that the essence and the inwardness confirm themselves only by stepping forward as appearance" (*EL* § 112A).

Part of what Hegel has in mind in these passages is expressed by Kant when he says that the good will is "not a mere wish, but the summoning of every means in our power" (*G* 394/10). People get no moral credit for mere wishes, and I need not trouble to congratulate myself on the "good intentions" that I find in myself but have never gotten around to acting on. But Hegel's position goes further than Kant's in the same direction, and is at odds with it in important ways.

Kant famously holds that the beneficial consequences of the good will, like the setting of a jewel, serve only to display it more favorably. They add nothing to its inner worth, which would not suffer at all if the good will failed completely to achieve the good results at which it aims (*G* 394/10). Kant distinguishes between the *satisfaction* we may take in the achievement of our purposes and the *contentment* we feel in ourselves when we are aware of having a good will – whether or not we succeed in accomplishing the good that we will (*TL* 386–387/46–47).

In this distinction Hegel sees the moralist's tendency to hypocrisy. The good will is supposed to consist in a concernful striving toward a good end. But if I fail to achieve the end, the moralist says, I may still feel perfectly content with myself, simply on account of my good will. Hegel wonders how far it can be consistent for me to feel such contentment when I have failed to achieve the end to which I was supposedly so devoted. To him it appears as if the moralist's struggle to actualize the good is really a sham-fight, which we dare not take seriously for fear of exposing our inner virtue to the assaults of evil (*PhG* ¶ 385).

The natural Kantian reply to Hegel at this point is to say that we can surely distinguish between my standpoint as an agent concerned to realize the good and my standpoint as judge of my actions and their inherent worth. Likewise, we can distinguish between the possession of a good will, which is up to me and my responsibility, and the success or failure of my efforts to actualize the good, which may not be my fault. As moralist I may feel disappointment and regret at not having accomplished my noble ends, but I may nevertheless be aware that my failure was not my fault, and so I may be content with myself as a virtuous moral subject, even if I am not satisfied with the wicked course of the world which has frustrated me.

Hegel's point, however, is that there are limits on how far we can press these two distinctions, especially when we take them in tandem. Admittedly a type of striving that generally leads to the good may, through no fault of the agent, fail to achieve it in a particular case. In Chapter 8, we will see that Hegel thinks I am not always to blame for the consequences of my actions, especially when I did not know they would occur. But Hegel holds that I am responsible for whatever belongs to my action by its very nature, and the nature of my action often involves the complex external circumstances in which I act. If the *nature* of my actions is such that they do not produce good results, then I cannot save the goodness of my will by hiding behind the profession of my good intentions.

Consider the following scenario:[4] Some moralists are sincerely concerned about the needy and oppressed of the world. They make great efforts and sacrifices to relieve their sufferings and bring them freedom and dignity. But suppose the system of oppression anticipates their charitable work, and knows how to exploit their efforts to its advantage. It has its own devices for extracting all the fruits, leaving the intended beneficiaries with none. Suppose, further, that receiving charity humiliates and demoralizes the poor, so that they are even easier prey to their oppressors. As a result, the moralists have accomplished nothing of their aims. They have enriched the exploiters, while the people they intended to help are even worse off than before.

Appealing to the Kantian distinction between the good will and its results, these moralists lay the blame for their failure entirely on the system that perverted their well-intentioned efforts, and the evil wills of those who have successfully thwarted their aims. If our motives are pure, they tell themselves, then, our consciences may be clear; the sad results of our efforts need not diminish our inner self-contentment.

Hegel's judgment is less consoling. If "the truth of the intention is just the deed itself" (*PhG* ¶ 159), then we must regard the subjectivity of these moralists as implicated in the results of their actions. The moral significance of their intentions must be interpreted in light of the natural consequences of the actions which manifest them. If our intentions issue in actions that natu-rally produce bad results, then we have *bad* intentions. The moralists are guilty of hypocrisy when they squander all their regret on the external world, leaving none for their own subjectivity.

Kant says that the good will without any good results "shines like a jewel, having its full value in itself" (G 394/10). In place of this, Hegel puts: "The laurels of mere willing are dry leaves that never have been green" (PR § 124A). He rejects the view that "presupposes a gap *(Bruch)* between what is objective in the action and what is inner, subjective in its motives" in favor of "the higher *moral* standpoint which finds satisfaction in the action itself" (PR § 121A). If I will to achieve some end, then I can be truly content with my willing only if the end is accomplished. There is no such thing as a purely inner volitional state, immune to the world of actions and consequences. The self-contentment found in such states is nothing but typical moralistic hypocrisy.

8

The moral will

1. Imputability

Morality is concerned with the subjective, but subjectivity is actual only insofar as it makes itself objective. The consequences of what I do are not appended accidentally to my moral subjectivity. They are its actuality, and it is from them that I must learn the meaning of what I am as a moral subject. It is equally true that from a moral standpoint I am interested in my actions and their consequences *only* insofar as they express my subjectivity. Hence from the moral standpoint it is important to decide for which external events my subjective will can be held accountable.

Anything I do changes the world in some way, or at least contributes to such changes. Hegel says that I "am responsible for" *(Schuld bin an)* any event in which my doing *(Tun)* is causally involved (*PR* § 115); but not everything for which I am responsible (in this causal sense) may be "imputed" *(zugerechnet, imputiert)* to me, treated as an expression of my subjective will. Hegel distinguishes my "deed" *(Tat)* from my "action" *(Handlung)*. Action consists only of that part or aspect of what I effect that lies in my conscious knowledge. This part or aspect of my deed Hegel calls my "purpose" *(Vorsatz)* (*PR* § 117). The extent of the consequences of my action lying within my purpose depends on my "representation" *(Vorstellung)* of the circumstances and of the likely results of what I did. If factors beyond my ken drive my action on to further consequences, then Hegel says I have the right to repudiate all consequences except the first one, since it alone lay in my purpose (*PR* § 118). Because my purpose depends in this way on my knowledge *(Wissen)*, Hegel also describes the right to repudiate alien consequences as the "right of knowledge" *(Recht des Wissens)* (*PR* § 117). Hegel contrasts the modern, subjective view of the scope of moral responsibility (recognizing the right of knowledge) with the "noble simplicity" *(Gediegenheit)* of the ancient Greeks, who had not yet attained the moral standpoint (*VG* 71/62). The Greeks thus accepted responsibility for the full compass of their deeds, even for things they did in ignorance or madness (as in the case of tragic heroes such as Oedipus and Ajax) (*PR* §§ 117A, 118R; *NP* 223–224; *PhG* ¶¶ 468–470).

Hegel clearly uses "purpose" *(Vorsatz)* in a highly technical sense. The "purpose" of my action includes not only those consequences at which I expressly aim, but also those whose occurrence I foresee in acting, even if I do not desire them at all. If I use my red flag to alter the path of a charging bull so that instead of goring your child it tramples your petunias, Hegel counts as part of my "purpose" not only the preservation of your child's life, but also the destruction of your petunias.

Further, Hegel counts as part of my purpose even consequences that I may not have known about, if they belong to "the nature of the action itself" (*PR* § 118R). In general, the "nature" of a thing for Hegel is what we grasp from rational reflection upon it and its connection with other things (*EL* § 23). In the case of an action, these connections are consequences (*VPR19*: 94; *PR* § 118). The nature of an action thus consists in those consequences of it that would be known by rational reflection: "In general it is important to think about the consequences of an action because in this way one does not stop with the immediate standpoint but goes beyond it. Through a many-sided consideration of the action, one will be led to the nature of the action" (*NP* 230).

Hegel apparently intends this to deal with cases like that of an arsonist who sets fire only to one house (or to one stick of furniture), but ends up burning up a whole neighborhood (*PR* § 119A). Hegel insists that the fully developed consequences of the act belong to the arsonist's purpose, because it belongs to the nature of an act of arson that the fire may spread out of control: "The *dolus directus* or direct purpose is, for example, setting fire to the first piece of wood, and the *dolus indirectus* contains all the further consequences. These belong to the nature of the action itself, which posits their possibility along with it. The man must know this" (*VPR 4*: 326; cf. *EG* § 505).[1]

An agent's "purpose" tells us which events are imputable to that agent, but it does not tell us everything we need in order to judge the agent's subjectivity. It tells us that both the saving of your child and the trampling of your petunias belong to my purpose. But the two results are related to my subjectivity in very different ways: One is the desired end of my action, the other a regrettable consequence I incur reluctantly for the sake of that end. This difference is important for understanding the two results as expressions of my subjectivity.

As a subject, Hegel says, I am a thinker, and so I bring my actions under a "universal," which Hegel calls the action's "intention" *(Absicht)*. By "universal" Hegel does not mean merely some general description under which my action may be brought ("burning," "killing"), but the whole complex of consequences that an act sets in motion, organized in a certain way by thought (*PR* § 119; *EG* § 505). Hegel points out that etymologically the word *Absicht* ("looking away") implies the abstraction of a particular side of a concrete deed (*PR* § 119R). The moral he draws from this is that the agent's intention is the aspect of the action that constitutes its "subjective essence" and explains why the subject did it (*PR* § 121A).

To put the point in non-Hegelian jargon, the "intention" of an action is its "desirability characterization" or the "description under which" the agent desires to perform it. Or again, we could say that the Hegelian intention is the "internal reason" for the action, the reason that explains why the subject did it.[2] For instance, my intention in waving the flag at the bull was to save your child, not to destroy your petunias. Hegel thinks that as moral subjects we have the right that our actions be judged under the appropriate intentional descriptions.

This "right of intention," as Hegel calls it, has two parts: First, an act can be imputed to me under a certain description only if I understand that description. A child too young to have any concept of property or immodesty cannot be guilty of theft or indecent exposure. The right of intention "carries with it a total, or a lesser, capacity on the part of children, imbeciles, the insane, etc. to have their actions imputed to them" (*PR* § 120R). Second, I have the right that my actions be considered in light of my intention in performing it. Destroying your petunias belonged to my "purpose" but not to my "intention," which is to save your child. It is my right of subjectivity to have my action evaluated morally in that light.

As in the case of an act's purpose, however, when we judge an act's intention we must take into account that a responsible agent is a thinker who must understand the nature of the action. Hence the right of intention is *not* a right to accept responsibility for an action *only* in terms of some preferred description. I must also accept responsibility for what I do under those descriptions that, as a rational agent, I ought to have known. Consequently, Hegel says that the right of intention corresponds to "the right of *objectivity* of the action, as it might be called, to assert itself as known and willed by the subject as a *thinking* being" (*PR* § 120). This means that if an act of mine violates a law or an ethical duty, or harms another individual, I am responsible for it under that description as well as under the description that supplies the reason for my doing it. Hegel cannot mean that these are all descriptions under which I *desired* the action. We must consider all the descriptions under which I knew (or should have known) the action to fall in their specific relation to my ends and desires. In a sense, then, the universal "trampling the petunias" is also part of my intention, but not in the same way as "saving the child."

2. Moral luck and negligence

One view of moral responsibility makes the agent responsible originally or fundamentally not for objective happenings in the world, but for the agent's own subjective states of willing or trying, whether or not they have any external consequences at all. It treats moral responsibility as a function of what morality may demand of us. We are responsible for doing only what lies within our control, and strictly speaking only our inner volitions are within our control. On this view it is not a simple matter to make sense of assertions to the effect that I am responsible for something that happens *in the world* (e.g., an accidental death, the prevention of a war) as distinct from what happens in my voluntary mental life (e.g., my trying or not trying to prevent an accident, my efforts to prevent the war). On such views, my responsibility for external events has to be indirect. These events are treated only as consequences of inner volitional doings or omittings, under the close supervision of some "ought implies can" principle.

Hegel's theory of responsibility, by contrast, makes the agent directly and originally responsible for external occurrences. This theory identifies my willing with the subjective side of an objective occurrence. My subjective willing is known through the interpretation of what it accomplishes, and has no actual existence in abstraction from that. Morality is interested in the subjective will; indeed, it is interested in nothing else. But Hegel thinks that the subjective will does not exist at all in separation from external deeds. Mere strivings or intendings, in abstraction from the actions that express them, are too inchoate and ambiguous to be objects of moral assessment. The significance of an intention can be grasped only when it is the intention of *this* act, with *these* consequences. An intention with no consequences at all has, in any case, only marginal significance. Deprived of its setting, Kant's jewel turns to glass.

Hegel's theory of responsibility plainly allows for a degree of "moral luck." It concedes that our inner moral worth is vulnerable to the hazards befalling our outward actions.[3] In Hegel's view, this is simply a consequence of the fact that our intentions have actuality only as embodied in the external world, where contingency is inevitable (*WL 6*: 544/820). "An old proverb rightly says, 'A stone once thrown is the devil's.' When I act, I allow for bad luck; so it has a right over me and is an existence of my own willing" (*PR* § 119A). The only way to keep your inner intentions free from the vagaries of good or bad fortune is to avoid acting on them at all; that is not moral purity, only hypocrisy (cf. *PhG* ¶¶ 658–660). Moral agents who understand the nature of subjectivity do not attempt to flee from contingency; they accept it as a condition of the possibility of expressing their subjectivity.

Karl-Heinz Ilting claims that Hegel's theory of responsibility makes no provision for a distinction between the foreseeable and unforeseeable consequences of actions, and cannot handle cases of responsibility due to negligence.[4] This judgment attends too one-sidedly to Hegel's insistence on the importance of the agent's knowledge and intention, without noticing his complementary remarks to the effect that we may impute to the agent whatever belongs to the nature of the action. If I am responsible for the nature of what I do, and if that includes the consequences that would be known by rational consideration of the action, then this entails that I am responsible for foreseeable consequences (but not unforeseeable ones). It also makes me responsible for consequences I *should* have foreseen and for my actions under descriptions that I *should* have known (but in fact did not know) to be true of them. In short, Hegel's theory makes me responsible not only for what I did while (in the usual sense) purposing or intending it, but also for what I knew would occur as a result of what I did, and even for what I did not know would occur if its occurrence would have been anticipated by a thoughtful or rational consideration of the action in light of the circumstances. That surely takes in everything we usually mean by culpable negligence.

Ilting may still have a point, though. Hegel's theory might be faulted for incompleteness regarding these distinctions. It distinguishes between what falls within the agent's "purpose" and what does not; and within that purpose, it enables us to say what belongs to the agent's "intention." This allows us to judge differently an agent who causes a death intentionally and one who causes a death knowingly but without desiring the death for its own sake. But does it account for the difference between the moral blame we would direct to the latter agent and the blame we would direct to an agent who causes a death unintentionally and without knowledge, but with culpable negligence?

Hegel remarks that someone who fires a gun into the woods, meaning to hit an animal but killing a human being, is guilty of manslaughter rather than murder (*VPR 2*: 423, *3*: 358, cf. *VPR 17*: 78). But it is unclear how his theory will draw such distinctions. The only questions on which it focuses are whether the death should fall within the agent's "purpose" and what the agent's "intention" was in acting. Issues of negligence and culpable ignorance usually also depend on the answers to other, quite different questions. How carefully did the hunter examine the thicket before firing into it? Whatever his knowledge and intention, why was he so reckless as to fire at something he couldn't see clearly?

Perhaps one reason Hegel tends to ignore these questions is that he does not always succeed in distinguishing issues of moral responsibility, judgment, and blame from issues of legal culpability. One sign of this is that Hegel's most immediate application of the proverb "A stone once thrown is the devil's" is to provide a rationale for a charge of felony murder in a case where an arsonist unintentionally causes someone's death (*PR* § 119R). Another sign of it is that Hegel sandwiches between "purpose" and "intention" a discussion of my "liability" *(Haftung)* for harm or damage caused to others or their property by things, animals, or children who are in my charge (*PR* § 116; *VPR 17*: 77–78; *VPR 3*: 356, *4*: 314). Hegel himself notes that there is an important difference between legal and moral imputability (*PR* § 113R), but he cannot be credited with explaining the distinction, or even with any great care in attending to it.

These are problems not so much with Hegel's theory of imputability itself as with its formulation and application. Hegel's theory holds us responsible for an occurrence if it gives outward existence to our subjective will. Because (as Hegel emphasizes) we are thinking beings, certain defects in our understanding have to be regarded as defects of our subjectivity. This plainly allows for the possibility of imputing negligent actions to people not only because they were not sufficiently motivated to acquire the knowledge they should have had, but also simply because they didn't know what a thinking subject should have known under the circumstances.

3. The good

The end of morality is the good, "freedom realized, the absolute final end of the world" (*PR* § 129). Hegel locates the good within the moral sphere because there the actuality and self-determination of the free will are found in their particularization (*WL 6*: 543/819). It is in the moral subject that the universal is united with the particular, achieving individuality (*PR* § 7). In other words, Hegel thinks that the self-actualization of reason in the world occurs only in and through the acts of self-conscious individual human subjects (cf. *VG* 78–110/68–93). To be sure, Hegel holds that I most fully actualize myself when I am devoted to higher ends than my own particular satisfaction; and the highest such end is the state (*PR* § 258). Nevertheless, these higher ends belong to the good, "the final end of the world," only because they are set as rational ends by free moral subjects who actualize themselves in pursuing the good. Moreover, the substance of these higher ends consists in the right and the well-being of individuals (*PR* § 265A; see Chapter 1, § 3). We should keep these points in mind when people tell us that Hegel's philosophy submerges the human individual in social collectives or abstract speculative universals.

The subject's actualization takes place when its universal rationality receives fulfillment through the satisfaction of its particularity. To this satisfaction Hegel gives the name of "well-being" *(das Wohl)* or happiness (*PR* § 123R; cf. Chapter 3, § 5). Well-being includes not only the satisfaction of our particular desires as natural beings, but also the "self-satisfaction" accompanying the success of projects in which we take an interest, even when the projects themselves are entirely unselfish (*PR* § 123). For Hegel as for Kant, the content of the good consists in rational agents' successful accomplishment of their ends, including the satisfaction of their natural needs (*G* 413/30).[5]

For both philosophers, well-being is a good only conditionally. Kant holds that the condition of its goodness is virtue or goodness of will. That is, I am worthy of well-being or happiness when I am virtuous enough (*G* 393/61; *KpV* 110/115; *TL* 481/155). Kant takes this position because he regards the moral agent as subject to an a priori law telling us which maxims to adopt prior to any end. The moral end (the good) is simply the ends determined by these morally required maxims. Goodness of will is the supreme or unconditioned end involved in morally legislative maxims; the well-being of rational agents is the conditioned end.

It is not open to Hegel to follow Kant's conception of the good at this point, even if he wanted to. As we shall see presently, Hegel conceives of the good will as the will whose insight and intention accord with the good (*PR* § 131). Given that conception of the good will, the Kantian conception of the good would involve him in a vicious circularity, because we would need a conception of the good in order to give content to the unconditioned component of the good. Instead of saying that good will or virtue is the condition for the worth of well-being, Hegel holds that well-being is good whenever it is consistent with abstract right (*PR* § 126; *VPR17*: 83), which (as we have seen) is independent of well-being.

For Hegel, then, right and well-being are lexically ordered.[6] Human happiness is something good, but only on the condition that no right is violated in acquiring it. The lexical ordering of the right and well-being is mitigated by the "right of necessity" (see Chapter 5, § 5) and in another way also: "Well-being is not something good without the *right*. Likewise, the right is not the good without well-being; *fiat justitia* [Do justice] should not have *pereat mundus* [though the world perish] as its consequence" (*PR* § 130). Well-being is subordinated to right, but the good requires that it be there just the same. A world of unhappy people who punctiliously respect one another's rights is not a good world.

4. Kant on the good will

It is illuminating to compare Hegel's conception of the good will with Kant's more famous one. This section discusses Kant's conception of the good will, in order to facilitate the comparison, which will occupy us for the rest of this chapter.

Kant distinguishes actions that are merely "according to duty" *(pflichtmäss-ig)* from actions that are done "from duty" *(aus Pflicht)*. Only the latter have moral worth and exhibit a good will, the only thing in the world or beyond it that is good without qualification (*G* 397–399/13–16; *KpV* 81/84; *TL* 389/50). To do an action from duty is to do it out of respect for the moral law, rather than from any inclination or from any liking for the actual, expected, or intended consequences of the action (*G* 399–401/16–17). Some actions accord with duty but are done from feelings of love and sympathy. They are fine *(schön)* and amiable *(liebenswürdig)*, deserving of praise and encouragement, but devoid of moral worth, and not deserving of esteem *(Hochschät-zung)* (*KpV* 82/85; cf. *G* 397–399/13–16).

We may be misled by Kant's claim that there is "no moral worth" in actions that accord with duty but are not done from duty. Kant clearly does not accept Fichte's more extreme view that all acts (even those commanded by the moral law) are *morally wrong* unless they are done from the motive of duty (*SL* 154/162–163, 310/326, 315–316/330). Kant asserts that these acts are fine, deserving of praise, and that they should be encouraged. These are plainly *moral* judgments about these acts, and they attribute *worth* to the acts. However, Kant wants to distinguish from this general moral approval a special sort of moral esteem belonging only to acts done from duty.

Sometimes both duty and inclination speak in favor of the same course of action. Here it makes an important moral difference to Kant whether we act from duty or from inclination. We need not forego the satisfaction of our inclinations. We may even have this as part of our *end*. But in our *motivation,* we ought to "abstract *(absondern)* ourselves from all incentives of inclination, so as to act solely from duty, and not from inclination (*TP* 278–279/64–65). The motive of duty is wholly distinctive for Kant because only in actions done from duty do we exercise our freedom – our capacity to act autonomously as beings independent of and superior to the natural or sensible world (*KpV* 86–87/89–90).

Kant's views here are striking, in some ways extreme. But it is easy (almost traditional) for Kant's readers to exaggerate their austerity. Kant does not think that it is desirable, or even possible, that every act should be done from duty, since he does not think that every action is even a candidate for moral worth. An action is a candidate for moral worth only if duty requires it (or if we look at its performance as a case of refraining from some other specific action that is contrary to duty); when we have a choice between two or more morally permissible actions, we inevitably make it on grounds other than duty. To want every one of our actions to have moral worth would be to want (in Kant's words) to "strew all our steps with duties," a wish whose fulfillment, according to Kant, would turn the "dominion" *(Herrschaft)* of virtue into a "tyranny" (*TL* 409/71).[7]

Even in cases where duty bids us do something, Kant does not think that we are required to act *solely* from duty. He thinks it is our duty to *strive* to make the thought of duty our sole and sufficient motive; but he holds that we may fulfill this duty even if our striving is not perfectly successful.[8] Kant does hold that perfect virtue, after which we do have a duty to strive, consists in performing morally lawful actions solely or purely from the motive of duty, without the need of any cooperating inclinations (*TL* 391–392/52–53; *KpV* 84–85/87–88; *R* 30/25). Thus those actions that accord with duty but are not done purely from duty – and which therefore deserve both praise and encouragement – are nevertheless viewed by Kant as exhibiting the "impurity" of the human will, the second of the three degrees of radical evil in human nature (*R* 29–30/25).

For Kant, my will is "pure," only where "no incentives of inclinations are the determining grounds influencing an action done as a duty" (*KpV* 160/165). The pure will does not necessarily lack nonmoral *incentives,* but it succeeds in abstracting itself from them in its motivation. In the pure will, the moral motive is not only strong enough to account for the agent's performance of the act in those particular circumstances, but also strong enough that the agent would still perform the dutiful action even if every conceivable nonmoral incentive stood opposed to doing it.

Kant invites us to imagine an honest man asked by a wicked sovereign to give false testimony against an innocent person (Kant's example is Anne Boleyn, falsely accused by King Henry VIII) (*KpV* 155/159). First the honest man is offered bribes and inducements to join in the unjust calumny. When he declines them, he is threatened with the loss of the affection of his friends and family, with the deprivation of his every happiness, even with the loss of his freedom and his life itself, if he refuses. True purity of will is to be found only in those who do their duty in such a way that they would still do it even in such an extreme situation (*KpV* 155–156/159–160). For Kant, we can have a good will without actually *having* a pure will in this sense; but to have a good will we must *strive* to the best of our ability after such purity of will in every act where duty is at stake (even in situations where no threats or enticements are present).

Kant famously denies a good will to the shopkeeper who serves customers honestly because he finds that honesty is good business. He does not mean that merely having the *incentive* of self-interest is sufficient to disqualify the shopkeeper from having a good will and performing acts of moral worth. The shopkeeper's action would have had moral worth if in the particular case he had acted from duty rather than from self-interest (i.e., if he had abstracted himself from considerations of self-interest, and striven for purity of will). A good will requires only that the agent should so abstract from nonmoral motives as to make the motive of duty *predominant* over them in the performance of this particular action.[9]

Kant's conception of the good will seems to be founded on the idea that genuine moral worth, the kind of worth that alone truly deserves esteem, could never depend on anything except our own use of our freedom. Thus Kant describes moral worth of character as the worth we *give ourselves,* as distinct from the various kinds of worth, such as talents of mind and qualities of temperament, which we might be given by nature or fortune (*G* 393/9, 398/15). Kant argues that true moral worth belongs only to actions done from duty on the ground that the lawfulness of actions done out of inclination is merely "contingent and spurious, for though the nonmoral ground may indeed now and then produce lawful actions, more often it brings about unlawful ones" (*G* 390/6).

This argument rests on a very dubious premise if it denies that people could ever be so happily constituted by nature or education that their inclinations reliably incline them toward lawful actions and away from unlawful ones. But Kant might mean that actions done from inclinations are only "contingently" lawful in a different sense. He might mean that their lawfulness (however reliable) is due only to good fortune and not to what I have made of myself through my own work alone. The true inner worth of a person, however, cannot be the result of good or bad fortune; it cannot vary with favorable or unfavorable natural endowment or circumstances. It must be up to each of us alone to give it to ourselves; and in respect of it, nature and fortune must place us all in exactly equal circumstances.

This concern to exclude the possibility of "moral luck" also explains why Kant insists that the good will consists of striving for purity of volition rather than in attaining it; for some people may be more happily constituted than others in this regard, and may have less work to do to achieve a given degree of purity. But the duty to strive to one's utmost for purity leaves everyone in the same situation. Likewise, it explains why Kant insists that even in comfortable circumstances we must strive to make the motive of duty so powerful in ourselves that it could withstand even the tyrant's threats and promises. After all, it is only good luck that separates us at any time from that unenviable position: "How many people who have lived long and guiltless lives may not be merely *fortunate* enough to have escaped many temptations?" (*TL* 392/52).

5. Hegel on the good will

Hegel describes the good will as one whose "insight and intention accord with the good" (*PR* § 131). My "insight" accords with the good if I have

148

reasonable and correct beliefs about what is good and about which actions further the good. My "intention" accords with the good if I believe that the description "furthers the good" applies to my action, and if my action's satisfaction of this description gives me a sufficient (internal) reason to act as I do.

From the moral standpoint, Hegel says, an action that accords with the good can be represented abstractly as a "duty." Hence a good will must have an intention that accords with duty. For this reason, Hegel agrees with Kant that a good will must do its duty for duty's sake (PR § 133). Hegel does *not* say (and does not believe) that a good will must do its duty *only* for duty's sake. He does not even think that a good will must strive for this. Hegel scorns the attitude of the moralist who criticizes the substantively good acts of great men on the ground that they intended and achieved happiness, fame, honor, or self-satisfaction for themselves. He finds no moral defect in those who do noble deeds for the sake of these satisfactions, so long as their intention and insight accord with the good. It is in this context that Hegel quotes the proverb "No man is a hero to his valet" – adding: "not because the man is not a hero, but because the valet is only a valet" (PhG ¶ 665; cf. PR § 124R, VG 104/87–88).

Let us turn to the humbler case of Kant's honest shopkeeper. Hegel would of course deny a good will to the shopkeeper who finds nothing attractive at all about moral goodness or dutifulness. A shopkeeper who cannot be relied upon to conduct business honestly would be a bad man no matter what his motives or intentions, simply because he would be deficient in the fundamental *ethical* virtue of "uprightness" *(Rechtschaffenheit)* (PR § 150). In Hegel's view, however, the shopkeeper counts as having a good will if the goodness or dutifulness of honest conduct is one feature (among others) that attracts him to such conduct, and if it is "the final ground" of the action (VPR 4: 354).

This means that the goodness or dutifulness of what he does must not only attract the shopkeeper, but also attract him *enough* (in this case) to be a *sufficient* (internal) reason to do it. If he were mildly attracted by dutifulness, but this were not enough to induce him to do his duty, then Hegel would not regard him as having a good will. To act for duty's sake is to have a "moral disposition *(Gesinnung)*" (VPR17 83, 246; cf. PR § 137); it is to perform the action "because it is good *(weil sie das Gute ist)* [or] because it is right" (VPR 4: 354). This "because" refers to the agent's intention, to the description or descriptions that specify the agent's (internal) reasons for performing that act on that occasion. Hegel holds that the agent has a good will if the moral goodness or dutifulness of the act belongs *among* those descriptions. It need not be the only such description, however. Nor does it need to have, in general, the highest priority among such descriptions. The agent need not try to improve its relative ranking, either.

Comparing Hegel's theory of the good will with Kant's, we see that Hegel's theory makes it harder in one way, but easier in another, to have a good will and to do actions with moral worth. Hegel requires that our "insight accord with the good," that is, that we act from objectively correct moral beliefs (*PR* § 140R; see also Chapter 10, this volume); Kant, however, requires only that we sincerely follow our conscience (*TL* 401/61). On the other hand, Hegel's theory does not require that the moral goodness or dutifulness of one's act should predominate over other motives, nor is it necessary to the moral worth of an action that it should be done solely or mainly from duty. Where the goodness or dutifulness of what I do attracts me enough to account for my performance of my duty, the relative strength for me of moral and nonmoral incentives is irrelevant to the moral worth of my act and the goodness of my will.

6. Moral worth and psychological causality

For Kant, whether or not one acts from duty is morally crucial because the autonomy or heteronomy of one's actions depends on how they are psychologically *caused*. Kant's strenuous denial that our free acts cannot be the result of *natural* or *phenomenal* causality should not blind us to the fact that his theory of action is a deterministic one in the sense that every act is seen as arising from a (supersensuous, noumenal) cause that brings about the act according to a law selected by the power of choice (*R* 35/30). Autonomy is, in Kant's words, "the causality of reason" (*KpV* 80/83). Thus the moral worth of an act depends accordingly upon the causal strength of the motive of duty, as compared with the agent's other motives, in the act's production. Goodness of will depends on the agent's disposition to acts whose sole or dominant cause is the motive of duty (*R* 28–30/23–26). Kant holds that we cannot judge the moral worth of our actions with certainty because he thinks that the causal mechanisms that produce them belong to the intelligible world, and are therefore unknowable by us. Accordingly, Kant denies that experience enables us to cite even a single sure example of the disposition to act from duty, on the grounds that we can never be absolutely certain that some "secret impulse of self-love, pretending to be the idea [of duty], was not the genuine determining cause of the will" (*G* 407/23).

From one point of view, Hegel's rejection of Kant's theory of moral worth can be understood as a rejection of its psychological determinism (i.e., of the crucial role played in it by causes, phenomenal or noumenal). For Hegel, the will has from nature a set of drives or original inclinations (*PR* § 11), but in relation to them it is also a "pure indeterminacy" which derives its contents not from nature but from an act of self-determination (*PR* §§ 5–7). His view, we may recall, is that we are "formally free" in the sense that our desires do not limit what we *can* do. Since causes necessitate their effects, Hegel denies that the will stands in any causal relation to its motives or to the other circumstances that determine it (*NP* 222; cf. *EL* § 195,A).

The idea that the will is free in relation to its desires and so is not causally determined by them makes Hegel look very much like an incompatibilist-indeterminist on the issue of free will. It is often said, however, that Hegel is a compatibilist or soft determinist.[10] This interpretation is sometimes based on a misreading of passages in which Hegel asserts that necessity is identical with freedom (*WL 6*: 239–240/570–571; *EL* §§ 157–159). It *is* a misreading, because in such passages the "necessity" intended is not causal necessitation but organic interconnectedness or teleological inevitability (cf. *PR* §§ 267A, 269A, 270A). That freedom is compatible with this sort of necessity does not entail that it is compatible with causal necessity.

There is nevertheless some truth in the compatibilist interpretation of Hegel if it is understood in another way. Precisely *because* Hegel rejects psychological determinism (a causal account of the will), his theory of human agency is conceived entirely in noncausal terms. Consequently, his theory of moral responsibility would be entirely compatible with any form of physical determinism that allowed (as compatibilists usually try to do) that (in some appropriate sense of "can") we always *can* act against our drives, desires, motives, and so forth. Also strikingly compatibilist in character is Hegel's theory of moral responsibility. Although Hegel believes that I always can do otherwise than I do, this belief plays no role at all in his theory of responsibility. For Hegel, I am responsible for doing a certain deed under a certain description if I in fact did the deed, knew I was doing it under that description, and intended to do it under that description. In principle, these conditions could all be satisfied even if there were no possibility that I could have done otherwise.

Hegel's theory of moral action concerns itself with what I did, whether I knew I was doing it, and the aspect or aspects of it that I intended. The two main factors are what actually occurred when I acted, and my way of conceiving of those occurrences. It is striking that motivation proper plays virtually no role in Hegel's theory of action, because Hegel's theory of action in effect replaces motives with intentions or (internal) reasons. Instead of asking what psychic factors motivated me, Hegel's theory asks for an explanation of my action in terms of the act-descriptions that supply the reasons I had for doing what I did. On Hegel's theory, to say that I acted "from duty" or "for duty's sake" means only that the dutifulness of my action belongs to my intention, that it counts as one description under which we might bring my action in explaining why I did it.

The published text of the *Philosophy of Right* contains no account at all of motivation. To get such an account, we must refer to two Additions drawn from Hotho's transcription of Hegel's 1822–1823 lectures (*PR* §§ 106A, 121A; cf. *VPR 3*: 330–331, 373–374). Both Additions emphasize that it is exclusively from the standpoint of morality that motives of an action are of interest. *PR* § 106A appears to identify the "incitement" *(Triebfeder)* of an action with its intention *(Absicht)* or its "principle" *(Grundsatz)*. *PR* § 121A is more specific, describing the "motive" *(Beweggrund)* of an action as "the universal in the purpose and the particular of the intention." The phrase "universal of the purpose" is precisely Hegel's formula for the intention (*PR* § 119), so the import of *PR* § 121A is that the motive of an action is a certain aspect or side of the intention, namely its "particular" side.

Hegel is evidently identifying the "motive" of an action with what he there calls the action's "particular content" or "moment of particularity," through which the action has "subjective *value, interest* for me" (*PR* § 122). An action's "motive," then, is simply the agent's interest in it. As we have seen, Hegel thinks that "interest" in this sense is present even in the most unselfish actions, since it derives from my awareness of the confirmation of my agency in a successful action, whether the action itself is oriented to my own good or not (*EG* § 475). But "interest" still always belongs to the agent's well-being or happiness, along with the satisfaction of the agent's needs, inclinations, and passions (*PR* § 123).

Hegel's view is that reason can be practical only when it relinquishes its purity and expresses itself through empirical desires. Universal ends get carried out only through the particular interests agents take in carrying them out. "The abstract universal end, insofar as it is done, since it steps into actuality, becomes a determinate end. My interest is in my doing in different ways. . . . That my well-being is my intention constitutes the scope of particularity. . . . This right lies immediately in particularity and is not for itself to be regarded as something bad" (*VPR19*: 96–98). As if to drive the point home against Kant, Hegel identifies the "motive" of an action with precisely that "particular" side of it that is necessary for setting and pursuing an end, and that in Kant's view is to be *contrasted* with the "universal," with the pure thought of duty or respect for the moral law.

7. Hegel's critique of Kant

This also means that Hegel's rejection of Kant's psychological determinism is not his basic reason for rejecting Kant's theory of the good will. Given Hegel's account of the good will, even if our actions are involved in a physical or psychological determinism, their causes are irrelevant to their moral worth, since that rests entirely on the nature of the act, the agent's knowledge, and the agent's intention (the features of the act that make it desirable enough for the agent to do). The crucial point is not that Hegel rejects Kant's psychological determinism, but that he regards the causal antecedents of acts as irrelevant to their moral worth and to the goodness or badness of the will that performs them.

When Kant's shopkeeper deals honestly with his inexperienced customer, there are at least two features of his action that recommend it to him:

1. Honest dealing helps to protect my reputation; it is good business.
2. Honest dealing accords with the good; it is my duty.

Let us suppose that he is both morally disposed enough and concerned enough for his reputation that (under the circumstances) *either* of these incentives would be reason enough for him to deal honestly. Aware of and attracted by both these features of honest dealing, the shopkeeper in fact chooses to deal honestly with the customer – though as a formally free agent, he could have acted against all these reasons and cheated the customer. That, as Hegel sees it, is an exhaustive report of the morally relevant facts of the case. They are sufficient for the shopkeeper to have a good will and his act to have moral worth.

Kant's conception of the good will requires us to probe much deeper into the shopkeeper's inner life. Kant wants the shopkeeper to ask which of the two motives *caused* him to act according to duty. He wants him to worry about the relative strength of the motives. He thinks it is important for determining the moral worth of *this act* what the shopkeeper would do if Henry VIII threatened him with torture and death if he does not cheat the customer. Hegel rejects these questions as having no answers, or at least no morally relevant answers. Kant himself agrees that the answers are all unknowable, since they inquire after information about causality in the intelligible world. Hegel merely draws the reasonable conclusion that if such matters are necessarily nothing to us, we have no business building our concept of moral worth upon them.

Kant emphasizes that we are finite beings. Kierkegaard and others who follow Kant in emphasizing the inwardness of the moral life have often accused Hegel of forgetting our finitude. But on the point we are now discussing, the truth is exactly the reverse. The Kantian and Kierkegaardian morality of inwardness seeks a freedom independent of everything that is other than freedom, independent of both nature and fortune. It is Hegel, however, who soberly faces up to the fact that the human condition is one of finite beings in a transitory world. Hegel makes no attempt to deny that, as the existentialists put it, we are "thrown" beings, conditioned by our natural endowments and the contingency of our situation; we ourselves and all our real concerns, including our innermost self-worth, are always to some degree delivered over to chance and absurdity.

Kant falsifies the finitude of the human condition when he attempts to place the good will beyond the reach of nature and fortune. This moral "displacement," or "pretense" *(Verstellung)* (as Hegel calls it; *PhG* ¶¶ 616–631), is neither innocent nor without cost. Every hidden value we hope to possess in the beyond must be paid for out of the real worth we enjoy in the here and now. When we displace morality to a beyond, locating it on the struggle of motives in an intelligible world, we alienate our practical reason from our self-satisfaction. When we locate our moral worth in a noumenal self that is hidden from us, we devalue the only self-worth we can actually possess. Our noblest actions and highest accomplishments become for us nothing but so much worldly splendor, the dazzling costume that cloaks a bad will. In the long run, the lie serves the ends only of envy and hypocrisy.

9
The emptiness of the moral law

1. The emptiness charge

In Chapter 7 we reviewed some of Hegel's complaints against the moral standpoint from his Frankfurt writings: its alienation of reason from sense, its tendency to hypocrisy, its abstraction from the relationships of social life, its commitment to an "ought" which can never become an "is." Hegel's best known criticism of morality, first appearing in the Jena writings, is the emptiness charge. It says that morality is doomed to be an "empty formalism," that from the moral standpoint there is no criterion at all of moral right and wrong (*PR* § 135R).

The emptiness charge is sometimes presented specifically as a criticism of Kantian ethics, especially of the first formulation of the moral law in Kant's *Foundations*, the so-called formula of universal law (FUL):

FUL: "So act that you can will the maxim of your action to be a universal law" (*G* 421/39).

The charge is that the test proposed by the FUL draws no real distinction between maxims. From one point of view all maxims pass it, whereas from another any maxim fails it.

The emptiness charge is also presented as a more general indictment against the moral standpoint as a whole. In this version it claims that no "immanent doctrine of duties" can be formulated from the moral standpoint at all, because this standpoint provides nothing but an "empty principle of subjectivity" (*PR* § 148R). Morality is the standpoint of the individual moral subject who judges actions by a standard of the good, whose content is drawn from both right and well-being, taking into account not only the agent's well-being but also the well-being of others. Thus Hegel might seem to be making the highly implausible claim that no principle formulated in terms of human rights and welfare could ever draw any distinction at all between good and evil or rule out any action whatever as immoral.

One way to make sense of Hegel's position here might be to distinguish also between a weaker and a stronger form of the emptiness charge. To say that the FUL, or Kantian moral philosophy, or the moral standpoint generally, cannot give us a completely satisfactory account of our duties is clearly weaker than saying that they can make no distinction between good and evil and are unable to exclude any action whatever as morally wrong. Even if the FUL shows some actions or maxims to be wrong, it may still fall short of

154

providing a fully adequate account of duties if there are some cases that it fails to cover or in which it yields the wrong results. A similar weakness might belong to every principle adopted from the moral standpoint if this standpoint abstracts from important factors in human life that any adequate theory of duties must take into account. Hegel did not vigorously pursue any argument in favor of this broader but weaker form of the emptiness charge. (We will have a little more to say about it, though, in § 11 of this chapter.)

It is plain that at least in his Jena period, Hegel regards Kantian moral philosophy as providing the moral standpoint with its most perfect theoretical expression. Using that as a starting point, we could develop a second interpretation of Hegel's emptiness charge (though it is not inconsistent with the first one). Other philosophers may formulate moral principles employing the notions of right and universal well-being, and such principles may succeed in being more than empty formalisms. But if Kantian morality is the only adequate expression of the moral standpoint, then none of these other principles is securely based in the moral standpoint itself. If Kant's principle is empty, then that would show that the moral standpoint as a whole is empty. Thus Hegel might see the emptiness of Kant's principle as a unique strength in Kant's moral philosophy from the standpoint of philosophical understanding, even if it is a fatal weakness in it from the standpoint of practical ethics. In § 6 we will see that this reading of Hegel's emptiness charge has at least this much confirmation: The emptiness charge is not only a criticism of the FUL, but also says that no contentful moral principle is available from Kant's philosophical standpoint.

2. Kant's formula of universal law

Hegel's emptiness charge against the FUL is also expressed by later philosophers, such as Mill:

> When [Kant] begins to deduce from [the formula of universal law] any of the actual duties of morality, he fails, almost grotesquely, to show that there would be any contradiction, any logical (not to say physical) impossibility, in the adoption by all rational beings of the most outrageously immoral rules of conduct. All he shows is that the *consequences* of their universal adoption would be such as no one would choose to incur.[1]

The charge was not original with Hegel either. In one of the very first critical discussions of Kant's *Foundations*, Gottlob August Tittel maintained that Kant's principle has no content unless interpreted in a utilitarian sense. The immorality (for example) of borrowing money with no intent to repay it can be derived from the principle only if Kant's argument is that the universalization of the agent's maxim would undermine the generally beneficial practice of money lending.[2]

Similar views were endorsed by Fichte, who insists that Kant's FUL must be treated as "merely heuristic," and "by no means constitutive" of morality.

> [The FUL] is not a principle but only a consequence of the true principle, the

command of the absolute self-dependence of reason. The relation is not that because something can be a principle of universal legislation, therefore it should be the maxim of my will; on the contrary, it is just the opposite, that because something ought to be a maxim of my will, therefore it can also be a principle of universal legislation. (*SL* 234/246)

Fichte's own fundamental principle of morality is unashamedly formalistic: "*Always act according to the best conviction of your duty*, or: *Act according to your conscience*" (*SL* 156/164, 163/173). Fichte holds that the content of duty must be arrived at independently of the fundamental principle, through a process of conscientious *theoretical* inquiry (*SL* 163–177/173–187; see below, Chapter 10, § 2).

   The FUL is Kant's first formulation of the principle of morality in the *Foundations*. He gives it the most extensive deduction, and develops its casuistical implications in greatest detail. Even so, it is a mistake for Hegel and other critics to fasten exclusively on the FUL in their attempts to prove that Kantian ethics is empty of content. The FUL is also casuistically the least ambitious of Kant's three formulations in the *Foundations*. As Hegel himself seems at times to appreciate (*PhG* ¶ 429), the FUL does no more than provide us with a permissibility test for isolated individual maxims. If a maxim can be willed as universal law, it is permissible to act on it; but if it cannot be so willed, then it is impermissible. Though Kant's illustrations of the formula are organized according to a taxonomy of positive duties, the FUL cannot tell us what any of our positive duties are. Kant's four arguments from the FUL, if successful, show that one may not follow the specific maxims concerning suicide, false promising, and so on, which he mentions. They cannot show that it is always contrary to duty to commit suicide or make false promises, since those acts might also be done from quite different maxims which (for all these arguments show) may pass the FUL test.

   By contrast, Kant's second principle, the "formula of humanity," forbids all conduct that treats rational nature as a means only and not at the same time as an end. It lays on us the positive (though wide and imperfect) duty of furthering the purposes of rational beings (*G* 428–431/46–49). The third principle or "formula of autonomy," though superficially similar to the FUL, does not merely forbid us to act on maxims that cannot be willed as universal law, but also enjoins us to act on any maxim belonging to a *system* of maxims suitable for universal legislation (*G* 432/50, 436/55).[3] Thus the formulas of humanity and autonomy both provide for positive duties in a way that the FUL cannot. Hegel and other critics will not have shown Kantian ethics to be empty of content until they have demonstrated the emptiness of these other formulas along with that of the FUL.

   Even against the FUL, however, Hegel's arguments will be seen to fail.

3. Contradictions and conflicting volitions

In the *Critique of Practical Reason*, Kant applies the FUL to a case in which a man, now deceased, has left a sizable deposit in my care without leaving any record of it. Kant argues that I cannot universalize the maxim of denying the deposit and appropriating the money, since then "the principal would annihilate itself, because the result would be that no one would make a deposit" (*KpV* 27/27). Hegel replies:

> But that there are no deposits – where is the contradiction in this? That there are no deposits would contradict other necessary determinacies, just as that a deposit is possible fits together with other necessary determinacies and thereby becomes necessary. But other ends and material grounds are not to be called upon. (NR 462/77)

Hegel insists that the test provided by the FUL is nothing beyond the principle of contradiction, and that this is a test that any maxim can pass (*EL* § 54; *PR* § 135R). Kant does speak of a maxim's "contradicting" or "annihilating" itself when considered as a universal law, and he does say that there would be a "contradiction" in a system of nature in which some maxims were universal laws (*G* 422/40). Yet Hegel is surely wrong to say that this is a test that any maxim can pass. There definitely are principles that one person can follow, but that it would be contradictory to suppose that all follow: For example, "I will never work, but always live by exploiting the labor of others." If everyone followed the principle, there would be no laborers left to exploit, and so it would be impossible for anyone to live by exploiting the labor of others. One problem for Kant, however, is that some maxims of which this seems to be true are morally innocuous: For example, "I will occasionally accompany others through a doorway, and on those occasions I will always go through the door last." Kant's test seems to yield false negatives in the case of maxims like this one. This is a problem that an adequate defense of the FUL would have to solve.

Hegel misunderstands the FUL's test for maxims, at least as it applies to the case of the deposit. Kant neither needs to show nor tries to show that the maxim would literally result in a self-contradiction if universally followed. His argument is rather that if my maxim of gaining money through the appropriation of the deposit were universalized, then people would not trust others with deposits. Consequently, it would be impossible for me to gain money by following my maxim, because I would never have been given the deposit in the first place.[4] This argument employs some empirical claims (about how people would behave if my maxim were a universal law of nature), but it appeals to no "other ends or material grounds," that is, none other than those contained in my maxim itself. The argument shows that I will an impossible or self-contradictory world in the sense that I will both (1) that I profit by appropriating the deposit and (2) that circumstances be such that I could never gain money in this way.

We might wonder whether there is any real impossibility in my willing here. It seems perfectly possible for me to will two incompatible states of affairs (such as having my cake and eating it, too), so why can't I will both that my maxim should be a universal law and that I should successfully act on it in this case? The answer depends on a more precise understanding of Kant's use of the verb "to will" *(wollen)*. Kant distinguishes "willing" from merely "wishing." "Willing" a state of affairs is not the same as wanting or desiring it. To will something, I must employ means to bring it about, or at least be prepared to employ some means (G 394/10). To will both that I have my cake and that I eat it, I must simultaneously try to eat the cake and try to keep myself from eating it. Conflicting volitions, unlike conflicting wants or wishes, are mutually incompatible.

Hegel's theory of ethical life derives our ethical duties from social relationships and institutions. Sometimes Hegel misunderstands the FUL because he imposes on it the assumptions of his own theory. Thus he interprets the example of the deposit as if it turned on the validity of the institution of private property. He appears to think that the FUL is applicable to cases like the deposit, only if it can be shown that the absence of this institution would result in a contradiction (*NR* 462–464/77–79; cf. *PhG* ¶¶430–433, *PR* § 135R, *VGP 3*: 368–369/460–461). This misconstrues the moral issue at stake in the example, which is the sanctity not of private property but of personal trust.[5] The question is whether I can consistently will that I should profit by betraying someone's trust and also will that all should betray the trust of another when they stand to profit from it. This issue could certainly arise in a society where property did not exist, and in that sense Hegel is quite wrong to suggest that Kant's argument about the deposit depends on the institution of property.

4. The universal law test

In the *Foundations* Kant distinguishes cases like this one, where the maxim as universal law involves an internal self-contradiction, from cases where the universalized maxim cannot be willed to be a universal law because such a will would necessarily conflict with itself on grounds external to the maxim. For example, Kant argues that we cannot will as universal law the cold-hearted man's maxim of refusing charitable help to those in need. The argument is that if we ourselves were in such need, we could not will that others should deny us the help we require. Here Kant plainly does need to call upon "other ends and material grounds" beyond what are given in the maxim to be tested. He supposes that all rational beings have ends they cannot hope to reach without the help of others. He takes for granted that we would not choose to deny ourselves that help if it were needed. Like the assumption about how people would behave if no one could be trusted with a deposit, this is an empirically founded assumption about how rational beings would behave under the envisioned counterfactual circumstances.

It might be objected that the assumption is normative rather than empirical, telling us not how they would behave but how it would be *rational* for them to behave. Even so, it is still an assumption that depends on empirical facts about what rational beings need and desire. It might also be possible to describe fictional beings whose needs and desires are such that it would not be irrational for them to forego all appeal to the charitable aid of others.[6]

Kant's argument depends on the empirical fact that we humans are not such beings. Moreover, if the assumption is normative, it is not *morally* normative. It deals with the rational pursuit of self-interest, not with moral duty.

But the result of the argument is moral, not prudential. Since it is a counterfactual circumstance that the cold-hearted man's maxim holds as a law of nature, there is no sense in which Kant's argument is based (as Schopenhauer falsely alleges) on a covert and corrupt appeal to self-interest.[7] Kant does not reason that I should help others because, if I do, they will help me. Kant's argument does rest on a supposition about the structure of our self-interested desires. It says that no human being could rationally will to sacrifice all her ends (even survival) whenever achievement of the end requires the beneficent assistance of someone else. But nothing in Kant's argument involves an "appeal to material grounds" in any sense that would contradict Kant's view that the good will acts solely from duty.

Tittel and Mill both try to portray Kant not as a covert egoist, but as a covert consequentialist. Kant's arguments never depend on the consequences of a maxim's actual adoption, though they do involve claims about the hypothetical consequences of its *universal* adoption. This interest in consequences seems properly consequentialist only if we add the premise (as Kant never does) that my following a maxim will somehow make it more likely to be universally followed. Moreover, the FUL does not reject a maxim simply on the grounds that its universal adoption would be *undesirable* (as Tittel and Mill both claim in Kant's behalf). Instead, the maxim is rejected because of a conflict of volitions, because willing the maxim as universal law conflicts either with the maxim itself or with something else that the agent wills.

These two tests may often have similar results. The fact that I find a certain practice undesirable often gives me a sufficient reason to refuse to participate in it, and this would be enough to prevent me from willing without contradiction that everyone participate in it. Conversely, if I regard everyone's behaving in a certain way as desirable, it appears as if I would be able to will without contradiction that everyone behave in that way. But neither of these generalizations holds universally, and therefore, the universalizability test for maxims is not the same as the consequentialist one. We can see this from Kant's own examples. In Kant's argument about the deposit, the issue is not whether leaving deposits with others is a desirable practice. Kant's argument should prove to those who dislike this practice and want it abolished that they must nevertheless deal honestly with any deposits left in their charge. In the other argument the issue is not how desirable it is for people to give and get charitable help, but whether I can will that they not help me when I need it. Kant describes a man who is able for the most part to get along without the help of others and who thinks that it would be best for everyone to be like himself in this respect; the argument is clearly supposed to apply to this man, showing him that he cannot will as a universal law the maxim of refusing charitable help to others (G 398/14–15). Kant's position is that he may try to abolish the practice of charity by encouraging people to develop self-reliance, but it is not permissible for him to pursue his end (as our rugged individualists in politics usually do) simply by refusing help to those who need it.

Hegel claims that anything can pass the test of the formula of universal law if it is considered merely in itself, as a "simple determinateness"; but he also thinks that nothing can pass the test if resolved into the distinct and opposed moments that constitute it (*PhG* ¶¶ 430–431). Thus he argues not only that Kant's principle permits immoral conduct, but also that it may forbid conduct that is praiseworthy.

Thus the determinacy of helping the poor expresses abolition of the determinacy that is poverty; the maxim whose content is that determinacy, when tested by being raised to universal legislation, would prove itself false, for it would annihilate itself. If it is thought that the poor should be helped universally, then either there would no longer be any poor, or there would be only poor and then there would be no one who could help them; and so in both cases the help ceases. (*NR* 465–466/80)

This argument purports to show that Kant's principle forbids us to follow the principle "Help the poor!" on the ground that if everyone helped the poor, there would no longer be any occasion for anyone to help the poor, and so the maxim of helping the poor (like the maxim of appropriating the deposit) would, if universalized, annihilate itself.

We can see what is wrong with Hegel's argument as soon as we distinguish two different meanings for the maxim "Help the poor!" If my maxim is simply that of trying to abolish poverty as far as possible, then there will be no self-annihilation if everyone follows the maxim and poverty is abolished. On the other hand, my maxim may be to engage in the activity of helping the poor, where the point is not so much to improve their condition as to busy myself with helping them. That maxim *is* threatened with self-contradiction if everyone follows it. But that maxim is morally suspect anyway: It is the maxim of those who help the poor in order to indulge their feelings of pity or because they have some vested interest in the institutions of poor relief.[8]

5. Some unsolved problems

I conclude that Hegel's criticism of the universal law test does not succeed. Even so, it might suggest a problem with the universal law test: How do we decide how to formulate an agent's maxim in a given case? The problem is not that we have to be able to distinguish between the intent of people who help the poor in order to abolish poverty and those who help the poor because they have a vested interest in charities; any moral theory must be interested in those distinctions. The problem is that the intentions of an agent often admit of distinct but equally correct descriptions from different points of view or at different levels of generality.

Suppose I invite you to dinner. I consider serving you granola and yogurt because, although you hate them, I enjoy them and they will be good for you. What is my maxim in this case? Is it, "I will serve my guest foods I like"? Or, "I will feed my guest foods that I know are good for people"? Or,

"I will feed my guest nourishing food that I like even though I know the guest won't like it"? Or is the maxim just "I will feed my guest granola and yogurt"? All these maxims seem to be accurate expressions of my intention, but some might be universalizable whereas others are not. How do I decide which maxim to use when I apply the universal law test to the action I propose? If we answer that the maxim ought to include all and only those things that are morally relevant, then this does not solve the problem but just restates it. For the problem is that the universal law test does not provide us with any way of deciding what is morally relevant.

Suppose I want to become a parent and I make it my maxim to marry and impregnate a woman who wants to have a child with me. This maxim seems quite innocent, but as stated it is obviously not universalizable. If everyone (including, of course, women) followed it, then there would be no women left for me to marry or impregnate, since all the women who wanted children would be busy trying to marry and impregnate other women.[9] Here it looks as if the problem is easy to solve by reformulating the maxim in more general terms using some such phrase as "marrying and having a child with a person of the opposite sex. . . ." But how can we be sure that such reformulations do not represent an arbitrary and ad hoc adjustment of the example to our moral prejudices? Not every maxim may pass the universal law test, but the test might turn out to be too vague and flexible to provide determinate results in many actual cases of moral reasoning.

There certainly are problems with Kant's universal law test; some of them might even turn out to be insoluble. Nothing I have said in this chapter should be taken as an endorsement of the FUL or as a denial that it might be shown to be empty of content. This is cold comfort to Hegel, who seems so far from a correct understanding of the universal law test that he cannot be credited with having identified any of the real difficulties with it. To make something of Hegel's criticisms of the FUL, we must use them as the occasion for raising problems Hegel never thought of. Thus it is not surprising that most scholars simply dismiss Hegel's criticisms of the FUL.[10]

6. Kant's deduction of the moral law

Hegel's emptiness charge appears at a disadvantage when it is regarded narrowly as an attack on the FUL. To regard it in this way is also partly to misunderstand it. Hegel thinks that the FUL is empty, but he never means to charge Kant merely with having formulated his principle badly, so that it turns out to be empty of content. Instead, Hegel consistently treats this emptiness as a *necessary* feature of the standpoint from which Kant thinks about morality. Hegel does not begin with Kant's FUL, interpreting (or misinterpreting) it as setting up noncontradiction as the sole moral criterion. On the contrary, he begins with the conception of the moral standpoint as that of the abstract subjective ego, founded on the pure concept of analytic unity; and then he infers from this that noncontradiction is the only criterion morality has at its disposal (NR 459/75; PhG ¶¶ 429–430).

Thus the Berlin *Encyclopedia* derives the emptiness charge from the claim that Kant never successfully distinguishes reason from understanding, since Kantian reason supplies nothing but a formal unity to an experience whose content must come from outside (*EL* § 52). From this Hegel infers that noncontradiction is the only moral criterion *available* to Kant: "For that which practical thought makes its law . . . there is again *nothing to hand* except the same abstract identity of the understanding, that there is no contradiction in the determination" (*EL* § 54, emphasis added). The *Philosophy of Right* criticizes Kant for remaining at the moral standpoint without going on to the standpoint of ethical life, claiming that from this standpoint noncontradiction is the only criterion of duty. Only then does Hegel allude to what he calls "the further Kantian form, the capacity of the action to be represented as a universal maxim," which (Hegel says) contains no principle beyond the absence of contradiction (*PR* § 135R). We have already seen that this last claim is based on a misunderstanding of Kant's principle; but Hegel's deeper and more interesting thesis is that Kant is not *entitled* to employ a principle with any content beyond the criterion of noncontradictoriness.

If Hegel's emptiness charge says that Kant is unable to provide an adequate deduction for a principle with any content and if the FUL is not empty, then we might pose Hegel's emptiness charge as a challenge not to the FUL but to its derivation. As we shall see in the next section, this is something that Hegel himself does at least once. In order to evaluate the challenge, we need to see how Kant proposes to derive the FUL.

Kant's deduction of the FUL, in both the *Foundations* and the second critique, attempts to show that the FUL is one that there is a special sort of reason or ground for following: an "objective" ground. An objective ground is "valid for every rational being as such" (*G* 413/30; *KpV* 19/17). But its universal validity cannot be merely a contingent matter of fact; it must be an a priori necessary ground for all rational beings. And it must be "valid in the same form for all rational beings" – that is, it must be "exactly the same determining ground for the will of all rational beings and in all cases" (*KpV* 21/20, 25/24). Thus unanimity among rational beings as to what pleases or pains them could not constitute the sort of universal validity necessary for an objective ground or an objectively grounded principle (a practical law). This unanimity would be merely contingent, and although each rational being might have a reason for promoting the universally pleasant, each one's reason would be different: My ground for promoting the universally pleasant is that it pleases *me;* your ground is that it pleases *you.* A genuinely objective ground for doing something would have to be something like: "because any rational being should do it," or "because it is rational to do it."

Kant thinks that if we can show that the FUL is objectively grounded, then that will show that we always have a sufficient and overriding reason to follow it. This is because he thinks that an objective ground is "supreme" *(oberste)* – deserving to prevail over any grounds that derive from "subjective differences between human beings" (*KpV* 32/32). This, in turn, is because he agrees with Hegel that we act more rationally when we act universally, from grounds deriving from our essence as rational beings, than when we act from particular grounds that we have only contingently and do not share with other rational beings.

Kant will have established that it is rational to follow the FUL if he can show that this formula expresses an objectively grounded principle or practical law. This is exactly what he tries to do. His deduction of the FUL can be divided into two stages. First, Kant argues that the FUL can be derived from the very concept of an objective ground, and second, he argues that there does in fact exist an objective ground. The first stage of Kant's argument is carried out in Part II of the *Foundations* and in Theorem III of the *Critique of Practical Reason*. Kant introduces the concept of a categorical imperative or practical law, a principle involving "an unconditional and objective, and hence universally valid necessity" (*G* 416/34); and then he proceeds to argue that "the mere concept of a categorical imperative is sufficient to provide the formula containing the proposition that alone can be a categorical imperative" (*G* 420/38; cf. *KpV* 26/26). The argument purports to show that the FUL is this formula.

In Part III of the *Foundations,* Kant undertakes the second stage of his argument, claiming that freedom, which can and must be presupposed as the property of every rational will, can belong only to a will that is subject to objective principles (*G* 447–448/65–66). In the second critique, the second stage of Kant's argument takes a slightly different form, for instead of arguing that there is an objective practical law for rational beings because such beings must think of themselves as free, Kant insists that rational beings must think of themselves as free only because they are aware of being subject to a practical law, which is given to them as a "fact of reason" (*KpV* 47/48). This difference, however, affects only the second stage of Kant's argument. The first stage, equally necessary to both versions of the argument, is also the same in both. It will be the target of Hegel's criticism.

7. The failure of Kant's deduction

Kant earns only praise from Hegel for grounding the moral law on freedom, "the positive infinity of practical reason," or "the [will's] faculty of determining itself in a universal way, *thinkingly*" (*EL* § 54A). Hegel grants that the will is free, and that its freedom involves self-legislation according to objective grounds. Thus Hegel agrees with the second stage of Kant's deduction of the FUL. He denies, however, that any content to the moral law can be arrived at from this starting point:

> Only with the recognition [of the will's freedom] the question of the *content* of the will or of practical reason is still not answered. When it is said that human beings ought to make the *good* the content of their wills, right away there recurs the question of the content, i.e., the determinacy of this content; and we get nowhere either with the mere principle of the agreement of the will with itself or with the demand to do duty for duty's sake. (*EL* § 54A)

This passage is not merely a repetition of the claim that the FUL is empty of content; it contains a denial of the first stage of Kant's deduction of the FUL, the stage that attempts to deduce the FUL from the concept of a categorical imperative, objective law, or objective practical ground. As we shall now see, if Hegel's emptiness charge is understood in this way, then it turns out to be correct.

Kant claims that "the mere concept of a categorical imperative . . . provides the formula containing the proposition which alone can be a categorical imperative." His argument is this:

> If I think of a categorical imperative, then I know straightway what it contains. For since the imperative contains, besides the law, only the necessity that the maxim agree with this law, but the law contains no condition which limits it, there remains nothing with which the maxim should agree except the universality of law in general, and it is this agreement alone which the imperative really represents. Hence the sole categorical imperative is this: Act only according to that maxim by which you can at the same time will that it should become a universal law. (G 420–421/38–39; cf. G 402/18, KpV 27/27)

Kant begins with the concept of an objective ground or objectively grounded principle (a categorical imperative). He first points out that the only conceivable ground for following such a principle is the agreement of your maxim with the concept of lawfulness or universal validity: You follow it because it is rational for any rational being to follow it. From this he concludes that this agreement, and hence the only possible objective ground, consists in the possibility of willing that your maxim be followed by all rational beings. The only possible objective ground is the conformity of your maxim to the FUL.

Kant's argument may be paraphrased as follows: A practical principle is objective, or a practical law, only if there is a ground for following it which is necessarily valid for every rational being as such. But a ground of this kind can consist in nothing but the agreement of the agent's maxim with the concept of a principle that is objectively valid. This agreement, however, can consist only in the possibility of willing that the maxim be universally followed. Consequently, the only possible objective principle is: Act according to a maxim that you can will to be universally followed.

This argument is fallacious. An objective ground is universally valid, and likewise an objective principle is one that every rational being has a reason (the same reason) for following. The universal validity of an objective principle thus consists in what we earlier called its "universality of applicability." But it does not consist, as Kant seems to infer, in the rational desirability (for someone, perhaps for anyone) of the state of affairs that would result if everyone followed the principle. Kant is arguing from the premise that it is rational for each person to follow a certain principle to the conclusion that it is rational (for someone, or anyone) to will that everyone follow the principle. But that inference is not valid. From the fact that it is rational for each of us to do something, we cannot derive any conclusion about the rational desirability of the state of affairs that would result if we all did that thing.

Suppose I am an egoist, who thinks that one objective principle is the principle of self-love: "Always seek your own happiness." In the second critique, Kant claims that if everyone followed this principle, the result would be a conflict between people's ends and the destruction of everyone's happiness. Let us suppose that Kant is right and that I (the egoist) agree with him. I admit I cannot will that everyone should follow the principle of self-love, since this would destroy my own happiness (along with everyone else's). But does this tend in the least to show that the principle of self-love is not an objective principle? No, it does not. Kant successfully refutes one argument in favor of the principle of self-love, an argument drawn from the universality of the desire for happiness. He points out that this desire is only contingently universal, and that it fails to provide a reason that is identical for all rational beings (*KpV* 26/25). But in my defense of the claim that the principle of self-love is an objective principle, I need not make the mistake of relying on this argument. To refute one bad argument for a view is not to show that the view itself is mistaken.

Yet if the first stage of Kant's deduction of the FUL were valid, then I could not even *claim* that the principle of self-love is an objective principle without falling into self-contradiction, for Kant's argument purports to show that the only principle consistent with the concept of an objective ground is the FUL. If Kant's argument were valid, it would be impossible to maintain without contradiction that a principle is objectively grounded and also that one cannot will that that principle be universally followed. But though it is doubtless false that the principle of self-love is an objective principle, the supposition that it is one leads to no contradiction. Hence Kant's argument is not valid.

8. Universal applicability and collective rationality

In framing his argument Kant seems to have been misled by the connotations of his terms "practical law" and "universal law." When conscientious legislators make laws for a community, they normally have in mind that the laws should have what we earlier called "universality of applicability" (Chapter 7, § 5): Everyone should be equally subject to them. Good legislators are also guided by what life will be like for the community if the laws are universally followed; they make the laws they do because they think that everyone's following those laws will result in a system of collective behavior that is rational and generally beneficial. Let us call this second feature of a good law "collective benefit." As we noted earlier in this chapter (§ 4), collective benefit in this sense is not identical with Kant's FUL test, which says that it must be possible to will without contradiction that the law will be universally followed. Let us call this feature of a law "collective rationality." For our present purposes, collective rationality is similar to collective benefit, since both have to do with the relation of the rational agent's will to the hypothetical situation in which a maxim is universally followed.

Now although Kant's conception of a practical law contains universality of applicability, it does not contain anything like collective benefit or collective rationality. The concept of a practical law involves the idea that taking each rational being individually, it is rational for that being to follow that law; but this leaves entirely open the question whether the result of everyone's following the law would be (collectively) desirable, or whether it would be something that a rational agent could will without contradiction. A priori we have no way of ruling out the possibility that a principle with universal applicability might dictate to each individual a course of action which she cannot will that others should follow too.

The mistake is an easy one to make because terms like "universally valid" and "universally rational" can be taken either individually or collectively. If I say that a principle is "universally valid," that might mean that for each individual, without exception, it would be rational for that individual to follow that principle. But it might also mean that any group of people all of whom followed the principle would behave in a way that is collectively beneficial or collectively rational. The phrase "what it is rational for everyone to do" contains a similar ambiguity. Of course, it might turn out that the referents of the phrase taken in the two senses are exactly the same: that the course which it is rational for each individual to take is identical with the course which, if universally followed, would result in a collectively beneficial or collectively rational system of action. To the extent that we can reasonably expect others to behave as we ourselves do, we have grounds for thinking that only collectively rational principles will turn out to have universal applicability. For if each of us can foresee that the consequences of following a certain maxim will be something we cannot consistently will, then that might provide us with a reason not to follow the maxim, and hence preclude its universal applicability. But it is only under certain contingent, empirical conditions that this would happen. We cannot infer (as Kant does) that a principle with universality of applicability is eo ipso a principle with collective rationality. Such an inference is simply invalid.

Someone might think that Kant could be saved from these objections by insisting that the concept of an objective ground should have been interpreted all along as containing both universality of applicability and collective rationality. Let us call this the "stronger" concept of objectivity, in contrast to the "weaker" concept that involves universality of applicability alone. If we employ this new concept of objectivity, then it will certainly be true that only a principle that can be willed as universal law can be objectively grounded, and hence that the FUL will follow from the very concept of an objective ground. This would, of course, trivialize the first stage of Kant's deduction of the FUL, but perhaps that is no reason to object to it: Kant himself seems to regard the point he is making as a trivial one: "A practical law which I recognize as such must qualify for universal legislation: this is an identical proposition and therefore self-evident" (*KpV* 27/27).

This is not a satisfactory way out of Kant's difficulties, however. The reason is that the first stage of Kant's deduction, which derives the FUL from the concept of an objective ground, needs to be combined with the second stage, which shows that there are objectively grounded principles. The deduction as a whole will not succeed if the stronger concept of objective ground is used in the first stage of the argument while the weaker concept is used in the second stage, for it will still be an open question whether the weakly objective principles established in the second stage are strongly objective too; indeed, it will be an open question whether there are any strongly objective principles at all.

Kant's arguments never attempt to establish the existence of strongly objective principles, but only the existence of weakly objective ones. The *Foundations* claims that a free will is subject to objective principles because an objective ground arises from the rational self rather than from inclinations for external objects (*G* 446–447/65, 457/76). Such an argument might show that a free will is subject to weakly objective principles (principles having universality of applicability), but it cannot show that the will is subject to strongly objective principles (having collective rationality as well). Even in *The Critique of Practical Reason,* where Kant treats the existence of objective principles as a "fact of reason," he maintains that the practical law that is such a fact is "reciprocally implied by" freedom and even "identical" with it (*KpV* 29/29, 42/43). The law that is given as a fact of reason is therefore only weakly objective. If we employ the stronger concept of objectivity in the first stage of Kant's deduction of the FUL, then we save that stage by trivializing it, but we only doom the deduction as a whole to failure.

Hegel may be mistaken in thinking that the FUL is empty, but he is not mistaken in thinking that Kant's starting point (in the idea of a free will and a categorical imperative) is purely formal, and incapable of leading to any determinate moral principles. Kant tries to derive a substantive moral principle merely from the concepts of an objective ground for acting and a principle that is objectively grounded. But we cannot tell, given these concepts alone, which principles, if any, are objectively grounded, are categorical imperatives. If Kant's FUL is not empty, that is because it does not follow from his starting point; this starting point is empty.

9. The emptiness of the moral will

A categorical imperative or practical law is an objectively grounded principle. Following such a principle because it is objectively grounded or acting from an objective ground is the same as acting from respect for law, or acting from duty (*G* 400/16). Thus Kant's attempt to provide a deduction of the FUL from the concept of a practical law or objectively grounded principle is the same as attempting to deduce the FUL from the idea of acting purely from duty. This is the way the deduction is in fact first presented in the *Foundations* (*G* 402/18). If Hegel's emptiness charge may be interpreted as the denial that any contentful moral principles may be derived from the mere concept of a categorical imperative or objective ground, then it might also be interpreted as the denial that any contentful moral principles may be derived from the idea of acting from duty.

Hegel's writings contain such denials. They go further, taking the position that the will that acts from duty is committed to act on a principle that is

167

purely formal and empty of content. In Chapter 8 we saw how Hegel rejects the Kantian conception of the good will as the will that acts from duty. Now we will see that at the root of the emptiness charge, as Hegel himself conceived it, lies the idea that if you embrace the Kantian conception of the good will, you are not merely unable to deduce contentful moral principles from it, but are also doomed only to empty principles. In short, the moral law is empty because the moral will is empty.

In Hegel's texts the emptiness charge is usually associated with an attack on the Kantian conception of the good will. The *Philosophy of Right* says that Kant's adherence to the moral standpoint without a conception of ethical life reduces his ethics of autonomy to "an empty formalism and the moral science to a prating about duty for duty's sake" (*PR* § 135R). In the *Lectures on the History of Philosophy,* Hegel puts it this way: "This is the defect of the Kantian–Fichtean principle, that it is simply formal. Cold duty is the last undigested lump in the stomach, the revelation given of reason" (*VGP 3*: 369/ 461). But in both these passages, it is unclear just how the emptiness charge and the Kantian conception of the good will are connected.

The emptiness charge came to articulation in Hegel's writings during the first years of his Jena period. It is first adumbrated in *The Difference Between Fichte's and Schelling's System of Philosophy* (1801) and developed further in Hegel's critique of Fichte in *Faith and Knowledge* (1802). Later presentations of the charge in the *Phenomenology, Encyclopedia, Philosophy of Right,* and the lectures are in fact only echoes and summaries of Hegel's most extensive exposition of the emptiness charge in the *Natural Right* (1802). It is in the early Jena writings that we must look for Hegel's clearest statements of the motivation behind the charge.

Faith and Knowledge is most explicit about the connection between the emptiness charge and his critique of the good will as the will that acts from duty. From the moral standpoint, Hegel says that "the content of the concept is some reality posited in an idea form as end and intention, some empirical given; only the empty form is the a priori." In morality there is a separation between the concrete action, whose content is contingent and empirical, and the pure form of duty, for whose sake alone the action is supposed to be done.

> Because the emptiness of the pure will and the universal is the truly a priori, the particular is something absolutely empirical. What right and duty are in and for themselves – to give a determination of this would be contradictory. For the content at once cancels the pure will or duty for duty's sake, and makes duty into something material. The emptiness of the pure feeling of duty and the content continually cross each other up. . . . So we are free to elevate every moral contingency into the form of the concept and procure a justification and a good conscience for what is unethical. (*GW* 426–427/183–184)

Hegel claims that if the pure moral disposition consists in acting from the pure thought of duty, then any "content" would destroy the moral purity of the will. Or, as Hegel more succinctly puts the point later in the *Phenomenology of Spirit:* "Since the *determinate* duty is an end, it has a content, its *content* is a part of the end, and so morality is not pure" (*PhG* ¶ 630). Suppose, for instance, that I try to think of a certain kind of action, such as keeping a promise or helping another in need, as my duty. To do this specific duty, Hegel seems to be saying, would be to act not from duty alone, but also from a more particular motive, that of keeping *this* promise or helping *this* person. But this more particular motive would cancel what Kant regards as the purity of my will. Hegel's contention is that to apply any determinate criterion of duty is to think of one's action as one's duty because it has certain determinate empirical features; and to perform it because it is a fulfillment of *that* duty is to perform it because it has *those* features.

The point could also be put by saying that if there are to be determinate duties, then to act from duty is to act from those particular duties under the empirical circumstances where they arise; but that means to act from empirical motives, and not solely from the pure motive of duty. This entails that Kantians must not apply any substantive criterion of duty, since to use such a criterion is to do the action not only from duty but also because it has whatever features satisfy the criterion. Hence the moral standpoint precludes any objective criterion for moral action; it is capable of procuring a good conscience for even the most unethical actions.

To this argument there seems a very natural Kantian reply. To act from duty is to perform the action because it satisfies the categorical imperative in one or another of its formulations. If promise keeping is entailed by some formulation of the categorical imperative, then to act from duty entails keeping promises. Thus in order to act from duty it is not only possible but even necessary to perform actions with the empirical features that make them acts of promise keeping. These empirical features should not motivate the acts, but it is a corollary of acting from the categorical imperative that one should perform acts with those features.

This reply, however, misses the point of Hegel's criticism. Hegel thinks that in order to do one's duty as this particular duty, even if one derives the empirical features of that duty from some moral principle, one must act from those empirical features, and that to act from the empirical features of the act in this way is also to act from something that has the stamp of "particularity" on it; it is to act from empirical inclinations, interests, drives, passions. Hegel's thesis is that to act from a contentful principle is always to act from empirical motives; therefore, the only way to avoid acting from empirical motives would be either not to act at all or else to act in a determinate way while abstracting entirely from the empirical content of what one is doing – and so any determinate way of acting will do. In other words, to act from pure duty is to act from a principle with no content. The motive of pure duty thus attaches just as easily to the unethical as to the right and good.

10. Ends and empirical motivation

Hegel's argument is perhaps most explicitly stated in the *Phenomenology*. According to the moral world-view:

I act morally insofar as I am *conscious* of performing duty only, and not *something else,* and this means in fact *when I do not* act. When I actually act, I am conscious of an *other,* an *actuality* that is at hand, and of an actuality I will to produce; I have a *determinate* end and fulfill a *determinate* duty. There is something in it that is *other* than pure duty, which alone ought to be intended. (*PhG* ¶ 637)

The crucial thesis here is that to act on a contentful principle is to pursue an end, and that to pursue an end is necessarily to act from something other than pure duty; it is to act from empirical desires. Hegel often makes this point in a very abstract way by insisting that the universal and the particular are identical (*EL* §§ 163–164), or that the universal is actualized only in the particular (*VG* 85/72). As applied to moral psychology, this means that duty or the moral law ("the universal") can be carried out or actualized only through the medium of "the particular" – through the agent's empirical desires, drives, and inclinations (*PhG* ¶ 622).

The meaning of Hegel's thesis is ambiguous. Sometimes it seems to be a point about human nature, the point that people are not disposed to carry out substantial projects unless they are driven to do so by "interest," or "self-satisfaction," or moved at the level of their sensuous nature by elemental drives or passions: "Nothing great," he says, "has ever been accomplished without passion" (*VG* 85/73; *EG* §§ 474–475; *PR* § 121). Such statements have an air of worldly wisdom about them, and they may even be true, but they do not pose a serious challenge to Kantian morality. They only confirm Kant's own suspicions, in his more cynical moods, that perhaps even the best human will is impure in its motivation, so that maybe none of our actions possesses true moral worth.

Sometimes, however, Hegel suggests something different: that all action is mediated by inclination because every action has an end and the setting and pursuing of any particular end necessarily involves acting from empirical drives and inclinations. Recall the passage quoted earlier from the *Phenomenology:* "Since the *determinate* duty is an end, it has a content, its *content* is a part of the end, and so morality is not pure" (*PhG* ¶ 630). Or, as he puts it much later in the Berlin *Encyclopedia:*

An action is an end of the subject, just as [the subject] is its activity of carrying out this end. There is an action at all only through the fact that the subject is in it, i.e. through its interest, even in the most unselfish action. . . . [According to some people] drives and passions are opposed as a whole to duty for duty's sake, to morality. But drive and passion is nothing but the vitality of the subject, through which [the subject] is in its ends and their execution. (*EG* § 475R)

Every action is itself one of the agent's ends, since in our actions we seek to vindicate our own agency through the accomplishment of our other ends. But the vindication of my agency is always an aspect of my particular good, my subjective interest or "self-satisfaction." From this Hegel concludes that the ethical worth of an action is not in the least diminished by the fact that it is performed from inclination or passion, since it is an inevitable fact about agency that this should be so. Instead, "the ethical has to do with the content, which as a *universal* is something inactive, and has its activation in the subject. The fact that this content is immanent in the subject is interest, and when it lays claim to the whole of the effective subjectivity, it is passion" (*EG* § 475R).

Kantians must take this argument more seriously. Kant himself holds that every action has an end, acts done from duty every bit as much as acts done from immediate impulse or prudential calculation (*G* 436/54–55). Kant even maintains that ends that are duties (ends that it is my duty to have) play the chief role in determining our ethical duties as distinct from our duties of right (*TL* 381/38). Kant agrees with Hegel that there can be no application of the moral law, no specification of what our duties are, without the specification of the determinate ends of dutiful actions. Kant also holds that an act is devoid of moral worth if its motive consists in the agent's desire for the end of the action; acts so motivated are done from what Kant calls a "material principle"; such principles, he says, are without exception empirical and fall under the principle of self-love or one's own happiness (*KpV* 21–22/19–20). An act whose motive coincides with its end is heteronomous, done from inclination and not from duty. If all acts were necessarily of this kind, then the whole of morality (as Kant understands it) would be nothing but a cobweb of the brain.

Kant thinks it is a mistake to suppose that the motive of an action inevitably coincides with its end. An act done from duty has an end, which sometimes even includes the satisfaction of the agent's inclinations or particular interests. Kant never claims that the agent has to forego this self-satisfaction in order for the action to have moral worth. But this end, which Kant calls the "matter" of the agent's maxim, is not the motive of an action done from duty; rather, the motive in this case is the "legislative form" of the maxim, the fact that the maxim can be willed as a universal law (*KpV* 26–29/26–29).[11] One meaning of Kant's thesis that freedom of the will means that pure reason can *of itself* be practical is that an action can be performed directly by legislative reason, without the assistance of inclinations (*KpV* 41–42/43).

Chapter 8 expounded Hegel's reasons for rejecting Kant's view on this point. For Hegel, the relevant question of moral psychology is not about an act's psychic causes but about the intentional descriptions that provide the agent with the (internal) reasons for doing it. Since Hegel agrees with Kant that the act must be done for duty's sake, the intention of an act done by a good will must include its promotion of the good. Since every successful act also appeals to the agent because of the self-satisfaction it provides, this self-satisfaction will also belong to the intention. So equally might other empirical or self-interested motives without taking anything away from the goodness of the agent's will.

In the context of Hegel's moral psychology, to try to act solely from duty is to attempt to bring your action under no intentional description at all except that it is your duty to do it. This means abstracting yourself from the self-satisfaction necessary to every action. Such a view of oneself is incompatible with acting according to any determinate or contentful principles, since such principles will always supply further intentional descriptions ("keeping that promise," "helping this person") under which the act is sure to be brought by an agent engaged in fulfilling a concrete duty. "Pure duty consists in the empty abstraction of pure thinking, and has its reality and content only in a determinate actuality – an actuality that is the actuality of consciousness itself, and this not as a mere thought-entity but as an individual" (*PhG* ¶ 637).

Kantians may object that abstracting from self-satisfaction with respect to motivation is not the same thing as ignoring the existence of these desires or trying to extirpate them – a course to which Kant is opposed every bit as much as Hegel (*R* 57/50). The morally relevant question is only whether our action is motivated by the desire for that benefit or by the thought of duty. If Hegel is correct, though, then this is *not* a morally relevant question at all; it may not even be a meaningful question. In practice, Kant's criterion of moral worth estranges moral worth from self-satisfaction. It encourages us to think that we cannot esteem ourselves unless we act from an outlandish supernatural motive which no one ever really has.

11. Emptiness and Hegelian morality

Kantians might take some comfort from a brief review of the history of the emptiness charge, because it reveals an ironic tension in Hegel's views. Hegel developed the emptiness charge in the Jena period, when "morality" was little more than a nickname for an erroneous standpoint, typified by the moral philosophies of Kant and Fichte, and firmly committed to the unhealthy idea that the good will acts solely from duty. The moral psychology that enables Hegel to defend the emptiness charge was made explicit only in the writings after 1816 – as part of a revised conception of morality that attempts to integrate it positively within a modern ethical life.

Hegel's mature conception of morality seems to open up the possibility of a morality based on the good (the right united with universal well-being) yielding contentful principles from which a doctrine of duties might be derived. But even in his later thought Hegel continues to hold that there can be no doctrine of duties from the moral standpoint, that this standpoint yields no criterion except noncontradiction, and that a contentful theory of duties requires the standpoint of ethical life (*PR* § 148R). This seems to be the emptiness charge in the weak form, which says only that morality cannot provide an "adequate doctrine of duties" (*PR* § 148R). At the same time, it would be a very broad form of the emptiness charge, since it applies even to the standpoint of morality as Hegel accepts it.

How might Hegel try to justify the emptiness charge in this form? If the moral standpoint is limited to considering nothing but the rights and welfare of individuals, then it might not be able to deal with the value we accord to social institutions, and that might prevent it from giving an adequate doctrine of duties. Hegel holds, for example, that the state is a higher end than individual well-being as such (*PR* § 258), and that we value the "leading of a universal life" in the state for its own sake (*PR* § 258R). He might argue that these purely collective values have a role to play in determining the substance of our duties. They might, for instance, impose on us duties to show respect for due process of law (*PR* § 221) or the person of the monarch, who represents the free personality of the state (*PR* § 279), even when these acts of respect are not really necessary for the state's institutions to fulfill their end of securing the right and well-being of individuals. Such duties could be comprehended from the standpoint of ethical life, but not from the standpoint of morality, even on Hegel's most sympathetic understanding of the latter.

This may be a promising line of thought, but nowhere does Hegel devote himself to a sustained defense of it. To make his case, Hegel would have to argue that the value of rational institutions is both genuine and irreducible to individual right and well-being. He would have to show how the higher end of the state and other institutions actually does shape our duties, and he would have to show how the standpoint of ethical life can give an adequate account of the matters for which the moral standpoint is insufficient.[12] It is the emptiness charge in this broad but weak form that poses the most serious threat to the moral standpoint. In Chapters 11 and 12 we will examine some features of Hegelian ethical life which may lend further support to the emptiness charge in this form (see especially Chapter 12, §§ 2–3).

10
Conscience

1. The role of conscience in Hegelian ethics

In the *Philosophy of Right,* the emptiness of morality leads to ethical life and its system of substantive obligations. The *Phenomenology of Spirit* suggests an answer to emptiness *within* the moral standpoint. This is *conscience,* where the subjective will gives iself content through the immediate conviction that a particular act fulfills its duty. Conscience also has an important role to play in Hegel's mature ethical thought.

The standpoint of conscience is what we might now call a "situation ethics." Here the subject leaves behind general rules and principles, looks at the concrete situation, and takes upon herself the responsibility of choosing the act which she thinks that situation requires. Conscience selects an act because it is good in some respect, but in other respects the act may appear to be bad or even wrong. Hegel thinks that within the moral standpoint there is no way to resolve such conflicts. Consequently, conscience involves an unavoidable element of arbitrariness. Hegel emphasizes that there are no rules that bind conscience absolutely. Even what looks to others like an act of theft or cowardice may be represented by conscience as a duty (*PhG* ¶ 644). This gives a positive meaning to the emptiness charge: Because morality cannot provide completely determinate duties, there are certain points in the moral life where the subject's arbitrariness must step in.

Conscience is morally ambiguous, in part owing to the complexity of human situations, but even more to the fact that the particular subject's insight is the only authority competent to resolve moral problems. Conscience relies on the individual's "moral genius, which knows the inner voice of its immediate knowledge to be a divine voice" (*PhG* ¶ 655). Hence conscience cannot altogether avoid an attitude of self-worship. Taken together with the possibilities of deception and hypocrisy that accompany it, this puts conscience very close to moral evil. Hegel likes to point out that the subjective self-certainty that makes conscience the supreme stage of morality has much in common with that self-centeredness that is the essence of sin in the Christian tradition (*PhG* ¶ 660; *PR* § 139; cf. *PhG* ¶ 777).

Hegel's treatment of conscience is correspondingly ambivalent. It involves a critique of post-Kantian moral thinking, following Fichte. The *Phenomenology* account, it seems, aimed at the German Romantics, especially Friedrich Schlegel, Schleiermacher, and Novalis,[1] whereas the *Philosophy of Right*'s lengthy treatment of conscience looks like a sustained attack on the so-called *ethics of conviction (Überzeugungsethik)* developed by Jakob Friedrich Fries. Most of the present chapter will be devoted to this theme. But Hegel also regards conscience as a necessary element in morality, which not even the structures ethical life can displace. This positive side of Hegel's theory of conscience also deserves emphasis, and we will devote the rest of this section to it.

If the standpoint of conscience is premised on the absolute moral authority of the individual subject's insight, then Hegel agrees with the premise:

The right of the subjective will is that whatever it is to recognize as valid must be *seen by its insight as good.* (PR § 132)

[Subjectivity] is the *judging* power for a content to determine from within itself only what good is. (PR § 138)

Conscience expresses the absolute justification of subjective self-consciousness, namely that of knowing *in itself* and *from itself* what right and duty are, and of recognizing nothing as good except what it knows to be so; and simultaneously the assertion that what it knows and wills in this way is in *truth* right and duty. (PR § 137R)

Even the institutions of ethical life have authority over a modern subject only because they may be "developed out of subjectivity" (PR § 138A). Hegel acknowledges that there are times in history when the ethos of social life has become "faithless to better wills"; he thinks that it is in such times that the wise turn inward to their own consciences, seeking to win back inwardly the self-harmony that outward actuality has lost (PR § 138R).

Even in happier times when subjectivity is fulfilled by ethical life, conscience plays an important role in individual morality. The objective content of my duties is determined by my social relationships (PR § 148R), but that cannot possibly determine every detail of my conduct. The duties imposed by different relationships leave important gaps, and occasionally come into conflict with each other. Conscience has the task of deciding between conflicting ethical duties (PhG ¶ 635; VPR17: 87; VPR19: 118; VPR 2: 485). It can resolve these conflicts only because before conscience no duty is absolute; rather, the only absolute is pure duty, whose content is known by conscience (PhG ¶ 643).

In morality Hegel sees a tendency toward casuistry, an attempt to bring every decision under rules and principles. The emptiness of the moral standpoint means that this attempt is ultimately doomed to failure. But Hegel would also have reservations about moral casuistry even if it were successful. He regards its rule-following mentality as destructive of character, which shows itself best where moral rules fail. "Decisive particularity is what we usually call "character"; a man can act only insofar as he is a particular. The demand for a casuistry involves expressing the wish that a man wants to be relieved of the trouble of having a character" (VPR19: 119).

"Naive, substantial action," ethical action as the ancient world performed and perceived it – Hegel thinks – "requires self-forgetfulness in regard to particularity" (VPR19: 119). Consequently, there character takes the form of an instinct for action of extraordinary ethical virtuosity or "virtue" *(Tugend)* (PR § 150R). Modern self-consciousness, by contrast, demands that particularity should become reflective. This is the meaning of the modern idea that moral genius takes the form of individual conscience. Like morality itself, conscience is not displaced by ethical life, but remains an element within modern ethical life.

2. Fichte's moral epistemology

We saw in Chapter 9 that Fichte's moral principle is purely formal: "*Act always according to your best conviction of your duty*, or: Act according to your conscience" (*SL* 156/164), leaving it to be determined what our conscience tells us to do. Fichte's scientific system of ethics also includes a lengthy taxonomy and transcendental deduction of the "material" of our duties (*SL* 206–365/217–378). But he regards this as only transcendental philosophy, which he distinguishes from the way ordinary moral agents know their duties (*SL* 15/19, 208/219). The ordinary knowledge of duty is for him simply a special case of theoretical knowledge, whose general criterion is coherence with the entire system of the individual's theoretical convictions (*SL* 163–164/173–174).

Fichte sees a problem with this, since it leaves open the possibility that my whole system of theoretical convictions may be in error. In most theoretical matters, we may resign ourselves to a certain degree of skepticism. But where our duty is at stake, Fichte thinks that any degree of doubt at all is intolerable, because it presents us with the specter of moral luck. If the content of our duty is in doubt to us, then to that extent we are leaving the morality of our actions and characters to mere chance, which no conscientious moral agent can ever do (*SL* 164/174). Since conscientious action is fundamental to our moral vocation, the possibility of the moral life depends on the existence of an infallible criterion for the correctness of our moral convictions, which must be equally available to all moral agents (*SL* 164–165/174–175).

When I inquire into any matter, my theoretical faculties present me with arguments and evidence of various kinds. While I consider the evidence, my imagination hovers (*schwebt*) between belief and disbelief regarding a proposition (*SL* 167/177). Sometimes this results in a judgment. A judgment is an act; it is practical in nature. Occasionally, the evidence gives to a particular judgment the distinctive quality of *certainty*. This happens when I am moved to the judgment by a *feeling* of certainty (or truth). This feeling is the final criterion of certainty in all matters. When the judgment is about our duty, Fichte calls the feeling of certainty "conscience" (*SL* 173/183). Fichte insists that the feeling of certainty must be possible in regard to every question of duty. Otherwise we could not be certain it is our duty, and so it could not be required of us (*SL* 168–169/178–179). Further, the feeling of perfect certainty must be unmistakable; if we could be sincerely mistaken in thinking we have it, then this would once again make it a matter of chance whether we have done what duty requires (*SL* 174/184).

Fichte's epistemology at this point has much in common with Descartes's. For both philosophers, we arrive at convictions by theoretically contemplating the evidence and then judging through our practical faculty or will. When the evidence is strong enough, it produces in us a special state of perfect certainty where belief is irresistible. Descartes calls this state "clear and distinct perception." Fichte considers it a feeling of the harmony of our pure and empirical ego, in which my contingent judgment experiences a harmony with the universal conditions of selfhood which serve as the norm of rationality (SL 166/176). Fichte's own explicit comparison, however, is with the Kantian theory of aesthetic judgment: The feeling of certainty claims objective validity but has an immediacy that precludes any conceptual or discursive demonstration (SL 167/176). Fichte does not mean that demonstrations and evidence are irrelevant to arriving at theoretical convictions; his point is rather that discursive arguments and evidence produce conviction in us only when they engage our practical faculty to come to a decision. Evidence can lead us to the trough, but we are convinced only when the practical self chooses to take the plunge. Doubt and uncertainty are states of the will, accompanied by anxiety and dissatisfaction, whereas conviction brings the self into a state of harmony with itself, which we experience as at once free and necessary, giving us peace and satisfaction (SL 167/177). Fichte shares with Descartes the view that belief or conviction, though occasioned by theoretical evidence contemplated by the intellect, is actually a state of the will.

Conscience does not supply the content of our duties (the theoretical understanding does that); it is rather the feeling that convinces us that something is our duty (SL 173/183). Fichte holds that we have a duty always to heed our conscience; that is, we must always inquire into the content of our duty until we arrive at the feeling of certainty, and then follow the conviction accompanied by that feeling (SL 174/183–184). Fichte admits that we are sometimes uncertain whether something is our duty. Sometimes we judge something to be our duty when it is not, and sometimes we believe we are following our conscience when we are not. He thinks that such things can occur only through the "darkening" of our moral consciousness by culpable self-deception (SL 192–196/202–206). The voice of conscience always speaks to us and its voice is infallible; but sometimes we choose either to pervert its message or not to listen to it at all. Moral uncertainty and moral error are always something for which we are to blame.

Both Kant and Fichte say there can be no such thing as an "erring conscience," but they mean different (even incompatible) things by the saying. Kant admits that we are fallible in our objective judgment whether something is our duty, but denies that I can err as to whether I have compared my action with my practical reason, and identifies conscience with the judgment that I have made such a comparison (TL 401/61). If we are fallible in the way Kant says, then conscience in Fichte's sense can err. On the other hand, if we can "darken" our moral consciousness in the manner Fichte describes, then it is possible to judge falsely that we have compared our action with our concept of duty, and that is an erring conscience in Kant's sense. Kantian and Fichtean theories aside, it looks as if an erring conscience (in both their senses) is a fairly common fact of life.

Fichte argues that because the feeling of certainty is the final epistemic court of appeal, it is impossible for a conviction accompanied by it ever to be in error (*SL* 174/183–184). This argument is not fully persuasive. What if we acquire a conviction (accompanied by the feeling of certainty) that an earlier conviction of ours (also so accompanied) was in error? This, or something rather like it, apparently happens in some cases when I change my mind on a moral question. Though I earlier felt perfectly certain of my position, I now feel equally certain that my earlier conviction was wrong, despite the certainty I used to feel. In such cases people do not always judge that they were not really certain before, or that they have been deceiving themselves. They sometimes judge that they used to feel perfectly certain, but now see that they must have been mistaken. Fichte nowhere argues that this could not happen, and he does not tell us how to reconcile it with his claim that conscience cannot err.

3. Fries and the ethics of conviction

Jakob Friedrich Fries (1773–1843) came to Jena as a *Privatdozent* at the same time as Hegel in 1801. He was promoted to professor at Heidelberg in 1805; Hegel succeeded him in 1816 when Fries moved to a professorship at Jena. The two men were personal rivals as well as disagreeing philosophically. In the Spring of 1819, one of Fries's students, Karl Ludwig Sand, assassinated the reactionary writer August von Kotzebue. It was this event that gave the Holy Alliance and Prussian reactionaries the pretext they needed to promulgate the Carlsbad Decrees, instituting censorship of academic publications and taking other repressive measures against academics perceived as subversive "demagogues." Fries had given a well-known speech, filled with republican and German nationalist sentiments, at the Wartburg Festival in 1817 (see *PR* Preface 17–20). Using this as an excuse, the authorities dismissed Fries from his professorship at Jena in 1820 as part of the so-called demagogue persecutions (the professorship was restored to him in 1824).

Fries accepts Fichte's principle that the fundamental moral duty is to follow your conscience, that is, to act according to your moral convictions: "The command of duties of virtue commands: to act from respect for the law according to one's conviction of what the duty of virtue requires" (Fries, *NKV* 3: 189). The "immediate command of virtue" is: "Give allegiance to your own conviction of duty!" (Fries, *HPP* 243; cf. *HPP* 158, 164).

Unlike Fichte, however, Fries allows us no infallible faculty for the knowledge of our duty. He thinks that sincerely following their conscience, moral agents sometimes do what is objectively wrong. Conscience, he insists is "educable" *(bildungsfähig)* (*HPP* 214). But like Kant and Fichte before him, Fries also defends the claim that conscience is "infallible," once again giving the claim his own interpretation.

It can easily appear that the doctrine of the infallibility of conscience stands against this doctrine of the educability of conscience. The following should clear this up. For

178

the man who has attained to purity *(Lauterkeit),* conscience is *infallible* according to an identical proposition; for no more can be demanded of any man than that he faithfully follow his *pure* conviction. Now since conscience expresses this conviction, it is always right for every individual man in the moment. *(HPP* 214–215)

For Fries, the infallibility of conscience means that those who act on errone-ous moral convictions should not be blamed; on the contrary, they should be most highly esteemed, since they show true "purity of soul" or respect for the practical spirit, which is the highest moral good *(JE* 49/20).

Fries holds that when we judge others, we ought to judge them only by the standard of *their* moral convictions, never by our own:

The first law of the philosophical theory of virtue is that of the good disposition of character: respect for the practical spirit. Correctness of conviction in respect of the command is by contrast only the second law. Hence the first rule by which I should compare the actions of others with the duty of virtue must be distinguished from the rule that tells me what duties are laid on me. For each can be judged only according to his own conviction, and what it would be wrong to do according to a correct convic-tion can for the individual be precisely what accords with duty. *(NKV 3:* 190)

It might appear that this still permits us to hold individuals blamable for their wrong moral convictions, since correctness of conviction is at least men-tioned as a "second law." But Fries intends this second law for the purpose of judging actions only, never agents; his principle for the moral judgment of individuals focuses exclusively on their motivation or "disposition" and not at all on the objective rightness or wrongness of what they do: "All legal estimation of individual actions as to their dutifulness or undutifulness be-longs only to the theory of right, and has no place in a proper theory of virtue, since this has to do only with dispositions" *(NKV 3:* 190).

Kant says that the shopkeeper who deals honestly with customers because it is good business performs acts that have "legality" but not "morality"; the acts deserve praise and encouragment, but they have no moral worth and do not deserve the esteem that is reserved for the good will *(KpV* 71/74; *TL* 219/ 17; *G* 397–399/13–16). Fries, however, thinks that this notion of "legality" belongs entirely to the theory of right, and has no place at all in morality. He apparently thinks that Kant's shopkeeper is no different morally from a shopkeeper who *cheats* his customers because he believes it to be good busi-ness, since both act from the same (impure, self-interested) disposition or motivation. On the other hand, Fries holds that if I am convinced that it is my duty to do something and do it from a morally pure disposition, then I should be esteemed rather than blamed for doing it, even if objectively it is morally wrong. Of course, if my action violates some positive law, then it is legally punishable, and if it violates another's right, then it may be con-demned from the standpoint of right; but Fries holds that morality or the theory of virtue can have nothing to say against it.

Fries's student Karl Follen, leader of the student *Burschenschaft* in Jena, drew extreme consequences from these teachings, combining them with a political radicalism which Fries shared only to a lesser degree. Follen espoused an extreme ethical individualism, which encouraged action on a personal moral code independent or even in defiance of accepted moral standards. In the political realm, he advocated a "theory of individual terror" in which even an act of political murder belongs to "a war of one individual against other individuals," and must be deemed a praiseworthy act if motivated by conscience. "Wherever there is a conviction won through free will and one's own cognition, for those so convinced, every means is permissible, even if it contradicts the common moral code. The only essential thing for the agent is to be responsible to one's own conviction."[2] Karl Sand came under Follen's influence. He believed (probably correctly) that Kotzebue was a Russian agent attempting to subvert the reform government in Prussia in the interests of the Tsar. Sand's murder of Kotzebue was apparently motivated by the conviction that it was his patriotic duty. (With Sand's help, of course, Kotzebue served the interests of the reaction far more effectively dead than he ever could have done alive.)

Fries probably did not share Sand's conviction that it was his duty to assassinate Kotzebue, but since he holds that we must judge agents morally only by their own convictions, not by ours, he must say that if Sand sincerely believed it was his duty to kill Kotzebue and acted out of a pure intention, then Sand is to be esteemed rather than blamed for what he did.[3]

4. A problem about moral error and blame

Fichte's moral epistemology and Fries's ethics of conviction may be viewed as two ways of dealing with a problem about moral error and responsibility. People often disagree with one another about what is morally right and wrong. Some hold that legalized abortion countenances mass murder, whereas others maintain that laws against abortion violate the basic human right over one's own body. If *either* of these beliefs is correct, then successful implementation of the incorrect belief (whichever it is) involves very serious wrongdoing.

Assume for a moment that abortion is murder of the innocent. Then physicians who perform abortions intentionally commit an act which, judged according to correct moral principles, is wrong. We will think such physicians blamable if we accept the following.

(1) It is blamable intentionally to do what is morally wrong; that is, if acts falling under description XYZ are wrong, then it is blamable to perform an act that is intentional under description XYZ.

To the extent that we are initially disposed to agree with (1), then, we are, with Hegel, disposed to reject Fries's ethics of conviction.

Now assume, on the other hand, that abortion is not murder, but rather that a physician who performs an abortion only aids a woman in the exercise of a fundamental human right. Even granting this, we ought to find it difficult to approve of physicians who believe they are butchering innocent babies when they perform abortions but who continue to perform abortions without qualm because it pays good money. We may think them blamable, even though a physician with different (as we are assuming, correct) moral beliefs would not be blamable. In that case, we are disposed to accept:

(2) It is blamable to do something you believe is morally wrong, to act against your own conscience, even if what you are doing is not really morally wrong.

Perhaps the strongest point of the views of Fichte and Fries that we have been examining is their fundamental commitment to (2).

Taken together, (1) and (2) threaten to conflict with another commonly held belief, which could be loosely stated as

(3) We can be blamable only for what is up to us.

Suppose that Sand, doing his best to discover moral truth, comes to the false conviction that it is his duty to kill Kotzebue. Then [by (1)] Sand is blamable if he intentionally kills Kotzebue, and [by (2)] he is blamable if he does not. But if Sand has done his best to find moral truth, then it was not up to him to avoid his error. Consequently, if both (1) and (2) are true, then Sand is blamable for something that is not up to him. That contradicts (3).

5. Some solutions to the problem

We could accept (1), (2), and (3) all without inconsistency, if we said that it is after all up to Sand to avoid incorrect moral beliefs. This seems to be the position Aristotle takes when he argues that we are responsible for the way the good appears to us because the appearance depends on our character, and our character is up to us because it is formed through our voluntary actions, which are up to us.[4] This position is not very satisfactory, though. It is doubtful that our characters are *wholly* a product of actions that are up to us. Even if they were, it would not necessarily follow that our character itself is up to us. When I add up a long column of figures, each stroke of my pencil is up to me, but that doesn't entail that it is always up to me to avoid making an error in the addition. Further, Aristotle does not explain how we can be blamed for the earliest actions through which our characters were first formed. These must have been chosen according to an appearance of the good that was not up to us.

Fichte's solution is similar, but not vulnerable to the same objections. He holds that if we inquire conscientiously into the content of our duty, we can always arrive at a conviction accompanied by the feeling of certainty; such a conviction is infallible, and only an action performed in accordance with such a conviction is performed according to conscience. If Sand had inquired conscientiously, he would inevitably have arrived at the correct conviction. If he arrives at an incorrect conviction, then he must be darkening his moral consciousness (either he has arrived at a correct conviction about his duty, and deceives himself as to what his conscience told him to do, or he has failed to convince himself fully concerning his duty and deceives himself in thinking that his conviction is accompanied by the feeling of certainty).

The main problem with Fichte's solution is that it is not plausible to think either that every case of moral uncertainty has to result from culpable neglect of our duty to inquire or that every moral error has to result from self-deception. Honest inquiry always has uncertainty as one possible outcome (skeptics even argue that it is the only possible outcome of any inquiry). Moral issues are often more complex than questions of mathematics, physics, or even history. Sometimes the only way to *avoid* self-deception is to admit that your moral convictions are not certain. When he insists that due consideration of a moral issue has to result in a conviction accompanied by the feeling of perfect certainty, Fichte commits himself to the position that we have not given due consideration to a moral issue until we have converted ourselves into rigid fanatics about it.[5]

Many are attracted to a less radical version of Fichte's view. Fichte insists that we have a duty to inquire carefully into the content of our duty (*SL* 163–164/173–174). Even if this inquiry involves no capacities for infallible knowledge, we still might blame people whose moral error results from a failure to inquire diligently, since that failure is up to them. Along these lines, Alan Donagan thinks that we are responsible for moral error only when the error is due to "negligence" or "want of due consideration."[6] But this offers no solution to our present problem. Unless we embrace Fichte's extreme view, the problem continues to arise whenever we have inquired diligently enough to fulfill our duty of inquiry, but have nevertheless arrived at the wrong result. It looks as though Donagan wants either to apply some notion of diminished responsibility to such cases, or else to treat moral error as simply irrelevant to the agent's moral worth.

In § 9 we shall consider the view that false moral convictions might be an excusing condition. At first blush, however, the other alternative would seem preferable. When I act on a false moral conviction, I am normally a full-fledged agent, engaging all my faculties and sentiments just as I would if my belief were correct. I may in fact have done everything in my power to do my duty, including a due consideration of what my duty is in this case. Rather than regarding me as not responsible for my actions, it might seem more appropriate to give me credit for doing my best.

In effect, that is Fries's position, which proposes to solve the problem simply by denying (1). Fries thinks that we have a duty to inquire after the correct answer to moral questions, but our intellectual powers are not infallible. Correct moral belief is a sign of an educated understanding, not of a pure will. The true measure of a person is not the intellect but the heart, not external acts and their consequences but inner purity of disposition:

> If we wish to pass judgment upon the true worth of someone else's life, we must remember that virtue is not the law. What is important is not the fact that an externally virtuous action has been performed but that virtue has been internally willed and practiced. . . . If we now ask, "What then is the good?" only the educated understanding could give a correct reply. The decision is no longer a matter of the will but

of insight, so that here even the purest and the best in earthly life could err and be mistaken. (Fries, *JE* 49/20, 55/23)

6. Mistaken criticisms of Fries

If you act on a mistaken moral conviction, some might blame you for the action only, whereas others might blame you for the belief as well. Hegel's attack on the ethics of conviction has to do with blaming actions, not beliefs. If Hegel thinks that people are blamable simply for holding erroneous moral convictions, he never says so. But he does insist that if such convictions lead me to do something wrong, then I am to blame for it.

Hegel's extended discussion of this point (at *PR* § 140R) plainly has Fries's ethics of conviction as its principal target.[7] So regarded, however, many of Hegel's criticisms miss their mark, since they are based on plain misunderstandings of Fries's position. It is important to get a clear view of where some of Hegel's criticisms go wrong if we are to appreciate where Fries's position is really vulnerable to Hegel's attacks.

Hegel criticizes a view according to which "*subjective opinion* is expressly given out as the rule of right and duty, since the *conviction that holds something to be right* is to be that through which the ethical nature of the action is determined" (*PR* § 140R: 272). He apparently takes this view to hold that whatever moral beliefs the subject holds are correct (at least for that subject), so that there is no such thing as an objective or impersonal truth about ethical matters. Thus Hegel charges that "with [the ethics of conviction] ethical objectivity completely disappears" (*PR* § 140R, pp. 272).

Hegel points out that when this view undermines the very possibility of objective truth and error in ethics, it also rules out many of its own claims. First, it can no longer mitigate crime and evil by saying they are "only errors" since it denies there is any such thing as moral error (*PR* § 140R, p. 275). Next, the view no longer permits me to quarrel with those who condemn the actions I perform out of my convictions, since their act of condemnation also accords with their conviction, and so it is entirely correct (*PR* § 140R, p. 276). Finally, this view no longer even gives us any reason to respect people's convictions, since the value of conviction is based on the fact that it is a serious attempt to possess the truth, and the view denies that there is any truth in moral matters. Conviction is "accidental and trivial, really something quite external, which could strike me this way or that way"; consequently, "my being convinced is in fact the most trifling thing if I cannot know the truth" (*PR* § 140R, p. 276).

These criticisms would be fatal against a moral relativist or antirealist who claims that there is no objective truth about right, wrong, and duty and then, in a liberal spirit, tries to infer from this that the only appropriate moral measure is the conformity of an action to the agent's own moral convictions. If you deny that there is any moral truth, then you have no business trying to correct people's erroneous moral judgments. If any conviction is as true as any other, then those who believe in *blaming* actions because they are performed according to the agent's moral convictions judge just as truly as those who believe in esteeming those actions.

Fries is not a relativist or antirealist of this kind. He does not deny the objectivity of moral truth and does not hold that an act is right or dutiful whenever the subject is convinced it is. His position depends on distinguishing between two questions:

(A) Is this act (objectively) right or wrong?
(B) Should I be esteemed or blamed for performing it?

Fries thinks that even when I have done what is objectively wrong, I should be esteemed rather than blamed if I followed my conviction. He does not think that my erroneous conviction thereby acquires any sort of truth.

Far from denying the possibility of erroneous moral convictions, Fries's view actually depends on it, since its central claims concern just those cases in which someone's moral conviction is in error. Since Fries agrees that our convictions aim at objective truth, he may also deny that it is trivial or incidental what I believe. The inner purity of my will does not depend on whether my convictions are correct, but the objective rightness of my actions does. If others, following their own convictions, blame me for my conscientious actions, then Fries is indeed committed to saying that I should not blame them for doing so. But he thinks that their convictions are nevertheless in error on this point, and he may try to convince them that their blame is misplaced.

According to Hegel, the ethics of conviction does away with the distinction between honesty and hypocrisy which appears to matter so much to a view emphasizing purity of heart: "Whatever a human being does can always be justified by the reflection on it of good intentions and motives and the conviction that it is good" (*PR* § 140R, p. 274). As Hegel presents it, the ethics of conviction considers an action justified whenever the agent represents it as good in any respect at all, and, since no act would be performed unless the agent found some good in it, it follows that any act (of lying, or theft, or cowardice, or murder) can be justified (*PR* § 140R, p. 271–272/97; cf. *PhG* ¶ 644). "The evil" (as Hegel puts it) "could be only what I am not convinced of" (*PR* § 140A).

This is plainly a gross caricature of Fries's position. Fries allows for cases of hypocrisy, since his theory allows the possibility that I may deceive others (or myself) about whether my action violates my own moral convictions. Clearly I can represent an act as good in some respect without representing it as my duty, so Fries need not approve of all agents who see some good aspect in what they do.

Further, I can be of the *opinion* that the act is my duty without being (in Fries's sense) *convinced* that it is my duty. Fries distinguishes "conviction" *(Überzeugung)* from mere "opinion" *(Meinung)*. Conviction, though fallible, is formed by a process of moral education and experience, yet "not by learning rules but by the exercise of the moral sentiment" (*NKV 3*: 206–208; cf. *JE* 54/23). Fries does not consider me blameless when I act on an erroneous moral opinion that has been formed carelessly, without the influence of a decent moral education or the exercise of my moral sentiments. In fact, Fries insists that my conviction must be "pure" *(lauter):* "By the virtue of purity I understand a man's truthfulness and sincerity toward himself and in himself" *(HPP* 344); self-deceiving moral beliefs and rationalizations do not count for Fries as "pure convictions."

If Hegel means to imply that on Fries's view there could be no such thing as acting blamably, then this is clearly mistaken. For one thing, Fries appears to think that we are blamable for acting on impure convictions, *even if they are objectively correct.* Whether my convictions are objectively correct or not, it is certainly possible for me to act against them, and Fries thinks that this violation of my own conscience is always blamable.

Fries was among the first of a long line of critics to charge that Hegel's philosophy of the state was shaped by professional ambition and personal timidity. Hegel's theory, he asserted, "has grown not in the gardens of science but on the dunghill of servility."[8] Fries may have been suggesting that Hegel was betraying his own political convictions, even violating his moral conscience in the process. If that suggestion is correct, then Hegel is guilty of something rather more serious than a logical blunder when he alleges that Fries's ethics of conviction makes it impossible to act blamably.

7. The emptiness of an ethics of conviction

In expounding his ethics of conviction, Fries usually considers cases in which a person acting on erroneous moral convictions is being judged by another person who does not share them. This displays the ethics of conviction to best advantage, by emphasizing the agents' common conscientiousness and leaving intact each one's moral commitments. Things look different if I apply the ethics of conviction to my attitude toward my own convictions.

If I am truly conscientious, I follow my convictions not because they are *mine,* but because (so I think) they are *correct.* I devote myself to a cause because I believe that this particular cause is right, and that indifference or opposition to it would be wrong. Further, I am usually moved to such devotion not only because I approve the cause in the abstract, but also because my self-worth is bound up with it. I esteem myself for serving it and would feel ashamed of myself if I let it down. The ethics of conviction tends to undermine this element of self-concern involved in our moral convictions. The ethics of conviction allows it to make a difference where moral truth lies, and whether I have found it. But it does not allow this to make any difference to my moral self-worth. The ethics of conviction tells me, in effect, that I would lose none of my moral worth by fighting on the other side of the barricades, provided only that I fought with a devoted spirit and had been sincerely duped by the enemy's lies. In this way, Hegel is not altogether wrong when he charges that the ethics of conviction makes the holding of one conviction rather than another into something incidental and trivial. This defect in the ethics of conviction seems especially serious in the context of an ethics which, like Fichte's, Fries's, or Hegel's, makes the agent's self-concern fundamental to the moral life.

It is as if the main point is to keep your soul busy at something or other; the struggle between good and evil matters only because it provides you with something to do. From this point of view, it makes no difference which side you are on, so long as you are devoted to some cause or other. If we take this attitude, however, it is not clear that we can really be devoted to any cause. The ethics of conviction says in effect that if you pray fervently, it does not matter whether you pray to Jaweh or to Baal. The problem is that the only way you are going to pray with any fervor to any deity is to leave the ethics of conviction behind you at the door of the temple.[9]

When Hegel claims that the appeal to conscience can justify anything at all (*PR* § 140R,A; *PhG* ¶ 644), he associates the shortcomings of the ethics of conviction with the emptiness charge. Prima facie the claim appears quite misdirected, since there is nothing in the ethics of conviction itself that precludes the existence of contentful moral principles. But Hegel is onto an important truth here as well. For Hegel, the good will is one whose insight and intention accord with the good (*PR* § 131). The ethics of conviction empties the good will of nearly all its content in the sense that it calls a will good even when its insight and intention are utterly opposed to what is objectively good. As Hegel describes it, the ethics of conviction holds that "goodness of will consists in *willing the good;* this willing of the *abstract good* is sufficient, indeed the sole sufficient requirement for making an action good" (*PR* § 140R, p. 269).

Fries allows that a pure will can perform an *act* that is bad, if it embraces a false conviction. But he thinks that the *will* itself is good whenever it does what it sincerely believes is good. Hegel is quite right to wonder whether this supplies the good will with enough content to distinguish it from a thoroughly evil will. Divorced from any specific conviction about what is good, the only constraints it places on the good will are those contained in the abstract concept of "goodness" itself. Thus Hegel uses the emptiness of an ethics of conviction to effect a dialectical reversal of the concept of moral good into moral evil (*PR* § 139; *PhG* ¶ 660). If we follow the ethics of conviction, Hegel alleges, we are committed to approve even an evil will as good.

Perhaps the abstract concept of "good" puts *some* limits on what can count as a good will. Philippa Foot has argued that the very concept of "morality" excludes certain beliefs, preferences, evaluations, and so on from being "moral."[10] But such purely conceptual constraints are nowhere close to sufficient. They allow the good will to be shaped by moral convictions that are tailored to the interests of those who hold them[11] or by systems of moral education whose content may be as barbaric, racialist, or ideological as you please.

Fries himself is an example. In an edict of March 12, 1812, Chancellor Hardenberg decreed that Jews were to enjoy full civil and political rights in Prussia. Hegel supported the edict (*PR* §§ 209, 270R, p. 421n), but Fries lent his support to the movement that wanted to overturn it or at least inhibit its enforcement. Fries's moral education and fallible sentiments led him to the sincere conviction that Jews are an alien people who can never become citizens of a German state (*GDJ* 3), and that "the whole Jewish caste should be extirpated root and branch" from German society because this "worthless caste of conniving second-hand peddlers" poses "the gravest danger to the state" (*GDJ* 18).

We ought to wonder how much worth there is in a "good will" if its "goodness" may be specified through convictions such as these. We may doubt that there is any reason to extend more moral credit to the sentiments and intentions that accompany those who oppress or persecute others on the basis of such convictions than to those who violate the rights of others simply from self-interest. If you are going to do wrong, it seems cleaner somehow to do it openly (either with a bad conscience or with none at all) than to sanctify your conduct with a convenient set of moral convictions. It is not only hypocrisy that bothers us here. Doesn't our repugnance for wrongdoing actually increase in proportion to the self-righteous sincerity with which the wrongdoers justify their conduct? Shouldn't we say of sincere belief in a bad cause exactly what Kant (*G* 394/10) says of resoluteness and self-control, that it makes a villain not only more dangerous, but also more abominable?

8. The hypocrisy of conscience

Hegel regards the appeal to individual conscience as a feature of the Germanic world and its appreciation of the right of subjectivity. He treats the validity of appeals to conscience as connected with the social practice of declaring them in language and having one's declaration recognized and accepted by others. Conscience is valid only in a moral community that extends moral credit to such declarations (*PhG* ¶¶ 647–653). But the possibility that I accept an appeal to conscience as justification for your action goes hand in hand with the possibility that I will treat this appeal as a sham. To the extent that you are free to justify any action by an appeal to your subjective conscience, I am equally free to interpret your act as evil and your declaration of conscience as hypocrisy (*PhG* ¶¶ 659–660).

Hegel thinks that this is part of the moral ambiguity that attaches inevitably to any subjective action. The ambiguity is limited to the extent that conscience has been given a content in the form of duties whose objective validity is recognized by the entire moral community. Thus he distinguishes "the truthful conscience" *(das wahrhafte Gewissen),* which is "the disposition to will what is good in and for itself" from the merely "formal conscience," which is an appeal to subjective conviction with no determinate content of its own (*PR* § 137). The truthful conscience relates to a system of objective principles and duties, founded in ethical life, and is nothing but the awareness of them by the moral subject. The formal conscience is nothing but the "infinite formal self-certainty of *this* subject." It may be either good or evil; its declarations may be accepted or not.

The appeal to formal conscience depends on a social framework in which there is objective knowledge of the content of good and duty. Formal conscience operates at the fringes of the system, where ethical standards are indeterminate, conflicting, or disputable. I accept your appeal to conscience as indicative of a good will only insofar as I am assured in advance that by and large you have a good will, that your insight and intention accord with the objective good. These assurances rest on the conformity of your conduct to what is objectively right in cases where this is determinate. To the extent that your conviction or intention deviate from what I accept as objectively good, the conscience to which you appeal becomes merely formal; your appeals to conscience lose their credit with me, and they deserve to lose it.

Hypocrisy, according to Hegel, involves two things: knowledge of the true universal, and an attempt to represent something conflicting with the universal as something conforming to it (the representation may be either to others or self-deceptively to oneself) (*PR* § 140R, pp. 267–268). If this is the nature of hypocrisy, then there seems nothing inherently "untruthful" or hypocritical about formal conscience, when used to justify action on erroneous moral convictions. Even formal conscience contains the agent's honestly held convictions; there seems nothing hypocritical in that.

Suppose, however, that we consider my appeal to formal conscience on the supposition that I subscribe to the ethics of conviction. If I acknowledge that my convictions about what is right may be erroneous, then my appeal to conscience is an attempt to pass off as objectively right something that may not be right at all. There is something inherently hypocritical in trying to justify myself by appealing to the principle that I should not be blamed as long as I am following my own moral convictions. For if I appeal *solely* to formal conscience in order to do this – as the ethics of conviction says I may do – then I am representing my fallible conviction as a standard of objective rightness – something which it is not, and which *I know* it is not. The appeal of conscience "solely *to itself* is directly opposed to what it seeks to be – that is, the rule for a rational and universal mode of action that is valid in and for itself" (*PR* § 137R). If I am honest with myself and others, I will not attempt to deny that to the extent that I act on moral convictions that are objectively wrong, my will is implicated in the evil that I do, and I am blamable for it.

Those who take objective moral truth seriously are sometimes confronted with the rhetorical question, But who is to say what the moral truth is? The question is rhetorical because its real purpose is to suggest that if you think that objective truth is important in morality, then you must arrogantly suppose yourself to be in possession of it. But that is wrong. The point is rather this: To the extent that we are uncertain whose moral convictions are correct, we are also uncertain about who has the good will and who deserves blame. If I hold you to blame because you are acting on moral beliefs I think are mistaken, then I must concede at the same time that if your beliefs turn out to be right and mine to be wrong, then it is I and not you who deserves blame. If we take moral truth seriously, that should not make us more arrogant about asserting the truth of our moral convictions, but more modest about assuring ourselves and others of our goodness of will.

Kant, too, thinks that we can never be sure whether we have a good will, because we are opaque to ourselves and can never be sure of the inner purity of our motives. Hegelian morality points to a different kind of uncertainty about the same thing, a different self-opacity coming not from inside but from outside. The goodness of our will is uncertain not because we cannot fathom the depths of our hearts, but because we live in a complex world where a good cause is sometimes difficult to distinguish from an evil cause.[12]

9. The right of insight

We noted earlier that Fries's ethics of conviction is not the only response to the problem about moral error and blame raised in § 4. Another option we mentioned was to regard moral error as an excusing condition. We might say that people who act on erroneous conviction are not to blame for the evil they do because they are not responsible for their acts. Hegel is aware of this option, and discusses it separately from the ethics of conviction.

We might even wonder whether Hegel shouldn't embrace this option himself, since he claims that the moral will has a "right of insight into the good":

> The right of the subjective will is that whatever it is to recognize as valid must be *seen by its insight as good,* and that an action, as an end stepping into external objectivity, should be imputed to it as just or unjust, good or evil, legal or illegal, according to its *cognizance (Kenntnis)* of the value that it has in this objectivity. (PR § 132)

This statement is carefully guarded. Hegel does not hold that the will can disown a wrong action whenever it fails to have insight into its wrongness. Instead, he claims that the will can repudiate only those actions of whose worth "in external objectivity" it has no "cognizance."

We are sometimes *cognizant* of things we don't know (or even believe). This happens when we have been apprised of them but have not taken in or accepted the information, or when we have sufficient grounds to believe them but have not drawn the right conclusions from these grounds. Hegel holds us responsible even for what we are ignorant of, so long as we are cognizant of it. In this sense, he agrees with Aristotle that "every vicious person is ignorant of the actions he must do or avoid and this sort of error makes people unjust, and in general bad" (PR § 140R, footnote)[13]; but only with an important qualification: Ignorance makes us bad only if we are cognizant of what we must do and avoid. It follows that ignorance in moral matters excuses only if the agent had no way of knowing the principles involved.[14]

Hegel's commitment to this view is indicated by several other things he says. He cites the right of subjectivity as a reason for saying that a state is unjust to its citizens unless its legal code is publicly known and intelligible to those who are expected to abide by it (PR § 215,R). More generally, Hegel maintains that the duties and institutions of ethical life must be "universal," so that the subject can understand their rationality and bindingness: "It is through the publicity of laws and through universal ethics *(Sitten)* that the state takes away the formality and contingency which the right of insight has for the subject at [the moral] standpoint" *(PR* § 132R). It is a function of moral education to put the subject in possession of the "cognizance" of what is objectively right and good *(PR* §§ 132R, 174, 187R, 315).

Hegel seems to presume that the modern state nearly always makes its members cognizant of the moral truths they need to know, so that the right of insight provides an excuse only for those ("children, imbeciles, lunatics") who lack the normal capacity to comprehend the rationality behind the laws and the prevailing ethical norms *(PR* § 132R). For the rest, Hegel regards the right of insight as involving only a moral duty imposed by subjects on *themselves:* "I can make the demand on myself and regard it as a subjective right that I have insight into an obligation from *good* grounds and a *conviction* concerning it, and still more, that I cognize it from its concept and nature" *(PR* § 132R).

This account is convincing if we suppose that there are social authorities (political, ecclesiastical, pedagogical) whose word on moral matters is reasonably trustworthy and provides us with a consistent set of moral standards. Such authorities might be taken to make moral agents cognizant of moral truth. Hegel doesn't suppose that conscientious moral subjects will follow the authorities blindly; they will think for themselves about moral questions and find their own reasons for embracing the correct convictions. As self-conscious subjects it is even their duty to do so *(PR* §§ 132R, 138).

But what if the social authorities are divided on moral questions? Worse yet, what if the most powerful of them advance errors or self-serving lies and ideology in the name of moral truth? In that case, the authorities do not make moral subjects "cognizant" of moral truth, but instead misinform (or disinform) them. Or again, suppose the authorities are seriously divided, and a moral subject, after carefully weighing all sides, ends up believing the wrong one. Does that count as being "cognizant" of the moral truth which the subject has rejected? Why is that subject more blamable than those who are not "cognizant" of the rejected truth because they have heard it only from quite untrustworthy sources?

In modern society as it actually exists, these are not merely speculative questions. Orthodoxy on many moral questions (if there is such a thing at all) is often rejected by dissenters representing a variety of different alternatives. Often these dissenters include some of the society's most sensitive, sophisticated, and articulate members. On many vital subjects, there is often no reliable moral authority. Thinking for oneself may often involve a rejection of moral orthodoxy rather than (as Hegel optimistically assumes) its subjective confirmation.[15] In this situation, Hegel's "right of insight" provides us with no clear way of deciding when people are "cognizant" of moral truth and when they are to blame for acting on wrong beliefs.

There is a part of the liberal tradition that is quite content with this ambiguous state of affairs, and even celebrates it as part of an "open society." Those who think this way mistrust the very notion of a "public moral truth." They say that the responsibility of society is not to set itself up as a moral authority, but only to police the open marketplace of moral ideas, in which individuals are to be free to adopt the convictions that most appeal to them. This view is threatened with inconsistency if it is pressed too far. It must at least allow the rules of the marketplace to pass for public moral truth, even though these rules are among the most prominent objects of controversy. But Hegel's objections go deeper than that.

Hegel holds that as moral agents we need to live in a society that can give a rational account of itself. Freedom, the harmony of our inner subjectivity with our outward life, is possible only where the reflection of the best minds on social norms and institutions result in their rational confirmation. Hegel thinks it is only in times of decay and disruption that the best wills are driven to dissent fundamentally from the accepted norms (*PR* § 138R). For this reason, Hegel is understandably reluctant to admit that some moral convictions supporting the basic institutions of the modern state could, in the end, be fundamentally problematic. He does occasionally admit it just the same (*PR* § 138A), though without noticing the dire consequences this would have for his conception of the right of insight.

10. Insight and responsibility

What is Hegel's own response to the problem raised in § 4? Even if we have been made cognizant of the objective rightness or wrongness of an action, it still does not necessarily follow that it is up to us whether we have insight into its rightness or wrongness. Through mere mistakes of intellect we may fail to appreciate the reasons we have been given. We may form a conviction directly opposed to the truth of which we have been made cognizant. If it is not entirely up to us to avoid errors of this kind, then Hegel's position still seems committed to the view that we are blamable for something that is not up to us to avoid.

Hegel's position that we are blamable only if we have been made cognizant of the relevant moral truth clearly amounts to a qualification of:

(1) It is blamable intentionally to do what is morally wrong.

It does not excuse all action based on moral error, even where the agent has given the matter due consideration and not behaved negligently in inquiring into moral truth. It does excuse those agents who are not cognizant of the relevant moral truth. But Hegel's solution to the problem apparently also involves a straightforward rejection of:

(3) We can be blamed only for what is up to us.

since it looks as though it may not always be up to us to avoid moral error even in cases where we have been made cognizant of the truth.

It all depends on what we mean by "up to us." The key to Hegel's conception of moral responsibility is that our actions are imputable to us because they are expressions of our subjectivity. Hegel emphasizes that a subject is essentially a rational being, a thinker (*PR* §§ 126, 132R). Hegel rejects the division of mind or spirit into distinct "faculties" (*EG* § 442) and especially the idea that theoretical mind is passive whereas only practical mind is active (*EG* § 444). My insight, as well as my volition, constitutes my subjectivity; that is why Hegel insists that my subjectivity is present as much in my insight into what is good as in my intention to achieve the good (*PR* § 131). We actualize our subjectivity in good judgment, and we are guilty of moral failure when our judgment is bad.

Thus Hegel rejects (3) if it is taken to mean that we are to blame for something only if we could have avoided it merely by making a different formally free choice. So understood, (3) would also rule out many things besides moral convictions as objects of blame: desires, emotions, attitudes, character traits. We often hold people to blame for wanting the wrong things, for being stingy, cowardly, ungrateful, or thoughtless of others, or for getting angry or resenting things when they shouldn't.[16] Thus if (3) is taken so that "up to us" means only voluntary choice, then it radically contracts the scope of moral responsibility in a number of ways that might be unwelcome even to those who think we are not responsible for moral errors.

Moral insight or error are "up to us" in the sense that they express what we are as rational subjects. If we accept (3) in that sense, then it does not conflict with (1) and (2). We are to blame for violating our conscience because it belongs essentially to our subjectivity; and in going against it, we perform actions in which our integrity as a subject is not present. We are also to blame for following erroneous convictions, because these convictions themselves are defects in us as subjects, and in acting on them we manifest those defects.

In Hegel's view, Oedipus was not guilty of parricide because he was not cognizant of the fact that the old man at the crossroads was his father, and so his killing him did not express his subjectivity in the way it would have if he had been cognizant of that. Sand, however, was guilty of murder because he was cognizant of the meaning of his act. His conviction that his act was not wrong represents a moral failure every bit as serious as if he had killed Kotzebue in the conviction that he was doing wrong.

Not every failure to grasp what has been placed within our cognizance represents so serious a defect of subjectivity. As Hegel says, our failure to remember whether we had *Kohl* or *Kraut* for dinner yesterday (*PR* § 140R, p. 276) is a matter of little subjective significance. He has no theory to distinguish errors that reflect on my subjectivity from those that do not, beyond the criterion that as rational beings we are responsible for knowing the nature of our action, its regular connection with the complex of objective circumstances in which it is involved (*PR* § 118R; see also Chapter 8, § 1). Plainly the nature of an action is taken by Hegel to include both factual and moral beliefs about the action – not only, for instance, that my act of arson is wrong, but also that the fire I start may spread farther than I intend it to. That also seems reasonable. The most vicious beliefs held by racists, for instance, usually do not concern matters of moral principle but matters of history, sociology, and anthropology.

IV
Ethical life

II
Ethical objectivity

1. What is "ethical life"?

In ordinary German, the word *Sittlichkeit* means something like "customary morality"; it calls attention to the close connection between ethical norms and social custom or usage *(Sitte)*. In English, these associations probably come through most strongly in the connection between "morality" and "mores"; but "morality" also has overtones of fussy "moralism," and this (together with the fact that it is a direct cognate) makes it the natural rendering of *Moralität*. That means we are more or less stuck with the word "ethics" to translate *Sittlichkeit*, even though its abstract (even theoretical) connotations are utterly inappropriate. *Ethisch* has the same connotations in German, however, and Hegel nevertheless occasionally uses it in place of *sittliche*, alluding to the Greek word *ethos* (PR § 148R; cf. *VPR 2*: 557, *VPR 2*: 565, *NR* 504/112).[1] It helps a little to translate *Sittlichkeit* as "ethical *life*," indicating that it refers to a way of living and not to a theory.

Largely owing to the connotations of the word, Hegel's conception of ethical life has often been interpreted as committing him to ethical relativism and traditionalism. Hegelian ethics is understood to rest on the thesis that it is always right to follow the customs of one's community and always wrong to violate them. We get the same impression from Hegel's association of ethical life with an unreflective and uncritical attitude toward traditional mores. He often quotes (with apparent approval) Antigone's stubbornly pious attitude toward the sacred law for which she was willing to die:

Not now and yesterday but everlastingly
It lives, and no one knows whence it came.
(*PhG* ¶ 437; cf. *PR* §§ 144A, 166R)[2]

To many, Hegel's view looks distressingly like the reverent atavism with which Romantic reactionaries wanted to replace the Enlightenment's critical rationalism. This is supposed to be Hegel's answer to the emptiness of the moral standpoint.

It would be a very poor answer. Since customs and traditions often represent a culture's dead past (what Hegel calls "positivity"), the ethical advice it yields would often be wrong and without any rational foundation. In the cases where we most need ethical guidance, moreover, it would often give us no clear advice at all. For in modern society, at any rate, many ethical questions are controversial, and there is no determinate custom or social consensus to guide us.

Hegel does hold that objective and determinate moral standards exist only in the context of a rational social order. Certainly he regards some Enlightenment moral theories as shallow and overly individualistic because they ignore this fact. But when we look at it more closely, we see that Hegel's conception of modern ethical life is not particularly conservative or traditionalist in its orientation. At least in its mature form, the conception of ethical life is intended to include rather than exclude individual moral reflection. *Sittlichkeit,* as Hegel means it, is a special kind of critical reflection on social life, not a prohibition against reflection.

2. The two sides of ethical life

Hegel uses *Sittlichkeit* to signify two apparently quite distinct things: First, it refers to a certain kind of social order, one that is differentiated and structured in a rational way. Thus "ethical life" is Hegel's name for an entire set of institutions – the ones anatomized under that heading in the *Philosophy of Right:* the family, civil society, and the modern political state. Second, however, the term also refers to a certain attitude or "subjective disposition" on the part of individuals toward their social life (*PR* § 141R), an attitude of harmonious identification with its institutions.

Hegel himself emphasizes this double use of the term. Ethical life, he says, is "the concept of freedom that has come to be a present world *and* the nature of self-consciousness" (*PR* § 142, emphasis added); it is both a "relation between *many* individuals" and the "form of the *concrete* subject" (*VPR 2:* 549). This does not mean that *Sittlichkeit* is an ambiguous term. It is rather a term referring to a single reality that has two complementary sides or aspects. Ethical life has both its "objective" side, in the form of a "present world" or social order (*PR* §§ 144–145), and its "subjective" side, in the self-consciousness of individuals (*PR* §§ 146–147). The objective side of ethical life is the "substance" of the individuals who belong to the ethical order (*PR* § 144), whereas the subjective side, the self-consciousness of individuals, is at the same time their consciousness of this substance (*PR* § 146).

The ethical is called a "substance" for several different reasons. Hegel wants to suggest that ethical life is something firm and unshakable: The individual can rely on its workings and be sure of the validity of its laws (*PR* §§ 146, 148). He intends to contrast "substance" with subjectivity, personality, or reflective thought (*WL 6:* 195/536–537), indicating that the ethical attitude toward laws, institutions, and relationships is a natural, habitual, spontaneous, and unselfconscious one, uncomplicated by any reflective doubts or by sophisticated calculations of personal advantage (*PR* § 146). Hegel also likens the relation between the social order and the individuals who belong to it to the relation between a substance and its accidents. The roles and relationships of a social order are something necessary and abiding, whereas the individuals who occupy them come and go contingently (*PR* § 145A). Individuals are "accidents" in the sense that the ethical order does not depend on those particular individuals for its existence. The laws of the ethical

196

order, Hegel says, are "powers" – such as "marriage," "piety," and "state" (*VPR 4*: 397) – which "govern the life of individuals, in whom they have their actuality as accidents, representation, and form of appearance" (*PR* § 145).

On the other hand, in Hegelian metaphysics a substance would be nothing actual without the accidents that manifest it (*EL* § 151). Consequently, a social order is nothing actual except through the action and consciousness of individuals. If spirit is a "group mind," then it is one that has its consciousness only in the consciousnesses of its individual members, who are aware of it: "In [the life of individuals], its *actual self-consciousness,* the [ethical] substance knows itself and becomes an object of knowledge" (*PR* § 146). In traditional metaphysics, substance is independent, and its accidents depend on it. For Hegel, the dependence of substance and accidents is reciprocal; just as individuals would lack substance without their ethical life, so ethical life would be nothing actual without the thoughts and actions of individuals.

By using the term *Sittlichkeit* to refer both to subjective attitudes and to social institutions, Hegel means to suggest that there is a close connection between the two. Institutions may foster certain attitudes on the part of the individuals who live under them – attitudes toward themselves and other individuals, and attitudes toward the institutions. Conversely, social institutions depend on the prevalence of certain determinate attitudes on the part of individuals. Without them the institutions could not arise, function, or perpetuate themselves. Hegel also means that the self-consciousness of individuals has, at bottom, something profoundly social for its content. My personality is constituted through the socialization I have received, and my sense of who I am is drawn from the social roles I am assigned.

Hegel rejects those modern (liberal, Enlightenment) conceptions of human nature which identify the human self with a set of natural faculties, needs, and dispositions, and regard the institutions of human society simply as a set of devices by which individuals make use of their relations with others in order to satisfy their needs (*PhG* ¶ 579). He endorses the Romantic view that Enlightenment liberalism proceeds from an abstract conception of human beings which ignores or impoverishes the content of human individuality, with disastrous results. Hegel's conception of ethical life is based on the idea that individual self-understanding cannot be had apart from an understanding of the social and historical process through which our social identities have come to be.

Hegel says that the concepts of "person" and "subject" are abstractions from the concrete individuals of ethical life (*PR* § 33). These concepts have a powerful hold on us, and Hegel does not want to break that hold. We demand our human rights because we understand ourselves as persons, and we demand subjective freedom because we understand ourselves as moral subjects. But Hegel maintains that abstract right and morality are *actual* in modern society only to the extent that their abstract conceptions of the individual are given real embodiment through modern social institutions. Conversely, we know the full meaning of our identity as persons and subjects only when we discover how these identities are actualized in the relations of a working social order.

3. Ethical life as spirit

"Ethical life" is intimately related to Hegel's concept of spirit. Spirit is also a unity of objective and subjective, in which "substance" becomes "subject" (*PhG* ¶ 18; *PR* § 152). Spirit is the self that becomes objective to itself through its action and then comprehends itself as what it is by being conscious of its object as its own work (*PhG* ¶ 351). Hegel thinks that spirit's activity takes a self-sufficient form only in a people or nation (*PR* § 156) that builds a self-contained world and achieves spiritual self-awareness in the forms of absolute spirit – art, religion, and philosophy (*EG* § 554).

For Hegel, the ethical is spiritual also because it rises above nature. In the ethical, custom (*Sitte*) becomes (in the words of the proverbial saying) a "second nature" (*PR* § 151). The ethical attitude imitates the immediate harmony through which a natural thing is immediately one with itself and its place in the natural order. But it is a *second* nature because its immediacy is essentially different from this. In fact, ethical life actualizes freedom only because it is *not* natural. The individuals who participate in ethical life are conscious of its laws. Ethical life, unlike nature, imposes its laws on itself, and is therefore free, something spiritual.

Insofar as the ethical exists only unreflectively, as habit or custom, ethical life is spirit's lowest, most immediate, or least developed form. Hegel says that it is in the form of unreflective custom that "spirit exists *for the first time* as spirit" (*PR* § 151, emphasis added). This implies that spirit *also* exists in other, later, more developed forms. The point is missed entirely by those who interpret Hegel's theory of ethical life as a Romantic traditionalism that is simply hostile to individuality or moral reflection. Ethical life is the basis of moral subjectivity, the condition of its possibility, and the true meaning of moral subjectivity can be properly understood only from the ethical standpoint. In that sense, as Hegel puts it, morality always falls short of ethical life; it is the "not yet" of ethical life (*PhG* ¶ 356). That is the meaning of Hegel's assertion that individual self-will and private conscience have "vanished" at the level of ethical life (*PR* § 152).

Equally, however, since ethical life proper indicates something immediate and unreflective, Hegel insists that the standpoint of morality is "a higher form than the ethical substance" (*PhG* ¶ 357). The unreflective harmony of ethical life is, from the higher reflective standpoint of morality, something that has been left behind, something that is "no more" (*PhG* ¶ 355). Human nature would stagnate and fail to develop its potentialities if left at the standpoint of ethical immediacy; it would be condemned to "spiritual death" (*PR* § 152A). In this respect, Hegel regards ethical life as merely the starting point for the development of morality as a higher form of spirit. Hegel's conception of a distinctively modern ethical life, as developed in the *Philosophy of Right*, is not an attempt to submerge or suppress the subjective, but rather to found it on the substantive. In § 8 we will see that ethical life, properly speaking, exists *only* in a society where individuality and subjective freedom have come into their full right.

4. The ethical order

In the *Philosophy of Right*, Hegel introduces ethical life by calling it "the *Idea of freedom*, as the living good" (*PR* § 142). Since the *Idea* is the unity of a concept with objectivity (*WL 6* : 461/754; *EL* § 213), this means that ethical life is the concept of freedom actualized in an objective world. Ethical life is *living* in the sense that it is self-moving: Unlike morality, it derives neither its content nor its motivation from something other than itself. It is also the self-moving *good*: It promotes the good through actions that are already actualizations of the good. Ethical life aims at the right and the well-being of individuals (the good), and achieves this aim through actions of individuals that are themselves right and constitute part of the well-being of the agents who perform them.

Though ethical life is described as living (self-moving), it is also compared to Aristotle's first or unmoved mover, which moves things in the way that an object of desire or thought moves them. The ethical order is substantial or unmoved in the sense that its fundamental principles are not at the mercy of individuals' whims. It moves individuals because it is their end (*PR* §§ 142, 152; *VG* 91/77). For its members, the ethical order itself is the final end, and a shared or collective end. It contains the right and welfare of individuals and can for this reason be identified with the moral good. But in the ethical order the good takes a concrete form. It is a rational institutional structure, whose rationality makes it desirable by individuals as an end in itself, and not merely as a means to individual good.

The objective ethical order is also "living" in that it is *organized*. In general, rationality for Hegel consists in the "Idea," a self-actualizing structure organized according to the concept (*EL* § 213). The "potencies" of ethical life are not "fixed" but mutually dependent and mutually reproducing, like the organs of a living thing (*NR* 518/122–123). Ethical life is a structure that sustains itself through the operation of its parts, "the movement through the form of its moments" (*PR* § 157). It "lives" by securing the right and promoting the well-being of its individual members; in this sense, too, it is the "living *good*." The right of individuals as free beings is fulfilled through membership in an ethical order (*PR* § 153), and their participation in it also guarantees their right to particular satisfaction, well-being, or happiness (*PR* § 154). Ethical life is modeled on the Kantian "realm of ends," in which the ends of all rational agents form a rational whole or harmonious system (*G* 438/57):

> The whole *as whole* becomes [the individual's] work, for which he sacrifices himself and thereby receives himself back from the whole. – Here there is nothing that is not reciprocal, nothing in which the self-dependence of the individual does not, in

the dissolution of its being for itself in the *negation* of itself, give itself its *positive* significance as being for itself. (*PhG* ¶ 351)

Only the realm of ends is an abstract ideal that merely "ought to be," whereas ethical life is an actuality.

An ethical order is "a world distinguished within itself, articulated (*gegliedert*) into separate spheres (*Massen*)" (*PhG* ¶ 445; cf. *PR* § 269A). On one level, the articulation of an ethical order refers to the fact that ethical life is a system of human relationships that objectifies freedom. Thus Hegel identifies ethical life with the free will itself, the "system of rational determinations of the will" in which freedom consists (*PR* § 19; *VPR19* : 122). The "articulation" of ethical life consists in the fact that within the ethical order institutions are differentiated. Each institution, like the organ of a living thing, serves a distinct function. Hegel emphasizes the way in which different institutions address different sides of society's individual members, answering to different human self-images and different human needs.

Oriental societies, in Hegel's view, were not truly ethical because they lacked articulation; there was in them no proper distinction between family and state, or between religion and government (*PR* § 355). True ethical life began with ancient Greece because there social life was for the first time articulated in its distinction between divine and human law, separating the family from the state and the "nether" world of religion from the "upper" world of political life (*PhG* ¶¶ 446–463).

5. Ethical individuality

The "articulation" of an ethical order also means that it allows systematically for social diversity, enabling different individuals to actualize different possibilities contained in the complex human self-image. This is especially clear in modern ethical life, where the emphasis on subjective freedom leads people to demand that they choose their own way of life for themselves (*PR* § 206,R) and causes them to value diversity in tastes and life-style for its own sake (*PR* § 185,R,A).

Hegel's views on this point have something in common with J. S. Mill's insistence that "individuality" is one of the elements of human well-being.[3] Unlike Mill, however, Hegel is concerned to identify the diversity of social types with the articulation of determinate socioeconomic roles, positions, or estates *(Stände)* which constitute the ethical order of civil society (*PR* § 202). Hegel stresses the diversity and complementarity of the estates, each with its own ethical "disposition" or "outlook" *(Gesinnung)* and way of life.

The "substantial" (or agricultural) estate is disposed to tradition and family life; it values individuality and diversity less than the urban estates (*PR* § 203). Within the "formal" or "business" estate, Hegel distinguishes the estate involved in manual craftsmanship from the estate that engages in manufacture, and both from the estate that concerns itself with trade or commerce (*PR* § 204). All three are marked off from the "universal estate" of civil servants, whose life is devoted to the universal interests of the whole community (PR § 205). It is distinguished from the military estate, which has "valor" *(Tapferkeit)* as its characteristic disposition (PR § 327). Hegel emphasizes the connection within each estate between life-style and values. He describes the ways in which self-worth for the members of different estates is sustained by quite different things (*JR* 253–262/163–171).

Because Hegel treats social diversity as determinate and socially organized, his conception of the value of individuality is less radical than Mill's, less experimental in spirit, and less open-ended in intent. This difference also reveals how Mill's notion of individuality owes more to the Romantic tradition than Hegel's does. Mill and the Romantics associate individuality with inspired eccentricity; individuality for the Romantics is the vehicle through which the boundless infinite intrudes into the finite world, disturbing and at the same time hallowing it. Hegel rejects the Romantic identification of individuality with idiosyncrasy; his philosophy aims, moreover, at reconciling infinitude with the finite, actualizing it by giving it residence within classical form.[4] He likes to compare ethical action with the work of a classical artist, a work that is great – and distinctive – precisely because it is "universal" and "vindicates the thing" rather than expressing the personal peculiarities of the artist:

> When great artists complete a masterpiece, we may speak of its inevitability, which means that the artist's idiosyncrasy has completely disappeared and no mannerisms are detectable in it. Pheidias has no mannerisms; his figures live and declare themselves. But the worse an artist is, the more we see the artist in the work, his singularity, his arbitrariness. (PR § 15A)

Hegel's point is that I don't find my authentic self or true individuality by detaching myself from my social identity, or by adding quirks and peculiarities to it. Individuality is achieved instead by taking over that identity thoughtfully, mastering it in the way that the great classical artists such as Pheidias have mastered their craft.

To be an individual is therefore always to be something determinate, to have a determinate *Stand,* a place, standing, or status in society:

> When we say that a human being must be *something,* we mean that he must belong to a determinate estate *(Stand);* for this "something" means that he is something substantial. A human being without a status *(Stand)* is a mere private person, not an actualized universality. (PR § 207A)

True human individuality consists in fulfilling in one's own way a determinate social function, having a specific job or profession *(Gewerbe)* (PR § 252R). Only in this way can an individual have a genuine social identity and a sense of honor or dignity *(Standesehre)* associated with it (PR §§ 207, 253). Individuality degenerates into alienation unless it is supported socially by solidarity with a "corporation" in which the individual's dignity receives recognition (PR § 253R; see Chapter 14, § 3). Without that solidarity, society dissolves into a heap of atoms (PR § 256R), abstract private persons whose personality has no ethical life. Where this occurs, even the right of personality no longer confers any dignity on people, and the "person" becomes an object of contempt (*PhG* ¶ 480; *PR* § 35A).

The thrust of Hegel's ethical thought is to value an individuality whose actualization is not a mere accident because it is socially situated. A human being is truly an individual only if given a determinate social identity to fulfill. On the other hand, the idea of individuality means so much to us in modern society because modern society is more completely articulated, because its system of social roles demands and rewards distinctiveness, diversity, and particularity. In this way, the reflective individuality of modern society also makes it *more* ethical – more organized and articulated – than other social orders, more ethical even than the social order of ancient Greece.

6. Romantic pluralism

Hegel prefers organism over mechanism as the metaphor for a society. Like Herder before him, Hegel infers from this metaphor that each culture is a self-contained whole that must be understood and appreciated in terms of its own internal laws and not measured by a rigid standard foreign to it. This thought might easily lead to the idea that different social orders and their corresponding ethical standards are also incommensurable; the norms and values of each ethical order are binding on the members of that order, but there is no universal standard by which any of them could be criticized or regarded as superior one to another.

Such a Romantic, pluralistic (even relativistic) attitude toward cultural differences in customs and ethical values is alive and well in our own day. There is a recent tradition of "communitarian" thinking, represented by such writers as Alasdair MacIntyre, Michael Sandel, and Bernard Williams, which criticizes the liberal tradition in ethical thought because it claims universal validity for some of its ethical standards, particularly for its conceptions of human rights and of the moral standpoint.[5] These critics, and their liberal opponents, habitually cite Hegel's notion of *Sittlichkeit* as the intellectual ancestor of pluralist, communitarian criticisms of liberal universalism.[6]

The connotations of the term *Sittlichkeit* also tend to suggest this reading of Hegel. When Hegel bases the content of an individual's duties on the *Sittlichkeit* of the people of which the individual belongs, it looks as though he is subscribing to some form of ethical relativism: Ethical truth varies with and depends on prevailing customs and moral beliefs. To understand the term *Sittlichkeit* in this way, however, you have to take it to refer indifferently to *any* community's system of customs, usages, and moral beliefs. You have to suppose that for Hegel every social order has an "ethical life," and that the ethical lives of different cultures are self-contained and equally valid or mutually incommensurable.

Some of Hegel's statements, especially in the Jena period, might suggest this. According to the *Natural Right* essay, society has its own geography, climate, and epoch; each actualizes its own idea in its own way, and so each historical stage is justified (*NR* 522–523/126–127). Even in the *Philosophy of Right*, Hegel says that different political constitutions are suited to different peoples, even that "every people has the constitution appropriate for and belonging to it" (*PR* § 274R).

Unlike many Romantics of his time, Hegel has no admiration for feudal society, which he regards as a confused hodgepodge of private privileges rather than as a rational organism (*PR* §§ 273R, 278R, 286R). But even feudalism, with its apparent positivity and its denial of personality through the institution of serfdom, may merely express the "weakness of ethical life" and a historical stage in which personality and right have "lost all conviction of truth"; where this is so, "the feudal constitution *(Lehensverfassung)* and servitude have absolute truth, and this relation is the only possible form of ethical life and hence the necessary, just and ethical one" (*NR* 524/128). If even feudalism can be an ethical order for Hegel, then perhaps anything can be one.

But we should be cautions in reading Hegel this way. Hegel does not claim that feudal institutions are *always* justified and ethical, only that they *may be* so, that they *are* so under the condition that they have become "necessary"; and that very condition Hegel describes as a "weakness of ethical life." Even when he calls feudalism "ethical," he does so in a way that implies that it is *less* ethical than other social orders. This suggests that the term "ethical" for Hegel does not signify adherence to a Romantic pluralism or relativism, but instead is being used to articulate some sort of standard for ethical conceptions and the social orders that embody them.

7. Hegel's universalism

There are a number of deeper features of Hegel's theory that point in the same direction. Hegel's ethical theory is a self-actualization theory. The object of self-actualization is plural in the sense that the human spirit forms different conceptions of itself at different times and places. But Hegel views these conceptions as stages of a single process, a series of attempts to grasp and actualize the nature of spirit. The process is progressive; spirit raises itself from less adequate conceptions of itself to more adequate ones. The *Philosophy of Right* purports to be the highest and most adequate cognition of objective spirit that has been attained so far. It is supposed to be the standard by which different human traditions, and earlier stages of the same tradition, are to be measured. That is why Hegel takes such a universalistic attitude toward the conceptions of modern ethical life, toward the "eternal human right" of persons, and toward the absolute claims of the free subject. It is also why he shows no patience with the ethical relativism which he (mistakenly) believes to be part of Fries's ethics of conviction.

At no time does Hegel ever apply the term *Sittlichkeit* to just any social order that happens to exist. As we have already noted, Hegel holds that Oriental societies have not yet risen to the level of "true spirit or the ethical" (*PhG* ¶ 700; cf. *PR* § 355). Hegel is willing to apply the term "ethical" only to peoples and societies that have attained to the level of culture represented by the ancient Greeks, or at least stand in a tradition related to them. Hegel's remark that every people has the constitution appropriate to it must be understood with this qualification if it is to be consistent with his general position. Indeed, Hegel seems not to regard peoples who fall outside such traditions as "peoples," properly speaking, at all. Even their claim on political sovereignty, he maintains, is at most merely "formal" (*PR* §§ 331,R,A, 349,R). Such statements no doubt reveal an unattractive European bias, even an ominous imperialist mentality. At the same time, however, they clearly exhibit Hegel's commitment to universal standards of rationality and right. These standards are not extrasocial and suprahistorical, but located in a cultural tradition. Reason locates this culture by viewing human history as a dialectical process, increasing self-awareness. The culture need not be your own, though it must be intelligible to you. Hegel's universalism is committed to discovering, comprehending, and developing whatever cultural tradition has so far achieved the deepest understanding of the nature of reason and the human spirit's vocation.

This approach, which we may call "historicized universalism," is inherently "ethnocentric" in the sense that it always proceeds from a given tradition and accepts its own unavoidable cultural and historical limitations. But the general approach, as distinct from Hegel's historically limited applications of it, has no particular tendency to be culturally exclusive or intolerant. On the contrary, it stands to reason that the most rational and progressive cultural tradition would also be the one that is most sensitive to its own fallibility and the most capable of appreciating what is valuable in other cultures. Tolerance has to rest on positive convictions about how one culture should treat others, about when, why, and to what extent we should allow others to do even what we think is wrong. If such convictions are to be rational, they must rest on principles that aspire to universal applicability. If these principles are to be contentful and effective, they must also rest on specific social forms that represent a culture and tradition of tolerance and openness. Hegel's historicized universalism looks like the best way to achieve rational tolerance.

In contrast, alternative doctrines such as romantic pluralism and cultural relativism are not at all well suited to defending a tolerant and receptive attitude toward other cultures. Relativism dogmatically claims that the values of different cultures are all equally valid, each for its own members. From this it follows directly that if you happen to belong to a narrow-minded and intolerant culture, then you are positively *required* to be intolerant. Relativism falls into this self-defeating position because it denies that there is a standpoint above and outside all cultures and then (self-contradictorily) tries straightway to occupy such a standpoint.

Hegel sees that the only possible way of really escaping ethnocentrism is gradually, through the actual self-development of reason, which is always rooted in a determinate cultural tradition. Of course, on this path there is always the danger that what the most progressive tradition calls rational may be a function of its own biases and limitations. No doubt its judgment of alien cultures and traditions will always be based to some extent on partial blindness and ignorance (as we can now see that Hegel's own judgments about non-European cultures often were). Yet a fallible, culturally conditioned, and historically limited reason is the only reason we have. Its unavoidable limitations do not take from it the right to comprehend and judge the world as best it can, while continuing to criticize and develop itself. Nowhere will we find anything with a better right.

8. Individuality as an ethical principle

Hegel's conception of the ethical is commonly understood to be an endorsement of cultural pluralism and relativism. But we have seen that on closer inspection it turns out to be just the opposite: a univeral standard for ranking the rationality of different social orders. Hegel restricts the term "ethical" to social orders that he takes to have attained a certain kind of articulated rationality. In the *Natural Right* essay, he calls a social order *sittlich* only when it adequately expresses a given historical stage of its people and only to the degree that it possesses a living and articulated organic structure. If Hegel believes that all or most (modern Western) nation-states do in fact exemplify these features, then that gives him a reason for thinking that all or most of these states are *to some extent* ethical.

When Hegel says that every people has the constitution appropriate to it, he does not mean that all constitutions are equally ethical, rational, or historically progressive, or that no change ever should occur in constitutions. If the saying is to be consistent with his other doctrines, it must be taken in the sense that every people tends to have the constitution best suited to its current stage of development. Recall his 1817 remark: "The rational must happen, because on the whole the constitution is only its development" (*VPR17*: 157).

In the Jena period, Hegel takes the Greek polis to represent the most perfect ethical order. In fact, the *Phenomenology of Spirit* appears to use the terms *Sittlichkeit* and *sittliche Substanz* simply as nicknames for ancient Greek society. Hegel describes ancient Rome as the "downfall *(Untergang)* of ethical substance," even the "death of ethical life" *(Tod des sittlichen Lebens)* (*PR* ¶ 357), where "the ethical shape of spirit has disappeared and another steps into its place" (*PhG* ¶¶ 475–476). In our time, he says, ethical life has long since been "lost," and the task of consciousness is to go in search of it; yet there is also the suggestion that ethical life has not been lost forever. Modern morality itself arises out of a distinctive kind of ethical life unknown to the Greeks (*PhG* § 357). This implies that there must be such a thing as a modern ethical life to be found at the end of the search, a higher ethical life than the ancient Greek one.

The Jena lectures distinguish three elements in modern society: (1) ethical life, which is the external social organization; (2) morality, which is the subjective "disposition" *(Gesinnung)* or self-consciousness of each individual as a member of a social estate; and (3) religion, the consciousness that each member has of the social whole, or "spirit knowing itself as absolute spirit" (*JR* 253/162). This parallels the *Phenomenology*'s progression from ethical life through morality to religion. It also means that modern society, like the Greek polis, has an ethical life, even an ethical life that has been deepened through the individual reflection that has given rise to the moral standpoint (*JR* 251/160).

In his later writings, Hegel continues to regard ancient Greece as the paradigmatically ethical society, but only if "ethical" is taken in the subjective sense, referring to the ethical disposition of individuals. In its objective sense, referring to the social order, Hegel regards the modern state as more ethical because it has greater structural articulation. This leads to a tension in Hegel's conception of the ethical, because a more articulated ethical order is also one that provides for greater subjectivity and individuality. In this way, the ethical turns out not to preclude the development of individuality, but actually *requires* it (*PR* § 356).

Hegel denies that there is ethical life in Oriental societies not only because they are unarticulated, but also because – owing to this – they do not give individuality its due (*PR* § 355). "No truly ethical existence is possible," he says, until individuals have gained a distinct consciousness of the ethical substance or "unmoved mover" that acts through them. "For this force to become effective, the subject must have developed to a condition of free individuality, in which it is fully conscious of the eternally unmoved mover, and each individual subject must be free in its own right" (*VG* 91/77).

Since an ethical order is one that liberates individuality, it follows that institutions that suppress individuality are "unethical" institutions, even in the ancient world: "Slavery falls in the transition from the natural state of humanity to a truly ethical condition" (*PR* § 57A). Likewise, the Roman practice of treating children as their father's property is "an offense against the ethical" (*PR* § 175R) and Roman laws that put a family's property under the father's arbitrary power are likewise "unethical" (*PR* § 180). In fact, Hegel argues that because a society can be fully articulated only where the principle of individuality is given its fullest development, perfected (objective) ethical life can be found *only* in modern society, and *not* in ancient societies:

The principle of individuality, of subjective freedom, has its origin [in ancient Greece], although it is still embedded in substantial unity. . . . The ethical life of Greece will therefore be an unstable one. . . . The aesthetic existence of Greece cannot be equated with true ethical life. (*VG* 249–250/202–203)
In ancient states, . . . ethical life had not progressed to [the modern state's] free system of self-dependent development and objectivity. (*PR* § 150R)

9. The ethical as a universal standard

The term *Sittlichkeit* is used by Hegel to convey the idea that the customs and traditions of a people deserve to have a deeper hold on us than the abstract, cosmopolitan ideals of liberal Enlightenment moralists. But we have seen that Hegel is no Romantic pluralist or cultural relativist about ethical norms. In *PR* § 3R, he follows Montesquieu's theory of the diversity of laws appropriate to diverse national minds or spirits; which is explicitly founded on the universal laws of human reason:

> Law in general is human reason, inasmuch as it governs all inhabitants of the earth: the political and civil laws of each nation ought to be only the particular cases in which human reason is applied. They should be adapted in such a manner to the people for whom they are framed that it should be a great chance if those of one nation should suit another.[7]

In fact, Hegel leaves even less room for ethical diversity than Montesquieu does. For he thinks that a thoughtful survey of the history of the human spirit reveals that the institutions of modern European society display a deeper comprehension of the human condition than those of other peoples. Though different customs may be necessary (and, in that sense, "valid") for other times and places, it does not follow that they deserve to be called "right" or "ethical" (*PR* § 57R).

If we look closely at Hegel's detailed discussion of modern ethical life, it is striking how little he concedes to ethnic diversity, how little room he leaves for the impact of varying cultural traditions on the social and political structure of modern states. Some of Hegel's general pronouncements sound like Romantic protests against the Enlightenment's tendency to modernize institutions, leveling customs and traditions, recasting all constitutions according to a single rationalistic model. But he is a false friend to Romanticism, just as he is to Prussian absolutism and to Christian orthodoxy. Hegel's own account of modern ethical life actually represents only a new, historicized version of that same aggressive, modernizing rationalism.

The ethical life of a modern social order requires the liberation of the bourgeois nuclear family from the traditional institution of the feudal extended family or clan (*PR* §§ 172, 180R). It needs an arena of civil society in which individuals participate in an open economic marketplace. The legal regulation of civil society must protect the personhood of each human being (*PR* § 209), and the laws should be explicitly and rationally codified [Hegel has no use for the English system, based on tradition and "unwritten" law (*PR* § 211R)]. The political structure of a modern state is defective unless it is a constitutional monarchy (*PR* § 273R), governed by a professional civil service (*PR* § 291) under the watchful eye of a representative estates assembly (*PR* § 302).

Hegel never suggests that we might appeal to the diversity of cultural traditions to justify (for example) common law in England, theocratic absolutism in Russia, republicanism in America, or the absence of representative institutions in Austria and Prussia.[8] In 1808, Napoleon attempted to impose on Spain the Constitution of Bayonne, based on French Revolutionary political principles. It provided for a limited monarchy, strong representative institutions, and the political disenfranchisement of the Church. The Bayonne Constitution was unpopular in Spain and it did not last. Hegel's explanation of its failure is revealing. He does not criticize Napoleon for doing violence to Spanish folkways, but says only that the Bayonne Constitution was *too rational* for the Spanish, who "were not yet educated up to it" (*PR* § 274A).

In practice, Hegel barely even pays lip service to the commonplace notion that different peoples require different laws and political institutions. The thrust of his theory of ethical life in the *Philosophy of Right* is to describe the social system that best actualizes the self-conception possessed by individuals in modern European (or "Germanic") societies, where Hegel thinks that the human spirit has reached its most complete development so far.

Hegel is anticosmopolitan in the sense that he stresses the sovereignty and self-containedness of the nation state (*PR* § 331), and the indispensable importance for individual self-actualization of the individual's devotion to it (*PR* § 259). But his celebration of a modern, universal conception of human beings and modern social institutions indicates that he, like the Enlightenment cosmopolitans, is an apostle of a single modern world culture founded on universal principles of reason, as opposed to the counter-Enlightenment view which favored a variety of parochial cultures with foundations in religion or some other traditional authority (*PR* § 209R).

Once we appreciate this, we can see how great a distance separates Hegel's conception of ethical life from all forms of Romantic–pluralistic communitarianism. We can also see how a misreading of Hegel on this point badly misinterprets his critique of Enlightenment liberalism. Hegel rejects liberal theories on the basis of their abstract, impoverished, and ahistorical view of human beings, their preference for a fictional human nature in place of a historically situated self-understanding. But he sides with the Enlightenment against Romantic pluralism, and its celebration of the diverse flourishing of cultural unreason. The real significance for us of Hegel's conception of ethical life is that it shows how we can accept a historicized and communitarian critique of liberalism without renouncing the Enlightenment's confidence in universal standards of reason.

12
Ethical subjectivity

1. The ethical disposition

The objective side of ethical life is the ethical order, a rationally articulated system of social institutions. The subjective side is the ethical disposition or attitude *(Gesinnung)*.

The ethical attitude is the truest actualization of freedom because in it individuals are completely "with themselves." Human individuals are products of their social order. The ethical laws they obey are self-given because the ethical order is fundamentally identical with the essence of the individual:

> [Ethical laws are] not something *alien* to the subject, rather the subject bears a *witness of spirit* to them as to *its own essence*, in which it has its *feeling of self*, and it lives in them as in an element not distinguished from itself – a relation more of identity than of *faith* or *trust*. (*PR* § 147)

The original experience of this identity is more fundamental than rational reflection, even more fundamental than any "faith" or any affective state. It is "the identity of living nature, which does not admit of grounds or reasons, yet also doesn't appeal only to feelings, but rather to a whole experience, the whole feeling of life, unity of the laws and the individual's nature. This is simple, natural ethical life" (*VPR 3*: 487–488).

The ethical disposition is Hegel's response to the Kantian duality of duty and inclination. In ethical life, the "universal" aspect of the self (the aspect represented by law and duty) is in perfect harmony with the "particular" side (the individual's drives and desires). In his very first use of *Sittlichkeit* in contrast to *Moralität*, Hegel describes the ethical as "a true identity of the universal and particular, of matter and form" (*GW* 426/183). The ethical attitude is heir to "love" as Hegel used it in the Frankfurt period, contrasting with the self-alienated will characteristic of Kantian morality. The ethical attitude includes love, especially in the context of family relationships (*PR* § 158), but it is supposed to be present whenever universal rationality is found in harmony with an agent's particular self-satisfaction under the auspices of an institution belonging to an ethical whole. Thus the ethical also includes patriotism (*PR* § 268R) and *Standesehre* – the sense of honor that binds us to our profession and those who share it with us (*PR* §§ 207, 253).

2. Ethical duty

Hegel describes the moral standpoint as the standpoint of the "ought" (*PhG* ¶¶ 425, 614; *PR* § 135R; *EG* § 512). Part of what he means is that moral

209

duties are experienced as external limits on the subject's particular desires, projects, and mode of life. Morality tells me which of my desires it is permissible to satisfy, and it reminds me of the deeds and ends on which I must expend my tithe of noble effort so that I may go about my grubby personal business with a clear conscience. Moral duties, as Kant often emphasizes, are experienced as constraints on the will; that is why Kant says that love, as a desire or feeling, cannot be a moral duty (*KpV* 83/86).

Ethical duties, on the other hand, are not constraints on my life; on the contrary, they are the best part of it, "the substance of my own being" (*PR* § 148). Ethical duties take the form of desires or "drives [whose] content belongs to my immediate will" (*PR* § 150R). Ethical duties include my love for my spouse, my parents, and my children, and the self-satisfaction I get from engaging in my profession or vocation (*PR* §§ 207, 255). The fulfillment of ethical duties involves having certain feelings and desires, such as the love for a certain person or the ambition to achieve some goal. Ethical duties are not only things I "ought" to do, they are usually things I spontaneously *want* to do. Leaving them undone does not so much offend my conscience as empty my life of its meaning. Morality takes, as our philosophers say, "the moral point of view." The point of view of ethical life, however, is nothing distinct from the concrete individual's total, unified perspective on the world.

Hegel does not reject the idea of moral duty as a constraint imposed by the universal on the particular will. Because morality is an aspect or abstract moment of ethical life (*PR* § 33,A), even ethical duties sometimes take a moral form. Certain duties (e.g., those of benevolent deeds rendered to strangers in contingent circumstances) are even moral in content, because they are *typically* experienced in their moral aspect (*PR* § 207). Hegel's point is rather that moral duty is not the only kind of duty, not even the fundamental or typical kind. In fact, if the fulfillment of all duty, following the model of morality, always involved a constraint by universal reason on the particular will, then we could not expect duty to be done reliably enough to produce the good. That is the sense in which the good for morality is forever an "ought," never an "is," whereas ethical life is the living good, the good that has become self-moving and self-achieving.

Hegelian ethical life involves a harmony between individual well-being and the needs of a rational social order. An ethical order provides individuals with a generally satisfying mode of life, so that they are seldom called upon to make great personal sacrifices for others. We identify with ethical duties because they fulfill us; they alone give us a meaningful life. This is not the same as saying that we are attached to them only (or mainly) by self-interest. On the contrary, ethical life involves concern for others and the recognition of claims that are more important to us than our own particular good. You do not experience professional or family life as a sacrifice of personal happiness, but you know that you could often do better for your own interests if you didn't fulfill the duties they impose. Ethical conduct would not fulfill you if it regularly cut too far into your happiness, but it seldom maximizes your self-interest.

Ethical life involves what Amartya Sen calls "commitment" – a disposition to choose acts that forego your own well-being to some degree for the sake of something you care about more than that (such as a loved one, or your profession or your country). Commitment is not "selflessness," though; it is not a case where self-interest is overridden by some universal moral principle such as utility or the categorical imperative. If Hegel is correct in believing that most of social life depends on ethical dispositions, then that means that by and large people's social behavior cannot be explained by either egoistic motives or adherence to a universalistic morality – the only two forms of motivation officially recognized at all by many ethical theories and most economic theories.[1]

According to Hegel, morality tries in vain to provide an "ethical theory of duties," but a theory of this kind can consist only in "the development of the *relationships* that are necessary through the idea of freedom, and hence in their whole range are *actual* only in the state" (*PR* § 148R). Our ethical duties are the demands made on us by other individuals and by institutions through the relationships in which we stand within a rational society, an ethical order. The *Philosophy of Right* does not really try to give us a doctrine of duties, since it attempts no detailed exposition of these relationships. But it does furnish an outline of the institutions within which these relationships are to be found, and so it might be seen as giving a sketch of that structure from which a doctrine of ethical duties can be derived.

3. Duties of relationships

Ethical duties are "duties of relationships *(Pflichten der Verhältnisse)*" (*PR* § 150). They arise from specific relationships to other individuals and to social institutions. Ethical duties have a universal content because I am aware of them as part of an ethical order, but I perform these duties on the basis of my particular desires and dispositions of character, not out of impartial benevolence or respect for a universal principle. For instance, I am devoted to the welfare of these individuals because they are my family and I love them, not because my conduct conforms to a system of universal legislation or maximally satisfies the utility functions of all sentient creatures.

Ethical life allows for what Christina Hoff Sommers calls the "differential pull" (or DP) of our duties to others, as distinct from the most prevalent moral theories, which begin from a standpoint of impartiality or "equal pull" (EP). I have special relations to such people as family members, friends, professional colleagues, comrades, or compatriots. Because of the ethical relations that bind us, I owe them a concern I do not owe to humanity generally. As Sommers puts the point:

> According to the DP thesis, the ethical pull of a moral patient will always partly depend on how the moral patient is related to the moral agent on whom the pull is

exerted. Moreover, the "how" of relatedness will be determined in part by social practices and institutions in which the agent and patient play their roles. . . . The gravitational metaphor may be suggestive. In DP morality the community of agents and patients is analogous to a gravitational field where distance counts and forces vary in accordance with local conditions.[2]

Like Sommers's version of DP morality, modern ethical life follows the Enlightenment tradition of providing (through the spheres of abstract right and morality) for some ethical obligations that are universalistic or EP. As Sommers notes, this version of DP is to be distinguished from anti-Enlightenment versions of communitarian ethics (such as that of Alasdair MacIntyre) which deliberately eschew universalistic principles.[3]

In a sense, however, even Hegel's commitment to DP itself is founded on universalistic principles. Hegel's is not an EP theory, because it is not founded, as Kantian and utilitarian theories are, on a universalism conceived as the "equal pull" individuals have on us as atoms of rational agency or repositories of pleasure and pain. But Hegel's theory is still universalistic because it appeals to principles that claim universal validity for all thinkers. As we saw in Chapter 11, the ethical is a universal, objective standard for the rational assessment of social institutions. A relationship is "ethical" only if it is capable of derivation from the universal concept of the free will.

Hegel does not agree with Sommers when she says that it is a "misconception of the job of ethics" to think that it should question the foundation of the social institutions out of which DP obligations arise.[4] On the contrary, the *Philosophy of Right* takes on the task of bestowing the "form of rationality" on the institutions of ethical life (*PR* Preface 13). Hegel thinks that it makes a difference whether I simply perform my DP duties out of habit, or also reflect rationally on the institutional setting of these duties and whether it can be vindicated before the bar of reason. He regards it as our "right of insight into the good" that we should "have insight into an obligation on *good* grounds" (*PR* § 132R). Here, too, Hegel appears closer to Enlightenment universalism than to the brand of contemporary communitarianism that exalts tradition and ethos at the expense of rational reflection.

4. Relational duties and universal reflection

Prima facie there is a problem reconciling DP duties with EP ethical theories, such as Kantianism and utilitarianism, which portray moral reasoning as adopting a detached and impartial standpoint. Moral impartiality seems to alienate us even from the love and commitment which even the theories themselves, from their impartial standpoint, tell us are good attitudes for us to have. Thus EP theories are threatened with self-defeat.

Some, however, deny that there is any problem here at all. If they are right, then Sommers is mistaken in thinking that DP obligations require any modification in the standard moral theories, and Hegel is wrong to suppose that duties of relation are comprehensible only from the standpoint of ethical life. Those who take this view, such as Peter Railton, think there is no problem with an EP moral theory that tells one to develop dispositions to think in terms of DP obligations.[5] Railton points out that there is a distinction between the *truth conditions* of a theory and its *acceptance* or *assertibility* conditions. EP theories may be true, even if they render themselves unacceptable or unassertible. He is untroubled by the objection that a true ethical theory must meet a publicity condition to the effect that it must be possible to believe and publicly assert it as true. "Any such condition," he says, "would be question-begging against consequentialist theories, since it would require that one class of actions – acts of adopting or promulgating an ethical theory – *not* be assessed in terms of their consequences."[6]

This reply does not cohere very well with the claim that an EP rationale *can be given* for DP obligations, for only if I actually *believe* the consequentialist theory (and am prepared to assert it) can I actually give myself (or others) consequentialist reasons for acting in the nonconsequentialist ways that have good consequences. The reply will be unconvincing, moreover, to those who think that there are independent reasons for imposing the publicity condition as a constraint on an ethical theory. There are such reasons, since ethical theories achieve their ends mainly by being taught and believed. Consequentialists ought to be troubled if they are forbidden by their theory itself to believe or promulgate it. There is nothing question-begging in pointing out that consequentialism is in a bind if it demands of us that we adopt beliefs on grounds other than their (evident or apparent) truth. Any view that makes such demands seriously conflicts with our fundamental sense of intellectual integrity. Pointing this out doesn't presuppose that consequentialism is false; it only provides a strong reason for thinking it must be.

A more reassuring reply from the EP theorist would be that the giving of EP reasons for acting in a DP manner does not as a matter of fact involve us in disbelieving our EP theory or refusing to assert it. The problem with this reply is that although it is possible that this thesis is correct for some EP theories, it is probably incorrect for many of them, especially (as Henry Sidgwick famously admitted) for consequentialist ones.[7]

Hegel himself might in principle have similar problems reconciling ethical duties of relation (many of which are DP duties) with his own theory, founded on universal reasoning about human freedom and the conditions of its self-actualization. That he faces such challenges is, in fact, a good thing for his theory. The possibility of being alienated from one's dispositions, affections, and spontaneous relationships is inseparable from all reason and reflection, since without it reason would lack the power to correct, or even properly to confirm such relations. It would be no advantage to an ethical theory – on the contrary, it would be a serious defect – if it did not allow even the *possibility* of such alienation.[8] It is reasonable to ask of an ethical theory only that it should in fact reconcile ethical reasoning with healthy and desirable traits, feelings, and ethical relations.

Generally speaking, a Hegelian self-actualization theory founded on freedom seems well suited to meet these challenges. It tells me to actualize a certain self-image that is the outcome of the dialectical process of experience.

This turns out to be a self-image that involves precisely those ethical relations with which our ethical duties are bound up. There would be a problem if the self-image involved the absence of self-awareness or self-determination.[9] Hegel's theory, however, proposes that we be self-consciously free (or "with ourselves") in what we do. Its whole point is to achieve rational self-knowledge and self-transparency in our ethical life. Such a theory gives us every reason to avoid a principle if the reflective attempt to follow it leads to self-defeat or self-alienation.

5. Ethical virtue

In Chapter 8, we looked briefly at a Kantian argument claiming that only pure respect for the moral law leads reliably to good acts:

> It is not enough that [action] should accord with the law; it must be done for the sake of the law. Otherwise, the accordance is merely contingent and spurious because, though the unmoral ground may indeed now and then produce lawful actions, more often it brings forth unlawful ones. (G 390/6)

Hegel's view is exactly the opposite of this. As we saw in Chapter 8, he thinks that the pure motive of duty, abstracted from our living desires, interests, and self-satisfaction, can never reliably produce the good. Rather, it is only when the good is brought to life by reconciling it with our empirical desires and self-satisfaction, that good actions become part of our everyday life, and *cease* to be "contingent and spurious." When Kant argues that "unmoral grounds" cannot reliably produce good actions, he seems to have in mind cases like that in which impulsive sympathy leads me to squander on the first needy person I meet some scarce resources that I already owe to someone else (BSE 216/58). To generalize from such cases is to suppose that a person's natural or empirical desires could never be so constituted that they aim reliably at the good.

That is simply to suppose the impossibility of *virtue* – "the ethical insofar as it is reflected in the individual character determined through nature" (PR § 150). Hegel's conception of ethical virtue is modeled on Aristotle's conception of virtues of character (PR § 150R). A virtue is a disposition *(Gesinnung)*, trait *(hexis)*, or habit *(ethos)*, but it is not only a disposition or tropism to behave in certain ways. Virtues are *intelligent* dispositions, dispositions to act for certain reasons, to be pleased or pained at certain things, to feel certain emotions.[10]

Hegel regards Aristotelian virtue as a direct answer to the Kantian duality of reason and inclination.

> Aristotle determines the concept of virtue more precisely by distinguishing a rational aspect of the soul from an irrational one; in the latter *nous* [reason] is only *dynamei* [potentially] – sensations, inclinations, passions, emotions apply to it. In the rational side, understanding, wisdom, reflectiveness, cognizance all have their place. But they do not constitute virtue, which consists only in the unity of the rational with the irrational side. We call it virtue when the passions (inclinations) are so related to reason that they do what reason commands. (VGP 2: 222/204)

This does not mean that the virtuous person simply acts out of goodhearted inclination. On the contrary, "if insight *(logos)* is bad or not present at all but passion (inclination, the heart) conducts itself well, then goodness of heart *(Gutmütigkeit)* may exist, but not virtue, because the ground *(logos, reason)* or *nous* is lacking, which is necessary to virtue" (*VGP 2*: 222–223/ 204–205).

There are two distinct ways of doing the right thing without exhibiting virtue. Kant is quite correct when he denies virtue to the person who does good to others simply because it happens to please him to spread joy around (*G* 398/14). There is also no virtue, however, in one of Kant's own examples of the good will, the misanthrope who thwarts his coldhearted inclinations and behaves kindly toward others solely from duty (*G* 398–399/14–15). Virtuous people know and will appropriate actions for good reasons, but their feelings and inclinations accord with reason, and so right actions also give them subjective satisfaction. Even for such a person, of course, right action can sometimes be painful, as when duty requires some personal sacrifice. But such cases will be due only to unfortunate external circumstances, not to deep conflicts between the demands of duty and the agent's emotional constitution. Moreover, in a rational system of ethical life, such circumstances should be comparatively rare, since a rational social order is one that is fundamentally satisfying to the needs and selfhood of its members. If they are virtuous, it will be unusual for them to find themselves in situations where the demands of duty come into serious conflict with their subjective needs and desires.

Virtues are "the ethical in application to the particular," dispositions finely tuned to particular circumstances (*PR* § 150R; *VPR19* 126). Virtue is not, as Kant would have it, our power of constraining ourselves to follow general principles (*TL* 404–406/66–68). It is rather the capacity to judge, feel, and act as each unique situation requires, to the degree that the situation requires. This is why both Hegel and Aristotle consider virtue to be a "mean."[11] As the fundamental ethical disposition, virtue is possible because it is the subjective condition of the possibility of an actual ethical order. Conversely, virtue is made possible by ethical institutions, in which the particular satisfaction of each subject is in harmony with the universal good (*PR* § 154).

6. Virtue and rectitude

Strictly speaking, though, virtue is not Hegel's ideal for modern ethical life. Hegel associates virtue *(Tugend)* with an earlier age, when the social order was less fully organized, and the ethical had to triumph through "ethical virtuosity" *(Virtuosität)* – the special ethical genius of individuals, such as Herakles and other heroes of ancient Greece (*PR* § 150R,A; *VPR 3*:490; *VPR19* 125).[12] Virtue in this sense is compatible with a good deal of what we would consider immoral or even barbarous conduct, because in a heroic age, the ethical is not yet established in a rational system, and is instead the work of the hero's arbitrary will (*VA 1*: 241/250).

In modern society, on the other hand, the ethical life of individuals is articulated into an organic whole composed of determinate roles, positions, or estates *(Stände)*. Each position has its own determinate duties and ethical disposition.

> Ethical disposition consists in everyone's having a position *(Stand)*: The human being must educate *(bilden)* himself for a position. . . . And he who has no position, is nothing. But through this existence, the human being must make himself actual, and preserve himself in this particularity. This is what is ethical in his position. . . . The position is the real content of duty. It provides determinate duties, which each can know. Virtue contains this, that individuality gives itself a character through its own determinate vocation *(Bestimmung)*. (VPR17 124)

Hegel has a preferred term for this more modern, less spectacular kind of virtue. "Insofar as [virtue] shows nothing but the simple conformity of the individual to the duties of relation that belong to him, it is *rectitude (Rechtschaffenheit)*" (PR § 150). Thus Hegel argues that where ancient drama focuses on heroic deeds, modern drama must deal with the success or failure of individuals in their quest for purely personal and subjective ends (VA *1*: 249–251/258–260). He realizes that we may regret the absence of the opportunity for heroism in the modern world. But he wants us to appreciate that this is simply the consequence of a more rational society and, at the same time, of a deeper self-understanding, which cannot help but view the ancient ideal of heroic virtue as something naïve, immature – in the end, ridiculous. Hegel is unimpressed with contemporary Romantic attempts to revive the heroic ideal in a modern context – as in Schiller's *The Robbers*. A truer insight into its fate, in his view, was provided in the early seventeenth century by Cervantes' *Don Quixote* (VA *1*: 253/262). Hegel's view implies that a society (like our own) whose popular fiction and drama are dominated by ideals of heroism, is seriously lacking a well-ordered and reflective ethical life.

We saw in Chapter 11, § 5, that Hegel is distinctly hostile to Romantic individualism. He is sensitive, however, to the rather Kantian thought that "from the standpoint of morality [rectitude] appears as something subordinate, above which other and greater things must be demanded; for [morality] seeks to be something *particular,* and is not satisfied with being the universal, or what is in and for itself; it finds the consciousness of authenticity *(Eigentümlichkeit)* only in what is exceptional" (PR § 150R). Hegel's response to this worry is to say that just as freedom does not lie in arbitrariness, so in a rational social order virtue does not lie in idiosyncrasies, through which I might hope to distinguish myself from others by some unique excellence of character. In a rational social order, virtue consists rather in perfecting myself in my particular vocation, bringing my character into conformity with the demands of my special position in society. For it is this that constitutes my real particularity: "The individual gives himself actuality only insofar as he steps into *existence (Dasein)*, hence into *determinate particularity,* and hence limits himself *exclusively* to one of the *particular* spheres [of modern economic life]" (PR § 207).

7. Ethical life and subjective reflection

In Chapter 11, § 8, we noted a certain tension in Hegel's view of the ethical. Hegel holds that the objective ethical order reaches perfection only in the modern state. The subjectively ethical, however, seems to be essentially unreflective. It is the attitude that follows ethical custom habitually and unquestioningly. Thus it might appear that the subjectively ethical, the ethical attitude or disposition, is essentially premodern, since it excludes the subjectivity found in the moral standpoint.

In the Jena period, Hegel argues that the moral consciousness of doing duty for duty's sake is Pharisaical, and poisons truly ethical conduct; "in a true ethical life, subjectivity is done away with *(aufgehoben)*" (*GW* 426/184). Even later, after he has come to terms with morality in a positive way, Hegel continues to speak of the ethical attitude as one that excludes reflection: "The ethical attitude *(Gesinnung)* of the subjects is a separation from reflection, which is always poised for a leap out of the universal substance over [and] into the particular" (*VPR17* : 90).

The ethical attitude described in such passages appears to have much in common with the second stage of moral consciousness in Piaget's theory of personality development, in which the child accepts rules as "sacred and untouchable, emanating from adults and lasting forever";[13] or again, it might remind us of the "conventional" stage of development in Kohlberg's theory, in which the child is oriented toward personal relationships, or at most toward institutions, but still lacks the capacity to formulate and follow self-chosen ethical principles.[14] The ethical attitude seems primitive or immature by comparison with the reflective moral attitude with which Hegel often favorably contrasts it.

In his mature writings, however, Hegel's usual position is that the ethical attitude does *not* preclude reflection after all. In those passages where Hegel still considers the "ethical" to exclude subjective reflection, the term suddenly acquires pejorative connotations. The arranged marriage is more "ethical" than a marriage in which the partners have chosen each other, but it clashes with "the subjective principle of the modern world" (*PR* § 162R). The "ethical will," together with the will of the child, the slave, and the superstitious person, is a will "sunk in objectivity," "without freedom" (*PR* § 26; *VPR 3* : 161; *4* : 146). More often, however, Hegel contends that the ethical attitude is the truest expression of freedom precisely because it is *compatible* with moral subjectivity.

> [In the ethical] subjective self-consciousness remains subjective will, but loses its one-sidedness, for it is subjectivity that has its foundation in the objective concept, the good. . . . Of course we can say that the ethical human being is unconscious, but consciousness is also there, though only as a moment. (*VPR 3* : 482–483)

Originally, I obey the ethical norms of my society because I feel completely identical or at home with them, and follow them habitually and naturally. This ethical attitude may still be present even if, supervening on it, there is also a moral or philosophical attitude of conscientious individual reflection or scientific criticism.

Faith and trust belong to the beginning of reflection and presuppose a representation and a difference: as, e.g., it is one thing to believe in a pagan religion and a different thing to be a pagan. Every relation, or rather this relationless identity, in which the ethical is the actual life of self-consciousness, can pass over into a relation of belief and conviction, and then through *further reflection* into an insight from grounds, which originate either in some particular ends, interests and considerations, or in fear and hope, or in historical presuppositions. But an *adequate cognition* of [these grounds] belongs to the thinking concept. (*PR* § 147R)[15]

The ethical attitude thus admits of a hierarchy of four levels:

1. Immediate experience of the individual identity with ethical norms
2. Reflective feelings of faith and trust
3. Insight of the understanding
4. Rational philosophical cognition of ethical norms as objectively right

The ethical disposition is fundamentally a living awareness of the individual's identity with the ethical order. This sense of identity can be wholly immediate, taking the form of custom and habit, or we can reflect on it. But reflection does not destroy what is ethical in the disposition. On the contrary, Hegel thinks that the better we understand the ethical order, the more profound will be our appreciation of its rationality. Reflective understanding and reason are there to confirm us in our habitual behavior, and they acquire the status not only of habit but also of moral conscience, since the truthful conscience is nothing but the subjective disposition to will what is objectively good (*PR* § 137). In this way, conduct that is at bottom habitual, arising out of a concrete life experience, does not cease to be so when it is reflected on; it retains its genuinely ethical character.

This presupposes that reason and reflection confirm the rightness and rationality of ethical norms. Hegel has every right to this presupposition since only an articulated and rationally organized society is truly ethical. Besides, the theory presented in the *Philosophy of Right* considers only the idea or rational essence of modern ethical life. It treats existing social orders only to the extent that they are actual and rational. Hence it is reasonable to presume that the ethical attitude discussed in this theory will relate to a society whose rationality will be confirmed by subjective reflection.

It bears repeating, however, that Hegel does not think that rational reflection inevitably endorses the existing social order. There are historical periods in which existing society is "faithless to better wills"; those are times when, in the manner of Socrates and the Stoics, moral reflection must turn inward and seek there for what outer social reality has lost (*PR* § 138). Hegel even thinks that reflection inevitably exposes the limitations of every ethical order, and so tends, in the long run, to undermine both the ethical attitude and the ethical order. In the next chapter, we will examine the radical conclusions Hegel draws from this thought.

13
The limits of ethics

1. The transitoriness of the ethical

In its objective aspect, ethical life is unified in the political state. Through the state people decide how they will live together, and this gives explicit rationality to the whole ethical community. That is why Hegel describes the state as "the actuality of the ethical Idea" (PR § 257), and "the actuality of concrete freedom" (PR § 260). The state is "the actuality of the substantial *will*, an actuality that it possesses in the particular *self-consciousness* when this has been raised to universality; as such, it is *rational* in and for itself" (PR § 258). Hegel even characterizes the state – in what might be regarded as blasphemous terms – as "the presence of spirit in the world" (PR § 270R), an "earthly deity" (PR § 272A), and "the march of God in the world" (PR § 258A).[1]

Hegel intends the terms "earthly" and "in the world" as significant qualifications on the state's claims to divinity. It is only the *Idea* of the state that Hegel calls "this actual God." This Idea is distinct from the *existing* state which, he says, "is no work of art; it exists in the world, and hence in the sphere of arbitrariness, contingency, and error" (PR § 258A). The state belongs to the practical sphere, "the standpoint of the merely finite, temporal, contradictory, and thus transitory, unsatisfied, and unblessed spirit" (VA 1: 129/128). In the state, "it is only the rational freedom of the *will* that explicates itself"; as rational beings we seek "the region of a higher, more substantial truth, in which all oppositions and contradictions of the finite can find their final resolution and freedom can find its full satisfaction" (VA 1: 137/137).

This higher region is that of "absolute spirit," the higher cultural realms of art, religion, and science (or philosophy). Art, religion, and philosophy, too, have their history, but the truth to which they give us access is absolute and timeless. This truth assumes three different forms in our threefold mental life: sensuous intuition (Anschauung), representation (Vorstellung), and the rational concept (Begriff). In art, absolute truth appears immediately to us in sensuous intuition as the ideal of beauty. In religion, we relate to truth through representative thought – in legends, myths, and doctrines held by faith. Only philosophy grasps the absolute truth in conceptual form, as the philosophical Idea.

The spheres of absolute spirit have a history because the stages of human history are stages of spirit's self-understanding. People actualize different concepts of their nature practically in different principles of ethical life. Likewise, their relation to eternal truth assumes different forms – in different aesthetic shapes, religious faiths, and philosophical theories. The cultures of different ages express the absolute differently, but the object presented us by art, religion, and philosophy – the one absolute truth – is the same in all ages. We might think that as much could be said of ethical life, since it strives to actualize the freedom of spirit, and its claim on us is conditional on its success in doing this. Cruder forms of art are less perfect intuitions of the aesthetic ideal, more primitive religious ideas represent the divine less adequately, and less developed systems of philosophy miss important parts of the truth of the Idea. In the same way, we might think, a less developed ethical order (one involving the institution of slavery, say, or failing to provide for subjective freedom) actualizes spirit's freedom less completely.

Hegel wants to distinguish ethical life from spheres of absolute spirit at this point. Because ethical life is practical, it involves a separation between the will and its end, whereas the spheres of absolute spirit deal with a perfection that transcends any such separation. Art, religion, and philosophy exhaust their true content in relating us to eternal truth; their proper aesthetic, religious, or philosophical claim on us consists only in their capacity to afford us access to that truth. If, owing to cultural and historical changes, a work of art, a cult, or a philosophical system loses its aesthetic, religious, or philosophical value for us, then it becomes a subject only for historians.

The same is not true of the ethical life of a community, because ethical life is spirit's way of giving practical actuality to freedom here and now, at a definite time and place. The ethical validity of laws and customs depends on people's confidence that they actualize freedom, but an ethical institution is not merely a theoretical statement about freedom; it is a practical attempt to actualize it. Thus Hegel says an institution can still "be valid" *(gelten, gültig sein)* in its own age even if, from the higher perspective of a later age, it involves the suppression of freedom. We have seen that slavery, for example, occurs "in the transition of humanity from natural to ethical conditions" *(PR* § 57R); it violates the "eternal human rights" of persons, and so it is absolutely wrong *(EG* § 433A). But in the ancient world it formed a part of the ethical structure that actualized spirit's freedom to the fullest extent possible at that time. Thus Hegel says that the ancient institution of slavery, though "wrong," was nevertheless "valid" *(PR* § 57A).

Hegel's ethical theory provides for a rational critique of social institutions in two ways. First, the Idea or actuality of a system of ethical life may differ from the contingent existence of this system because the latter belongs to the sphere of contingency, where human wickedness may pervert and deform it. Second, even the ethical Idea of a society may be seen as defective when it is viewed from a higher, more developed standpoint. But Hegel does not think that an institution altogether loses its validity as soon as we find out that it is at odds with what is rational or right. Valid ethical norms are not merely theoretical statements about the right or the good. They belong to practices that (to some degree, or at some time and place) actualize the freedom of spirit. Even when they are seen to be defective, institutions remain a part of practical life until they are abolished in practice. Defective art, religion, and philosophy, to the extent that they are seen to be defective, cease to belong to the realm of absolute spirit. But even a defective ethical life retains its validity until it is abolished in practice and replaced with something better.

Hegel does not conclude from this that we are bound absolutely by the institutions of the existing order (no matter how evil and irrational they may be). Perhaps some will think his conclusions is even more scandalous, for it is that there is a limit to the whole realm of the ethical and its rational authority over us. The claim of all duties on us depends on the rationality of an actual social order. Yet there is no social order whose rationality is perfect, permanent, or unconditional. Every system of ethical life is transitory and conditioned by the extent to which spirit has reached self-knowledge in that time and place. Consequently, each shape of ethical life necessarily falls short of actualizing the idea of freedom in all its inexhaustible depth. The claims of the ethical are therefore always conditional, imperfect, ultimately unsatisfying to our reason. Kant and Fichte got things backwards when they tried to make morality or ethics the foundation of the highest things, even of religion and speculative philosophy.

2. The ethical life-cycle

The ethical is limited not only by the timeless realm of absolute spirit, but also bounded *within* time. The ethical life of any state always occupies a determinate place in world history, which is the progress of the world spirit toward self-knowledge and self-actualization. The right of the state supersedes that of abstract right, morality, the family and civil society, but it is limited by an even higher right – that of the world spirit "whose right is the highest of all" (*PR* § § 33, 340).

Hegel sees world history as a progressive succession of spirit's attempts to know and actualize its own freedom. "The history of spirit is its *deed,* for it is only what it does, and its deed it to make itself, as spirit, into an object of its consciousness, to grasp itself interpretingly *(auslegend)* for itself" (*PR* § 343). Spirit's successive attempts to interpret and actualize itself constitute a series of "principles." These are the principles of peoples or nations *(Völker):* "Nations are the concepts which spirit has formed of itself" (*VG* 59/51). A people actualizes its principle when it forms itself into a state. "States, peoples and individuals involved in this concern of the world spirit emerge, each with its own *particular and determinate principle,* which has its interpretation and actuality in [a nation's] *constitution*" (*PR* § 344).

A people does not begin as a state (*PR* § 349), but becomes one in the course of its regular life cycle, during which "it blossoms, grows strong, then fades away and dies" (*VG* 67–68/–58). In youth, a nation is "ethical, virtuous and vigorous" (*VG* 67/58). The people grows to maturity when it becomes a state, so that its principle "produces an ethical, political organization" (*VG* 178/145). "The transition of a family, horde, tribe, group, etc. into the condition of a state constitutes the *formal* realization of the Idea in it" (*PR* § 349). Each stage in the world spirit's development is represented by a determinate national principle. A nation becomes historically dominant when its principle corresponds to the level of self-awareness attained by spirit. "For at any time the timely nation, the one which rules, is the one which has grasped the highest concept of spirit" (*VG* 69/60).[2]

When the principle of a nation no longer corresponds to spirit's highest conception of itself, then the time of that nation is past, and it grows old and dies. It may be conquered by another nation, with a higher principle, or it may die a "natural death" in which the ethical life of the nation stagnates and continues to subsist in the senescent condition of mere habit (*VG* 68–69/59–60). Hegel sometimes insists that a nation's time can come but once, and that once the time of its principle is past, it has no further role to play in world history (*PR* § 347R; *VG* 69/60, 180/148). This suggests that historical development occurs only transiently, through the successive prominence of a series of different nations or national principles. According to this picture, each nation embodies a determinate but unchanging principle, and progress consists in the passing of the torch of civilization successively from one nation (or nation-kind) to another (e.g., from Persia to the Greek city states to Rome to the "Germanic" nations of modern Europe).

Hegel suggests quite a different picture when he describes a second sort of "death" that a nation may suffer when its hour is past. A nation's maturity consists in the expression of its national principle in a rational political constitution; this process goes hand in hand with the development of the nation's self-consciousness. "This spiritual self-consciousness of a nation is its highest point" (*VG* 177/146), but at the same time the nation's downfall. In reflecting on its ethical life, a nation ceases to follow its ethical principles spontaneously; it begins to demand rational grounds to follow them. The answer to these demands can consist only in the reflective awareness of its own principle and of the rational basis of that principle. In the course of becoming reflectively aware of its principle, it also inevitably becomes aware of the limitations of that principle and of the grounds for following it: "This lies inevitably in any demand for grounds" (*VG* 178/146). "For thought, as universal, dissolves [its objects]. . . . Spirit has the property of dissolving every determinate content it encounters" (*VG* 179/147). In this way, Hegel says, the death of a nation appears not as a merely natural death, but as a kind of suicide, the "killing of itself by itself" (*VG* 70/60).

Reflective self-knowledge leads inevitably to demoralization: "Thus enters the isolating of individuals, from one another and from the whole, the intervention of their selfishness and vanity, the seeking of their own advantage at the expense of the whole" (*VG* 178/146). When we behold a principle in its limitedness, we perceive that it is not truly universal or ultimately valid.

What is universally valid now appears to us as something different, as a new principle (*VG* 179/147).[3] But the new principle cannot be grasped reflectively in its determinacy until much later in history, after it, too, has been actualized.

The irony in the life of a people is that its deepest aspiration and highest achievement, the self-knowledge of its actualized principle, always amounts to that principle's self-destruction:

> The life of a people brings a fruit to ripeness; for its activity is directed to carrying through its principle. But this fruit does not fall back into into its lap, into the womb from which it was born; the nation does not get to enjoy it. On the contrary, it becomes a bitter drink. Yet the nation cannot refuse it, for it has an infinite thirst for it; but the cost of the drink is its annihilation, and at the same time the rise of a new principle. (*VG* 72/62–63)

Following this picture, history is not merely a series of nations or national principles. It is also the immanent production of each successive principle out of the one that preceded it. A national principle is not really overcome from outside, but overcomes itself, by revealing its own limitations to itself. In other words, history is dialectical.

3. History's supreme right

According to Hegel, a new ethical order achieves ascendancy over an older one because the principle of the new order represents a deeper and truer conception of spirit's freedom. Since the actualization of spirit's freedom is the foundation of the ethical, we might think of the transition from one ethical order to another as an *ethical* advance, the result of a growth in ethical knowledge. But it would be a fallacy to infer that we *must* think of it in that way. The ethical belongs only to practical or objective spirit. Spirit's freedom is the ground of the ethical, but not everything founded on spirit's freedom is ethical, and some things founded on spirit's freedom may be higher than the ethical. A new and higher order embodies ethical knowledge, and superior knowledge of spirit's freedom, but it does not follow that it embodies superior *ethical* knowledge. Given Hegel's concept of the ethical, in fact, exactly the opposite follows. The ethical order's highest right is the right of the state; but the right of the state is superseded by the right of the world spirit in history (*PR* §§ 33, 340). This higher right is asserted at precisely those points where the state or the ethical order is seen to be limited and inadequate in its rationality. Thus the right of world history is a right that supersedes the ethical. It is, if you like, a right that is beyond the ethical, beyond good and evil.

It might be argued that the right of the world spirit in history always supersedes one ethical order in favor of another, superior ethical order, and so its right has to be identified with the *ethical* right of the new order. This argument would also be fallacious. There are two distinguishable features of the situation:

1. The old order actualizes spirit's freedom in a way that is seen to be limited, hence inadequate.
2. A new order comes on the scene which actualizes freedom better, or less inadequately.

For Hegel, (1) and (2) are closely connected, because he thinks (rather optimistically) that people's awareness of the inadequacy of one principle always gives rise to a new and superior principle.[4] Even if connected, however, (1) and (2) are still distinguishable. The world spirit's right over a decadent ethical order is based on (1) only, not on (2). The old order loses its right and its hold over people because people are aware that its principle is limited and the rational justification for its institutions is inadequate. It is a separate question whether there is ready to hand a new principle or new institutions that have a better justification. Besides, until the old institutions have been abolished in practice, they still have *ethical validity*, even if they have lost rational justification. The right of the world spirit over the declining ethical order is, if you like, only a right to destroy what is seen to be dead and hollow. The right to create something better is perhaps consequent on this first right, but it is quite separate from it.

We can see this point illustrated in Hegel's account of the consciousness that lives through the historical transition and effects it. Hegel stresses the moral decadence of the declining ethical order, the isolation of individuals from one another and from the ethical whole, their retreat into selfishness and vanity. Their experience is disillusionment with the old order, not enthusiasm for any new one.

There are good reasons, in Hegel's theory of the historical dialectic, and even in his basic conception of spirit, for describing the transition in exactly this way. A spiritual being is only what it does; its self-understanding consists in an interpretation to itself of what it has done. People are capable of acquiring a clear conception of the ethical order only after it has been fully actualized, "only at a time after the actuality of its process of formation has been completed" (*PR* Preface 25). It follows directly that the individuals who create a new ethical order cannot have a clear conception of what they are creating, and cannot be in possession of rational knowledge of its superiority over the old order.

As an ethical order matures, its members become reflective, and this makes possible a positive comprehension of it (such as Hegel tries to provide for the modern state in the *Philosophy of Right*). But when the ethical order's time of maturity is past, negative reflection on it also comes within their reach, and the ethical loses its right over the individual will. The old order now comes into collision with forces animated by a new principle. It is impossible that those forces should take the form of a rationally worked out plan or ethical "ideal," which might display the superiority of the new order to the old. Given Hegel's conception of spirit, it follows that such an ideal form can make its appearance only after the new order is fully actual. For this reason, even if those who create the new order were motivated by high-

224

minded ethical conceptions or moral ideals, their ideals would have to be inchoate and there could be no cogent moral or ethical justification, available to themselves for their actions. We shall see in § 5, however, that Hegel thinks world historical change typically involves no such high-minded motivation.

4. History and relativism

In Chapter 11, it was argued that Hegel's theory of ethical life is not committed to cultural relativism. We may now begin to wonder whether Hegel's theory of history does not force us to revise this conclusion. Hegel clearly does hold that different forms of ethical life prevail at different stages of history, and even that a form of ethical life may be "valid" even when a correct insight reveals its institutions to lack rational justification. It looks as though the validity of an ethical order consists simply in the fact that its institutions exist. That looks like a form of ethical relativism.

Hegel holds that a system of ethical life has validity because, and for as long as, it actualizes the highest stage of self-awareness that spirit has thus far achieved. That is not a feature that belongs to a social system merely because it exists. He also maintains that different ethical orders have validity at different stages in history. But it is a mistake to call a view relativistic simply on that account. Hegel thinks different ethical orders are valid in different ages only because he thinks that spirit's knowledge of its freedom grows and deepens through history, and so spirit's attempt to actualize that freedom takes different forms in different ages. The validity of a duty, for instance, depends on its being part of a system of ethical life that (for a time) actualizes spirit's freedom.

This need not distinguish Hegel's view radically from hedonistic utilitarianism, for instance. If utilitarians thought that people's history shows them passing through different stages in their awareness of pleasure and how it is to be acquired, then they might very well adopt a view analogous to Hegel's. Hegel's view is more analogous to rule- than to act-utilitarianism, because it is a self-actualization theory in which the human good consists in manifesting a certain identity in action rather than achieving certain ends. Rule-utilitarians might very naturally distinguish between different historical systems of rules for the promotion of pleasure, and say that one set of rules is valid so long as people hold one conception of pleasure and its pursuit, whereas a different set of rules becomes valid as soon as people acquire greater knowledge about these matters. The historical variability of ethical standards in Hegel's theory is closely analogous to this.

Where Hegel's view is significantly different from utilitarianism, as well as from most other moral theories, is in the idea that ethical standards generally have only a limited role in humanity's pursuit of the final goal. For Hegel, the actualization of spirit's freedom sometimes justifies conduct that directly violates the only applicable ethical standards. This happens in periods of historical transition, when one ethical order is dying and another is being born.

5. World historical individuals

The the world is still not conscious of its condition; the end is to bring this about. This is the aim of world historical human beings, and in this they find their satisfaction. They are conscious of the powerlessness of what is present, of what still coasts along but only appears to be actuality. Spirit, having cultivated itself inwardly, has outgrown its world and is about *(im Begriff ist)* to pass beyond it; spirit's self-consciousness no longer finds satisfaction in this world, but this kind of dissatisfaction has not yet found what it wills – for this is not as yet affirmatively at hand – and so it stands on the negative side. It is the world historical individuals who have then told people what it is that they will. (*VG* 98–99/84)[5]

World historical individuals serve a cause – that of "the higher universal" (*VG* 97/82, 98/83) – but they do not serve this cause consciously, intentionally, or with knowledge of so doing. Their knowledge of the higher universal or new principle of spirit is not knowledge of "the Idea as such"; it is not rational comprehension of the movement of history. It is only a practical insight into what must be done next in order to further their own personal ends – ends that just happen to coincide with the larger ends of spirit. "Since these individuals are the living expressions of the substantial deed of the world spirit and are thus immediately identical with it, they cannot themselves perceive it and it is not their object and end" (*PR* § 348). Hegel distinguishes the "immediate" insight of the world historical individual from a reflective or rational knowledge of the idea, which is the prerogative of the philosophical historian who comes along later and comprehends what they have achieved (*VG* 98/83).[6]

World historical individuals help to actualize the freedom of spirit by bringing to birth a new order of things. That puts them among humanity's greatest benefactors. Their conscious intentions, however, are by no means philanthropic. On the contrary, world historical individuals are men of affairs, statesmen, and military commanders, such as Alexander of Macedonia, Julius Caesar, Charlemagne, or Napoleon Bonaparte. Along with their practical insight into the higher universal to be actualized, they usually have a sense of their own historical destiny, but they are motivated less by the needs of the human race than by their own personal ambition and glory. Their insight into the needs of the time thus typically takes the form of a knowledge of the way to enhance or protect their own power (*VG* 103/87).

Hegel says that Caesar's crossing the Rubicon, for example, was done only with the intention of preserving himself, protecting his command against those who were on the point of becoming his enemies (*VG* 90/76). Caesar defied the laws and commands of the Roman Republic because he saw that it had become a "lie," "that this hollow structure had to be replaced by a new one and that the structure he himself created was the necessary one" (*VG* 105/89). Nor are world historical individuals fastidious in the means they use to achieve their ends. They are often ruthless and unprincipled, "treating other intrinsically admirable interests and sacred rights in a carefree, cursory, hasty and heedless manner. . . . A mighty figure must trample many an innocent flower underfoot, and destroy much that lies in its path" (*VG* 105/89).

We have seen (Chapter 12, § 6) that for Hegel a "hero" is someone who creatively brings to birth something new, and that this is incompatible with displaying the "rectitude" characteristic of a member of a rational social order. World historical individuals are "heroes" (*VG* 96/83) in something like this sense. Yet because they emerge in periods of decadence and transition, not in the first blossoming of a new order but at the end of an old and decadent one, Hegel does not see them as characterized by "virtue" (or "ethical virtuosity"), any more than they are by rectitude. However, he does not represent world historical individuals as selfish or egoistically motivated in the sense that they seek their own personal *happiness*. They are driven by what Hegel calls "passion": the concentration of the whole individuality on a single goal (*VG* 85/72–73, 92/78).[7] Nor, in Hegel's view, are world historical individuals typically happy people: "When their end is attained, they fall aside like empty husks. They may have undergone great difficulties in order to accomplish their end, but as soon as they have done so, they die early like Alexander, are murdered like Caesar, or deported like Napoleon" (*VG* 100/ 85). This is what Hegel calls the "cunning of reason" in history, "that it sets passions to work in its service, so that the agents by which it gives itself existence must pay the penalty and suffer the loss" (*VG* 105/89).

Judged by moral or ethical standards, world historical individuals are typically *bad* men. They benefit humanity, but they receive no honor and no gratitude, either in their own time or in subsequent ages. All they receive from posterity is undying fame as "formal subjectivities" (*PR* § 348). Hegel does not dispute this judgment of posterity, or claim that its ingratitude does them any injustice. Nor does he try to disguise or mitigate the wickedness of world historical individuals. On the contrary, the morally good and ethically virtuous are those who oppose the world historical individual, resisting the progressive course of spirit: "Those who, with an ethical vocation and a noble disposition, have resisted what the progress of the idea of spirit has made necessary, stand higher in moral worth than those whose crimes have been transformed into means to higher order" (*VG* 171/141).

In Hegel's view this is how it must be, since the interests of spirit represented by world historical individuals are precisely those that require the destruction of the existing ethical life, overriding all moral or ethical claims in favor of the higher right of the world spirit:

> In the course of history one essential moment is the preservation of a people, a state, and the preservation of the ordered spheres of its life . . . that is, the preservation of ethical life. But the other moment is that the subsisting of a people's spirit as it is must be broken through, because it is exhausted and has worked itself out, in order that world history, the world spirit, should go forward. . . . It is precisely here that there arise those great collisions between subsisting, recognized duties, laws and rights, and new possibilities which are opposed to this system, which violate it, and even destroy its foundation and actuality. (*VG* 96–97/82)

If it is the task of world historical individuals to help bring a new ethical order to birth by destroying the old one, it is hardly to be expected that their deeds will exhibit ethical virtue. World historical individuals share their time's cynical insight into the hollowness of the existing ethical order, which they therefore treat with contempt (*VG* 104/88). Their passions can achieve the destruction of the dying ethical world precisely because "they do not heed any of the restraints which right and morality seek to impose upon them" (*VG* 79/68). Passion is the force that brings the new ethical order to birth, because it is the only force powerful enough to break the bonds of the ethical.

6. Beyond the ethical

There is nothing new in Hegel's idea that some of humanity's greatest bene-factors have been criminals and evildoers. This idea stands squarely in the tradition of Mandeville's "private vices, public benefits," Adam Smith's "invisible hand," Turgot's views about the role of war and ambition in human progress, and Kant's theory (derived partly from Rousseau) that our rational capacities (including our capacity for morality itself) are developed only through social competition and the drive for unjust ascendancy over others (*IG* 20–22/44–45). What perhaps makes Hegel's view more scandalous than its precursors is the further idea that these wicked individuals are absolutely *justified* in their unethical conduct. When they violate abstract right, moral-ity, and ethics, they "have the absolute right on their side, but a right of a wholly peculiar kind" (*VG* 98/84).

The assertion that someone could have a *right* to do what is morally or ethically wrong may already seem like a straightforward self-contradiction. But in fact it follows quite naturally from Hegel's ethical theory that there should be such a right. "Right," in the most general and fundamental sense, refers to whatever gives existence to the will's freedom (*PR* § 29). The more completely and less conditionally something actualizes freedom, the higher its right. Moral subjectivity actualizes freedom more fully than abstract right, so its right is higher. Ethical life, in turn, gives greater actuality to freedom than morality, and so its right is higher than theirs. The right of any ethical order itself is also limited by the imperfect way in which its principle actual-izes spirit's freedom. These limits show themselves in an era of world-histori-cal transition, when people's wills no longer find satisfaction in the existing ethical order but no new form of ethical life has arisen to take its place. At such a time, the freedom of spirit is given existence by those who violate and overturn the old order. In fact, these actions give freedom a higher existence than does the decadent ethical order they are violating. In the most general and fundamental sense, then, their unethical actions constitute a "right," in fact a higher right than the ethical order those actions offend. There can be a right that overrides the ethical because the justification of ethics itself, through the way it actualizes spirit's freedom, has always been only a limited and conditional justification. In that sense, no moral or ethical imperative can ever be categorical.

For Hegel, the sphere of world history is higher than that of the ethical. From its higher standpoint, ethical right and wrong do not cease to exist, but they no longer matter. It is to the sphere of "conscious actuality" – of

228

practical life lived in the present – that such things as "justice and virtue, wrongdoing, violence and vice, guilt and innocence" have their "determinate significance"; it is in this sphere alone that "talents, passions, the splendor, independence, happiness or unhappiness of individuals and states" are to "find judgment and (always imperfect) justice." But "world history falls outside these points of view" (*PR* § 345). Philosophical historians should not make moral or ethical judgments, not because their discipline is "value free" but because its standpoint on human freedom – the ultimate value – is higher than the ethical standpoint.

[From the world-historical standpoint] the deeds of the great men who are the individuals of world history, appear justified not only in the inner significance of which those individuals were unconscious, but also from a worldly standpoint. From this point of view, no claims must be raised against world-historical deeds and their perpetrators by moral circles, to which they do not belong. The litany of private virtues – modesty, humility, charity, and temperance – must not be raised against them. World history could wholly dispense with the circle in which falls morality, and the often mistakenly discussed dichotomy between morals and politics. (*VG* 171–172/141)

Hegel is particularly interested in attacking those moralists who see in great men and their deeds only wicked passions and vices, and treat the study of history chiefly as a gymnasium in which to exercise our capacity for moral indignation:

What schoolmaster has not demonstrated of Alexander the Great or Julius Caesar that they were impelled by such passions and were therefore immoral characters? – from which it follows that the schoolmaster himself is a more admirable man than they were, because he does not have such passions (the proof being that he does not conquer Asia or vanquish Darius and Porus, but simply lives and lets live). (*VG* 103/87)

Hegel's writings contain two quite distinct defenses of "great men" against small-minded moralists. In both contexts he quotes the French *bon mot*: "No man is a hero to his *valet de chambre*" – with the barbed addition that this is not because the hero is not a hero, but because the valet is only a valet (*PR* § 124A; *VG* 103/78; cf. *PhG* ¶ 665).[8] But the two defenses are very different in import. One is a *moral* defense of the great man, claiming that those who achieve great things within the sphere of morality and ethical life should not be criticized morally on the ground that their achievements were satisfying to them and motivated partly by personal ambition, so long as their insight and intention accord with the good (*PR* § 124; cf. Chapter 8, §§ 3–7). Here the small-mindedness of the moralist consists in dwelling one-sidedly on motivation, and in perversely drawing pointless distinctions between different motivational frames of mind which (Hegel alleges) are all morally creditable to the agent.

The other defense of "great men" is not moral but *amoral* in its import. It applies to the deeds of great men that are admittedly wrong, plain violations of people's rights, or other ethical principles. This defense says that the wickedness of great men, though blamable from a moral or ethical stand-point, has no significance from the higher standpoint of world history. The small-mindedness of the moralist here does not consist, as in the first case, in an error in *moral* judgment. It consists instead in failing to see that great men have a justification for the crimes they commit which transcends the moral and ethical spheres altogether. Here the small-mindedness of moralists consists in the fact that when they consider world historical deeds, they think it appropriate to make any moral judgments at all.

7. Exercising the right to do wrong

Though he ridicules the banal moralizing of the schoolmaster, there is some-thing rather trite about Hegel's own admiration for the men nineteenth-cen-tury schoolboys read about in their history books, and something very schoolmasterish about the way Hegel turns the history lesson into a "time to praise famous men." Some of us might have preferred an alternative history curriculum, in which what Marx called "the high-sounding drama of states and princes" is supplemented by an account of how history is really shaped incrementally by the deeds of countless people whom the schoolmaster never heard of and would in any case not have time to name. If Hegel must view history as a military museum, some of us would prefer it if his gallery also contained portraits of people like Spartacus, Wat Tyler, Jeanne d'Orleans, and Stenka Razin.

These, however, have not been people's only, or deepest, qualms about Hegel's philosophy of history. What scandalizes more people is Hegel's no-tion that there can be actions that morality (even ethics) has no right to judge. We may be repulsed by the thought that there are people who, though wicked and destructive, have an "absolute right" or supramoral justification for their evil deeds, so that it is inappropriate and small-minded to raise any moral objections against them. It may frighten us to think what people might do if they got the notion that they possessed such a right. Some of Hegel's critics have even thought that his doctrines might, without any distortion or misunderstanding, be used to justify the deeds of all those ruthless individu-als through whose cruelty human history appears to us (in Hegel's all too candid words) as the "slaughter-bench on which the happiness of peoples, the wisdom of states, and the virtue of individuals have been sacrificed" (*VPG* 35/21; cf. *VG* 80/69).

Hegel denies that the "absolute right" of history belongs to just any power-ful person, or to anyone who takes it into his head to oppose the established ethical order. Individuals have the "absolute right" of world history on their side, he says, "only insofar as their end is in accord with the end of spirit as it is in and for itself" (*VG* 98/84), in other words, only insofar as their deeds really do serve to bring about the further actualization of spirit's freedom. Those of whom this is not true (even if they think it is) are merely crimi-nals and wrongdoers, who deserve every just punishment they receive. For that matter, the fate even of *genuine* world historical individuals, as Hegel depicts it, is usually a harsh one; and he nowhere claims that they deserve better.

As Hegel conceives it, the "absolute justification" of world historical individuals is relevant only from the standpoint of the reflective historian. Its point is not to promote the careers of world historical individuals or to protect them from the consequences of their deeds, but only to protect philosophical historians from missing the rational meaning of history by making moral judgments of deeds whose significance transcends the sphere of ethics or morality.

If, as a practical matter, you wanted to avail yourself of the absolute right of the world spirit in history, you would have to have reason to believe of your own crimes and ambitions that they promote the further actualization of spirit's freedom is history. It is Hegel's view that no one could ever have reason to believe this. The historical significance of spirit's deeds can be understood only after those deeds are there to reflect on. What we can appreciate, as a matter of practical reason, is the relation of our deeds to the fully formed ethical order of our age – as conforming to this order or violating it, or at most as helping it more fully to actualize its own idea.

Consider the reflections of Rodion Raskolnikov, as he sits in prison, contemplating his murder of the two old women he has killed:

> "Why does my action strike them as so hideous?" he kept saying to himself. "Is it because it was a crime?" What does 'crime' mean? My conscience is clear. No doubt I have committed a criminal offense, no doubt I violated the letter of the law and blood was shed. All right, execute me for the letter of the law and have done with it! Of course in that case many of the benefactors of mankind, who seized power instead of inheriting it, should have been executed at the very start of their careers. But those men were successful and so *they were right* and I was not successful and therefore I had no right to permit myself such a step."[9]

Raskolnikov is supposed to be a student of philosophy, but he still has a lot to learn about the subject. If some criminal acts have a supramoral justification, it doesn't follow from this that all criminal acts might have it. Still less does it follow that there is no longer any such thing as criminality, or any distinction (except in terms of the letter of the law) between what is criminal and what is not. If Raskolnikov is reasoning from a Hegelian theory of history, then he is committing a grotesque error if he tries to justify his crime by appealing to the absolute right of world history, for such a justification is never available to world historical individuals themselves. Nor would genuine world-historical individuals ever think of looking for one; as Hegel describes them, they are driven by such powerful passions that they will not be deterred by moral scruples, and they will be uninterested in philosophical arguments, whether moralistic or amoralistic. From the mere fact that Raskolnikov needed to justify his crime to himself by bad philosophical arguments, he might have known that he was not of the same ilk as the bold, unscrupulous heroes Hegel had in mind.[10]

8. Historical self-opacity

Raskolnikov's reasoning from a Hegelian philosophy of history is inconsequent, but the direction of his thinking may nevertheless raise some serious issues for Hegel's views. Once we admit the possibility of an absolute, supraethical right of world history and what we might call a "teleological suspension of the ethical" for world historical individuals, it seems inevitable that we should wonder, with Raskolnikov, how far our own actions might fall under this right. This, in turn, seems inevitably to open the door in practice to a frightening amoralism.

Hegel's way of avoiding these conclusions depends on his skepticism concerning the historical meaning of our own actions. In a period of historical transition, the meaning of our deeds depends on the new and higher principle of spirit, which those deeds help to bring to actuality. But that actuality, together with the possibility of rationally comprehending the principle, depends on a future growth in spirit's self-knowledge. Consequently, the historical meaning of such deeds is beyond the comprehension of the individuals who do them. They are necessarily ignorant of the historical meaning of what they do; they are opaque to themselves.

The main point of Hegel's argument for this historical self-opacity was later articulated by Karl Popper. Popper argues that we cannot predict the course of human history to the extent that it depends on the further growth of human knowledge, since that growth is in principle not predictable by us.[11] During periods of historical transition, Hegel thinks we cannot understand the meaning of our world historical deeds, because that meaning depends on the future; but we cannot foresee (and, a fortiori, cannot comprehend) that future, because in it a new principle of spirit is at work. To comprehend that new principle and its ethical life will require a further growth in spirit's self-knowledge, to which we have in principle no access in the present.

The practical conclusions Hegel draws from this point are evident throughout the *Philosophy of Right,* but especially emphatic in the Preface: we cannot overleap our own time any more than we can "jump over Rhodes"; the only self-transparency available to us lies in philosophy, which "comprehends its own time in thoughts" and rejoices in the rational comprehension of the historical present. This it can do only when a "form of life has grown old": "the owl of Minerva begins its flight only with the falling of the dusk" (*PR* Preface 27–28). As we have observed before, these doctrines are not necessarily conservative in their import, since they allow for rational action to actualize the existing social order, reforming it by correcting (as far as we are able) its (inevitable) contingent flaws and bringing it as fully as possible into harmony with its rational idea. But they do rule out the possibility of radical social change based on historical reason. Popper, though with some changes of emphasis, draws similar (antiradical) conclusions from his argument. Since we cannot predict the historical future, he warns us against undertaking radical social change and urges us to content ourselves with cautious, piecemeal social experimentation.[12]

Both Hegel and Popper exaggerate the skeptical conclusions to which this line of argument entitles them. Popper's argument does not rule out the possibility of radical social action, even with rational predictions as to its success, founded on what we *already* know. For all Popper's reasoning shows, it might be evident that the present social order is ethically unacceptable, that some radically different social order is both required by the ethical knowledge we already have and historically inevitable based on our present sociological knowledge.

Hegel is in a better position to rule out such a possibility, based on his conception of ethical life and his theory of spirit. Hegel's ethical theory says that ethical standards are rationally knowable only as part of an actual form of ethical life; his theory of history says that we can gain such rational comprehension only after a form of ethical life has grown to maturity. Thus Hegel's view does justify saying that we cannot undertake radical social change on ethical grounds. It also denies us a rational comprehension of the social order we are creating. But it does not follow from Hegel's view that we cannot undertake radical social change with a rational knowledge of the fact that we are creating a new and higher social order. We can do this if we can form a conception of the historical meaning of our actions that is not ethical in character and not dependent on a determinate conception of the social order we are in the process of creating.

Processes involving the growth of our knowledge are in principle unpredictable in certain respects, but not in all. A team of scientists searching for a cure for AIDS cannot predict precisely what the cure will be. But after some preliminary research, they might be in a position to make justified predictions concerning such things as whether the cure will be found at all, the type of research that will lead to it, the general nature of the cure, and the approximate length of time it will take to find it. In a similar way, even if Hegel's theory of history is correct and it is impossible to predict the nature of next ethical order, it still might be possible to identify in the present ethical order the social problems that the future one will have to solve. It might be possible to say something about the general character of the coming ethical order (e.g., to say whether it will have to be more egalitarian or more meritocratic than the present one). It might even be possible to identify the type of social movement that will bring it into being.

Whether or not Marx's conception of revolutionary practice was devised with Hegel's philosophy of history in mind, it serves to illustrate the point that has just been made. Marx pretends to no clear conception of what future, postcapitalist society will be like. He declines to write "recipes for the cookshops of the future" because, he insists, future society will depend on "a series of historic processes, transforming circumstances and men" – in Popper's language, on "the further growth of our knowledge."[13] Marx does think that we can now comprehend the class structure of present-day society, identify the class movement that will bring about the higher social form, and so rationally align ourselves with that movement. This is what Marx and Engels mean when they say that "communism is not for us a state of affairs to be brought about, an ideal to which reality will have to adjust itself; we call communism the actual movement that is abolishing the present state of affairs."[14] As communists, in this sense, we engage in what Hegel would call "world historical" action, we consciously engage in the creation of a new social order – and we do so with historical self-transparency.

Marx may very well have been mistaken about the working-class movement; the history in which we are involved may in fact have been as opaque to him as it is to the rest of us. But if, consistent with Hegelian principles, it is even conceivable that he might have been right, then we must admit that Hegel's theory of history does not preclude the possibility that there might be such a thing as self-transparent world-historical agency. If there is, then it might be possible for you to know of your own action that it possesses a supramoral justification. You might be able knowingly to exercise the world historical right to do wrong.

9. Hegel's amoralism

Revolutionary practice, as Marx thought of it, also illustrates one aspect of the amoralism in Hegel's theory of history. For Marx, world historical agency assumes the shape not of the "great man" but of the revolutionary class, and so the lever of historical change is not the passionate ambition of the world historical individual, but class interest, conceived not as the private interest of the class's individual members, but as the interest that the class as a whole has in fulfilling its historic mission. Like individual ambitions, class interests fall outside morality or ethics. For Marx, class moralities are only the false, mystified ideological forms taken by class interests. When world historical agents conceive of their actions in moral or ethical terms, they are victims of ideological illusion and their agency becomes self-opaque. For this reason, Marx consistently rejects all appeals to moral conceptions or ideals within the working-class movement.[15] Once again, even if Marx's view is in fact mistaken, as long as we agree that it might have been correct, then we must recognize that (whether Hegel himself admits it or not) the Hegelian philosophy of history does allow for the possibility that someone might self-consciously and justifiably exercise the "absolute right" of world history, which transcends and overrides all moral and ethical claims.

Hegel's philosophy of history contains a second sort of amoralism, involving not a right to do wrong, but a case in which unethical conduct is rational, or at least not contrary to reason. Hegel holds the view that when a culture becomes reflectively aware of the principle underlying its ethical life, it passes through two main stages. In the first stage, the culture becomes reflectively aware of the reasons for ethical conduct; in this period, not only is ethical conduct objectively rational but also its rationality is grasped by people reflectively and subjectively. In the second stage, however, as its reflection continues, the culture eventually comes to see the limits of that principle. Now when it examines the reasons for following ethical duties, it finds these reasons insufficient. Ethical conduct that was rationally justified in relation to its earlier reflection, now ceases to be so, and this leads to a period of subjective self-indulgence, vanity, and decadence (*VG* 178–180/145–146). People's right to belong to a rational ethical order (*PR* § 153) is no longer satisfied. Ethical duties are no longer rationally binding on them. They are, if you like, free of their duties from the standpoint of reason. In the deepest sense, however, they are less free than they were in a more harmonious time, because they are no longer with themselves in their social life.

According to Hegel, one possibility for agents at this stage is to turn inward, abandoning the ethical life (which has become "faithless to better wills") in favor of a subjective and personal moral code (*PR* § 138R). Another possibility is simply to put one's own selfish interests and caprices ahead of ethical conduct – "seeking [one's] own advantage and satisfaction at the expense of the whole" (*VG* 179/146). Hegel's view implies that in a decadent age people are *justified* in turning away from their ethical duties. Vanity, selfishness, and the abandonment of ethical virtue constitute a *rational* mode of conduct.

Some may find it paradoxical that the same conduct that is supposed to be rationally justified by reflection at one time ceases to be so at a later time. They may think that this involves Hegel in some sort of relativism either about ethical truth or about rationality. Such reactions are mistaken. No matter how objective we take ethical truth and rationality to be, any judgment of the rationality of a course of conduct is always relative to someone's epistemic situation. It is always possible that conduct that is rational for me relative to the reasons I have at my disposal at one time will turn out to be irrational relative to the reasons I have at a later time. Moreover, as objective circumstances change, there may also be a change in the course of conduct that it is objectively rational to follow. When an ethical order is in its prime of life, it will be true that it actualizes spirit's freedom (according to the highest conception of itself that spirit has thus far attained), and it will be rational for people living in that age to display ethical virtue and do their ethical duties. As reflection deepens, however, spirit's conception of itself begins to change, and the old ethical order is no longer sufficient to actualize the emerging conception. Reflective individuals begin to realize this, and ethical duties lose their rational justification for them. In such an age, the question "Why be ethical?" has no rational answer. There is no good reason to be ethical.

Hegel's philosophy of history is not innocuous. It includes a genuine amoralism, though a restricted and conditioned one. Ethical conduct lacks rational justification, but only in ages of decadence and historical transition. There is an absolute right to do wrong, but it belongs only to those whose deeds really do clear the ground for a new order of things. Only someone as demented as the hero of a Russian novel could think this right is applicable (for example) to the murders Raskolnikov committed. If Hegel's doctrine frightens us because we think it justifies indiscriminate wrongdoing, then our fear is based on a simple misunderstanding.

This is not likely to quiet our deepest fears, however. We know only too well how insanely people can behave when a sense of historical mission takes possession of them. We see all around us that the usual effect of political violence is not to benefit or liberate humanity, but merely to inflict pointless harm on innocent people. Our most basic reluctance to accept Hegel's historical amoralism probably derives from the thought that anyone who countenances the idea of justified wrongdoing in history no longer has any clear way in practice of drawing the line against some of the worst examples of senseless inhumanity that people have committed against one another.

We should not attempt to deny that Hegel's amoralism is a dangerous doctrine. Our defense should rather be that the danger is not Hegel's creation; he is only the bearer of bad news. Moral restraints should not bind us when they stand in the way of human liberation. If there really are times when the human spirit can be emancipated only through doing wrong, then it would be dreadful if we let our fear of wrongdoing keep us forever in chains. On the one hand, if it were always possible for the human spirit to advance in a calm and orderly way, in accord with right and morality, then Hegel's historical amoralism would never find application. On the other hand, if it were always easy for people to know precisely when terrible and immoral actions were required in the interests of human freedom, then there would be little danger of the doctrine's ever being abused. But human affairs are complex and beset with ambiguity. We sometimes do have difficulty distinguishing senseless crimes and detestable atrocities from extraordinary historical deeds necessary to the advancement of the human race. Moreover, some of those necessary deeds may at the same time *be* detestable atrocities. Hegel is not to blame for those troubling facts of human life.

14
Problems of modern ethical life

1. The principle of the modern state

The *Philosophy of Right* is both an ethical theory and a social theory. It is an ethical theory based on the conditions for human self-actualization in the modern world, and an attempt to show that modern social institutions provide for self-actualization. In this chapter, we will look at selected parts of Hegel's attempt to defend modern society, and at some of his problems. As a social observer, Hegel was subtle and far seeing. The difficulties he encounters in demonstrating the rationality of the modern state are seldom merely theoretical mistakes. They usually point to practical problems of the modern ethical life we are still living.

Hegel says that the distinctive principle of the modern state is the principle of subjective freedom (*PR* § 273A; cf. *PR* §§ 185R, 206R, 260, 262A, 299R, 316A; *VPG* 540/456). But this is not to be understood in the sense of Kant's liberal political theory, that the end of the state is to maximize individual freedom under law. Hegel rejects the view that takes the end of the state to be "personal freedom and the protection of property, or the interest of the individual as such" (*PR* § 258R; *VPG* 434/542); that is to confuse the state with civil society or the "necessity state" *(Notstaat)* (*PR* § 183). On the contrary, for Hegel the state is an "absolute unmoved end in itself" (*PR* § 258; cf. *VPG* 540/456), or "the universal, having the universal as such for its end" (*VPR 4* : 635). The point is rather that unlike any previous culture, the ethical life of the modern world recognizes that subjective freedom turns out to be an indispensable part of that absolute end.

The end of spirit in history, and the foundation of Hegelian ethical theory, is the self-actualization of freedom. The modern state, however, is "the actuality of concrete freedom"; concrete freedom consists in "the complete development of personal individuality and the recognition of its right for itself" combined with their "transition through themselves and with knowledge and will into the interest of the universal, so that they recognize it as their substantial spirit and are active for it as their final end" (*PR* § 260.) In other words, concrete freedom is actual when free people, whose individuality is fully developed and protected by right, choose to devote themselves to a universal or collective end which they acknowledge as the foundation of their individual worth itself. In the rational modern state, the common end is not put ahead of individual interests or promoted by coercing or manipulating individual wills. At the same time, individuals do not lead lives devoted to

237

their own private good or the good of their family of class. Their deepest individual self-actualization is found in their promotion of the common good. "Neither is the universal accomplished and given validity without particular interests, knowledge, and will, nor do individuals live only for the latter as private persons without at the same time willing in and for the universal, consciously being effective in behalf of this end" (PR § 260).

This is freedom in the Hegelian sense of "being with oneself in an other" because in it the free individual person and subject achieves rational awareness of its own final end as an objective, social end, with universal significance. "My substantial and particular interest is contained and preserved in the interest and end of another (the state) in its relation to me as an individual – so this other is immediately not an other for me, and in that consciousness I am free" (PR § 268; EG § 535).

Thus it is a serious distortion of Hegel's view to say that he regards true freedom as the freedom of a collective rather than the freedom of individuals. The state is an objective and collective end, but the freedom it actualizes is the freedom of the individuals who are active in its behalf: "If you ask how individuality achieves its highest right, then this is the spiritual universality which the state is. Only in the state does the individual have objective freedom" (VPR19 : 209–210). Individuals are free only through the state because the deepest need of individuals is to actualize their rational nature, their universality, and they can do this only by contributing to the state as a collective end and an end in itself.

2. Rationality and subjectivity

Individuality and subjective freedom also have an essential role to play in the content of this collective end. Although the state is not a means to the freedom or happiness of its members, the way in which it provides systematically for their well-being and subjectivity is what makes it into an end in itself. The state is an end in itself for our rational nature because the state itself is rational (PR § 258). "Abstractly considered, rationality in general consists in the interpenetrating unity of universality and individuality; in content here concretely it consists in the unity of objective freedom and subjective freedom" (PR § 258R). Rationality in deliberation consists in harmonizing and adjusting different aims so that they form a coherent and self-justifying combination. What makes the state rational is that its institutional arrangements combine the freedom and interests of many individuals into a single organized whole.

The city-states of Greek antiquity were rational in this sense, because they harmonized the happiness of their citizens into a larger happiness of the whole people.[1] But in classical culture, the harmony between the interests of the individual and the interests of the whole was something "immediate" or direct: "Particularity had not been released, set free, and brought back to universality, i.e., to the universal end of the whole" (PR § 260A). That is why differences between the interests of the state and particular interests, such as those of the individual or the family, were wrenching and tragic for the ancients (*PhG* ¶¶ 475–476). In the modern state, the harmony is not only between collective and individual happiness, but also between the collective good and the subjective freedom of individuals:

> The essence of modern states is that the universal is combined with the complete freedom of particularity and the welfare of individuals, . . . so that the universality of the end cannot progress without the proper knowledge and willing of particulars that preserve their right. Thus the universal must be activated, but on the other side subjectivity must be wholly and vitally developed. Only through the subsistence of both moments in their strength is a state to be regarded as articulated and truly organized. (*PR* § 260A)

Hegel's theory of the modern state demands a special kind of social cohesiveness, unknown to any earlier society. The state's institutions must not only protect individual interests but also individual freedom, and they must even provide for the development of individuality in ways that satisfy individuals and so bind them the more firmly to these institutions. Our "political life" must not be an extraordinary activity that draws us away form our normal professional responsibilities, or our freely chosen plans for our own or our family's well-being. Individuals must experience devotion to the common good not as a sacrifice of the private for the sake of something "higher," but simply as the ever-present deeper purpose behind everyday life which prevents it from being a mere private self-seeking (*PR* § 268).[2]

Perhaps, contrary to Hegel's firm convictions, the experience of such a free and rational social life is also quite foreign to us. That would explain why some of Hegel's readers can interpret his vision of the state only as the totalitarian intrusion of the state into every corner of private life, or else as the expression of the complacent self-deception that identifies patriotism simply with minding one's own business and letting the state do whatever it likes. If the modern state is not really as Hegel portrays it, then the attempt to persuade yourself that it is, or the unsuccessful attempt to force it to be what it is not, might very naturally lead in one or both of those unattractive directions. But even more basic to Hegelian ethics than the claim that the state exhibits this special unity of universality and particularity is the claim that it *must* do so *if* our freedom is to be actualized. This means that if the community we live in is not already a Hegelian state, we cannot be whole or free until it becomes something like one.

3. Civil society: subjective freedom and corporate spirit

Hegel believes that the modern state's successful unification of universality with particularity is due to the one institution that is unique to it: civil society. Civil society provides the public social space in which individuals as free persons and subjects pursue their own welfare in their own way, choose their own way of life, and enter into voluntary relations with others who are likewise free choosers of their own ends and activities (*PR* § 182). Without it, we would have a state "based on a patriarchal or religious principle or on the principle of a more spiritual but simpler ethical life, but always on an original natural intuition, which cannot withstand the division arising as self-conscious became infinitely reflected into itself" (*PR* § 185R). In Plato's state, for instance, economic life is left entirely in the hands of the rulers. Modern individuals would experience such an arrangement as a denial of their human rights and a violation of their inner life (*PR* §§ 185R, 206R, 262A). In this way, Hegel anticipates the perennial critique of all forms of state-run or collectivized economy.

At the same time, Hegel thinks that civil society also determines the distinctive kinds of social cohesiveness that make it possible to unify subjective particularity with a universal end. For one thing, civil society determines the shape of both the modern family and the modern political state. Unlike the *Stamm,* the clan or wider kinship group, the modern family is not an economic organization.[3] The family's sole remaining function is to provide individuals with social bonds based on the immediate feeling of love, a refuge from the spirit of individuality, rational reflection, and self-seeking which characterizes civil society. Civil society also determines the form of the modern state. As free subjects, individuals can no longer belong to the state without becoming conscious of the public business and wanting to participate in it. Consequently, the modern state must include representative institutions.[4] Hegel also thinks the principle of subjective freedom determines the the essentially *monarchical* principle of the modern state. In the modern world, we must see the state's laws and policies not merely as results of a collective decision-making process, but as the decisions of a subject. Hence the state's sovereignty must assume the shape of an individual human being.[5]

Just as important, civil society itself generates its own social solidarity, which effects the transition from individuality to universality. Hegel thinks that without the special form of community engendered by civil society, it is not even possible for individuals to actualize their subjective freedom. This crucial point is missed entirely if we think of civil society only as a marketplace where economic agents meet to further their private ends.

When Hegel opposes the tendency to "atomicity" in modern society (*VPG* 534/452; *VPR17* : 143), he is not only rejecting the idea of society as a disorganized aggregate of individuals. He is also attacking a merely abstract conception of social individuals themselves, as mere nondescript units – as legal persons and moral subjects, or as economic calculators, desire-satisfiers, and resource-deployers – whose lives and individualities receive their content merely through private choice and chance and are not a matter of social concern. In a civil society where people live out this conception of themselves, individuals will never achieve what Hegel calls "existence" or "determinate particularity."

Hegel insists that each individual's social position must be mediated through that individual's arbitrary choice (*PR* § 185). But the options between which individuals choose must be meaningful:

The individual attains actuality only by entering into *existence,* and hence into *determinate particularity;* he must accordingly limit himself *exclusively* to one of the *particular* spheres of need. The ethical disposition within this system is therefore that of *rectitude* and *the honor of one's estate,* so that each individual, by a process of self-determination, makes himself a member of one of the moments of civil society. (*PR* § 207)

In order to achieve "existence" in civil society, individuals have to be conscious of themselves as engaged in activities whose objective worth is recognized by others. In order to have "determinate particularity," their activities must be specifically recognized as part of society's ethical life. The individual's social position or estate must be a definite vocation, profession, or trade *(Gewerbe).* In order to achieve explicitness and public recognizability, these trades must organize themselves, as *corporations.*[6]

Corporations have several different but related functions. The members of a corporation collectively assume responsibility to civil society for performing the social task of their specific trade or profession (*VPR19* : 203). To this end, the corporation is to recruit, educate, train, and certify its members in appropriate numbers (*PR* § 252). The corporation also has responsibilities to its members. It "comes on the scene like a second family" for them (*PR* § 252), providing them with a sense of identity and honor, as well as an assurance of economic security in the times of hardship that are unavoidable in the life of civil society (*PR* § 253,R). Because members of a corporation have common interests and a common ethical disposition, Hegel also sees corporations as the proper avenue for ordinary citizens' political participation in the state (*PR* § 311).[7]

4. Hegel's dilemma: subjective freedom or ethical goals

Perhaps the corporation's most important function is to provide its members with "ethical goals" (*VPR19* : 206). Unless an individual belongs to a corporation, Hegel says, he lacks the "honor of his estate":

His isolation reduces him to the selfish aspect of his trade, and his livelihood and satisfaction lack *stability.* He will accordingly try to gain *recognition* through the external manifestations of success in his trade, and these are unbounded, because it is impossible for him to live in a way appropriate to his estate if his estate does not exist. (*PR* § 253R)

Without the ethical integration provided by corporation membership, the only identity I have in civil society is that of a freelance hustler of whatever resources, skills, or other commodities I may have for sale. My destiny is simply to sell myself, and my only aspiration is to do so at the highest price and on the most favorable terms. My self-worth in civil society will be simply the market price of whatever it is I have to sell. Consequently, I find myself in the condition Émile Durkheim described as "anomy."[8] Because I have no determinate ethical identity, there are no proper bounds or measures for my life, for either my needs or my accomplishments. My life in civil society can bring no self-satisfaction, because there is no determinate self for me to satisfy. Without ethical goals, directing my activity to the needs of others and to a larger universal good, I likewise find myself in the condition Durkheim called "egoism."[9] My participation in civil society is reduced to boundless individual self-seeking, which is self-defeating by its very nature because it can never lead to happiness or self-actualization.

Hegel insists that he is not telling the world how it ought to be, but only teaching us how the actual modern state is to be rationally understood (PR Preface 25). Yet Hegel was generally a proponent of the Stein and Hardenberg political reforms, and plainly favored their continuance in the direction of constitutionalism and representative government. He clearly had mixed feelings, though, about some of their economic reforms, motivated by the free-trade doctrines of Adam Smith and C. J. Kraus. The edicts of November 2, 1810 and September 7, 1812 abolished guild monopolies that stood in the way of occupational freedom and assured the livelihood of individual artisans or tradesmen, protecting them from open market competition. Hegel attacks the "spirit of atomicity" in modern civil society which has brought the corporations to ruin (VPR17: 143). He insists that he wants no restoration of the "miserable guild system," but on closer inspection, he seems to oppose only the privileges of guilds to resist the state's economic controls (PR § 255A).

In fact, Hegel's conception of the corporation in civil society can be seen as quite radical. Perhaps it is even utopian, unworkable in the context of a market economy. No doubt in actual market economies some of the functions Hegel assigns to corporations do sometimes get fulfilled for some people – by professional organizations, corporate firms, or labor unions. But no institution fulfills them in the combined and systematic way a Hegelian corporation is supposed to.

This may be no accident. Insofar as corporations assure a livelihood to individual members of each trade, to that degree their conduct of business and their fortunes cannot be sensitive to market factors. If offical corporations determine what trades are recognized, and even regulate the numbers of people engaged in various trades, then these matters cannot be vulnerable to the open market. In a corporate civil society, it would be not the market but the state's decision to recognize various corporations that determines whether people engage in the production of microchips or buggy whips.

Hegel wants to have it both ways: a free market system for the full blossoming of subjective freedom, and a corporate organization of civil society for ethical existence and determinate particularity. Hegel even *needs* to have it both ways, since both subjective freedom and ethical existence are equally indispensable if the modern self is to actualize its freedom through the institution of civil society. If Hegel's account of civil society turns out to be utopian, then perhaps it is only through an illusion that people continue to believe that a market-based civil society offers the possibility of subjective freedom.

5. Substantiality and reflection

Civil society is the institution in which subjective freedom is to be actualized. But in Hegel's state, the genuine participants in civil society are a distinct minority of the adult population. The "universal estate" (of civil servants) shares in the educated and reflective spirit of civil society, but only the "formal" or "business *(Gewerbe)* estate," the urban bourgeoisie, lives essentially through the market system, and organizes itself into corporations *(PR §§* 204, 250). Hegel regards the rural nobility and the peasantry as essentially unsuited to the reflective spirit of civil society. Among them "reflection and the will of the individual play a lesser role, and its substantial disposition in general is that of an immediate ethical life based on family relationship and on trust" *(PR §* 203). Hegel puts it even more bluntly: "The agricultural estate is thus more inclined to subservience, the business estate to freedom" *(PR §* 203A).

In Hegel's rational state, women are also excluded from civil society, and from public life generally. "Woman has her substantial vocation in the family, and her ethical disposition consists in this [family] piety" *(PR §* 166; cf. § 164A). Though formally women are persons with abstract rights *(PR §* 49R; *VPR17 :* 47), marriage is the mutual surrender by both parties of their independent personality *(PR §§* 163, 167–168). Since women are restricted to the family by their ethical disposition, the rights of personality and subjective freedom apply to them only in abnormal circumstances, when they are out of their proper element (as when they find themselves in a divorce court or earning an independent living) *(PR §§* 158–159). Hegel finds women unsuited by nature for a rational and reflective education, and consequently for life in civil society and the state: "Women may well be educated, but they are not made for the higher sciences, for philosophy and certain artistic productions which require a universal element. Women may have insights *(Einfälle),* taste, and delicacy, but they do not possess the ideal" *(PR §* 166A). Though he recognizes individual exceptions to this, "these exceptions are not the rule"; when women trespass into what are properly male provinces, "they put the provinces themselves in danger" *(VPR 3 :* 525). "When women are in charge of government, the state is in danger" *(PR §* 166A).

Such remarks are no doubt quaintly repugnant reminders of the social practices of Hegel's age and the prejudices of his class. But we should not miss the deeper motivation behind them. Hegel's theory of modern ethical life is based on the idea that the modern spirit reconciles two contrasting principles, which might easily be seen as hostile, opposed, even incompatible. On one side is the *substantial* principle both in the individual character and in social life, which shows itself in the human character dominated by habit and feeling, and in social institutions emphasizing trust and tradition or concrete relationships between individuals. Its social center is the family, and its cultural expression is chiefly religious. On the other side is the modern *reflective* principle, which favors personal insight and reason, in the guise both of self-interested calculation and of impartial, impersonal moral thinking. Reflection also predominates in the specifically modern social institutions, civil society, and the modern political state; it triumphs culturally in the modern world through the sciences of the understanding and through philosophical reason.

Hegel's thesis is that spirit is substance that becomes subject: The substantial principle is spirit's basis, whereas reflection is its essence and vocation (*PhG¶* 18; *WL 6*: 198/539; *EG* § 564; *VG* 28/27). For Hegel, the error of the Enlightenment was to dismiss the substantial and place exclusive reliance on reflection, whereas the error of Hegel's Romantic contemporaries was to restore the substantial by attempting to revoke or suppress reflection. In opposition to both, Hegel thinks that the modern spirit can be actualized, individually and socially, only through the reconciliation of both principles.

Hegel's theory of this reconciliation is founded on his idea that a developed ethical order must be "articulated" *(gegliedert)* – an organism composed of differentiated social institutions with complementary functions. (Generally speaking, the substantial principle has its place in private family life, whereas the reflective principle predominates in the public domains of civil society and the political state.) Next, Hegel holds that differentiated institutions require a social differentiation among individuals. Each principle must have its proper representatives and guardians. Hence even in the ethical order whose distinctive principle is subjective freedom, there will be many whose character and life-style do not exemplify that principle.

6. Man and woman

For Hegel these considerations legitimate the agricultural estate's "inclination to subservience," as well as the exclusion of women from "the universal element." Our indignation at Hegel's condescending opinion of women's intellectual abilities may prevent us from seeing that this is not his basic reason for holding that women's vocation is properly restricted to family life. On the contrary, he insists that the natural differences between the sexes are founded in reason, and that is what gives them "an *intellectual* and *ethical* significance" (*PR* § 165). In other words, Hegel contends that there are sound ethical reasons why women should devote themselves exclusively to the family, and this makes sense of whatever natural proclivities and limitations we find in them that point in this direction.

Hegel's theory is that the two sexes represent the contrasting principles of ethical substantiality and subjective reflection. The female is "spirituality that maintains itself in unity as knowledge and volition of the substantial in the form of concrete *individuality* and *feeling*," whereas the male is "spirituality that divides itself up into personal self-sufficiency with being *for itself* and the knowledge and volition of *free universality*, i.e., into the self-con-

sciousness of conceptual thought and the volition of the objective and ultimate end" (*PR* § 166). Hegel's view of the sexes is undeniably traditional,
but not as one-sided as it might appear from the remarks I have thus far
quoted. He thinks that men are naturally superior to women in the reflective
abilities needed for "life in the state, in science, and struggle with the external
world and with himself." The other side of this view is that women are naturally superior in the qualities that foster "a subjective ethical life of feeling"
(*PR* § 166).

In other words, men are better at grasping abstract ethical principles, but
women are more perceptive about particular ethical relationships and better
at responding emotionally to them. The woman "orders things according to
her feelings, and thus governs [the family] in a genuine sense, deriving what
should happen from her individuality" (*VPR 3*: 530–531). It should not be
forgotten that the feminine ideal for Hegel is Antigone's heroic defense of
divine law and family obligation: "Antigone is the most beautiful description
of femininity; she holds fast to the bond of the family against the [state's]
law" (*VPR 1*: 301; cf. *PR* § 166R; ¶¶ 464–468, 473–475; *VA 2*: 60/215, *3*:
550/4:318). This is hardly a vision of woman as generally stupid, submissive,
weak, or incapable. It even has something in common with some contemporary feminist theories, such as those of Nancy Chodorow and Carol Gilligan,
which emphasize women's distinctive moral capacities and viewpoint.[10]

The main problem with Hegel's theory is its attempt to combine three
ideas that don't go well together:

1. The reconciliation of the substantive and reflective principles requires a
   differentiation of social roles, confining women to the sphere of family
   life.
2. The principle of the modern world is subjective freedom; for modern individuals self-actualization involves the actualization of personhood and subjectivity through civil society.
3. Christianity has taught us that all individuals are equally persons and subjects.

Points (1) and (2) create a problem because they assign a role to women
that is socially necessary, yet devalued because it does not represent the principle given priority in the modern ethical order. Points (1) and (3) conflict
to the extent that the exclusion of women from public life is experienced as
a denial of their personhood and subjectivity. Points (2) and (3) create a
difficulty because they tend to turn everyone into a guardian of the reflective
principle, leaving the substantive principle underemphasized in social life.
Hegel's rational state, in effect, grants subjective freedom only to the male
bourgeoisie, at the expense of women and the rural population. Hegel thinks
that this is acceptable because the substantial disposition of the feminine personality and the naturally servile inclination of the peasantry guarantee that
women and peasants will not miss the subjective freedom of which they are
deprived. We now know Hegel was seriously mistaken about this. Once you
grant points (2) and (3), those who do not enjoy the status of person and

subject to the fullest extent will inevitably see themselves as oppressed and degraded by their social role.

Hegel's main problem, however, is how to reconcile the substantive and reflective principles. That problem will not be solved by turning everyone into a representative of the reflective principle. Hegel's critique of the moral standpoint is an attack on the idea that ethics can be founded on abstract principles of autonomy. His theory of ethical life, like the feminist theories just mentioned, emphasizes the foundation of the ethical in feelings, dispositions, and personal relationships. His theory does give priority to the masculine principle of reflection, but it also recognizes the indispensability of the feminine or substantive principle.

The problem has not gone away. Modern civil society needs to admit women to full membership, but it also fears doing so. It is deeply torn over whether officially to accord women the status of persons with equal rights under the law, and there is terrible moral ferocity behind the proposition that women's natural reproductive vocation must place limits on their jurisdiction over the life processes going on within their own bodies. Modern society is polarized by the fact that there is a contradiction in the idea of a woman who is a full and free member of civil society.

One attractive way out of Hegel's problem might be to reject his idea that the substantive and reflective principles should be assigned each to one gender. Instead, it might be proposed that we integrate both principles within each human personality. On this view, every human being should be a whole, and individuals would relate to one another as equals fully and concretely, within all ethical relationships.

Hegel never considers this option. He shows no sympathy for the views of his Romantic contemporaries Karl Ludwig von Haller and Adam Müller, who think that the principle of social hierarchy – paradigmatically, the principle of patriarchy – is intrinsically right and good, legislated to us by nature or God. But neither does Hegel see anything inherently bad (as long as the formal equality of persons is maintained) about ethical relations involving relations of power and personal authority. One development in modern ethical life since his time is that such relations are increasingly regarded as unacceptable, or at least undesirable.

The implications of this solution, however, may be more radical than we would like to realize. Hegel's remarks about the alleged natural incapacities of the female sex are easy to deride, and it is easy to agree with the platitudes that men should be more sensitive, women more self-confident. But we have never really seen what human personalities would be like if they were not socialized through the traditional system of gender stereotypes. We do not know what role gender differences might play in personalities balancing the substantial principle with the reflective. Moreover, the modern social order as it actually exists is not one in which such personalities could develop or thrive. It is understandable, if not admirable, that many fear the unknown path to new possibilities more than the present contradictions they are living.

7. Poverty in civil society

Hegel regards the de facto exclusion of both women and the peasantry from direct participation in civil society as justified by their social position and ethical disposition. But he recognizes that modern civil society effectively excludes many others in a way that cannot be so justified. In civil society, Hegel argues, the accumulation of wealth is facilitated by the "universalization" both of human needs and of the means of their satisfaction (in other words, by mass production and marketing). Mass production leads to the "individualization and limitation" of detail labor, which produces the greatest profits precisely because it is unskilled, and so can command only a low wage. As a consequence, many people fall into a condition of "dependence and want" (*PR* § 243).

Along with its industry, moreover, civil society is also constantly expanding its population (*PR* § 243). Much of this increase, especially in urban centers, consists of individuals with few resources or salable skills. The displacement of the wider kinship group by the nuclear family leaves these individuals without any protection against the contingencies of the market system (*PR* § 241). They can command only the lowest wages, and they live with the constant threat of unemployment. The wealth in civil society tends to accumulate in a few hands (*PR* § 244), and in the hands of those who benefit most from the existence of poverty: "When there is great poverty, the capitalist finds many people who work for small wages, which increases his earnings; and this has the further consequences that smaller capitalists fall into poverty" (*VPR 4*: 610). Poverty is not an accident, a misfortune or the result of human error or vice. Rather, "the complications of civil society itself produce poverty" (*VPR17*: 138; cf. *PR* § 243; *VPR 4*: 605; *VPR19*: 194).

What is to be done about poverty in civil society? In a society where there is widespread poverty, there is always ample scope for private morality to engage in works of charity. But Hegel regards moral charity as no real remedy at all. By their very nature as well as in their effects, moral acts of charity are contingent and cannot be counted upon (*PR* § 242). Charity tends to humiliate its recipients, to undermine their self-respect (*PR* § 253R). Thus charity even aggravates the fundamental ethical problem posed by poverty, since it violates the basic principle of civil society that individuals should come by a decent livelihood through their own work. Hegel thinks that civil society as a whole, through the public authority of the state, must "endeavor to make [private charity] less necessary by identifying universal aspects of want and taking steps to remedy them" (*PR* § 242).

This is all the more necessary since in Hegel's view civil society always remains a *society*, a "universal family" (*PR* § 239) that exists for the purpose of satisfying the needs of its members, including their need for freedom and self-actualization. Each member of civil society has a duty to work for it, but also a right to a self-fulfilling livelihood earned through labor. It is the state's responsibility to protect that right, a responsibility belonging to the state's "police"[11] power (*PR* § 238,A; *VPR 4*: 609).

At the same time, Hegel admits that he does not see how this responsibility is to be fulfilled without contradicting the basic principles of civil society itself. On the one hand, the state might provide the poor directly with the necessities of life, perhaps through taxes levied on the rich. That would contradict the principle of civil society that all are to earn their own livelihood by their own labor. On the other hand, the state might provide the poor with the opportunity to work. But the original problem that created widespread poverty was that there was an excess of goods and services in relation to effective demand, and the state's sponsorship of more labor will only exacerbate that situation. "This shows that despite an *excess of wealth*, civil society is *not wealthy enough* – i.e., its own distinct resources are not sufficient to prevent an excess of poverty and the formation of a rabble" (*PR* § 245). Hegel's reflections on the problem of poverty conclude with a virtual counsel of despair: In England, he says, it has been found that the best way of dealing with poverty is simply "to leave the poor to their fate and direct them to beg from the public" (*PR* § 245R; cf. *VPR 4*: 612).

8. Does Hegel have an answer?

It is easy to understand why Hegel says that "the important question of how poverty can be remedied is one that especially agitates and torments modern societies" (*PR* § 244A). But Hegel never shared the optimistic opinion of his friend and follower Eduard Gans, who thought that because the existence of an impoverished class "is only a fact, not something right, it must be possible to get to the basis of this fact and abolish it."[12] Hegel plainly regards the best measures against poverty available to the state as mere palliatives, an "endless progress" that will never attain to a "final solution."[13] Hegel discusses the colonial export of civil society's surplus population, but only as an effect of poverty, not as a cure for it (*PR* §§ 246–247).

How is the problem of poverty related to Hegel's larger project of presenting the modern state as the actuality of reason and the objectification of freedom? Shlomo Avineri regards Hegel's discussion of poverty as a striking anomaly in his system – simply a problem to which the system offers no solution – a victory of Hegel's farsightedness and honesty as a social analyst over his zeal and ingenuity as a speculative system-builder and theodicist.[14] Against this, it is sometimes suggested that it is precisely such insoluble problems that drive Hegel's dialectical system of categories. Abstract right, ending with wrong (*PR* § 81), passes over into morality, which ends with evil and hypocrisy (*PR* §§ 139–140); Hegel's treatment of the family ends with its dissolution as its members take their place in civil society (*PR* § 181). Likewise, according to Klaus Hartmann's version of the suggestion, Hegel's "esoteric" answer to the problem of poverty in civil society is "that there must be a higher categorial structure, a structure with a more affirmative relationship of the many to one another than obtains in the antagonisms typi-

248

cal of civil society." This structure is the state, in which society for the first time becomes "truly universal."[15]

Even the state, however, is a limited and finite realm, as we see from its inevitable involvement in war (*PR* § 324,R), and every state is doomed to succumb to the transitoriness of its principle in world history (*PR* § 347). Thus it is never in the finite and temporal realm of the practical that our reason can find satisfaction, but only in the higher realms of absolute spirit. This view in effect locates Hegel's real answer to the problem of poverty in his speculative theodicy, which provides the grounds for philosophical resignation in the face of the contingency and imperfection of everything finite.[16]

Such tidy resolutions of the problem of poverty certainly are "esoteric," in the sense that they are never found anywhere in Hegel's own discussions of that problem. Hegel never describes poverty as an inherent limitation of a finite sphere within his system. His discussion of poverty does not conclude his treatment of civil society, as wrong concludes the treatment of right, or evil the treatment of morality. Instead, poverty arises in connection with the state's police power, which is charged with the task of dealing with poverty, but turns out to be necessarily incapable of fulfilling its responsibilities. Hegel's treatment of civil society actually ends with his discussion of corporations, and he explicitly identifies the limit of the sphere of civil society as the restricted and finite character of the corporation's ends, which must therefore pass over into the universal ends of the state (*PR* § 256).

As we saw earlier (Chapter 13, § 1), Hegel thinks that philosophy can demonstrate that all temporal existence is subject to defects and accidents, and therefore the wise do not expect perfection of anything in this world. All things human are marred by contingency, particularly the contingency of the finite will, with its irrationality, caprice, and wickedness. Appeal to these considerations is an important part of Hegel's rational theodicy of the state. The actual state is rational, but the existing state is never wholly actual (see Introduction, § 5). It is always to some degree marred by the error and misconduct of those individuals who are in charge of public affairs (*PR* § 258A).

This theme in Hegel's philosophy provides no solution to the problem of poverty, because poverty in civil society is no accident. It is not a result of contingent imperfections that befall a rational system when it achieves outward existence, or of the arbitrary will of individuals. Part of the evil of poverty is that it subjects people's lives to contingency, but poverty is not itself a contingent feature of civil society. On the contrary: "The emergence of poverty is in general a consequence of civil society and on the whole arises necessarily out of it" (*VPR19*: 193). Moreover, it is the basic principles of civil society itself that stand in the way of the state's attempts to prevent poverty or remedy it (*PR* § 245).

There is a very hollow ring to Hartmann's suggestion that the problem of poverty is solved when Hegel's system moves on to the "universal" community of the state. Part of what worries Hegel about poverty is the fact that the poor are systematically excluded from the benefits of social life. They have no participation in the state, however indirect. The state's police power bears the responsibility for dealing with their distress, but it necessarily fails. Appeals to rational theodicy are unpersuasive for similar reasons. The poor are said to be excluded especially from the *spiritual* benefits of modern society – from the education necessary to appreciate art and philosophy, even from the consolation of religion (*PR* §§ 241, 243; *VPR17*: 138; *VPR19*: *VPR4*: 606). Hegel is no friend, in any case, to those who regard religious consolations as an appropriate response to social evils: "If the proposition [that the state needs religion as its foundation] means that individuals must have religion in order that their fettered spirit can be more effectively oppressed within the state, then the meaning is a bad one" (*PR* § 270A); it is simply "a mockery to dismiss resentment towards tyranny by declaring that the oppressed should find consolation in religion" (*PR* § 270R).

Closer to the mark is John McCumber's suggestion that Hegel's writings contain a "covert" but "radical and systematic indictment of the state."[17] Closer, but still not very close. Hegel never set himself to argue *against* the thesis that the modern state is a fundamentally rational system. On the contrary, that is his own most fundamental thesis about the state. The most reasonable view, I think, is either Avineri's – that poverty is simply an unsolved problem for Hegel's system – or else a modified version of McCumber's, which says that Hegel's theory of poverty in modern civil society might support an indictment against it, but not one that Hegel was ever inclined to draw up. In § 10, we will look at a wayward strand in Hegel's thought where this possibility is pursued to the furthest extent.

This leaves Hegel's position messy, maybe inconsistent. But it is not an implausible interpretation. Even now, apologists for modern capitalism sometimes realize that poverty is an unavoidable feature of the system but do not relinquish their basic loyalty to it on that account. If intelligent people can still take this position even in the late twentieth century, then surely it must have been possible for Hegel to take it in the 1820s, without the additional 170 years of capitalism staring him in the face.

9. The rabble mentality

Despite massive changes in technology, economics, and the sociology of poverty since Hegel's day, most of his observations about poverty in civil society are still applicable. When Hegel wrote that "for people who have money and keep to the main highway, the world is in good shape," he was on a visit to the Low Countries in 1822 (*B 2*: 433/594); but he could have been describing any flourishing capitalist society that is enjoying the upside of its trade cycle.

Hegel's treatment of poverty in civil society is characteristically hardheaded. He wastes little pity on the sufferings of the poor, and does not place moral blame for their condition on them, or on anyone else. Instead, he devotes his mind with remorseless honesty to considering the causes of poverty, its consequences, and its ethical significance. It is also characteristic that Hegel's deepest reflections have to do with poverty's *spiritual* effects on people – its impact on their self-understanding, and their relation to the social institutions and ethical norms that structure their lives. Hegel was unfamiliar with widespread drug-dependency and other self-destructive life-styles often associated with poverty, nor was poverty as he knew it reinforced by the effects of racism. But his analysis of the *Weltanschauung* that poverty produces in those subject to it still has much to say to us.

When the poor form a concentrated mass, as they do in cities, Hegel calls them the "rabble" *(Pöbel)* and he gives the name "rabble mentality" *(Pöbelhaftigkeit)* to the characteristic attitude of mind that develops among them. Hegel describes the rabble as a "class" rather than an "estate" *(PR §§ 243, 245,A)*. Estates rest on "concrete distinctions" between functionally different and complementary social positions or roles. Class distinctions rest on mere *"inequalities"* of birth, wealth, education, social status, and self-valuation *(NP 63)*. The rabble is a class drawn from those whose wealth, education, and skills are minimal, and therefore have either a marginal place in civil society or none at all. Though they are products of civil society, the rabble are "more or less deprived of all the advantages of society" *(PR § 241)*, and unable "to enjoy the wider freedoms of civil society, particularly its spiritual advantages" *(PR § 243)*. Lacking in economically valuable skills or general education *(VPR 4: 606)*, they also lack the economic means to preserve their physical health *(VPR19: 195)*, to protect their rights as persons in the formal legal system of civil society *(VPR 4: 606)*, or to share fully in its culture or its religion *(VPR19: 195; PR § 241)*.

This leads to a deeper separation of the poor from civil society, one of "mind" or "emotion" *(Gemüt):* The poor see themselves simultaneously as human beings and as beings deprived of humanity, as beings whose humanity is constantly violated and degraded by the very society from which they derive the principle that it should be recognized and respected. They respond to this treatment with an indignation that is drawn directly from the ethical principles of modern society, but is also directed back against these principles: "The poor man feels himself excluded and mocked by everyone, and this necessarily gives rise to an inner indignation. He is conscious of himself as an infinite, free being, and thus arises the demand that his external existence should correspond to this consciousness" *(VPR19 : 195)*. It is above all this indignation, born of a sense of exclusion from society, that turns the poor into a "rabble": "Poverty in itself does not reduce people to a rabble; a rabble is created only by the disposition associated with poverty, by inward rebellion against the rich, against society, against the government, etc." *(PR § 244A)*.

The poor do not suffer merely a contingent denial of certain rights, which might leave intact the subject's dignity and will to defend them. Poverty destroys the sense of self which is the necessary vehicle of moral self-consciousness and the ethical attitude in modern individuals. If the poor retain the sense that they are infinite and free beings with rights, this remains merely an abstract notion, which never reaches as far as the affirmation of a concrete life of duties done with self-satisfaction. It sustains envy, indignation, and hatred against those who seem to enjoy the humanity of which they are deprived, but not a sense of honor, dignity, or respect for their own worth. The rabble mentality is therefore a condition of ethical vice and moral degradation: "Poverty is a condition in civil society that is on every side unhappy and forsaken. It is not only external distress that burdens the poor, but this is also accompanied by a moral degradation" (*VPR19* : 194). Moral vices do not cause poverty, but they are caused by it.

It is the loss of "self-feeling" that turns "ingenuous poverty" *(unbefangene Armut)* into the rabble mentality:

> When individuals have not progressed to a self-consciousness of their right, then they remain in ingenuous poverty. But then this ingenuous poverty progresses at least as far as the condition of the idle and unemployed, who are in the habit of just loafing around. With that, the modifications of self-feeling are totally lost. In the poor there arises an envy and hatred against all those who have something. (*VPR19* : 195–196)

When the poor lose "the feeling of right, of the integrity and honor of subsisting through one's own activity and work" (*PR* § 244), they become lazy, and their sense of right degenerates into the demand that civil society should provide a living for them: "Here is laziness and at the same time the consciousness of a right to find subsistence in civil society. . . . The rabble is the greediest after its rights, always hammering away at civil society's obligation to maintain it" (*VPR 4* : 609). The fundamental principle of civil society, that each individual should be self-dependent and live through their own work, has now turned into its opposite: The only right remaining to the rabble is the right to live by the work of others.

In the rabble mentality, the very concepts of right and free personhood themselves are put in jeopardy. Living under conditions of poverty, I experience in myself that the ideas of freedom, personhood, and right are a mere sham – empty notions lacking any real existence. Since I do not experience my recognition by others as a free person, I cease in turn to recognize the personhood of anyone else: "Self-consciousness appears driven to the point where it no longer has any rights; freedom has no existence. [Consequently,] the recognition of universal freedom disappears. From this condition arises that shamelessness that we find in the rabble" (*VPR19* : 195). The rabble mentality concerns Hegel because for him the rabble is in one respect at least what the proletariat was later to be for Marx, "a class in civil society that is not of civil society." The rabble live amid civil society, but they are systematically deprived of the rights pertaining to its members, and consequently of their duties as well: "The rabble is a dangerous [social] ill, because they have neither rights nor duties" (*VPR 1* : 322).

Though the rabble mentality is an effect of poverty, Hegel realizes that it can also find its way into other classes of civil society, most especially the rich: "The rabble is distinct from poverty; usually it is poor, but there are also rich rabble" (*VPR 4* : 608). The degraded condition of the poor puts them at the rich man's disposal. This teaches him as well as them that in civil society there is no such thing as human dignity beyond price, that no one's universal human rights mean anything when the particular will to violate them has enough wealth at its disposal.

The rabble disposition arises also with the rich. The rich man thinks that everything can be bought, because he knows himself as the might of the particularity of self-consciousness. Hence wealth can lead to the same mockery and shamelessness that we find among the rabble. The disposition of the master over the slave is the same as that of the slave. (*VPR19*: 196)

10. The class with neither rights nor duties

Hegel does not approve of the rabble mentality. In his vocabulary, *Pöbel* is always an epithet of abuse. But he agrees that the members of civil society have a duty to work for it only to the extent that they have against it a right to an education and social position enabling them to find an honorable and self-fulfilling livelihood through their work (*PR* §§ 239, 238,A). Thus the condition of the poor in civil society is not merely sad or regrettable, it is a systematic wrong or injustice: "Against nature no one can assert a right, but within the conditions of society hardship at once assumes the form of a wrong inflicted on this or that class" (*PR* § 244A).

Hegel grants explicitly that the rabble have the rights on which their indignation is based. He further admits that civil society violates those rights to such an extent that the poor are deprived of their personhood. Consequently, he regards the indignation that drives the rabble mentality as quite justified. When the rabble regard their poverty as a wrong or injustice, they are entirely correct:

The [rabble's] disposition is founded on the fact that everyone has the right to find his subsistence; insofar as he does not find it he is poor, but because he has the right to subsistence his poverty becomes a wrong *(Unrecht)*, an offense against right, and this produces a dissatisfaction which simultaneously assumes the form of right. (*VPR 4*: 609)

In another passage, Hegel speaks of the rabble mentality as the result of generalizing, apparently with justification, the "right of necessity" which takes priority over the abstract right of persons (*PR* §§ 127–128; see Chapter 5, § 5). The right of necessity is usually supposed to apply only under extraordinary conditions of momentary danger or distress. But when you are poor, the right of necessity ceases to apply only in exceptional moments, because your whole life goes on beneath the minimum level recognized as necessary for a member of civil society (*PR* § 244). Consequently, the right of necessity comes to apply universally; necessity overrides everyone's rights, no one any longer has rights. In this way, the rabble mentality turns into a criminal mentality, for which any violation of right is justified. If crimes are sometimes punished, this no longer has any ethical meaning for the rabble, but becomes merely a piece of bad luck, another contingency to which the life of poverty is exposed.

Earlier we considered the right of necessity as referring to a momentary need. [In the case of poverty, however,] necessity no longer has this merely momentary character. In the emergence of poverty, the might of the particular against the reality of freedom comes into existence. This produces the infinite judgment of the criminal. Crime can of course be punished, but this punishment is contingent. . . . So on poverty rests the rabble mentality *(Pöbelhaftigkeit),* the nonrecognition of right. (VPR*19*: 196)

As Hegel presents it, the rabble mentality involves a kind of argument. The premises of the argument are drawn from norms of modern ethical life and facts about the actual status to which modern society consigns the poor, and the conclusion is that at least for the poor, there is no validity to the whole idea of personal right. In one version, the argument brings together the ethical idea that all human beings are equally persons with rights and the brutal fact that civil society necessarily generates a class of poor, in whom "self-consciousness no longer has any rights, freedom has no existence." The conclusion is that the entire idea of persons and their rights is a sham, "the recognition of universal freedom disappears" *(VPR19* : 195). In another version, the argument rests on the idea that people in a condition of distress or necessity *(Not)* have a "right of necessity" which overrides the abstract right of persons.[18] It combines this with the observation that civil society consigns whole classes of people systematically and permanently to the condition of distress. From this it follows that the abstract right of others in general has no claim to their recognition.

These are sound arguments, though some of their premises may be controversial. Some might not agree that poverty is systematically produced by the workings of civil society *(PR* §§ 243–245), treating it instead as the product of social factors extraneous to the market system as such, or else of bad luck or human error or wickedness. Hegel acknowledges that poverty can be a result of bad luck or of individual failings and improvidence, but maintains that civil society has both the right and the responsibility to compensate for such factors and protect individuals against them *(PR* §§ 239–240). It might also be disputed whether all members of civil society have a right to a satisfactory livelihood through their own work. In some places, Hegel seems to hold that to be a person with abstract right, the only requirement is that one owns some property *(PR* § 49,A). But later he claims a broader conception of a person's right, on the ground that civil society is not merely a natural order arising contingently out of the free acts of individuals, but a genuine society with a "form of universality" *(PR* § 182) which can demand participation by its members because, like a "universal family," it undertakes to provide to their welfare *(PR* §§ 238A, 239).

11. Ethical self-destruction

Given Hegel's premises, the conclusion follows that for the poor, there are neither rights nor duties *(VPR 1* : 322). At least these conclusions follow within the context of Hegelian ethical theory. There, ethical duties and rights are closely bound up with actual social practices. If there are to be valid rights and duties, then the practices must succeed, at least within the limits of the contingency and imperfection afflicting everything finite, in actualizing the spiritual principles they express. When a social order systematically fails to actualize its own ethical principles, that amounts to the self-destruction of those principles.

The main purpose of Hegel's theory is to exhibit the rationality of the ethical order. Plainly, the line of thinking Hegel pursues in his analysis of the rabble mentality does not cohere well with that purpose, because it leads to the conclusion that the poor have neither rights nor duties – a conclusion Hegel himself sometimes explicitly draws. This suggests some even more drastic conclusions. It is a fundamental principle of modern ethical life that all individuals are equal persons with rights. If civil society systematically produces a class whose existence violates that principle, then that tends to undermine the rationality of the ethical order as a whole. In a social system that undermines its own principles, can anyone really be said to have valid rights or duties? Can the participants in such a system truly be "with themselves" as rational beings in its institutions and practices? I suggest that Hegel is worried by and hostile to the rabble mentality in part because he correctly sees it as a threat to the rationality of modern ethical life as a whole, hence to the fundamental aim of his entire theory of objective spirit.

The rabble mentality also *coheres* with an important theme in his philosophy of history. In Chapter 13 we saw that every ethical order must ultimately destroy itself through the reflective awareness of its own principles and their limits. If the rational state as Hegel presents it is "a form of life grown old," then we may expect on the basis of Hegelian principles that its time of destructive self-awareness and decadence cannot be too far off. Hegel's reflection on the modern state, though positive in intent, may also begin to reveal the limits of its principle.

If the rabble mentality represents such an awareness, then it fits in with Hegel's philosophy of history in another way as well – with its amoralism. The rabble is seen by Hegel not as the creator of a new order, but only as the corrupter of the old. Its mentality contains nothing so respectable as "ideals" of a better world, nor even a "right of revolution" against the old one.[19] It is simply an alienated mentality of envy and hatred, a derisive rejection of all duties and ethical principles, a contemptuous refusal to recognize anyone's rights, a bitter denial of all human dignity and self-respect – supported by a cogent rational justification through the self-destruction of modern ethical principles.

Hegel often cites Plato's suppression of the emerging historical principle of free subjectivity as the most serious limitation of his political thought (*PR* §§ 46, 184A, 185R, 206R, 262A, 299R). But he insists that despite this, Plato "proved his greatness of spirit" by the fact that the point that most troubled him was "the pivot on which turned the impending world revolution" (*PR* Preface 24). It may still be too soon to say, but perhaps by the same standard Hegel's attempt to grasp his time in thought also displays spiritual greatness where it reaches its own limits.

Conclusion

1. Ethics and society

Hegel's ethical thought does not dissolve ethics in sociology or reduce it to politics, but social relationships and institutions do play an important role in the way Hegel's theory grounds ethical standards on the self-actualization of spirit's freedom. Ethical duties and principles rest on universal reason, but they must also be the principles of an actual social order. The actual is always rational, but no existing social order is ever wholly actual. In its existence, the rational Idea of an ethical order is always to some extent disfigured by contingency, error, and wickedness. The present social order must be measured not by a timeless standard but by its own immanent Idea, simply because "in the most recent time, the perfection of the Idea is always the highest" (*VPR 4*: 717). There is plenty of room in Hegel's ethical theory for criticism of the existing order as an immature or imperfect embodiment of its own Idea.

Hegel's ethical thought has an outward, social orientation. Its theory of personal morality stresses particular situations and social relaltionships, and finds the good will only in outward actions and results, not in empty, unactualized intentions. Hegelian morality treats the subject as a thinker, and holds inward earnestness to objective standards of rightness. Because moral action takes place in the objective world, Hegelian ethics sees the moral worth of agents as delivered over to the laws and contingencies of that world.

The principles of an ethical order are valid only so long as that order is rational. Because spirit is always advancing in its self-knowledge, there are no determinate ethical principles valid for all times and places. What had rational validity yesterday no longer has it today, and what has it today will lose it tomorrow. The foundation of the ethical is its actualization of spirit's freedom. The cause of that freedom is served not only by the structure of a rational social order, but also by the destruction of an order that has lost its rationality. Consequently, the ethical itself has only a limited and conditional justification.

Inevitably, Hegel's ethical theory focuses critical attention on prevailing social institutions: Does the existing order actualize its Idea? Is the ethical order itself rational, or has it lost its foundation in spirit's struggle to actualize freedom? Through its conception of the self-actualization of spirit's freedom, Hegel's theory also proposes standards by which these questions are to be answered. Because the *Philosophy of Right* defends the rationality of the modern state, the intent of the theory is supposed to be apologetic, a defense of modern society – and of the existing order to the extent (but only to the extent) that it actualizes the Idea of objective freedom.

Hegel tries to show that the institutions of modern society – the family, civil society, and the state – actualize human freedom in the modern world. That attempt presupposes the possibility that modern society might *fail* to meet those same critical standards. In that case, the real import of Hegel's ethical theory would be radical. The possibility of a radical Hegelian "left" is inherent in Hegel's ethical thought, along with the possibility of a conservative or apologetic Hegelian "right" and a moderate or reformist Hegelian "center." The historical Hegel was pretty clearly a "centrist," but to decide in a more properly philosophical sense which camp has the right to claim "the real Hegel" is to decide whether modern society really is rational according to the standards of Hegelian ethical theory.

2. Hegel as liberal

For Hegel, the rationality of the modern state turns ultimately on its actualization of *freedom*. A free society is one in which individuals are with themselves in their ethical institutions. In the modern world, this requires that social institutions guarantee the right of persons and provide scope for the subjective freedom of individuals. As a person, I must have an external sphere of freedom over which society respects and protects my right to arbitrary freedom. As a subject, the direction of my life must, in the respects that matter most to me, be at the mercy of my choices and conscience. Hegel argues that this means I must have civil freedom and the opportunity to choose a place in civil society, and give my individuality determinate existence through my own labor there.

These Hegelian doctrines have much in common with the liberal tradition (whose success in the West may be measured by the fact that it encompasses the exhaustive polarity of "liberalism" and "conservatism" as those terms are commonly used in contemporary politics). Moreover, the constitutional monarchy described in the *Philosophy of Right* is quite liberal by the standards of the time in which it was written. It provides not only for nearly all of the political and economic liberalization that had been accomplished by the Stein and Hardenberg administrations in Prussia between 1808 and 1818, but also for most of the further intended reforms which were successfully resisted by the reactionaries who had just come to power when the book was published. The contents of Hegel's theory simply can't be reconciled with the assumption that he was intending an uncritical endorsement of restoration Prussia as it existed in 1820 and after. The French philosopher Victor Cousin had Hegel's actual political views in mind when he said that, like himself, Hegel was "infused with the new spirit; he considered the French Revolution to be the greatest step forward taken by humankind since Christianity. He was profoundly liberal without being the least bit republican."[1]

It is no wonder that Rudolf Haym, who is chiefly responsible for the tradition of reading Hegel as an apologist for the Prussian reaction, also found it necessary to charge Hegel's whole political theory with "duplicity." Haym was well aware that Hegel's state is a liberal reformed Prussia, not a reactionary, absolutist Prussia. Thus Haym had to claim that when Hegel professes allegiance to restoration Prussia in the *PR* Preface, he at last shows his true colors, or (in Haym's words) "strips [his system] of its liberalistic sheen."[2] Less informed liberal critics rob Haym's position of this subtlety by simply taking for granted that Hegel is an apologist for reactionary Prussia and ignoring the fact that Hegel's state has a very liberal look to it.

Haym's deeper intention was to demonstrate that, despite these appearances, the philosophy of German idealism is antiliberal in its implications. Haym's argument for this conclusion is superficial and flawed, but the conclusion itself is essentially correct.

3. Hegel versus liberalism

When we consider them in their historical context, Hegel's political ideas leave the liberals' state pretty much intact. Hegel's ethical theory, on the other hand, shreds the liberal rationale for it. Hegel attacks the subjectivistic, atomistic, and moralistic foundations of modern liberalism, and he provides an alternative rationale for quite similar social institutions, based on a combination of communitarian principles and the radical German idealist conception of absolute freedom. Thus Cousin's remark needs correction: Although the *state* Hegel favors may be quite liberal, the ethical theory through which he justifies it is not liberal at all.

In Hegel's theory, personal, subjective, and civil freedom are valuable because they serve determinate purposes in the context of actualizing absolute freedom. I do this only when my private life takes on meaning within a larger, collective life, when my particular ends pass over into the ends of the community. Hegelian ethical theory provides a defense of the value of individual freedom, but at the same time also a criterion for deciding when individual freedom matters and when it does not. Its handling of these matters might very well point us in quite a different direction from some standard liberal theories of individual freedom.

The specific function of subjective freedom is to actualize the individual's particularity. Subjective freedom is subordinated to the end of individual self-actualization. Hegel is worried about the "spirit of atomism" in civil society because he thinks that too little social structuring of individual possibilities and expectations (too much of what liberals usually value under the name of freedom) might actually frustrate the whole aim of subjective freedom. Hegel plainly fears that a market system without the sort of ethical structure he assigned to corporations might well be self-defeating in just this way.

Hegel also diverges from the liberal tradition when he insists that collective goods have a value in themselves not reducible to the private good of individuals. In Hegel's theory, collective goods do not normally compete with individual good or individual freedom. On the contrary, the state's rationality, which makes it an end in itself, consists in the systematic identification of its institutions with the actualization of subjective freedom and private good for individuals. Nor is Hegel denying the virtual tautology that collective goods have value because they have value *for individuals*. His claim is that what has the most value for individuals, what actualizes their freedom most completely, is the pursuit of a universal or collective end, not the pursuit of their own private ends as such. If a liberal state is one that has no universal, collective goals but exists only to serve the particular whims and desires of its individual members, then Hegelian ethical theory says that the members of a liberal state, for all their personal, subjective, and civil freedoms, are fundamentally *un*free.

4. The free society

To accept Hegel's thesis that the modern state actually meets the demands of his ethical theory is to propose an antiliberal vision of what modern society is and how we should try to keep it true to itself. Communitarian theories of modern society lie in that direction, though (as I have suggested in Chapters 11 and 12) Hegel is more rationalistic and universalistic than most communitarians are today.

This book, however, has suggested a few reasons for doubting Hegel's thesis. Plainly the nation-state cannot serve the exalted function in human life which Hegel assigned it (Chapter 1, § 7). Neither it nor any other modern institution provides for the transition of individual into communal life in the way Hegel's theory demands. This is true to such a degree that Hegel's very conception here is hard for us to grasp, and we are apt to interpret it either as an advocacy of totalitarianism or else as a complacent sophistry (Chapter 14, §§ 1–2). Reflective individuals in modern society are typically so far from being able to identify themselves rationally with their social roles that Hegel's notion of liberation through ethical duty is to strike them as either dangerous humbug or a bad joke (Chapter 2, § 10).

It is doubtful that the market system of modern civil society can provide both subjective freedom and the social structure necessary to a sense of individual identity (Chapter 14, § 3–4). Modern society's failure to reconcile the principles of substantiality and reflection shows itself in the untenability of Hegel's conception of the family and the social role of women, along with the absence of any alternative that satisfactorily addresses the same problem (Chapter 14, §§ 5–6). Finally, Hegel himself calls our attention to poverty as a systematic product of modern civil society (Chapter 14, § 7–8). He sees how it violates modern society's own conception of personal right (Chapter 14, § 10; Chapter 4, § 10, Chapter 5, § 7) and how it threatens to undermine its rationale for criminal justice (Chapter 6, § 5) and even modern ethical life as a whole (Chapter 14, §§ 9, 11).

Our recognition of this failure of modern society does not provide us with anything like an alternative "Hegelian" vision of the free society, which might be set over against Hegel's own vision of the modern state. But it might point

Hegel's ethical theory in a radical direction, since it suggests several different ways in which modern civil society cannot satisfy the demands to which Hegel's ethical theory gives rise. It suggests that modern civil society cannot fulfill its own principles of universal human freedom and dignity, because it systematically consigns whole classes to conditions of life that are subhuman by its own standards. Moreover, modern society seems unable to fulfill the individuality even of those who escape this fate, because it is not structured enough to prevent anomy and not cohesive enough to weld people's personal rights, subjective freedom, and individual well-being into a universal end that can be collectively pursued.

The same considerations, however, might raise doubts about Hegelian ethical theory itself. If modern society has not satisfied the demands of Hegel's ethical theory, we might wonder about the reasonableness of those demands. Are Hegelian freedom and self-actualization goods that a social order can be expected to provide? Self-actualization, it may be said, means different things to different people, and one individual's meaningful life structure is always going to be someone else's oppressive social constraint. Individuals are notoriously unable to agree when it comes to deciding the higher, collective purposes of society. In theory, liberals will tell us, the vision of Hegel's free society is very tempting. But in practice, we have good reason to reject and even to fear it, because attempts to realize it always lead toward a society that smothers individual freedom and well-being under some set of collective goals whose bogus "universal validity" turns out to be nothing but a pretext for the exercise of tyrannical power.

These fears may be exaggerated, but we miss the point if we are too quick to allay them. Hegel himself was a political moderate, but his thought has certainly been implicated in political movements, both right and left, some of whose deeds have been monstrously destructive. On the other hand, the aim of this book has been to present Hegel's ethical theory as a well-conceived articulation of the modern Western image of humanity and human self-actualization. That theory sets ambitious standards for any society that wants to call itself free, and grounds these standards in both reason and history. Until its vision is actualized, we cannot exclude the possibility that the Hegelian demand for a free society may be just another symptom of our culture's most incurable disease. But no theory of society that fails to acknowledge that call to liberation will ever understand the modern world or what it is about; no society that leaves it unanswered can be rooted in the deepest needs of its members. Radical hopes themselves are actual as long as they have their roots in us. The dangerous self-deceiving utopian dreamers are those who turn against these hopes, harboring the complacent wish that they will just go quietly away and let our broken dream world slumber in peace.

Notes

Introduction

1. It is surely paradoxical to say first that philosophy depends on the empirical sciences and then that philosophy will turn this empirical knowledge into a priori knowledge. But this might seem appropriate if, as Hegel contends, philosophy demonstrates that these empirical facts are posited by nothing but the thinking mind, dependent on no external inputs. Perhaps the right conclusion is just that the a priori/empirical distinction, as traditionally understood in the Kantian tradition, is one which Hegel means to challenge. In his excellent book, *Hegel's Theory of Mental Activity* (Ithaca: Cornell University Press, 1988), pp. 14, 27–28, 31–35, Willem deVries suggests that a priority for Hegel is something that always admits of degrees; different claims have different degrees of empirical sensitivity.

2. The claims about Hegel's methodological project made in this paragraph have been argued very convincingly by Michael Forster in his excellent book *Hegel and Skepticism* (Cambridge, MA: Harvard University Press, 1989).

3. For two good discussions of Hegel's reading of the Kantian antinomies, and its influence on his own conception of dialectic, see Martial Gueroult, "Le jugement de Hegel sur l'Antithétique de la Raison Pure," *Revue de Metaphysique et de Morale 38* (1931); a German translation of this article is to be found in Rolf-Peter Horstmann (ed.), *Seminar: Dialektik in der Philosophie Hegels* (Frankfurt: Suhrkamp, 1978); and John Llewellyn, "Kantian Antinomy and Hegelian Dialectic," in Stephen Priest (ed.), *Hegel's Critique of Kant* (Oxford: Clarendon Press, 1987).

4. Ludwig Wittgenstein, *Bemerkungen über die Grundlagen der Mathematik/Remarks on the Foundations of Mathematics,* ed. Von Wright, Rhees, Anscombe (Oxford: Blackwell, 1964), §§ 12, 80, pp. 51, 104.

5. See G. E. Mueller, "The Hegel Legend of 'Thesis–Antithesis–Synthesis'," *Journal of the History of Ideas 19* (1958), 411–414.

6. Michael Rosen, *Hegel's Dialectic and Its Criticism* (Cambridge: Cambridge University Press, 1982), p. 179.

7. See Herbert Schnädelbach, *Philosophy in Germany 1831–1933* (Cambridge: Cambridge University Press, 1984), pp. 77, 241.

8. Ernst Cassirer, *The Myth of the State* (1946) (Garden City, NJ: Doubleday, 1955), p. 311.

9. Raymond Plant, *Hegel* (Bloomington, IN: Indiana University Press, 1973), p. 184.

10. Charles Taylor, *Hegel* (Cambridge: Cambridge University Press, 1975).

11. At this point, the PR Preface echoes a noteworthy passage toward the beginning of Hegel's unpublished essay of 1800 on German politics, customarily entitled "The German Constitution":

The thoughts contained in this essay can in their public expression have no other end or effect than promoting the understanding of what is, and thus furthering, both in actual contact and in words, a more peaceful outlook on and a moderate endurance of what is. For it is not what is which makes us irascible and passionate; rather, it is that it is not as it ought to be. But if we recognize it is as it must be, i.e. that it is not arbitrariness and contingency which make it what it is, then we will also recognize that it ought to be that way. (*DV* 463/145)

12. Georg Lukacs, *The Ontology of Social Being: Hegel,* trans. David Fernbach (London: Merlin Press, 1978), p. 47.
13. Søren Kierkegaard, *Concluding Unscientific Postscript,* trans. Walter Lowrie (Princeton University Press, 1942), p. 108; W. H. Walsh, *Hegelian Ethics* (New York: Garland Publishers, 1984), pp. 11, 55; Herbert Marcuse: *Reason and Revolution: Hegel and the Rise of Social Theory* (Boston: Beacon Press, 1968), p. 200.
14. See also Taylor, *Hegel,* pp. 282–286.
15. See Manfred Riedel, *Between Tradition and Revolution: The Hegelian Transformation of Political Philosophy,* trans. Walter Wright (Cambridge: Cambridge University Press, 1984), p. 28.
16. Hardenberg's constitutional plan can be found in an Appendix to Alfred Stern, *Geschichte Europas 1815–1871* (Berlin: Wilhelm Hertz, 1894), *1*: 649–653. For Humboldt's much longer draft, see Wilhelm von Humboldt, *Gesammelte Schriften* (Berlin: Behr, 1904), *121*: 225–296. See also Friedrich Meinecke, *The Age of German Liberation, 1795–1815* (1906), ed. P. Paret and H. Fischer (Berkeley: University of California Press, 1977); and Walter Simon, *The Failure of the Prussian Reform Era* (Ithaca: Cornell University Press, 1955), pp. 201–207.
17. Hegel's lectures of the period just preceding the publication of the *Philosophy of Right,* which have been edited only quite recently, shed considerable light on the old but perennially sensational question of Hegel's relation to the restoration Prussian state which employed him after 1818. See Karl-Heinz Ilting's introductions to *VPR 1* (pp. 25–126), *VPR 4* (pp 45–66), and *VPR17* (pp. 17–34); and Dieter Henrich's introduction to *VPR19* (especially pp. 9–17, 24–30). For further illuminating discussion of these issues, see Shlomo Avineri, *Hegel's Theory of the Modern State* (Cambridge: Cambridge University Press, 1972), Chapter 6; and Michael Theunissen, *Die Verwirklichung der Vernunft. Zur Theorie–Praxis Diskussion im Anschluss an Hegel,* Philosophische Rundschau, Beiheft 6 (1970); cf. Theunissen, *Sein und Schein* (Frankfurt: Suhrkamp, 1980), pp. 472–486. The definitive recent account of the long history of this controversy is Henning Ottmann, *Individuum und Gemeinschaft bei Hegel,* Bd. 1: *Hegel im Spiegel der Interpretationen* (Berlin: DeGruyter, 1977).
18. See Thomas Nipperdey, *Deutsche Geschichte 1800–1860: Bürgerwelt und starker Staat* (Munich: C. H. Beck, 1983), p. 479; John Edward Toews *Hegelianism* (Cambridge: Cambridge University Press, 1980), pp. 253–254.

Chapter 1

1. See Samuel Scheffler, "Moral Skepticism and Ideals of the Person," *Monist 62* (1979).
2. Derek Parfit, *Reasons and Persons* (Oxford: Clarendon Press, 1984). Korsgaard suggests that this difference between Parfit and the Kantians lies in the fact that

for Parfit, as for all empiricists, the stuff of which selves are made is simply the passive having of experiences (so that even acting is interpreted as a kind of undergoing of the experience of agency), whereas the Kantians regard agency as fundamental to selfhood, and fundamentally different from any passively enjoyed experience [Christine Korsgaard, "Personal Identity and the Unity of Agency," *Philosophy and Public Affairs 18* (1989)]. For other relevant discussions of Parfit on selfhood, see Susan Wolf, "Self-Interest and Interest in Selves," *Ethics 96* (1986); and Robert Merrihew Adams, "Should Ethics Be More Impersonal?" *The Philosophical Review 98* (1989).

3. John Locke, *Second Treatise on Government* ed. T. Peardon (Indianapolis: Bobbs-Merrill, 1952), § 87; cf. §§ 6, 27, 59.

4. "Germanic" in this sense of course includes "Germany proper" (*das eigentliche Deutschland*) – which Hegel understands to include the Franks, the Normans, and the peoples of England and Scandinavia (*VPG* 421/349). But it is not limited to that; equally "Germanic," in Hegel's sense of the word, are the "Romanic" peoples of France, Italy, Spain, and Portugal: the Visigoths, Ostrogoths, Lombards, and Burgundians (*VPG* 420/348), and even the Magyars and the Slavs of Eastern Europe (*VPG* 422/350). But the prominence he gives both to Tacitus's image of the Teutonic character and to the Lutheran Reformation indicates that Hegel regards German culture in a fairly narrow sense as playing a very prominent role in the development of the modern spirit (cf. *DV* 465–467/146–150, 532–533/202–203; *VPG* 494/414).

5. As Manfred Riedel has shown, before Hegel the term *bürgerliche Gesellschaft* – along with its equivalents in Latin, French, and English – was always equated with the political state, and distinguished from the family, the only recognized form of "private society." See Riedel, *Between Tradition and Revolution* (Cambridge: Cambridge University Press, 1984), Chapter 6.

6. The error is quoted from an otherwise illuminating discussion in Alan Ryan, *Property and Political Theory* (Oxford: Blackwell, 1984), p. 134. For a better discussion of this particular point, see Shlomo Avineri, *Hegel's Theory of the Modern State* (Cambridge: Cambridge University Press, 1972), Chapter 7; and Bernard Cullen, *Hegel's Social and Political Thought* (New York: St. Martin's Press, 1979), Chapter 5, especially pp. 91–94.

7. John Stuart Mill, *Utilitarianism* (Indianapolis: Hackett Publishing Co., 1979), p. 33.

8. See T. O'Hagan, "On Hegel's Critique of Kant's Moral and Political Philosophy," in Stephen Priest (ed.), *Hegel's Critique of Kant* (Oxford: Clarendon Press, 1987), p. 157.

9. The uniqueness of the *type* of theory found in the *Philosophy of Right* is appreciated by Hans-Friedrich Fulda, "Zum Theorietypus der Hegelschen Rechtsphilosophie," in D. Henrich and R.-P. Horstmann (eds.), *Hegels Philosophie des Rechts: Die Theorie der Rechtsformen und ihre Logik* (Stuttgart: Klett-Cotta Verlag, 1982), pp. 393–427. I believe, however, that Fulda underestimates the degree to which Hegel's ethical theory has a content analogous to that of other types of ethical theory.

10. What I am calling a "self-actualization" theory bears a close resemblance to what Julius Moravcsik calls an "ideal ethical theory" – a type of theory he claims to find in certain classical Greek texts, for example, in the *Eudemian Ethics* of Aristotle. J. Moravcsik, "Ideal Ethics in the *Eudemian Ethics*," unpublished paper.

11. Richard B. Brandt, *A Theory of the Good and the Right* (Oxford: Clarendon,

1979), Part I; Peter Railton, "Moral Realism," *The Philosophical Review* 95 (1986), 171-184.

12. I owe this point to a conversation with Milton Wachsberg.

13. Marx, *Werke* (Berlin: Dietz Verlag, 1961-1966), 23: 23; *Capital* (New York: International Publishers, 1967), 1: Marx–Engels, *Selected Works* (New York: International Publishers, 1968), p. 295.

Chapter 2

1. See E. F. Carritt, "Reply" in Walter Kaufmann (ed.), *Hegel's Political Philosophy* (New York: Atherton Press, 1970), p. 38. This echoes the more famous criticism of Rudolf Haym: "The system of right, as [Hegel] defines it in one of his first paragraphs, is 'the realm of actualized freedom.' The whole book has to do with nothing but freedom. . . . Only the word 'freedom' is a coin whose rate of exchange finds itself in constant fluctuation. Only one's disposition determines the sense of the word. The version of it that Hegel gives will betray the fundamental weaknesses of his philosophy" [Haym, *Hegel und seine Zeit* (Berlin: Rudolf Gaertner, 1857), pp. 369-370; cf. Manfred Riedel (ed.), *Materialien zu Hegels Rechtsphilosophie* (Frankfurt: Suhrkamp, 1975), p. 376].

2. I owe this remark to Ernst Tugendhat.

3. See Gerald G. McCallum, "Positive and Negative Freedom," *The Philosophical Review* 86 (1967).

4. It is not clear whether Hegel means to say only that (1) we are able to act against *any* of our desires, however powerful; or whether he means to make the even stronger claim that (2) we are capable of acting against *all* our desires at once – in effect, that we are capable of acting in a way prompted by none of our desires and against which all our desires speak. In favor of (1) is the fact that Hegel insists (*PR* § 5) that the power of abstraction is incapable of any positive action; in order to do anything, he holds, the will must particularize itself (*PR* § 6), and this apparently means bringing into play at least one of its particular desires. But in favor of (2) is Hegel's apparent belief that there is such a thing as "negative freedom," which attempts to actualize the self as nothing but the power of abstraction. Hegel plainly regards negative freedom as irrational and wholly destructive, but if he thinks it is possible at all, that would seem to imply a kind of action that defies all particular desires at once.

5. Isaiah Berlin, *Four Essays on Liberty* (Oxford: Oxford University Press, 1969), p. 122.

6. Paul Guyer has called my attention to a passage in the *Lectures on Ethics*, where Kant distinguishes between "the capacity for freedom" and "the state of freedom" or "inner freedom," and where it might look as though the latter is the same as autonomy or freedom as a state of actuality. However, a closer look reveals that here, too, Kant is thinking of freedom as a capacity – namely the capacity to compel oneself, or the ability to do so with relative ease: "The more a man can compel himself, the freer he is. The less he need be compelled by others, the greater his inner freedom. . . . The more a man practices self-compulsion, the freer he becomes. Some men are by nature more disposed to magnanimity, forgiveness, righteousness. It is easier for them to compel themselves and they are to that extent freer" (*VE* 37-38/30-31). "Inner freedom" in this passage is not autonomous action itself but the virtue of character which gives one a greater capacity to act autonomously. When Kant says, "The more a man practices self-

compulsion the freer he becomes," he is not asserting the tautology that the more one acts autonomously the more one acts autonomously; rather, he is saying that frequent acts of self-compulsion make it easier to compel oneself, or increase one's capacity for self-compulsion; that is what "inner freedom" is.

7. John Locke, *Second Treatise on Government*, ed. T. Peardon (Indianapolis: Bobbs-Merrill, 1952), § 22, p. 15. In the same vein, Locke says: "That ill-deserves the name of confinement which hedges us in only from bogs and precipices" (*Second Treatise* § 57, p. 32); and he asks: "Is it worth the name of *Freedom* to be at liberty to play the Fool, and draw Shame and Misery upon a Man's self? If to break loose from the conduct of Reason . . . be *Liberty*, true Liberty, mad Men and Fools are the only Freemen" [*An Essay Concerning Human Understanding*, ed. Peter Nidditch (Oxford: Oxford University Press, 1975), Book II, Ch. 21, § 50, p. 265].

8. "Liberty can consist only in the power of doing what one ought to will" [Charles Louis de Secondat, Baron de Montesquieu, *Oeuvres Complètes* (Paris: Gallimard, 1951) 2 : 395; cf. *The Spirit of the Laws* (New York: Hafner, 1949), p. 150]; "Liberty consists in being able to do whatever does not injure another" [*Declaration of the Rights of Man and Citizen* (1789), § 4]. Kant follows Rousseau in holding that the transition from the state of nature to the civil state is one in which no real loss of freedom is involved (Kant *RL* 316/80–81).

9. Jean-Jacques Rousseau, *Oeuvres Complètes* (Paris: Gallimard, 1964), *3* : 364; cf. *The Social Contract and Discourses* (New York: E. P. Dutton, 1950), p. 18.

10. John Stuart Mill, *On Liberty*, ed. Elizabeth Rapaport (Indianapolis: Hackett, 1978), p. 12, italics added.

11. Isaiah Berlin, *Four Essays on Liberty*, p. 148.

12. Jeremy Bentham, *Of Laws in General*, ed. H. L. A. Hart, in J. H. Burns (ed.), *Collected Works of Jeremy Bentham* (London: Athlone Press, 1968-), Chapter 6, § 3.

13. Berlin, *Four Essays on Liberty*, p. 152.

14. Berlin, *Four Essays on Liberty*, pp. 151–153. There is this much to be said for Berlin's position: Hegel thinks that a free society is one in which rational institutions (specifically: institutions protecting personal and civil freedom for the sake of subjective freedom) are "universal" or common ends to be pursued collectively for their own sake. But suppose some "Hegelians" altogether forgot the content of these ends, and retained only the thought that social institutions must be ends in themselves pursued by the whole community. In that case, we can easily imagine that they might have few scruples about foisting different ends on the community, without appreciating that it is essential for these ends to harmonize with people's subjective freedom. At the same time, it is easy to imagine that the ends they want to impose might be resisted by many members of the community, making coercion, manipulation, and thought control all the more necessary to getting society to accept them. In that sort of case, it would certainly be "psychologically and historically intelligible" that a society run by "Hegelians" might move in a totalitarian direction (see Chapter 14, §§ 1–2). It is a separate question, however, whether anything like this is the correct explanation for the development of totalitarian states in actual cases. The main point not to miss is that this would be self-defeating for Hegelians in exactly the same way that it is self-defeating for liberals to suppress these same freedoms in the name of protecting the "free" society from subversion.

15. Berlin, *Four Essays on Liberty*, p. 153.

16. "A thing is said to be free when it exists solely from the necessity of its nature, and is determined to act by itself alone. . . . [It is] constrained if it is determined by another thing to exist and to act in a definite and determinate way," Spinoza, *The Ethics*, trans. S. Shirley (Indianapolis: Hackett, 1982), ID7, p. 31.

17. For Fichte, this entails that legitimate government always rests on the actual consent of the people and is always responsible to the people. Realizing how far the political institutions of his time were from meeting this condition, he concludes: "Any constitution of the state is in accordance with right which does not make impossible the progress, in general and for individuals, toward something better; and one can serve it with a good conscience. Only that constitution is completely contrary to right which has the end of preserving everything as it presently is" (*SL* 361/375).

18. See *Marx*–Engels Werke (Berlin: Dietz Verlag, 1961–1966), *1*: 514, *3*: 67; *Marx–Engels Collected Works* (New York: International Publishers, 1975–), *3*: 274, *5*: 87.

19. See, for instance, Bernard Yack, *The Longing for Total Revolution* (Princeton: Princeton University Press, 1986). Yack excuses Hegel from such criticisms because of the right-Hegelian interpretation he gives of the *Philosophy of Right*. According to Yack, Hegel recommends "resignation to the limitations of our ability to achieve our practical ends in society" (p. 220) because he has arrived at the "realistic" position that no form of society can ever eliminate "the social sources of human dissatisfaction posed by the indifference of nature to our practical ends" (p. 222). The dourly complacent views just quoted appear to be Yack's own. They are clearly not Hegel's: "Reason [is not] content with that cold despair which submits to the view that in this earthly life things are truly bad or at best only tolerable, though they cannot be improved, and this is the only reflection that can keep us at peace with the world" (*PR* Preface 25).

20. Isaiah Berlin, *Four Essays on Liberty*, p. 135.

21. Epictetus, *Enchiridion*, trans. T. Higginson (New York: Liberal Arts Press, 1948), p. 17.

22. Actually, Hegel's first use of the term *bei sich* to mean "freedom" occurs in the *Phenomenology of Spirit* (*PhG* ¶ 197). But there it is used to characterize the completely self-contained and therefore limited freedom of Stoicism, which is at best an abstract version of "being with oneself" as it appears in Hegel's later writings, since Stoicism (as Hegel presents it) excludes otherness rather than conquering it. Hegel's conception of freedom is not merely "being with oneself" but "being with oneself *in another*." Of course, this conception of freedom, expressed in other terms, goes back at least as far as Hegel's Jena period: "A freedom for which something is genuinely external and alien is no freedom; the essence and formal definition [of freedom] is just that nothing is absolutely external" (*NR* 447/89).

23. Hegel does not regard my end as something simply existing in me, which, when I achieve it, gets supplemented by an external state of affairs. Instead, he insists that the very subjectivity of my end, the fact that it is something in me, is a defect in it, something which needs to be made good through the objective actualization of that same end (*PR* §§ 8–9). My end (*Zweck*) itself is, most properly speaking, that which is simultaneously subjective and objective; it is the thing I subjectively willed, but it is that thing in the form of an object which stands over and against that willing as what it has created (*PR* §§ 108–109).

24. On the sense of "interpretation" relevant to Hegel's philosophical method, see

Willem deVries, *Hegel's Theory of Mental Activity* (Ithaca: Cornell University Press, 1989), p. 16.

25. See Harry Frankfurt, "Freedom of the will and the Concept of a Person,"*Journal of Philosophy 67* (1971).
26. It appears so, for instance, to Ernst Tugendhat, *Self-Consciousness and Self-Determination*, trans. Paul Stern (Cambridge, MA: MIT Press, 1986), Lecture 14.

Chapter 3

1. Aristotle, *Nicomachean Ethics 1*: 5, 1095b15–1096a10.
2. Cf. Plato, *Gorgias* 468a–470e.
3. Descartes, *Passions of the Soul*, in John Cottingham, Robert Stoothoff and Dugald Murdoch (eds.), *Philosophical Writings of Descartes* (Cambridge: Cambridge University Press, 1985), *1*: 381–382.
4. Hobbes, *Leviathan 1*: 11 (Indianapolis: Bobbs-Merrill, 1958), p. 86.
5. See Nicolas Malebranche, *Oeuvres Complètes*, ed. A. Robinet (Paris: J. Vrin, 1959–1978), *5*: 96; Antoine Arnauld, *Oeuvres* (Paris: Sigismond D'Arnay, 1780), *39*: 367–368. Compare St. Thomas Aquinas, *Summa Contra Gentiles* L. 3: C. 26. Like Aquinas, most Scholastics identify true happiness not with any earthly condition but with the beatific vision of God in a future life. A disputed issue concerns whether this vision is an act of the intellect (Aquinas's position), or an act of the will – the view of most Franciscan thinkers (compare Duns Scotus, *Opus Oxon.* Q. 1, Dist. 25). For the Scholastics, beatific vision is an act of the soul, but it is not a subjective state, and most flatly deny that it is to be identified with the pleasure or enjoyment (*delectatio*) involved in it. Even a dissenter on this point, such as the Franciscan Peter Aureol, emphasizes that it is enjoyment of the object, not of the state of seeing the object (Peter Aureoli, *Scriptum super Primum Sententiarum*, Distinctio 1, Sect. 7): The beatific vision of God is supreme happiness because it is a vision *of God*, not because of any subjective qualities it may possess.
6. Locke, *Essay Concerning Human Understanding* 2:21:42, ed. Peter H. Nidditch (Oxford: Oxford University Press, 1975), p. 259.
7. Locke, *Essay Concerning Human Understanding* 2:21:43, pp. 259–260.
8. Anthony Ashley Cooper, Third Earl of Shaftesbury, *Characteristics of Men, Manners, Opinions, Times* (1711) (Indianapolis: Bobbs-Merrill, 1964), Vol. 1, Treatise IV: *An Inquiry Concerning Virtue or Merit II/1*, 293–295.
9. Locke, *Essay Concerning Human Understanding* 2:21:43, p. 259.
10. Epicurus, "Letter to Menoeceus," *Letters, Principal Doctrines and Vatican Sayings*, trans. Russel M. Geer (Indianapolis: Bobbs-Merrill, 1964), pp. 55–58.
11. See Richard Kraut, "Two Conceptions of Happiness," *The Philosophical Review 88* (1979).
12. Kierkegaard, *Either/Or*, trans. Walter Lowrie (New York: Doubleday, 1959), especially the Diapsalma "Either/Or: An Ecstatic Lecture" (pp. 37–39) and the essay "The Rotation Method" (279–296).
13. Kierkegaard, *The Sickness Unto Death*, trans. H. Hong (Princeton: Princeton University Press, 1980), pp. 30–33. It is arguable that Romantic irony was the first form of the outlook on life that has since been called "hip" or "cool." I remain deliberately alienated, uninvolved, aloof, bitterly smiling at the world, refusing

my emotional complicity in anything the outside world chooses to take seriously. Hegel regards Romantic irony as an attitude of monstrous arrogance and self-conceit (*PR* § 140R,A), since the ironic self treats itself as superior to everything else, including even the most sacred things. But Hegel was assuming that our life in the world (especially the social world) can be rationally satisfying, and gives us no good reason not to take it seriously. In its more recent versions, the ironic attitude seems more appropriately interpreted as basically a defensive one, protecting my dignity as a subject against an ethically bankrupt world that refuses to recognize me and constantly outrages my sense of justice and decency. In either form, however, we have to take seriously Hegel's critique of the ironic attitude as a deception that fails to deliver the freedom it promises.

14. Rudolf Reicke, *Lose Blätter aus Kants Nachlass* (Königsberg: Ferd. Beyer, 1889), *1*: 11–12, cf. Paul Arthur Schilpp, *Kant's Pre-critical Ethics*, 2nd ed. (Evanston: Northwestern University Press, 1960), p. 129.

15. This suggestion was made to me in a conversation by Gottfried Seebass.

16. Hegel's rejection of utilitarianism in this context has much in common with John Rawls's rejection of hedonism as a way of devising a decision procedure for a plan of life [Rawls, *A Theory of Justice* (Cambridge: Harvard University Press, 1971), pp. 554–560].

17. Martin Heidegger, *Being and Time,* trans. John Macquarrie and Edward Robinson (New York: Harper & Row, 1962), p. 343.

18. Dieter Henrich, Editor's Introduction to *VPR 19*: 31–35.

Chapter 4

1. Philonenko emphasizes this when he points out that Fichte posits mutual recognition not simply as a condition for self-consciousness, but as a condition in which self-consciousness *becomes* possible: "Fichte in fact writes not that a man is a man only among men, but that a man *becomes* a man only among men." Alexis Philonenko, *L'Oeuvre de Fichte* (Paris: J. Vrin, 1984), p. 46.

2. See Jean Piaget, *The Moral Judgment of the Child* (New York: Harcourt Brace, 1932); cf. Calvin S. Hall and Gardner Lindzey, "Psychoanalytic Theory and Its Applications in the Social Sciences," in Lindzey (ed.), *Handbook of Social Psychology,* Vol. 1 (New York: Addison Hall, 1954), pp. 143–180. This reading of Fichte's theory of recognition, implying a form of socialization and moral education, has also been developed very creatively by Andreas Wildt, *Autonomie und Anerkennung* (Stuttgart: Klett Cotta Verlag, 1982), pp. 259–283.

3. "My freedom is possible only through the other's remaining in his sphere; hence in demanding my freedom for all the future, I demand that he limit himself; and since he is free, I demand it for all the future: and all this immediately, in positing myself as an individual. . . . But he can limit himself only in consequence of a concept from me as a free being. But I demand this limitation absolutely; hence I demand *consistency* from him, i.e., that all his future concepts should be determined by a certain previous concept, his cognition of me as a rational being" (*GNR* 52/78).

4. Again, see Andreas Wildt, *Autonomie und Anerkennung* (Stuttgart: Klett Cotta Verlag, 1982), pp. 259–283.

5. For an illuminating discussion of the relation of Hegel's Jena theory of self-consciousness to his overall philosophical project, see Robert Pippin, *Hegel's Idealism* (Cambridge: Cambridge University Press, 1989), Chapter 7. Probably the

best study of Hegel's Jena period theory of recognition itself is Ludwig Siep, *Anerkennung als Prinzip der praktischen Philosophie* (Munich: Alber, 1979).

6. Thomas Hobbes, *Leviathan II/20* (Indianapolis: Bobbs-Merrill, 1958), p. 165.
7. Hobbes, *Leviathan II/20*, p. 166.
8. Hobbes, *Leviathan I/14–15*, pp. 109–132.

Chapter 5

1. Rights as "permissions" may be regarded as Hohfeldian "privileges" or "liberties," whereas rights as "warrants" may be taken as Hohfeldian "claim-rights." Wesley Newcomb Hohfeld, *Fundamental Legal Conceptions* (New Haven: Yale University Press, 1964).
2. Locke, *Second Treatise on Government*, ed. T. Peardon (Indianapolis: Bobbs-Merrill, 1952), § 27.
3. This point is emphasized by Alan Ryan, *Property and Political Theory* (Oxford: Blackwell, 1984), pp. 130–131.
4. G. A. Cohen, "Self-Ownership, World-Ownership and Equality," in Frank Lucash (ed.), *Justice and Equality Here and Now* (Ithaca: Cornell University Press, 1986), pp. 108–135; "Self-Ownership, World-Ownership and Equality: Part II," *Social Philosophy and Policy 3* (1986), 77–96.
5. Locke, *Second Treatise on Government*, § 87.
6. See Christine Korsgaard, "Kant's Formula of Humanity," *Kant-Studien 77* (1986), 196–197.
7. John Rawls, *A Theory of Justice* (Cambridge, MA: Harvard University Press, 1971), pp. 12, 505, 561.
8. This is the way it is read, for instance, by Alan Ryan, *Property and Political Theory* (Oxford: Blackwell, 1984), p. 122.
9. That Hegel was thinking of Rehberg is indicated at *VPR4*: 196; cf. *VPR17*: 295.
10. cf. Ronald Dworkin, *Taking Rights Seriously* (Cambridge, MA: Harvard University Press, 1978), p. xi.
11. Thomas Hobbes, *Leviathan I/14–15, II/17*.
12. The state has its "absolute right" only because it is a *rational* state, that is, a human community structured in certain determinate ways which ensure that the values and interests involved in a modern rational self-understanding are protected and actualized. Among other things, a modern state is a community that treats its members as persons and protects their abstract right; to the extent that some existing state fails to do this, it is defective as a state. A "state" that systematically failed to protect the abstract rights of its citizens, or that wantonly trampled on these rights, would not be a state at all; it would be a despotism (*PR* § 270R, p. 428/173). As we noted earlier (Chapter 3, § 10) Hegel prefers to speak of individuals having rights *within* the state rather than rights *against* the state (*PR* § 261R); what we might regard as an individual's rights against the state, Hegel prefers to see as a feature of the state as an institution that recognizes and guarantees individual rights.
13. Carole Pateman, *The Problem of Political Obligation* (Berkeley, CA: University of California Press, 1985), pp. 112–113.
14. Hegel ignores the fact that restrictions on private property apply only to the guardians in Plato's state, and that they do not necessarily forbid all private property, even for the guardians. See *Republic* 416–417.
15. If Hegel's doctrine on this point shocks us, we might compare it with the teaching

of Fichte, who holds that in marriage it is the wife only who surrenders her personality; married men remain persons as before, whereas married women do not: "The wife belongs not to herself but to her husband" (*GNR* 312/401, 325–326/418).

16. Locke, *Second Treatise on Government*, § 27.

Chapter 6

1. See John Rawls, "Two Concepts of Rules," *Philosophical Review 64* (1955).
2. Thus in his 1939 paper "Punishment," J. D. Mabbott errs in regarding himself as a retributivist for arguing that the institution of punishment (which he thinks we adopt for various consequentialist reasons) requires violations of the law to be punished simply because they are violations of law. The distinction on which his error turns is that between justifying a practice and justifying a particular action falling under it, which was the subject of John Rawls's 1955 paper "Two Concepts of Rules." Both papers have been reprinted in Robert Baird and Stuart E. Rosenbaum (eds.), *Philosophy of Punishment* (Buffalo: Prometheus Books, 1988).
3. It has sometimes been alleged that Hegel's justification of punishment rests on the idea that it has a morally educative effect on the person punished. See J. E. McTaggart, "Hegel's Theory of Punishment," *International Journal of Ethics 6* (1896), reprinted in Gertrude Ezorsky (ed.), *Philosophical Perspectives on Punishment* (Albany: SUNY Press, 1972); and Jean Hampton, "The Moral Education Theory of Punishment," in *Philosophy and Public Affairs 13* (1984), 208. But this ideas has no real textual basis, and it flies in the face of Hegel's assertion that the punishment of children by their parents is different from the punishment of criminals precisely because the latter aims at justice whereas the former aims at moral education and not at justice (*PR* § 174).
4. "Punishment is not an absolute end. When this is asserted either expressly or through propositions that take such premises as a tacit presupposition (e.g., the unmodified categorical assertion that whoever has killed must die), no thought at all is being expressed. Punishment is only a means for the state's final end, public safety, and its only intention is that harm can be prevented by threatening it" (*GNR* 262/345). "Against our theory of punishment generally . . . an absolute right to punish is set up, according to which judicial punishment is considered not a means but as itself an end, founded on an inscrutable categorical imperative. But . . . we can reject this theory on the ground of the inscrutability of the proofs for its assertions" (*GNR* 282–283/372).
5. David E. Cooper, "Hegel's Theory of Punishment," in Z. B. Pelczynski (ed.), *Hegel's Philosophy of Right: Problems and Perspectives* (Cambridge: Cambridge University Press, 1971); cf. also Lew Hinchman, "Hegel's Theory of Crime and Punishment," *Review of Politics 44* (1982); Peter Steinberger, "Hegel on Crime and Punishment," *American Political Science Review* (1983).
6. Joel Feinberg, "The Expressive Function of Punishment," in Gertrude Ezorsky (ed.), *Philosophical Perspectives on Punishment* (Albany: SUNY Press, 1972).
7. Cooper, "Hegel's Theory of Punishment," p. 163.
8. Cooper, "Hegel's Theory of Punishment," p. 164.
9. Hegel's concepts of "appearance" *(Erscheinung)* and "show" *(Schein)* are related to his theory of truth, reflective being, and essence. This is a complex and subtle matter, the most definitive discussion of which is probably Michael Theunissen, *Sein und Schein* (Frankfurt: Suhrkamp, 1980). See also Charles Taylor, *Hegel*

(Cambridge: Cambridge University Press, 1975), Chapter 11; and Robert Pippin, *Hegel's Idealism* (Cambridge: Cambridge University Press, 1989), Chapter 9.

10. In this last passage, Hegel is paraphrasing Kant (*RL* 333/102).

11. Cesare Beccaria, *On Crimes and Punishments,* trans. Henry Paolucci (Indianapolis: Bobbs-Merrill, 1963), pp. 12–13.

12. A contemporary defender of a similar view is C. S. Nino, "A Consensual Theory of Punishment," *Philosophy and Public Affairs 12* (1983).

13. A similar theory of punishment, ascribed (somewhat creatively, I think) to Kant, but lacking the foundation provided by a Fichtean or Hegelian theory of recognition, is developed by Edmund Pincoffs, *The Rationale of Legal Punishment* (New York: Humanities Press, 1966), Chapter 1.

14. See David Lyons (ed.), *Rights* (Belmont, CA: Wadsworth, 1979), Introduction, pp. 3–4.

15. Of course if the argument of § 5 of this chapter is correct, then Hegel's theory does not "mandate" or require that a criminal should be punished at all, but only indicates what may with right be done to a criminal. If that is right, then it is open to a follower of Hegel's theory to choose for its good consequences any punishment that the theory says is not unjust.

16. This is not at all to say that theft or robbery of $100 should be punished by a fine of only $100. Clearly a theft, involving the forcible entry into my house, or worse yet a robbery involving a threat against my person, is a much worse serious violation of my right than my being ordered by a court to pay $100.

17. Beccaria, *On Crimes and Punishments,* p. 45. Beccaria also considers the possibility that the state might kill the offender not by the right of punishment but by the right of war, deeming this to be necessary for the preservation of the state. He rejects this defense of the death penalty also, on the grounds that life imprisonment at hard labor would always be a greater deterrent to any act than the death penalty (pp. 46–52).

18. Even those of us who believe that people have a right to commit suicide or permit euthanasia might think that letting yourself be killed as part of a contractual exchange is wrong in much the same way that selling yourself into slavery is wrong.

19. For example, see Jeffrey H. Reiman, "Justice, Civilization and the Death Penalty," in R. Baird and S. Rosenblum (eds.), *Philosophy of Punishment* (Buffalo: Prometheus Press, 1988).

20. Beccaria, *Of Crimes and Punishments,* p. 46.

21. Jean Hampton, "The Moral Education Theory of Punishment," in *Philosophy and Public Affairs 13* (1984), 237.

22. Jean Hampton, "The Moral Education Theory of Punishment," *Philosophy and Public Affairs 13* (1984), 208.

Chapter 7

1. See H. S. Harris, *Hegel's Development: Toward the Sunlight 1770–1801* (Oxford: Oxford University Press, 1971); and Raymond Plant, *Hegel* (Bloomington: Indiana University Press, 1973). These are two of the many accounts of Hegel's early development. See also Bernard Cullen, *Hegel's Social and Political Thought* (New York: St. Martin's 1979), Chapters 1–4; Charles Taylor, *Hegel* (Cambridge: Cambridge University Press, 1975), Chapter 2; Shlomo Avineri, *Hegel's Theory of the Modern State* (Cambridge: Cambridge University Press, 1972),

Chapter 2; G. Lukacs, *The Young Hegel,* trans. Rodney Livingstone (Cambridge, MA: MIT Press, 1975); Laurence Dickey, *Hegel: Religion, Economics and the Politics of Spirit 1770–1807* (Cambridge University Press, 1987).

2. Hegel had, of course, used the term *Sittlichkeit* before, for instance, in the *Difference* (*D* 93/153–154); but it is only in *Faith and Knowledge* that he began to use the term in its distinctively Hegelian sense, in which it is opposed to *Moralität.*
3. Concerning the term "police state," however, see Chapter 14, note 11.
4. The economics and sociology presented in this example is intended to be purely hypothetical. To look at the extent to which Hegel might endorse it, see Chapter 14, § 7.

Chapter 8

1. The meaning of this last sentence is unclear. Does Hegel mean that no arsonist (however thoughtless) could possibly have been ignorant of the fact that a set fire might spread out of control? If so, then he probably underestimates the thoughtlessness of some arsonists. Does he perhaps mean that we are justified in treating the arsonist as if he knew it, whether he did or not? That thought would seem more appropriate to a discussion of legal accountability than moral responsibility; Hegel did not always adequately attend to this distinction (see § 2 of this chapter). Whatever Hegel's meaning is, the intent of the remark is plainly to reconcile this provision of his theory of responsibility with the implications of his term "right of knowledge."
2. See Bernard Williams, "Internal and External Reasons," *Moral Luck* (Cambridge: Cambridge University Press, 1981), pp. 101–113.
3. See Thomas Nagel, "Moral Luck," *Mortal Questions* (Cambridge: Cambridge University Press, 1979); and Bernard Williams, "Moral Luck," *Moral Luck.*
4. *VPR17,* note 125, pp. 303–304.
5. See Christine Korsgaard, "Kant's Formula of Humanity," *Kant-Studien* 77 (1986), 196, 200–202.
6. That is, just as in the dictionary any word beginning with "A" comes before any word beginning with "B," so any right has priority over any amount of well-being. See Rawls, *A Theory of Justice* (Cambridge, MA: Harvard University Press, 1971), pp. 42–43.
7. See Barbara Herman, "On the Value of Acting from the Motive of Duty," *The Philosophical Review* 90 (1981), 374–376.
8. See Paul Dietrichson, "What Does Kant Mean by 'Acting from Duty'?" in R. P. Wolff (ed.), *Kant: A Collection of Critical Essays* (Garden City: Doubleday, 1967); and Allen Wood, *Kant's Moral Religion* (Ithaca: Cornell University Press, 1970), pp. 245–247.
9. See Herman, "On the Value of Acting from the Motive of Duty," pp. 376–382.
10. See Richard Schacht, "Hegel on Freedom," in A. MacIntyre (ed.), *Hegel: A Collection of Critical Essays* (Garden City: Doubleday, 1972), p. 309; and G. H. R. Parkinson, "Hegel's Concept of Freedom," in M. Inwood (ed.), *Hegel* (Oxford: Oxford University Press, 1985), p. 156.

Chapter 9

1. J. S. Mill, *Utilitarianism,* ed. George Sher (Indianapolis: Hackett, 1979), p. 4.
2. Gottlob August Tittel, *Über Herr Kants Moralreform* (Frankfurt: Pfahler, 1786),

pp. 14–15, 32–36. Cf. Fred Beiser, *The Fate of Reason* (Cambridge, MA: Harvard University Press, 1987), pp. 185–186.

3. See Thomas Pogge, "The Categorical Imperative," in Otfried Höffe (ed.), *Grundlegung zur Metaphysik der Sitten: Ein kooperativer Kommentar* (Frankfurt: Vittorio Kostermann, 1989).

4. Here I follow the interpretation of the formula of universal law developed by Onora Nell (O'Neill), *Acting on Principle: An Essay on Kantian Ethics* (New York: Columbia University Press, 1975), Chapters 1–5.

5. I owe this point to the text of an unpublished lecture on Hegelian ethics by Ernst Tugendhat.

6. The novels of Ayn Rand sometimes provide moderately persuasive fictional accounts of such fantastic beings.

7. Arthur Schopenhauer, *The World as Will and Representation*, trans. E. F. J. Payne (New York: Dover, 1969), *1*: 525.

8. Hegel may also intend slyly to suggest that the latter has to be the real maxim of those who help others. He may intend to call our intention to the hypocrisy of those who engage in charitable deeds in order to exercise power over those they "help" – or at least to feel superior to them. Or he may have in mind the point that those who give real, effective help to others on a regular basis must take on that task as a concrete vocation, and find self-satisfaction in it. He is certainly right to be suspicious of moralists who exhort us to help others without explaining how our efforts are to be rationally integrated into our own lives or the larger life of society. These points may all be well-taken, but they do not show that the maxim "Help the poor!" (taken in the sense Kant means it) contradicts itself.

9. This example is from Bruce Aune, *Kant's Moral Philosophy* (Princeton: Princeton University Press, 1978), pp. 123–125.

10. See Marcus Singer, *Generalization in Ethics* (New York: Alfred Knopf, 1961), pp. 292–295; Dieter Henrich, "Das Problem der Grundlegung der Ethik bei Kant und im spekulativen Idealismus," in P. Engelhardt (ed.), *Sein und Ethos* (Mainz, 1963); Andreas Wildt, *Autonomie und Anerkennung* (Stuttgart: Klett-Cotta Verlag, 1982), pp. 84–96; Christine Korsgaard, "Kant's Formula of Universal Law," *Pacific Philosophical Quarterly 66* (1985); and Onora Nell (O'Neill), *Acting on Principle*, especially Chapter 5. An exception to the rule is Michael Hardimon, *Individual Morality and Rational Social Life: A Study of Hegel's Ethics* (University of Chicago, Ph.D. dissertation, 1985), Chapter 1.

11. See my book *Kant's Moral Religion* (Ithaca: Cornell University Press, 1970), pp. 40–52.

12. Later, however, we will explore the possibility that ethical life deals more satisfactorily with duties to others involving "differential pull" (see Chapter 12, § 3).

Chapter 10

1. See E. Hirsch, "Die Beisetzung der Romantiker in Hegels Phänomenologie," *Deutsche Vierteljahrschrift für Literaturwissenschaft und Geistesgeschichte 2* (1924), 510–522; Otto Pöggeler, *Hegels Kritik der Romantik* (Bonn: Abhandlungen zur Philosophie, Psychologie und Pädagogik: Bd. 4, 1956).

2. Richard Pregizer, *Die politischen Ideen des Karl Follen* (Tübigen: Mohr, 1912), p. 70; and K. G. Faber, "Student und Politik in er ersten deutschen Burschen-

schaft," *Geschichte in Wissenschaft und Unterricht 21* (*21* (1970), 77. Cf. Karl-Heinz Ilting, *VPR 1*: 48–49.

3. Such sentiments were actually expressed by Hegel's colleague, the Friesian theologian Martin Leberecht de Wette (1780–1849) in a letter to Sand's mother; the letter was intercepted by the authorities, and de Wette was dismissed from his professorship in theology at Berlin (restored in 1823). (See K. A. von Müller, *Karl Ludwig Sand* [Munich: C. H. Beck, 1925], p. 176; and Ilting, *VPR 1*: 48.) Though Hegel apparently sympathized with de Wette's plight (contributing to a fund for his support), he strongly disapproved of his statement. Ilting argues that prior to 1819 Hegel had taken a more permissive attitude toward such acts as political assassination and tyrannicide, and hence that he must have changed his mind (Ilting, *VPR 1*: 49–50, 63). But this conclusion is unwarranted. Throughout his career Hegel always insists that a "moral intention" can never excuse or justify an act that is wrong (*PhG* ¶ 425; *VPR17*: 83; *PR* § 126,R). At the same time, Hegel always thought that political assassination (or at least tyrannicide) could be justified in some circumstances. Hegel evidently believed that Sand's assassination of Kotzebue, however, was not such a case, and that Sand's conviction to the contrary could not justify either him or his act of murder.

4. Aristotle, *Nicomachean Ethics 3*:5, 1114a–1114b.

5. Of course, sometimes those who take the wrong side in moral disputes deceive themselves and are wedded to their position by interest or prejudice rather than argument. But this can equally be the psychology of those who take the right side of the dispute. It seems gratuitous and pernicious to assume a priori that it must be the psychology of at least one side in every moral dispute. If we go into every moral dispute with this assumption, then we preclude taking the arguments of both sides at face value; we seem compelled to interpret one side's attempts at rational argument as no more than rationalizations of a position that the arguer cannot really believe. That precludes from the start the sort of honest and open dialogue on moral questions which Fichte himself regards as indispensable to the common life of free rational beings (*SL* 236–241/240–246).

6. See Alan Donagan, *The Theory of Morality* (Chicago: University of Chicago Press, 1977), pp. 130–134.

7. Although Fries's name is never mentioned, the allusions to him in *PR* § 140R are plain enough. Hegel's brief mention of the ethics of conviction in the Preface does mention Fries explicitly (*PR* Preface 17, 23). Hegel also interprets Fries's (Kantian) denial that we can know the thing in itself as the "so-called philosophy which says that the truth is unknowable" (*PR* Preface 17), and it is under this same label that he describes the ethics of conviction in *PR* § 140R (p. 273). Hegel's references in this context to political assassination (*VPR 4*: 388–389) also suggest that he has Follen and Sand in mind.

8. J. F. Fries, letter of January 6, 1821, in Gunther Nicolin (ed.), *Hegel in Berichten seiner Zeitgenossen* (Hamburg: Felix Meiner, 1970), p. 221. Of course this is really not true at all; it is about equal in viciousness and unfairness to Hegel's charge that Fries's ethics of conviction provides a justification for any misdeed. The most that could be said is that Hegel's depiction of his own theory (chiefly in the Preface) is designed, from motives of self-protection, to deemphasize and disguise its progressive and reformist aspects. It is not at all certain that Hegel was violating his conscience in doing this, though it is understandable that, Fries – already a proud martyr ar the hands of the reaction – might want, in such matters, to hold Hegel to standards that Hegel never shared.

9. This way of putting it brings out a similarity between the ethics of conviction and Kierkegaard's "truth is subjectivity":

> If one who lives in the midst of Christendom goes up to the house of God, the house of the true God, with the true conception of God in his knowledge, and prays, but prays in a false spirit; and one who lives in an idolatrous community prays with the entire passion of the infinite, though his eyes rest upon the image of an idol; where is there most truth? The one prays in truth to God though he worships an idol; the other prays falsely to the true God, and hence worships in fact an idol. [Kierkegaard, *Concluding Unscientific Postscript*, trans. Walter Lowrie (Princeton: Princeton University Press, 1941), pp. 179-180]

This story makes sense only if we suppose that the true God (unlike the God of Israel) is entirely free of jealousy – very partial to worshippers, but indifferent as to whether they decide to make him or something else their object of worship. If it turns out that you are saved equally no matter what you believe in, then (contrary to Kierkegaard's usual protestations) there ceases to be any risk at all in taking the leap of faith. Or rather, the only real risk is that you will come to believe the doctrine that truth is subjectivity; for, since on that doctrine all faiths are equally saving, and none of them involves any risk for me and I cannot believe anything with the passion attending an infinite risk, the doctrine that truth is subjectivity guarantees that any leap will be to safety, and thus insures that my belief (whatever its content) will be comfortable, lukewarm, and lacking in passion.

10. Philippa Foot, "Moral Beliefs," *Proceedings of the Aristotelian Society* (1958).
11. We need only think of Pascal's account of Jesuitical casuistry, to which Hegel alludes (*PR* § 140R). Pascal imagines the Jesuit giving moral advice to a wealthy patron, shaping the advice more to the desires and interests of the patron than to the demands of morality or religion. In this connection, he quotes the opinion of the Jesuit Father Layman: "A doctor, when consulted, may give advice not merely probable according to his opinion, but contrary to his opinion, if it is considered probable by others, when this view, contrary to his own, happens to prove more favorable and attractive to the person consulting him" (Blaise Pascal, *The Provincial Letters*, trans. A. J. Krailsheimer (Harmondsworth: Penguin, 1967), p. 84).
12. The only way to preserve a total allegiance to one's subjective conviction, Hegel suggests, is to go a step further than the ethics of conviction does, and say that

> [Goodness itself] is something constructed by my conviction, sustained by me alone, and that I, as lord and master, can make it come and go. As soon as I relate myself to something objective, it ceases to exist for me, and so I am poised above an immense void, conjuring up shapes and destroying them. This supremely subjective point of view can arise only in a cultivated age in which faith has lost its seriousness, which exists essentially only in the vanity of all things. (*PR* § 140A)

This view Hegel associates with Friedrich Schlegel's theory of irony, whose import he takes to be openly immoralistic: "In this shape, subjectivity is conscious of *the vanity* of all ethical content in the way of rights, duties, and laws, and is accordingly evil" (*PR* § 140). This clearly involves a misunderstanding of Schlegel (perhaps a deliberate and malicious one). The Romantic concept of irony is not a mere lack of seriousness, but a response to what Schlegel sees as the paradoxical human situation of being (religiously) conscious of absolute infinitude, yet incapable of expressing this consciousness adequately in language, which belongs to the everyday finite human world. [See Ernst Behler, "Friedrich Schlegel und Hegel, *Hegel-Studien*" 2 (1963); and Hans Eichner, *Friedrich Schlegel* (New York: Twayne, 1970), pp. 69–75.] But Hegel's polemics are not wholly a result of misunderstanding. Schlegel thinks that as finite creatures we are doomed to a condition of alienation from the infinite or divine, and so our most profound relation to it must always involve a kind of self-detachment. Hegel's philosophy, on the contrary, is an attempt to find the infinite immanent in the world, to overcome the Romantics' alienation through a rational comprehension of the actual which enables us to feel at home in our everyday lives, in our relationships to others, in human language, even in the life of state. The Romantic attitude, usually without religious scenery in the background, flourishes in our own century. Usually it takes the form of a sophisticated survival-mechanism in response to social alienation and despair – ranging from popular attitudes ("hip" and "cool"; see Chapter 3, note 13) to the highly intellectualized aesthetic of much twentieth-century poetry, and trends in recent philosophy, which view reason itself as the deepest enemy of freedom, and clever self-destructiveness as thought's only means to liberate itself.

13. Aristotle, *Nicomachean Ethics 3*: 3, 1110b29.
14. This sensible principle is, however, one that would be difficult to accept if you are a moral skeptic or noncognitivist, since if there is no such thing as moral knowledge at all, then our moral ignorance is always total; so, following Hegel's principle, no one is ever to blame for anything. The conclusion I draw from this is that Hegel's principle is perfectly all right, and that moral skepticism and noncognitivism have absurd consequences. Cf. Nicholas Sturgeon, "What Difference Does It Make If Moral Realism Is True?" *Southern Journal of Philosophy 24* (1986), 126–127.
15. This point is forcefully directed against Hegel by Ernst Tugendhat, *Self-Consciousness and Self-Determination*, trans. Paul Stern (Cambridge, MA: MIT Press, 1986), Lecture 14. But Tugendhat overstates his case in supposing that Hegel is *hostile* to critical reflection on social norms. Instead, for the purposes of the *Philosophy of Right* he is supposing a *rational* state (see above, Introduction § 6), and hence that correct reflection will always discover that the norms of society are rational. As we shall see in the next chapter, Hegel's conception of ethical life itself involves something like a critical reflection on society as it exists, though Hegel has his reasons (both philosophical and political) for not emphasizing this in the *Philosophy of Right*.
16. See Robert Merrihew Adams, "Involuntary Sins," *The Philosophical Review 94* (1985), 3–31.

Chapter 11

1. Sometimes Hegel also uses *Ethik* to signify *Moralität* and *Sittlichkeit* taken together (see *Werke 18*: 444–445).
2. Cf. Sophocles, *Antigone*, lines 455–457.
3. John Stuart Mill, *On Liberty*, ed. Elizabeth Rapaport (Indianapolis: Hackett, 1978); Chapter 3.
4. "When I will what is rational, then I act not as a particular individual but in accordance with the concepts of ethics in general. In an ethical action, what I

vindicate is not myself but the thing *(Sache)*. . . . The rational is the high road where everyone travels but no one is conspicuous" *(PR* § 15A).

5. See Michael Sandel (ed.), *Liberalism and Its Critics* (Oxford: Blackwell, 1984).
6. For instance, Onora O'Neill, "Ethical Reasoning and Ideological Pluralism," *Ethics 98* (1988), refers to these critics repeatedly as "Hegelians" and uses the term *Sittlichkeit* to denote the various folkways that the critics exalt above the standards of Western liberalism. No liberal moralist, however, could be any more hostile than Hegel is to MacIntyre's notion that we would be better off in a premodern society governed by habit and tradition than we are in a modern social order founded on the conceptions of human individuals as right-bearing persons and reflective moral subjects.
7. Charles Louis de Secondat, Baron de Montesquieu, *The Spirit of the Laws,* trans. T. Nugent (New York: Hafner, 1962), *1* :1 :3, p. 6.
8. Hegel does argue that the American states are republican only because they are "physically not fully developed, and even less advanced in terms of their political organization. . . . North America will be comparable with Europe only after the measureless space which this country affords is filled and its civil society begins to press in upon itself" *(VG* 209/170).

Chapter 12

1. Amartya Sen, "Rational Fools," in Frank Hahn and Martin Hollis (eds.), *Philosophy and Economic Theory* (Oxford University Press, 1979), pp. 87–109.
2. Christina Hoff Sommers, "Filial Morality," *Journal of Philosophy 83* (1986), 445.
3. Sommers, "Filial Morality," pp. 453–454.
4. Sommers, "Filial Morality," p. 456.
5. Peter Railton, "Alienation, Consequentialism, and the Demands of Morality," *Philosophy and Public Affairs 13* (1984), 134–171.
6. Railton, "Alienation, Consequentialism, and the Demands of Morality," p. 155.
7. Henry Sidgwick, *The Methods of Ethics* (Indianapolis: Hackett, 1981), pp. 492–495. The best-known recent argument for this conclusion is by Bernard Williams, "A Critique of Utilitarianism," in J. J. C. Smart and Bernard Williams (eds.), *Utilitarianism For and Against* (Cambridge: Cambridge University Press, 1973). It has also been argued recently that consequentialists have an especially hard time reconciling their doctrine with the kinds of commitment involved in personal relationships; see William Wilcox, "Egoists, Consequentialists and Their Friends," *Philosophy and Public Affairs 16* (1987).
8. Railton does a good job of making this point ("Alienation, Consequentialism, and the Demands of Morality," pp. 146–148).
9. Perhaps Hegel comes dangerously close to demanding this in the "antinomian" phase of his ethical thought, during the Frankfurt period (see above, Chapter 7, § 3). For there he thinks that the good will acts spontaneously out of love, and every moral reflection on its acts renders them impure and hypocritical.
10. See Aristotle, *Nicomachean Ethics* 1065a12, 1106b15–30.
11. Aristotle, *Nicomachean Ethics* 1107a, *PR* § 150R; cf. Kant's rejection of the idea that virtue is a mean, *TL* 404/65.
12. "The Greek heroes step forth in a pre-legal age, or they are themselves the founders of states, so that right and social order, law and custom *(Sitte)*, proceed from them, and actualize themselves as their individual work, remaining connected to

them. In this way Hercules was praised by the ancients themselves, and stands there as an ideal of original and heroic virtue. His free and self-dependent virtue, in which he championed the right and battled against the monstrosities of men and nature, is not the universal condition of the age, but belongs exclusively and properly to him" (*VA 1*: 240–241/250).

13. Jean Piaget, *The Moral Judgment of the Child*, trans. Marjorie Gabain (Glencoe, IL: Free Press, 1960), p. 18.

14. Lawrence Kohlberg, *Essays in Moral Development*, Vol. 2: *The Psychology of Moral Development* (San Francisco: Harper and Row, 1984), pp. 172–177. Cf. the philosophical use made of this developmental psychology by Jürgen Habermas, "Moral Development and Ego Identity" and "The Development of Normative Structures," *Communication and the Evolution of Society* (Boston: Beacon Press, 1979). The emphasis placed by Habermas ("The Development of Normative Structures," pp. 116–129) on institutional differentiation and rationalization in modern society accords well with Hegel's treatment of modern ethical life.

15. For a good discussion of this passage, see Ludwig Siep, "The *Aufhebung* of Morality in Ethical Life," in L. Stepelevich and D. Lamb (eds.), *Hegel's Philosophy of Action* (Atlantic Highlands, NJ: Humanities Press, 1983), pp. 146–153.

Chapter 13

1. Hegel uses such language not because he "worships the state," but because he wants to insist on the immanence of God in the world – particularly in the spiritual world of human society and history. He opposes what he sees as the "monstrous disbelief in nature" found in ancient Hebrew religion, for which the world, "if not a nothing, is supposed to be sustained by a God alien to it, who is to partake of nothing in nature, but by whom everything is to be dominated" (*TJ* 274, 279/*ETW* 182, 187); Hegel equally criticizes the "unhappy consciousness" of medieval Christianity, which views God as an unchangeable "beyond," separated from the finite human self sorrowing over its sinfulness, consuming itself in yearning, devotion, and self-mortification, relating to God only through degrading subservience to a priesthood (*PhG* ¶¶ 206–230). He wants his philosophy to be more in the spirit of ancient Greek folk religion, which viewed nature both within us and around us as a manifestation of the divine, and united people's religious life with their service to the state. Hegel wants to be the philosopher of a truer Christianity, for whom God actualizes himself in the world by taking a human form and is directly present to us in the "spirit" – the human community.

2. Hegel regards political supremacy, and even military success, as playing a role in a nation's historical dominance. Thus Hegel treats the Greek victory over the Persians as the victory of the Greek principle over the Oriental one (*VPG* 313–316/256–268); and the defeat of the Macedonian King Perseus by the Romans in 146 B.C. as the transition of the Greek principle into the Roman one (*VPG* 337–338/277). Further, Hegel's theory of history harmonizes with the imperialist mentality of nineteenth-century Europeans. "Civilized" nations, he says, are correct to treat backward ones as barbarians, having an "unequal right" and only a "formal" independence (*PR* § 351). At the very least, Hegel sees the world historical nation as one that possesses political autonomy (*PR* § 322); when a once dominant nation loses its autonomy, Hegel takes this as a sign that its time is past (*PR* § 347R). Yet the dominance of a nation for Hegel *consists* not in political rule over other nations but in the currency of its principle, as expressing the highest concept that

spirit has yet formed of itself. This is not something that could be created by mere military, political, or economic might; at most, Hegel sees military conquest and political or economic hegemony as instruments by which the dominant nation disseminates its principle.

Hegel's account of his theory is also highly misleading if it sometimes suggests that each nation has a distinct principle and that at any given time there is only a single dominant nation state. When we look at the four "world historical realms" into which Hegel divides history (the Oriental, the Greek, the Roman, the Germanic), we see that only one of them (the Roman) is characterized by the dominance of a single nation state. More typically, a world historical realm typically involves the prevalence of a certain *kind* of state, or the preeminence of a family of states, sharing a single world historical principle. This is clearly the way in which Hegel views the modern world (the Germanic realm), in which the European nations are the dominant ones: "The European nations form a family, in accordance with the common principle of their legislation, their customs *(Sitten)*, and their culture *(Bildung)*" (*PR* § 339A).

3. "This dissolution through thought is necessarily at the same time the production of a new principle. The universal essence [of the nation's old principle] is preserved, but its universality as such is lifted out of it. The previous principle is transfigured by universality. Spirit, in its new inward determination, has new interests and ends beyond those which it formerly possessed" (*VG* 179/147).

4. This same optimistic belief was later expressed by Marx when he said: "Humanity sets itself only such tasks as it can solve" [*Marx Engels Selected Works* (in one volume) (New York: International Publishers, 1977), p. 183].

5. Hegel does not have a "great man" theory of history in Carlyle's sense. He does not believe that the course of history is determined by what certain extraordinary individuals happen to will, or that things will go better in human affairs if people honor their heroes than if they don't. For Hegel the course of history is set by the needs of spirit and the growth of its self-knowledge. The individuals who facilitate the satisfaction of these needs are simply the necessary instruments of spirit's purpose. They achieve their ends because they have a kind of insight into what the time requires. If this individual had not happened to articulate the needs of the time, someone else would have. Hegel's view was very well articulated later by Plekhanov, in his critique of "great man" theories:

> [The great man] points to the new social needs created by the preceding development of social relationships; he takes the initiative in satisfying these needs. He is a hero. But he is a hero not in the sense that he can stop or change the natural course of things, but in the sense that his activities are the conscious and free expression of this inevitable and conscious course. Herein lies all his significance; herein lies his whole power. But this significance is colossal, and the power is terrible. [G. Plekhanov, *Fundamental Problems of Marxism*, (1898) (Reprint: New York: International Publishers, 1969), p. 176]

6. Shlomo Avineri [*Hegel's Theory of the Modern State* (Cambridge: Cambridge University Press, 1972), p. 233] finds Hegel's view inconsistent at this point, claiming that Hegel describes the world historical individual "as, alternatively, (1) wholly conscious of the idea of history and its development; (2) only instinctively conscious of it; and (3) totally unaware of it." Hegel probably held (2); I doubt that he held either (1) or (3). Avineri cites no passage, however, in which Hegel commits himself to *any* of (1)–(3), much less to all three simultaneously. In the

case of (1), the passage Avineri quotes is the one quoted at the beginning of this paragraph; it says only that the world historical individual "knows" the higher universal and makes it his end; it does not say that either the knowledge or the purposiveness involves conscious rational comprehension of the universal. The passage he quotes in favor of (2) says that "[Caesar] acted instinctively to bring to pass what the times required," and says nothing either way about Caesar's *awareness* of what the times required. The passage Avineri quotes in favor of (3) says that world historical individuals have "no consciousness of the Idea as such"; that obviously does not say that they are totally unaware of it. In the paragraph to which this note is appended, I have tried to indicate the kind of historical awareness Hegel attributes to world historical individuals.

7. Passion is not far from what we earlier (Chapter 3, § 7) called "monomania," and distinguished from the total, harmonious satisfaction of desires that constitutes happiness.

8. "No man is a hero to his *valet de chambre*" is usually attributed to Marie de Rabutin-Chantal, Marquise de Sevigné (1626–1696). But the best evidence, a letter by Charlotte Elisabeth Aissé (1695–1733), attributes it to Mme. Cornuel (1605–1694): "I remind you of what Mme. Cornuel said, that there is no hero at all for his *valet de chambre,* and no fathers of the church for their contemporaries" (*Lettres de Mlle. Aissé à Mme. Calendrini* (Paris: Stock, Delamain & Boutelleau, 1943), letter of August 13, 1728. Cf. also: "Few Men Have Been Admired by Their Domestics" [Montaigne (1533–1592), *Essays 3*: 2]; when the Macedonian general Antigonus (c.382–301 B.C.), was described by Hermodotus as "Son of the Sun," he replied: "My servant is not aware of it" (quoted by Plutarch, *Apothegms,* "Antigonus"). Hegel was the first to add: "Yet not because the former is no hero, but rather because the latter is only a *valet de chambre*" (*PhG* ¶ 665). Two years later, Goethe used the saying (with a slightly different version of Hegel's wry addition) in the novel *Die Wahlverwandtschaften* ("Elective Affinities") (1808): "There is, it is said, no hero for his chamber servant. That is only because a hero can be recognized only by a hero. The servant will probably know how to evaluate only his equals" [*Elective Affinities,* Part 5, Chapter 2: "Ottilie's diary"; Goethe, *Werke,* ed. Erich Trunz (Munich: Beck, 1982), *6*: 398; cf. *VG* 104/87].

9. Dostoyevsky, *Crime and Punishment,* trans. David Magarshack (Harmondsworth: Penguin, 1951), p. 552.

10. The point was appreciated by the Devil who appears to Ivan Karamazov in his delirium: " 'All things are lawful', and that's the end of it! That's all very charming; but if you want to swindle, why do you want a moral sanction for doing it? But that's our modern Russian all over. He can't bring himself to swindle without a moral sanction" [Dostoyevsky, *The Brothers Karamazov,* trans. Constance Garnett (New York: Random House, 1950), pp. 789–790].

11. Karl Popper, *The Poverty of Historicism* (Boston: Beacon, 1957), pp. ix–x.

12. Popper, *The Poverty of Historicism,* pp. 83–88. Because Popper's discussions of Hegel and Marx are characterized everywhere by unrelenting hostility founded on ignorant bigotry, he never appreciates the extent to which Hegel anticipates both his own conclusions and his "antihistoricist" argument for them; nor does he realize the extent to which Marx has taken the same considerations into account in formulating his theory of revolutionary practice.

13. See Marx, *Capital* (New York: International Publishers, 1967), *1*: 17; *Marx Engels Selected Works* (in one volume) (New York: International Publishers, 1968), pp. 294–295.

14. *Marx Engels Werke* (Berlin: Dietz Verlag, 1961–1966) *3*: 35; cf. *Marx Engels Collected Works* (New York: International Publishers, 1975–), *5*: 49.
15. I have discussed this point at length in other writings; see "Marx Against Morality," in Peter Singer (ed.), *A Companion to Ethics* (Oxford: Blackwell, 1990); "Marx's Immoralism," in Chavance (ed.), *Marx en perspective* (Paris: Editions de l'Ecole des Hautes Etudes en Sciences Sociales, 1985); "Justice and Class Interests," *Philosophica* 33 (1984); *Karl Marx* (London: Routledge, 1981), Chapters 9–10.

Chapter 14

1. Cf. Plato, *Republic* 420b; Aristotle, *Nicomachean Ethics I* :2, 1094b7–10, *Politics I* :1 1252a5.
2. "[Private] ends constitute and reproduce themselves for the well-being of individuals, but resolve themselves into the well-being of the universal. The universal in the state does not let the particular ends ossify as such, but makes them resolve themselves ever again into the universal end" (*VPR17* :144).
3. Since individuals must enter the sphere of labor and need satisfaction as free persons, then there is no longer any social legitimacy for the *Stamm*, around which feudal society, and much of earlier agrarian life, were organized (*PR* § 177). The modern family, unlike the clan, is not an abiding social structure; its duration is limited to a single generation, since it is destined to dissolve as the children reach maturity and take their place as persons in civil society (*PR* § 180) and found new families of their own (*PR* § 177). The only legitimate family is the bourgeois nuclear family – typically a husband, a wife, and their minor children (*PR* § 172). From the standpoint of civil society, each family constitutes a single person, whose property or resources are owned in common (*PR* § 169). The individual family members retain the status of persons with rights, even though these rights appear as such only with the dissolution of the family itself – as in cases of divorce (*PR* § 176) or the division of the family resources when the head of the family dies (*PR* § 178).
4. Like that other great nineteenth-century antidemocrat John Stuart Mill, Hegel is a firm believer in government, not by the populace generally but by an educated class of experts (*PR* § 291). Mill expresses Hegel's position quite well in passages like the following:

> The proper duty of a representative assembly in regard to matters of administration is not to decide them by its own vote, but to take care that the persons who have to decide them shall be the proper persons. . . . It is equally true, though only of late and slowly beginning to be acknowledged, that a numerous assembly is as little fitted for the direct business of legislation as for that of administration. There is hardly any kind of intellectual work which so much needs to be done, not only to experienced and exercised minds, but by minds trained to the task through long and laborious study, as the business of making laws. [John Stuart Mill, *On Representative Government,* ed. C. Shields (Indianapolis: Bobbs-Merrill, 1958), pp. 74–76]

> Yet Hegel also insisted that in an ethical life characterized by the principle of subjective freedom, citizens are concerned about the universal business of the whole; they form subjective opinions about it, and demand that their views be brought to bear on the political state. Thus like Mill, Hegel also regarded repre-

sentative institutions as essential to the modern state, serving not only as an ultimate check on the power of the government (*PR* §§ 297, 302), but also, most importantly, as a vehicle for the free expression of public opinion in political affairs through the public exchange of everyone's views on matters of universal concern (*PR* §§ 309, 314). Again, Mill's words are apt:

Instead of the function of governing, for which it is radically unfit, the proper office of a representative assembly is to watch and control the government; to throw the light of publicity on its acts; to compel a full exposition and justification of all of them which anyone considers questionable. . . . In addition to this, the Parliament has an office, not inferior even to this in importance: to be at once the nation's Committee of Grievances and its Congress of Opinions – an arena in which not only the general opinion of the nation, but that of every section of it, and as far as possible of every eminent individual whom it contains, can produce itself in full light and challenge discussion; where every person in the country may count upon finding somebody who speaks his mind, as well as or better than he could speak it himself, not to friends and partisans exclusively, but in the face of opponents, to be tested by adverse controversy. (Mill, *On Representative Government,* pp. 81–82)

5. It may help us to take Hegel's position on this more seriously if we reflect on the importance (especially in this latter age of mass communication) of the president's or prime minister's function, in a modern representative republic, as the symbolic representative or personification of the state. The Hegelian constitutional monarch differs most from the heads of state with which we are more familiar in having less actual political power than they do (*PR* §§ 279A, 280A). Real power in the Hegelian rational state is supposed to lie with a professional governing class, under the watchful eye of a representative estates assembly with the power to recall any particular ministry and replace it with another (*VPR17* : 187). It is important to Hegel that the state's personified sovereignty should remain inviolable, and hence that it not be confused with the ministers who must bear responsibility for controversial acts and policies of the state (*VPR17* : 164; *VPR19* : 246). Hegel argues that it is precisely because the state's policies are *not* at the mercy of the individual judgment of the sovereign prince that it is appropriate for this to be an "immediate" individual who comes by the position "naturally" through heredity (*PR* § 280).

6. In Hegel's German, of course, the term "corporation" *(Korporation)* does not mean (as in English) the *Aktiengesellschaft* or incorporated limited liability firm (in English, Ltd. or Inc.; in German, *GmbH – Gesellschaft mit beschränker Haftung*). It refers instead to a fellowship or guild *(Genossenschaft, Zunft)* made up of people who follow the same trade or profession. Strictly speaking, for Hegel a "corporation" is any society officially recognized by the political state that is not itself a part of the political state. Thus Hegel counts municipal governments (*PR* § 288) and churches (*PR* § 270R) as "corporations," along with professional guilds. He seems to intend that estates representation should be organized around corporations in this broader sense, as when he speaks of representatives drawn from "associations, communities and corporations" (§ 308; municipal representatives were prominent in the Prussian estates proposed in the 1819 constitutional plans of Humboldt and Hardenberg, to which the political constitution of *PR* bears a strong resemblance). In this chapter, however, we will be concerned with

corporations in the narrower sense, as trade or professional organizations within the economic sphere.

7. The "estates" *(Stände)* as a representative body must be founded on the corporate organization of the *Stände* of civil society *(PR* § 303R). Deputies to the estates are to represent determinate, organized branches of civil society *(PR* § 308). Only in this way can we make provision for all to feel that their concrete interests and viewpoint are represented; when representatives are elected from the populace at large or by mere geographical districts, individuals are alienated from the state rather than integrated into it by the election process. "As for mass elections in large states, it should be noted that the electorate inevitably becomes *indifferent* in view of the fact that a single vote has little effect when numbers are so large; however highly they are urged to value the right to vote, those who enjoy this right will simply fail to make use of it" *(PR* § 311).

8. Emile Durkheim, *Suicide,* trans. John A. Spaulding and George Simpson (Glencoe, IL: Free Press, 1951), pp. 241–276.

9. Durkheim, *Suicide,* pp. 152–216.

10. Nancy Chodorow, *The Reproduction of Mothering: Psychoanalysis and the Sociology of Gender* (Berkeley: University of California Press, 1978); Carol Gilligan, *In a Different Voice: Psychological Theory and Women's Development* (Cambridge, MA: Harvard University Press, 1982).

11. Hegel defines "police" as "the state insofar as it relates to civil society" *(VPR19:* 187). This usage was in his day not the least idiosyncratic. Until the midnineteenth century, the word *Polizei* in German included all the functions of the state that supported and regulate civil society, including public works, building regulation, fire protection, public health, and poor relief. It was not until after 1840 that the term came to be limited to the state function of maintaining peace and order. See G. C. von Unruh, "Polizei, Polizeiwissenschaft und Kameralistik," in K. G. A. Jeserich, Hans Pohl, and G. C. von Unruh (eds.), *Deutsche Verwaltungsgeschichte* (Stuttgart: Deutsche Verlagsanstalt, 1983), *1:* 388–427.

12. Eduard Gans, *Naturrecht und Universalrechtsgeschichte,* ed. M. Riedel (Stuttgart: Klett-Cotta, 1981), p. 92.

13. Henning Ottmann, "Hegelsche Logik und Rechtsphilosophie. Unzulängliche Bemerkungen zu einem ungelösten Problem," in Dieter Henrich and Rolf-Peter Horstmann (eds.), *Hegels Philosophie des Rechts: Die Theorie der Rechtsformen und ihre Logik* (Stuttgart: Klett-Cotta, 1982), p. 388.

14. Shlomo Avineri, *Hegel's Theory of the Modern State* (Cambridge: Cambridge University Press, 1972), p. 154.

15. Klaus Hartmann, "Towards a New Systematic Reading of Hegel's *Philosophy of Right,*" in Z. A. Pelczynski (ed.), *The State and Civil Society: Studies in Hegel's Political Philosophy* (Cambridge: Cambridge University Press, 1984), p. 120. The same solution is suggested in the same volume by Garbis Kortian, "Subjectivity and Civil Society," p. 205.

16. Bernard Yack, *The Longing for Total Revolution* (Princeton: Princeton University Press, 1966), pp. 220–222. See above, Chapter 2, note 19.

17. John McCumber, "Contradiction and Resolution in the State: Hegel's Covert View" *Clio 19* (1986).

18. Hegel's conception of the right of necessity is broader than the idea of a right to secure one's physical survival in case of a momentary emergency. When he takes this right, for instance, to ground the Roman legal notion of a *beneficium compe-*

tentiae guaranteeing that a debtor will not be deprived of the resources necessary to carry on his trade (*PR* § 127R), Hegel indicates that he interprets the right of necessity in close association with civil society's duty to provide a livelihood for each of its members. [When he takes the right of necessity in his broad sense to override other rights, Hegel merely moderates Fichte's contention that when the extent of your property leaves you unable to earn your livelihood, the property of others immediately ceases to be theirs and becomes yours (*GNR* 212–214/293–294).]

19. McCumber describes Hegel's references to the "right of distress" and the rabble's "indignation" as culminating in "the rage of a justified revolution" ("Contradiction and Resolution in the State," p. 382). I hope I have made it clear already why this has to be regarded as a misinterpretation.

Conclusion

1. Victor Cousin, "Souvenirs d'Allemagne," *Revue des deux mondes* (August, 1866), 616–617.
2. Rudolf Haym, *Hegel und seine Zeit* (Berlin: Rudolf Gaertner, 1857), p. 368; cf. Manfred Riedel, *Materialien zu Hegels Rechtsphilosophie* (Frankfurt: Suhrkamp, 1975), 1, 375.

Index

INDEX

estate *(Stand)*, 13, 27, 200–2, 216, 283
Estates *(Stände, Ständeversammlung)*, see
  estate; representative government
ethical *(sittlich)*, pejorative use of term, 217
ethical life *(Sittlichkeit)*, 22, 25–6, 50, 98,
  127, 130, 131–3, 193–236, 256, 272, 278;
  ancient Greek, 22–3, 57, 127, 140, 192,
  200, 204, 206, 215–16, 222, 238, 277, 278;
  as harmony of reason and sense, 132;
  modern, 25–30, 175, 205–8, 237–55;
  objective side of, 195–208; as organism,
  132; subjective side of, 196–8, 209–18
ethical theory: classical, 7, 20, 31, 53–8;
  Hegelian, xiii–xiv, 6–74; kinds of, 30–1;
  self-actualization theory as distinct kind of,
  30–3; self-defeat of, 212–14
ethics, limits of, 219–35, 249, 256
ethics *(Ethik)*, 94, 195, 276
ethics of conviction *(Überzeugungsethik)*,
  178–89; see also Fries, Jakob Friedrich
ethnocentrism, 204–5
eudaimonism, 31, 70–1, 164–6; see also
  happiness
Eudoxus, 55
evidence, 176–8
evil *(Böse)*, 174, 184–5, 186–7
existence *(Dasein)*, 10–11, 71–2, 216, 240
existentialism, 5, 153
experience *(Erfahrung)*, 19, 213
expressivism, 6

Faber, G., 273
fact of reason, 167
fallibility, 177–8
family *(Familie)*, 26–8, 106, 207, 209, 210,
  240, 243, 246, 281
Feinberg, Joel, 110, 270
feudalism, 43, 203, 281
fiat iustitia, pereat mundus, 146
Fichte, Johann Gottlieb, 3, 7, 12, 23, 36, 51,
  95, 100, 146, 174, 181–2, 221, 265, 268,
  274, 284; alleged atheism, 131; concept of
  freedom, 39, 43–5, 47–8; moral
  epistemology, 156, 176–8; principle of
  morality, 156, 176; as representative of
  "morality," 131–2; theory of punishment,
  109, 270; theory of recognition, 77–83, 89,
  91; theory of self-awareness, 17–18, 77–81;
  views on marriage, 269–70
Filmer, Robert, 41
finitude, 153
Follen, Karl, 179–80, 273, 274
Foot, Philippa, 186, 275
Forster, Michael, 261
Franciscans, 267

Frankfurt, Harry, 267
freedom *(Freiheit)*, 20, 32, 36–52, 199, 200,
  217, 230, 237–8, 256, 259–60, 265–6;
  absolute, 38–40, 70–1, 191; abstract and
  concrete, 38; civil, xiv, 38, 41, 51; formal,
  37, 41, 77, 150, 264; kinds of, 38; and
  necessity, 151; negative, 38, 48, 77;
  objective, 38; personal, 22–3, 38, 41, 51;
  political, 38; positive, 38; subjective, 23–5,
  28, 38, 51, 57, 220, 238–43, 245, 255, 257–
  9, 281–2
French Revolution, 38, 41, 100, 207, 257, 265
Friedrich Wilhelm III, King of Prussia, 13
Friedrich Wilhelm IV, King of Prussia, 14
Fries, Jakob Friedrich, 175, 178–87, 203,
  274; antisemitism of, 186–7; ethics of
  conviction, 178–87; rivalry with Hegel,
  178; as victim of persecution, 178, 274
Fulda, Hans-Friedrich, 263

Gans, Eduard, xiv, 248, 283
Gediegenheit, see noble simplicity
Geist, see spirit
Geisteswissenschaften, see human sciences
Gemüt, see heart
gender differentiation, 243–6
genius, moral, 174, 176
Germanic realm *(germanische Reich)*, 23, 134,
  208, 222, 263, 279
Gesinnung, see disposition
Gewerbe, see business estate; profession
Gilligan, Carol, 245, 283
God, 4, 10, 24, 219–20, 275, 278; beatific
  vision of, 57, 267; jealous, 275
Goethe, Johann Wolfgang von, 7, 280
good *(Gut)*, 17, 31, 57, 199; abstract, 186;
  living, 199, 210
Greek realm *(griechische Reich)*, see ethical
  life, ancient Greek
ground, objective, 162–8
Gueroult, Martial, 261
Guyer, Paul, 264

Habermas, Jürgen, 278
habit *(Gewohnheit, ethos)*, 214, 218
Hall, Calvin, 268
Haller, Karl Ludwig von, 246
Hampton, Jean, 270, 271
handicraft estate *(Handwerksstand)*, 200
Handlung, see action
happiness *(Glückseligkeit)*, 20, 53–71, 145,
  152, 227, 229, 267, 280; indeterminacy of,
  63–6; as issue of objectivity, 53–6;
  subjectivity of, 55–8, 60–3; why we care
  about it, 66–70; see also eudaimonism

287

INDEX

Hardenberg, Friedrich von, *see* Novalis
Hardenberg, Karl August von, 13, 186, 242, 257, 262, 282
Hardimon, Michael, 273
Harris, H. S., 271
Hartmann, Klaus, 248–9, 283
Haym, Rudolf, 257–8, 264, 284
heart *(Gemüt)*, 24–5, 215, 251
hedonism, 62, 225, 268; *see also* pleasure
Hegel, Georg Wilhelm Friedrich: Berne and Tübingen period, 127–8; conception of good, 146; conception of philosophical science, xiii, 1–6; *Difference Between Fichte's and Schelling's System of Philosophy* (1801), 6, 9, 131, 168; *Encyclopedia of Philosophical Sciences* (1817, rev. 1827, 1830), 4, 21, 78, 84, 88–90, 134, 162, 168, 170–71; ethical theory, xiii–xiv, 8–10, 15–74; *Faith and Knowledge* (1802), 131, 168–9, 272; Frankfurt period, 128–31, 209, 277; influence of, xiii–xiv, 5, 259–60; Jena period, 1, 4–5, 119, 131–3, 155, 158, 160, 168, 202–3, 205–6, 217, 266, 268; *Jena Realphilosophie*, 85–6, 119, 201, 205–6; lectures on right, xiv–xv, 13, 151, 261; *Natural Right* (1802), 131–32, 202–3, 205; obscurity of his writings, xiv; *Phenomenology of Spirit* (1807), 1, 4, 83–8, 90, 133, 153, 168, 170, 174–5, 187, 205–6, 278; philosophy of history, 219–36; *Philosophy of Right* (1821), 6, 8, 11–14, 20–1, 31–2, 43, 49–51, 58, 90, 134, 168, 172, 174–5, 196, 198–9, 203, 208, 211–12, 218, 224, 232, 237, 256–8, 282; philosophy of the state, xiii–xiv, 5–6, 10–13, 219–21, 237–43; *Science of Logic* (1812, 1816), 7, 63, 72, 137; "The German Constitution" (1801), 261–2; theory of recognition, 83–93; theory of universals, 63–4; views on non-European peoples, 93, 204–5; views on political obligation, 105; views on women, 26, 93, 243–6
Hegelianism, 5
Heidegger, Martin, 7, 268
Henrich, Dieter, 74, 262, 268, 273
Henry VIII, King of England, 147, 153
Herakles, 215, 278
Herder, Johann Gottfried, 202
Herman, Barbara, 272
Hermodotus, 280
hero *(Held)*, 149, 215–16, 226–8, 277–8, 279–80
Hinchman, Lewis, 270
"hip," *see* "cool"
Hirsch, E., 273
history, *see* world history

Hobbes, Thomas, 41, 91–2, 102, 267, 269; concept of happiness, 54; on despotical dominion, 87
Hohfeld, Wesley Newcomb, 269
Holy Alliance, 178
honor of one's estate *(Standesehre)*, 27, 201, 241
Hotho, H. G., 151
human being *(Mensch)*, 27
human sciences *(Geisteswissenschaften)*, 5
Humboldt, Wilhelm von, 13, 262, 282
Hume, David, 17
Husserl, Edmund, 1
hypocrisy *(Heuchelei)*, 130, 137–9, 143, 153, 174, 184, 187–9, 217, 273, 275, 277

I *(Ich)*, the, 18, 48, 84
Idea *(Idee)*, 4, 9–10, 72, 77, 199, 219–20, 222, 226, 256
idealism, xiii, 3, 43–4
identity, personal, 18, 45, 262–3
identity, social, 197, 201, 209, 241–3, 258
illusion *(Schein)*, 10, 112, 270–1
Ilting, Karl-Heinz, 143–5, 262, 274
imagination, 48, 176
imperative, 30–1, 270; hypothetical, 64–6; of right, 31, 94
imputability *(Imputabilität, Zurechnung)*, 140–4; *see also* responsibility
individual *(Einzelne, Individuum)*, 21, 23–5, 28, 42, 106, 179–80, 205–6, 210, 216, 258; world historical, 226–31, 279–80
infinity *(Unendlichkeit)*, 2, 60, 96, 276
inheritance, 106
inner and outer, identity of, 137–9
insight *(Einsicht)*, 175, 192, 218; right of, 189–91
institutionalism, 74
intention *(Absicht)*, 137, 141–2, 151, 171–2, 256, 274; right of, 142
interest *(Interesse)*, 152
interpretation, 46, 221, 224, 266–7
intuition *(Anschauung)*, 219
irony, 60, 267–8, 275–6

Jeanne d'Orleans, 230
Jesuits, 275
Jesus, 127–9
Judaism, 24, 127–8, 186–7, 278
justice *(Gerechtigkeit)*, 109–10; *see also* right

Kant, Immanuel, xiii–xiv, 1–2, 5, 7, 12, 23, 29, 31, 55, 57–8, 67, 70, 88, 97, 102, 127–8, 135, 143, 177, 179, 189, 209–10, 212, 214, 215, 216, 221, 228, 237, 261, 262, 263–4, 268, 271, 274; concept of freedom, 39,

288

www.ingramcontent.com/pod-product-compliance
Ingram Content Group UK Ltd.
Pitfield, Milton Keynes, MK11 3LW, UK
UKHW042152130625
459647UK00011B/1298

For EU product safety concerns, contact us at Calle de José Abascal, 56-1°,
28003 Madrid, Spain or eugpsr@cambridge.org.